STORMRIDER

"A Historical Novel Based on True Events."

GORDON L. "BOX" BOCHER

Paperback ISBN: 978-1-09833-098-9
eBook ISBN: 978-1-09833-099-6

"War is an ugly thing, but not the ugliest of things. The decayed and degraded state of moral and patriotic feeling which thinks that nothing is worth war is much worse. The person who has nothing for which he is willing to fight, nothing which is more important than his own personal safety, is a miserable creature and has no chance of being free unless made and kept so by the exertions of better men than himself."

John Stuart Mill

English economist & philosopher (1806 - 1873)

"For the ultimate measure of a man is not where he stands in moments of comfort and convenience, but where he stands at times of challenge and controversy. And there comes a time when we must take a position that is neither safe nor politic nor popular, but one must take it because it is right."

Dr. Martin Luther King, Junior

AC-130A CREW CONFIGURATION

AC   CP

    FE   TN

AG

AG

                IR   BC

              (The Booth)

              FCO TV

AG

AG

AG

IO

AC: Aircraft Commander   CP: Copilot   FE: Flight Engineer

TN: Table Navigator AG: Aerial Gunner IR: Infrared Operator

BC: Black Crow Operator/EWO   FCO: Fire Control Officer

TV: Lowlight TV Operator IO: Illuminator Operator

TABLE OF CONTENTS

PREFACE — 1

ANNA 1 — 3

ANNA 2 — 10

1: Introduction — 34

2: The College Years — 44

3: The Wasted Years — 61

4: First Tour — 68

5: Sandy — 78

6: Loss — 109

7: Adjustment — 124

8: Recovery — 146

9: The Rabbi of the Booth — 175

10: Spring Offensive or Second TET — 194

11: A Gunner's Moon — 204

12: Spectre 11 Gulf — 214

13: The Rainy Season — 227

14: End of Tour — 236

15: Back in the World — 262

16: The Best Job — 293

17: 33rd ARRS — 310

18: 55th ARRS — 342

19: Getting Out — 376

20: Civilian Life — 405

21: New York Center — 434

22: Elmira Flight Service — 447

23: The Long Goodbye — 470

24: Joshua Paul — 505

EPILOGUE — 535

PREFACE

I retired from air traffic control and all full-time work in 2008. My son Joshua, over the course of his life, has heard some stories regarding the kind of life that I lived. He urged me to write them down so they would not be lost to the generations that follow. I did not want to write a full autobiography as I did not want to embarrass the innocent and the not-so-innocent who are not public figures. So, this is a work of fiction, but it is based upon fact. The chapters that deal with combat, rescue and air traffic are absolutely the best description of events that I can recall. Any person or document that is italicized really did exist. The actions and character traits ascribed to these people are all ones that I personally witnessed.

One chapter which will vary from the "accepted" written history is the one that deals with the Second Tet offensive thrust which occurred in the spring of 1972. History records that the city of An Loc, which was at the very center of the enemy's focus (true), was defended by some 2,000 South Vietnamese troops. Not true. My crew was in voice contact with the three forward air controllers (FACs) who directed our fire power against the enemy. They told us (Crew number 1, 16th SOS) that the friendly forces consisted of 600 South Vietnam

Rangers and three US Army FACs. That city was held, and the Second Tet Offense was crushed by the AC-130 Spectre gunships. History says that the battle ended in June. History is wrong . . . it was over by the end of April, 1972. I know because I was there.

Finally, I wish to dedicate this work to my wife, Betsy. We have been married for thirty-seven years now. Living with a Viet Nam combat veteran is 'no walk in the park.' Throughout all that I had to endure to find balance in my life, Betsy has been there providing the support I needed. We have a wonderful son who is the product of our love for each other. I can honestly say that I trust Betsy with anything and everything. She is not only my wife; she is also my best friend.

ANNA 1

It had been six months since Anna's father died. His brother, Uncle John, phoned her. "Are you up to receiving a visitor?" he asked after the usual greetings. Anna heard the urgency in his voice and told him that she was free in the morning but that she did have an appointment with her gynecologist in the afternoon just after lunch. Uncle John told her that he would be there in less than half an hour. She did not know why, but she sensed that what he had to say would greatly affect her. Anna's instincts, as usual, were correct. She got out of her chair which took some doing as she was six months pregnant with her second child. Anna walked to the window and looked out. There on the U-shaped driveway she saw her chauffeur and protector, Liam O'Reilly, washing the family limousine. Seeing him as she pushed the window curtains aside while patting her extended midsection warmed her.

Liam O'Reilly, a large agile man, was hired by Anna's father, Dr. Stephen Blithe, when she was less than two years old. Liam, at a height of 6'2", looked as if he weighed about 180 pounds. He actually weighed 198 pounds and was a superbly conditioned warrior. Liam, a former Green Beret who left the Army in 1974, answered a want ad posted in a military publication. The ad listed the required skills of a very well-paying position, and Liam knew that he possessed all of them. Dr. Blithe interviewed him and was duly impressed. Liam possessed black belts in several different martial arts and had a superb military record which included two combat tours in Vietnam. In a word Liam was courageous and dangerous with a very strong moral base. Dr. Blithe knew, after an hour of conversing with him, that he had found the right man. He offered Liam the job, and he accepted. Liam became Anna's protector from that time on. At first, protecting Anna and her mother was just a very well-paying job. However, it didn't take long for this cute little girl with soft blonde curls and large blue eyes to burrow her way into his heart. She became like his own, and there was nothing that he would not do for her. Liam, due to wounds he received in combat, would never be able to father his own child. This circumstance intensified his protective instincts toward her.

As Anna grew and developed from a child into a startlingly pretty woman, Liam was always there. Even when she went on dates, he made sure that the young men in her life knew not only her boundaries, but his. Anna, all 63 inches and 120 pounds of her, sometimes resented Liam's intrusion into her personal life. But as she matured, she appreciated his instincts regarding the character of the men that she would see socially. Anna was and is the major beneficiary of her father's estate, which at the time of his death, exceeded more than $50,000,000. Her wealth made her a target, and she relied more and more on Liam's judgment as she knew with every fiber of her being that her welfare was his only concern. In her sophomore year at Brown University she met Mark Shellholm who was at least as wealthy as she. When Liam approved, she freely gave her heart to him, and they were married three years later. Her father's estate also made arrangements to pay for Liam's services for the rest of his life. Whatever the ups and downs of her life, Liam was always there. That thought comforted her.

When Anna turned twelve years old, her mother, Joan Clare Blithe nee Revere, passed. Joan was a small, slightly-built, blond woman who was never very healthy. Joan possessed a very weak heart, and the strain of childbirth probably shortened her life by at least a dozen years. Not having Anna was never a consideration for Joan. Motherhood was the single most important aspect of her short life. Anna's mother died in her sleep and her father, who was completely devoted to her, was devastated by her death. His grief was so intense and so personal that it was difficult for him to comfort her. But Liam was there and he grieved with her. It broke his heart that there wasn't more he could do. But he also knew that in time Anna would come back to life. By the time Anna was fourteen, she was like any other teenage girl, but she had a twinge of sadness that a perceptive person would eventually notice. Liam attended all her soccer games, as Anna was a varsity player on her preparatory school's team. Even when Anna went to Brown, Liam was there. He kept a discreet distance to allow her some personal space. Sometimes Anna would really resent his intrusive presence, but those times were rare. When she met Mark in her sophomore year and Liam approved, he gave her all the space that safety would allow. Since Mark's intentions were honorable, and he truly loved Anna, he came to appreciate Liam's presence and protection. Mark, a scion of wealth, knew that members of his economic class were targets, and he appreciated what Liam did for his fiancée.

Both Anna and Mark's families came from old line Protestant lineage whose faith was based upon Calvinism. They were raised to believe that their wealth was a sign from God that they were selected by Him to achieve salvation. In addition, having that great wealth was not only a privilege, but a moral obligation to help others, including tithing. Although they possessed great wealth, they did live rather simple lives. When they married, Dr. Blithe presented them with their own home which included an attached apartment for Liam, which was his, rent free, for life.

Anna opened the front door and called to Liam. He stopped what he was doing and asked what she needed. Anna answered, "Uncle John is coming to visit. He should be here in about 15 minutes and, when he arrives, ask him to wait for me in the study and I will meet him there." Liam nodded his assent and continued to clean the car. She went upstairs to the second floor that contained five bedrooms, four bathrooms and the large sitting room which was Anna's destination.

She found her son, Andrew, playing with his nursemaid, Trudy, who was a gentlewoman in her mid-40s. When Andrew saw his mother enter, he immediately ran to her. Anna gave him a big hug and told Trudy that she would be busy in the study and did not want to be disturbed. Anna gave her son a big kiss on the cheek and told him that if he got hungry, Trudy would take him to the kitchen for lunch. She promised Andrew when she returned from the doctor, she would spend the rest of the afternoon playing and reading with him. That assurance seemed to satisfy him, and he returned to Trudy. Anna closed the door and went downstairs to the study to await her uncle's arrival.

Ten minutes later, her uncle arrived. John Blithe was even taller than Liam. He was very thin, like her father, with deep-set blue eyes and dark hair with gray streaks. Anna could see the worry lines on his face and knew that her instincts were correct. She invited her uncle to take a chair facing hers. Uncle John sat and reached inside his suit pocket for an envelope which he gripped tightly. John usually had a small tremor which affected his hands, but Anna noticed that his hands were shaking more than usual.

"You know that your dad and I were very close. I was not only his brother, but his friend, his confidant, and the executor of his estate.

Stephen knew he was dying. About two or three months before he passed, he instructed me to give you this envelope. I think I know what's in it, but as you can see, it is still sealed. Frankly, although I loved your father, I wasn't sure until today that I wanted to comply with his request. I am still not sure that I am doing the right thing. But when in doubt, the right thing to do is usually the harder thing to do. If you have any questions, I will answer them to the best of my ability." And with that, Uncle John handed Anna the envelope. With trepidation she unsealed it, removed the pages and began to read:

My Dearest Anna,

This is one of the most difficult tasks I must do while there is life still left in me. As you know, I loved your mother with every fiber of my being. I was more than 20 years her senior, yet we were soul mates. One of the reasons that we were hesitant to marry was the fact that we were second cousins, and we both came from basically the same gene pool. Over the past 300 years since our ancestors arrived in this country, our family has married within a very small select group. Over those long years, this practice has caused some genetic diseases associated with generally recessive traits. Mom and I discussed this and what to do about it. I wanted to spend the rest of my life with Joan but I could not take a chance of fathering a child with her. Mom and I faced a very large dilemma. We loved each other, but could not have children with each other without the strong possibility that a child we conceived would suffer some devastating genetic disease. We talked about artificial insemination, but your mother was totally against carrying a child from a man that she did not know. After much discussion, we came up with a solution which I will now explain.

Mom decided to go to Paris in order to study French. She would spend the summer there, and if she met someone who could provide a child for both of us to call our own, she would be intimate with that person and stay in Paris until she was pregnant. I agreed, as long as the man involved never knew that he impregnated her so that when the child was born, I would be considered the child's father.

As a result of that agreement, your mother went to Paris in May, 1971. She stayed there almost three months. Mom and I talked over the phone almost every week during that time. Your mother met a man over there that she liked very much. He attended the same beginning French class, and that's where she met him. Your mother told me that he was about 5'8" tall, weighing about 150 pounds, with blonde hair and blue eyes. Mom also indicated that he was very athletic and physically strong. He was an officer in the United States Air Force. He was very bright with a tremendously inquiring mind. His family came from Eastern Europe and because of that, he offered a potential gene pool with none of the recessive traits that has plagued our extended family.

Around the first or second week of August of that year, Mom called and told me that she had missed her period and that she thought she was pregnant with you. She got a test from a French doctor confirming the pregnancy and left two days later. We were married within two weeks of her return to the States. You were born on March 10, 1972. That is still the happiest day of my life. You were a beautiful and healthy baby, and you grew into a beautiful and healthy woman which is exactly what both Mom and I wanted for you. What I want you to know is how completely loved you were by me and your mother.

One of the last conversations I had with Mom was about your conception. Joan always believed that the truth would come out. She made me promise to tell you as much of the truth as I knew. This letter is my final act to fulfill the oath I made to my beloved as she lay dying. I hope you can forgive us both. I do know that Uncle John has more of the details of the man who biologically sired you. I will leave it to you if you want to pursue your history. I instructed my brother to answer whatever questions you may have as honestly as he can. Please don't think badly of me. I write this with love.

Dad

Anna read and then slowly reread the entire letter while crying softly. John Blithe kept his distance and gave her time to absorb what he knew to be shocking information. Finally, Anna put the letter in her lap and looked at her uncle, and asked, "Do you know what's in this letter?"

"Yes. Stephen and I discussed what he intended to write in general terms. I did not read this letter. I was with your mother and father when she made him promise that he would tell you about the circumstances regarding your conception. I talked with Mom at some length just before she died, and I asked her for more details . . . or at least what she wanted to confide in me without upsetting your father. Would you mind if I read the letter?"

Anna nodded her assent. John read the letter in its entirety and when he was done, he passed it back to Anna. "Do you have any questions?" he asked.

Anna sat silently for several minutes. Her brow was furrowed in thought. She considered whether she really wanted to pursue her parentage or let it go. If she went down this road, she might pass a point of no return that would possibly alter who she was and how she thought of herself . . . a very big decision. Finally, after taking a deep breath and a cue from her mother, she said, "Tell me everything you know about my biological father." Uncle John complied with her request.

ANNA 2

After Uncle John left the house, Liam, sensing something was amiss, entered the study and saw Anna softly crying. She had a letter in her left hand, and she was softly caressing the bulge created by the baby she was carrying inside of her. "What's wrong?" he asked. Anna, without saying a word, held up the letter which Liam quickly retrieved. With Anna staring at him intently, he read the letter in its entirety. The content was not a total surprise to this quick-witted man. Anna's startling blue eyes, the fact that she was left-handed, and the fact that she was generally much healthier and hardier than either her father or mother was sufficient information for Liam to have questioned her true lineage, but he never pursued it, as there was nothing to gain by proving what he suspected. He loved Anna as a daughter and who sired her was never an important issue to him. So, he let bygones be bygones. But now the situation was different. He needed to know what she wanted to do in order to help her. And so, he asked.

Anna got up and reached for Liam whose big arms engulfed her small frame. She cried quietly for ten minutes while tightly holding onto her protector. She looked up at him and said, "I want to know who my biological father was, or is. Right now, I am numb . . . I don't know whether to be angry or forgiving . . . I just don't know."

Liam responded, "Don't judge your parents. They were faced with choices fraught with difficulties. I can tell you that they made these decisions with the very best of intentions. You are a beautiful and healthy woman, and it appears to me that your children will share your good health. That is a gift worth cherishing. Now, what do you want to do about finding your biological father?"

"But what would happen if I find that my true father is someone I could not respect or even like?"

"Nonsense!" he replied. "I knew your mother. She would never, and I mean never, share intimacy with somebody who was not worthy. The reason she went to Paris was because she didn't want to take a chance on an anonymous sperm donation. She wanted to know the character of the man who would sire a child for her and her beloved Stephen. She obviously wanted you to know about the circumstances of your conception. That's why she made your father make a deathbed oath."

Anna listened. The truth of his words sunk in as she asked him to sit in the chair that Uncle John recently vacated. "I want to find my biological father. At least, I would like to know who he is and what he's about, and then I can make a decision as to whether I wish to include him in my life. Regardless, I will always love my parents no matter what happens from this point on."

Liam reached into his pocket and retrieved the small notebook that he always carried. He had a habit of taking notes of anything of interest or things that had to be done so he would not forget later. He opened up to a fresh page and asked, "Tell me everything that Uncle John told you as well as you can remember it, particularly information not included in the letter." She nodded her agreement and gave Liam the information he requested, pausing to allow Liam time to write down her responses.

Uncle John knew that the school her mother attended in the summer of 1971 was the Sorbonne University. Her mom took a beginning French course and met her biological father there as he was also a student attending the same class. Joan told her brother-in-law that he was very adventurous and, she thought, very good looking. But what really appealed to her was the breadth of knowledge that he possessed. His intellectual curiosity was intense. Yet as strong a physical person that he was, he was always careful with her mother, who was always very frail. Her mother only loved two men in her entire life. She knew that her Paris lover was too intense over the long haul. The man who she spent the summer loving lived life on the edge. That was okay for a summer, but she knew that for a lifetime his intensity would be too much for her. She told John that her paramour rode a Harley-Davidson motorcycle and that he, in her words, dressed roughly. She also told Uncle John that he was in Paris awaiting orders from the United States Air Force.

Liam stopped writing and looked up at her. "I think we have enough here to get started. Do you have any memorabilia that belonged to your mother?"

Anna looked up quietly and thought for a minute. "Yes, I think I do. If I remember correctly, there are some sealed boxes which I inherited from my mom. They are stored in the basement. I haven't thought about them in years. I will have some time this evening to look through them. I must see the doctor this afternoon, and I promised Andrew that I would read with him when I returned. Mark should be home around five or six this evening and that's when we will eat dinner. I will share the letter with him at that time. About eight o'clock this evening,

I will be free to look through those boxes." Anna, lost in thought for several moments, resumed speaking. "I have an idea. Why don't you join Mark and me for dinner, and we can discuss the matter together?" Liam readily agreed.

About 6:30 that evening, Liam joined Mark and Anna. Mark knew that something was unsettled as Liam always gave them their personal space. After they were seated, Anna excused the kitchen help and told them to take the rest of the night off as she would be serving. Andrew, already fed, was upstairs with Trudy who had instructions not to disturb them unless something of great importance happened. Their privacy assured, Anna served the salad course, gave Mark the letter, and explained how and when she received it. He quietly read the letter and with a totally surprised expression said, "Wow! What do you want to do about this?"

"What would you suggest?" she asked her husband. Anna looked intensely at the man she loved. Mark was 5' 11" and weighed just about 200 pounds. When Anna had met him, they were taking the same economic, business and finance courses. Both their respective parents insisted that they take these classes because both would inherit large fortunes. They had to be able to handle the responsibilities that accompanied great wealth. For his part, Mark fell for her the first moment he laid eyes upon her. He asked if she wanted to have some coffee after they attended an introductory economics course at Brown. Anna readily accepted, as she was physically attracted to him. He was very good looking and physically fit. She liked the contrast between his light blue eyes and dark wavy hair. As they chatted together over coffee, she found herself enjoying his company and his subtle, dry humor. They started dating immediately and within a few short weeks, they were a solid couple.

Mark played on the varsity football team both as a running back and a defensive back. His athletic abilities were sufficient for the Ivies, but fell short of what major football conferences such as the Southeast or the Big Ten would require. His playing weight in college was 180 pounds. But three years of marriage and long office hours caused him to put on a few pounds, mostly around the middle. After college, Mark attended law school for three years at Harvard University, and at the end of his second year, he married Anna. He passed the Massachusetts bar exam six months after graduating. He spent many hours overseeing both fortunes. Mark also created a law firm which provided first-rate legal advice and representation to indigenous people who otherwise would be poorly served in the court system. This firm was totally paid for by a tax-free trusteeship that he set up. This was his way of tithing and doing something worthwhile with his time. Overseeing the family fortune was his duty. Providing legal help to the poor was his calling.

After reading the letter, he took his time before answering. He looked up at his wife and stated, "Whatever you want to do is fine with me. I love the person you are. My only concern is what is best for you. What do you want?"

Anna reached for his hand with hers which he engulfed with his much larger hand. Anna told him about the entire conversation that she had with Uncle John and then later with Liam. Mark knew many of the prosecutors who worked the court system in Massachusetts. To say he was well-connected was a major understatement. He suggested that he could "nose" around to get information that would answer some of her questions. He would do so discreetly as he did not want the media to make a scandal out of the circumstances of her birth. While Anna served the main meal, they agreed that Liam would make discrete inquiries as to the person who became Joan's paramour. They spent the remaining time discussing the best way of dealing with these inquiries without raising the specter of a news sensation. After all, this would affect two major families who were among the "pillars of the community."

After dinner, all three went downstairs to the basement. In the far corner were boxes neatly sealed and placed in wooden shelves which occupied one full wall of the basement. Mark and Liam set up a large portable table near the shelves and started to take the boxes down one at a time. Many of the boxes contained financial information and other mundane paraphernalia, but there was one small square box measuring 12" x 12" x 5" in dimensions carefully sealed with duct tape and marked "personal." Liam carefully opened it using his pocket knife and then let Anna be the first to look at the contents.

With some trepidation, Anna carefully removed the top. The first item she saw was a man's long-sleeved white dress shirt which was carefully folded. Anna reached for the shirt and allowed it to unfold in front of her. The shirt was much larger than Anna's mother and obviously belonged to the man she was with. Anna noticed that the shirt was made of a good cotton fiber and was soft to the touch. She put the shirt aside and reached for the next object. That was a small journal that contained a pressed flower inside of it which fell to the top of the table as she opened the small book. Anna immediately recognized her mother's fine handwriting as she scanned the contents of what was essentially a diary of her stay in Paris. She put that aside, knowing that she would look at this diary in more detail after she examined the remainder of the contents of the box. The next item she pulled out was a small black box of matches with "*CAFE LE GENTILLY*" emblazoned in red on top. The box was full of matches that were never used. She carefully placed the matchbox on top of the table and reached for the next item which was a small, slim book titled, <u>The Little Prince</u> written by Antoine de Saint-Exupery. The last item in the box was an 11" x 10" book titled, <u>Meester-Weken in het Van Gogh Museum</u>. This book contained excellent photographs of Van Gogh works whom Anna knew to be Mom's favorite master. A cursory examination of both books revealed that they were read and reread many times. Anna turned her attention back to the journal now that the box was empty. With some trepidation, she opened the diary. Each entry was headed by date or dates followed by the events of that particular time period. Some entries were single dates and some spread over a period of several days, and in one case, over a period of two weeks. Anna turned to the first page:

> May 24: Arrived in Paris. Class is supposed to start today, but I'm too tired, so I'll go tomorrow. Hotel is simple, but nice. Can you imagine—no shower, but they do have a bidet!

> May 25: I'm not used to the time zone. I overslept, and I had to take a taxi to the Sorbonne. It took a while for me to find the right classroom. I was about an hour late when I entered the class—so embarrassing, but I was anxious to start. The class is taught by Mme. C. The class has 16 students of which 11 were women and five were men. About an hour after I arrived, Mme. C. gave us a 30-minute coffee break. As we were leaving, one of the men came quickly to my side and introduced himself. He was not my usual type, as he was very athletic, very strong, and dressed in blue jeans, a T-shirt covered with a leather vest, and large black boots. He asked me, with a twinkle in his eye, if I always arranged to come late to make an entrance. Normally, I would never answer such a person, but something told me that he may be worthwhile. After a few minutes of light banter, I agreed to have coffee with him. His name is B. What I discovered quickly is that B. has a quick mind and a very good sense of humor. We were

having such a good time that we were late returning to class. Mme C. admonished both of us, and I'm sure that I turned quite scarlet. I do blush easily.

Oh well! After class, B. asked if I would care to join him for dinner. I quickly agreed, and told him where I was staying. B. asked if I would mind riding on the back of his motorcycle. I told him that I would try, and he suggested that I wear slacks. He came on time, and I was waiting for him by the hotel's street entrance. We went to a wonderful restaurant and had a fabulous meal. I asked B. how he found this restaurant. He laughed and told me that if he heard English being spoken in a restaurant, he would not eat there. Besides, his brother recommended this particular one. B.'s rule was simple: He would eat in restaurants where only French was spoken. I had a great time! Aside from his rough exterior, B. is extremely intelligent, well-educated, and very interesting. B. told me that I was the first woman he'd dated since his fiancée died, almost two years ago. It was very difficult for him to talk about her. I do believe that hint of sadness is one of the reasons that I found him appealing. Around 2:00 AM, he took me to my hotel and kissed me good night, and told me that he would see me the next day in class.

May 26: B. and I spent the afternoon touring Paris on his bike. I thought I would be very nervous riding on the back of a huge motorcycle, but B. is a very competent rider. He told me to lean with him . . . sort of follow his lead. And that's what I did. We went in and out of traffic, but after a while I became very relaxed. After about three hours of exploring the city, B. took me back to his room at the Citee

Universitaire so we could freshen up and go to his favorite restaurant, *Le Gentilly*, which was only two blocks away from where he was living. His room was in a men's dormitory, and B. would stand guard by the bathroom while I used it. His room was very Spartan as the furniture was a single bed, a desk and chair set, and one lounge chair which B. placed near the windows. B. did not have much in the way of clothes, so he would do laundry about every fourth day. On his desk, he had the three-volume paperback version of <u>The Lord of The Rings</u>. He told me that he was not a big fan of poetry in general, but he loved the poetry in Tolkien's masterpiece. He even read some of it to me, and I found that I was enjoying it, even though I am not a fan of fantasy literature. That evening we walked to Cafe Le Gentilly and B. introduced me to the friends that he'd made while living in the Citee. After visiting with them for about an hour, we got our own table and proceeded to have a wonderful meal. I liked the fact that B. would let me proceed at my own speed. I know he was interested in me, yet he made no advances that were untoward, even when we were alone in his room. His friends, sensing that we wanted to be alone, gave us our privacy. That is when I told B. about Stephen, of course, without using his real name. I also told B. that if we are to proceed to intimacy, that our affair must end when I left Paris and that he would have to swear on his honor that he would not seek me out anytime in the future. B. took a few moments and then agreed. I had his word. I asked him to take me back to my hotel and told him that the next time we went out, we would spend the night together. We rode together on his bike back to the hotel and before I entered the doorway, B.

gave me a long passionate kiss goodnight. That night I called Stephen and confirmed with him that what I was planning to do was still okay with him. He told me that nothing I could do would change the way he felt about me. I told him that when I returned from Paris, he would be the only man in my life forever.

May 27: B. asked me during class break if I wanted to "dine" with him that evening. I agreed and told him to pick me up at my hotel so I could bring a few things. He came for me about six, and we rode to the *Le Gentilly* and had another wonderful meal. That night we joined some of his friends and the conversation was marvelous. B.'s friends consisted of a truly odd grouping. Several were leading professors in their fields. One was a major union leader. Another was a lieutenant in the French military. All wanted to practice their English and all, including B., were very aware of history and current events. The conversation was highly intellectual, very animated, and punctuated with many hand gestures. Everyone at our table smoked Gauloises, a very strong French cigarette while drinking red wine. I mostly kept quiet, but B. was right at home. His intellect was competitive with anyone there. I could see that his friends respected his opinions and his breath of knowledge. Around midnight, we walked back to his dormitory room. When we got in his room, B. gently kissed me, and when I responded, the kiss became more passionate. That night, B. made love to me. I was very nervous, as no man other than Stephen had ever seen me without clothes in my entire life. B. was very gentle with me. It was the first time I saw him totally naked. His body is beautiful. He is well muscled, very strong and very gentle with me.

And when I saw how aroused he was, I became more relaxed, because I knew that he wanted me as much as I wanted him. A Great Night!

May 28-June 1: B. awoke well before I did. He did a laundry so that I would have a clean towel to use after taking a shower. B. gave me his shirt, the only one he had, to use as a bathrobe. The sleeves extended well past my hands, so I rolled them up and the bottom of the shirt extended past my knees. Frankly, a very modest outer wear, except I wore nothing beneath it. Again, B. would stand guard while I used the bathroom and showered. I used the freshly dried towel and told him that it was "toasty!" This caused him to laugh out loud. We had to hurry as not to be late for class. We did stop at *Le Gentilly* for breakfast before going to school. When class was over, we returned to his room and literally spent the weekend making love. The only time we came "up for air" was to walk to *Le Gentilly* for food. Monday was a holiday, so we did not go back to class until Tuesday, June 1. After class we went to the English bookstore on the Rue de Rivoli. It was B.'s habit to go to there on Tuesdays to pick up the *International Herald Tribune* which he read from cover to cover. I told him that every Tuesday I would spend my day in my hotel room alone. He looked at me quizzically, but he nodded his assent. That evening, he dropped me off at the hotel. We kissed, and I told him that I would be with him after class tomorrow until the following Tuesday. That night I called Stephen, and we talked for about four hours over the phone. Stephen and I agreed to talk at length every Tuesday evening until I returned home. This time would give me the opportunity to make my entries into this diary which I will keep in my hotel room. I trust B., but it's better to be safe than sorry.

June 2-7: After class on Wednesday, B. and I went to the Louvre. It was my suggestion. B. agreed only because he knows how much I love art. That was sweet of him. The museum is huge, far bigger than what I had imagined. B. walked quietly by my side until we entered a large room which was almost the size of a basketball court. The walls had to be at least 20 feet high, and on them were heroic paintings from the French neoclassic period. B. was mesmerized. He asked me if I would mind if we spent "some fair amount" of time there. I readily agreed. It was fun for me to watch this man who had little or no interest in great art, as he put it, "have his eyes watered." That little time turned into almost three hours. B. was fascinated in particular by Anne-Marie Girodet's rendition of *The Deluge* and Jacques-Louis David's painting entitled *Leonidas at_Thermopylae.* Because we spent so much time with the neo-classics, we decided to come back again the next day and visit more of the Louvre. In fact, we spent the next six days, when we were not in class, going through that magnificent museum. During one of the meals that we shared together, B. explained that the neoclassic paintings that he so much enjoyed were the visual reflections of the classical economic and political theories which were bubbling to the surface and dominating the latter part of the 18th century and at least the first quarter of the 19th century. The great economists such as *Ricardo, Malthus* and *Smith* produced an economic theory based upon reason that reflected the artwork of the day. Similarly, and not just coincidentally, B. went on to explain how the political doctrine of the day was reflected by the classical economic theory and the art work of the French Neo-classics—each part affecting the others. (I love art, particularly the Impressionists of the late 19th century and early 20th century.) It was fascinating for me to watch B. shape his theory as he explained it to me. I really enjoyed watching him work this out and seeing how his mind works. I am more confident now in my decision to create a new life with B., although he will never know about it. We now spend six nights a week together. B. is a very good lover who is very gentle with me. We also eat almost every meal at *Le Gentilly*. The food is wonderful and the conversation is even better. I'm fascinated, as we spend almost every evening discussing all kinds of topics with an eclectic group of intellects who congregate in that small café. For me, it is a nonstop educational safari.

June 8-14: During this period there were two things that stood out. First, on this Thursday we went to the English bookstore. While we were there, I found an English version of The Little Prince written by Antoine de Saint-Exupery. B. bought two copies and gave me one. The day was perfect, with beautiful sunshine, a gentle breeze and temperatures in the low 70s. We walked to the Place de la Concorde and onto the Avenue des Champs-Elysees. After walking for about a half hour, I was really tired and B. suggested that we take a break. He led me to a very old maple tree located in a beautiful park on the north bank of the Seine River. I was a little chilled, so B. gave me his green flight jacket and had me sit on the very lush grass with my back supported by this very large maple tree. He laid down with his head in my lap. B. closed his eyes while I read the entire The Little Prince book to him. He told me later that hearing my "soft voice" read the story out loud was like being part of the book and being in the book. He really enjoyed it. In fact, he told me that was one of the best afternoons of his life. We spent about three hours in that small park. By the time we left, it was really getting chilly. B. and I walked back to the parked motorcycle. His flight jacket kept me warm while we drove back to his dormitory room. B. saw how tired I was and let me sleep. I woke several hours later from my nap, and we made love. It's getting better and better, and I hope it will not be too difficult to leave him.

The next day we went to *Le Gentilly* again for the evening meal. B.'s friend Andre was there, and after greeting us, he explained excitedly that his favorite dish was being served as the special of the day. Andre, a very tall thin man, was fluent in English because he was a doctoral student in the field of theoretical mathematics. That discipline requires French students to learn either Russian, German or English as a second language, as the French language did not have sufficient words to properly convey complex mathematical concepts. Andre was fluent in English. He was also best known as the "gourmet of *Le Gentilly*." The dish was Coquille St. Jacques, a delicate seafood dish in a magnificent wine sauce. B. loved it so much that he ordered a complete second meal for himself. *Le Gentilly* is owned by a couple. The husband is a small, dark-haired man with a well-trimmed mustache. His wife towers over him as she is at least 5 foot 10 in her stocking feet. She is a woman of robust figure with a very hearty laugh. When she heard that B. ordered a second meal, she came out to ask why. The answer he gave was simple: "It was just about the best meal I ever ate!" That lady just beamed. During the meal, Andre explained that it took the Madame (every one called her by that title) the whole day to make that dish. She went to the market area of Paris and purchased all the ingredients on the day she cooked to ensure that they were truly fresh. Then after several hours of shopping, she prepared enough servings to satisfy a large number of their regular customers. That, combined with all her other duties, made preparing that dish a once-a-month offering.

June 15-21: We only have two weeks of class left. B. and I generally go to some park near the school to practice our French. During our weekly trip to the English bookstore, I noticed that a special Van Gogh exhibition was opening for several weeks. After class was over on Wednesday, we went directly to a small museum where his paintings were on display. We spent the whole afternoon there. For me, it was like a little bit of heaven. There is no artist in any medium that speaks to me the way Van Gogh does. I think B. enjoyed himself, although he still prefers the neo-classic painters. He told me that knowing how much I enjoyed this exhibit was very gratifying to him.

On Friday, we went to *Le Gentilly* for the evening meal. There we met Andre, the mathematician and resident gourmet, who joined us for supper. We sat down and asked what the nightly special was. Madame took our order and told us that Coquille St. Jacques was the special. That answer delighted all of us but angered Andre. After she left, I asked Andre why he felt this way. He explained that for years he had begged Madame to make this dish a weekly offering. He was delighted that he would be able to eat it again this week, but he was angry because the Madame ignored his pleas, the pleas of a Frenchman, yet responded to the request of an American! Both B. and I howled with laughter. After a while, Andre joined in and finally was laughing with us. B. told him "to sit back and enjoy the ride!"

On the weekend we rode out to the countryside and visited several castles. One castle in particular had a beautiful flower bed arrangement. I can't believe it, but B. managed to cut a single flower using his pen knife. He carefully wrapped the flower in his handkerchief and placed it in the pocket of his flight jacket. I didn't know he did this until we got back to his room where he presented the flower to me. I wrapped it in tissue and put it in my pocketbook. I will put the flower in the back of this diary and keep it there. I told him that we could've gotten into a lot of trouble. He laughed. He told me that he loved living on the edge. I enjoy the excitement of being with him. Even traveling on his motorcycle is like an adventure for me. B. goes fast. He weaves in and out of traffic with impunity. He relies on his unbelievably fast reflexes. He senses situations well before I am aware of them. Normally that would set me on edge, but for some reason, and I don't know why, I am totally relaxed sitting behind him on that rather large motorcycle.

B. and Stephen are total opposites in many ways. Stephen is much taller, yet B. is much stronger and much more physical. Stephen is a very reasonable, sedate person. B. is adventurous. Stephen is dark-haired with dark eyes. B. has light brown hair and luminous blue eyes. Stephen is always serious and is very wise. B. just enjoys life as it comes. He savors life as he does a good meal! When I am with B., I find myself doing more whimsical things. However, they both share some very good traits: both are honest, caring men with good hearts. I know I love Stephen. I think I am somewhat in love with B.

June 22-28: I am really excited. I missed my period, and I am usually very regular. I'm going to give it another month to see if it comes or not. I thought about this all my adult life. I want a child more than anything else in this world. If I am pregnant, then this will be the answer to my prayer and Stephen's. God, I hope so.

This Friday we went to *Le Gentilly* and, as usual, we dined with Andre. And guess what? Madame had Coquille St. Jacques again as a special and informed us that it will be the special every Friday until their vacation time in August. She really likes B.! This time, Andre, still miffed, enjoyed what is also his favorite dish. I was careful to have only one glass of wine, and I did not smoke after the meal. Can't be too careful! B. did not notice, as he was deeply involved with a philosophical discussion with Andre. I am sure that Stephen would have noticed. He does pay attention to these little details. I suppose this is one of the reasons I do love him so much. I just hope that I'm not being overly cautious.

June 29-July 5: Last week of class. I will miss our morning sessions as my French has really improved. B. tries hard, but languages are difficult for him, particularly annunciating the nasal twang that proper French requires. B. took me back to the museum displaying the Van Gogh paintings. After spending another afternoon there, B. purchased a book of the master's paintings for me. The book is written in Dutch, but the displays of the paintings are beautiful. I will always treasure it.

July 7-19: I missed making an entry last week, as B. and I spent every day exploring this beautiful city. Most of the time we took the Metro, as it was easier than trying to find parking spaces for the motorcycle. Besides, it allowed B. to have wine with his meals. Although he is adventurous, B. absolutely refuses to mix alcohol and driving. One afternoon we went to Montmartre Butte. On top of it were a collection of artists. There you could see them create a painting, and if you liked it, buy some of their works. The only way to this location was up a large flight of stairs. By the time we got to the top, I was totally winded. B. let me set the pace, and so it took a long time to get to the top. After regaining my breath, we spent a delightful afternoon watching various painters apply their craft. The elevated view was spectacular, as you can see all the major sites in the city. When we descended the stairs to return to the Metro, B. noticed a kosher Jewish delicatessen. So, we had lunch there. I really enjoyed it.

July 21-27: I missed my period again! I made an appointment with a gynecologist next Tuesday. I have my fingers crossed. In the last two weeks, B. and I, after going to the English bookstore, would travel to the main American Express office in Paris. B. wanted to check to see if there were any messages from his parents. He is awaiting orders from the Air Force, and the service knows that his parents are his main point of contact. Well, on Monday we went to the American Express office as usual. But this time, there was a message from B.'s mom telling him that his formal orders were sent to the American Embassy in Paris, and he was to go there to receive them. We got directions as to the location of the embassy and proceeded there immediately. It's a large gated building that had American Marines as guards. B., dressed in his usual jeans and T-shirt, walked up to a very large, impeccably uniformed Marine. B. then pulled out his wallet and presented his military ID to the Marine guard. The guard, in turn, realizing that B. was an officer, sharply saluted which B. returned. B. asked where to go to pick up his orders, and the guard promptly responded with the directions. As we walked to the appropriate desk, I was finally struck that the man with whom I am currently sharing my life and my love is part of the military. Before this event, our temporary life together has been a beautiful vacation . . . a pause from the harsh realities of life . . . almost dreamlike. We approached a State Department official who again examined B.'s ID and gave him an envelope. B. signed a receipt and we left the embassy. When we got outside, B. opened the letter and read the orders. He had to be home in two weeks in order to take a physical at McGuire Air Force Base. We went back to the American Express office, where B. arranged his return flight back to New York on Saturday, August 7. He was lost in thought as we returned to his room. I think I found a way to distract him!

July 28-Aug 2: I am much more tired than usual—another sign that I might be pregnant. I told B. that I wanted to go to the English bookstore and purchase some more books that I could read on the trip home. We took the Metro to the appropriate stop, and we spent several hours in the bookstore.

B. was excited because he was able to purchase a recently printed copy of Theodore H. White's new book, <u>The Making of the President, 1964.</u> When we returned to his room, I told B. that I needed to sleep, which I did. I stripped down to my undies and his large cotton shirt and immediately fell asleep in his bed. B. sat in the overstuffed chair and started reading his new book. I woke up about two hours later, and I marveled at the intensity in which he read. I was up and stirring, yet he was so focused on the book that he was unaware that I was even awake. I lay on my back, snuggled under the blankets, and observed my lover for more than half an hour. Seeing such fervor during the act of reading really turned me on. I called to B., and he put the book down and came to me. I was so turned on that I experienced an orgasm almost the moment he entered me!

On Friday, we met Andre at *Le Gentilly*. Of course, we ordered Coquille St. Jacques. It was our Friday ritual. While we were eating, Madame came to our table and told us that Wednesday, August 4th would be the last day that the restaurant would be open before they left for a four-week holiday. B. told them about the orders that he just received. It was like fate bringing closure to a perfect summer.

On Saturday, B. and I went "caving." We took the Metro to the Cardinal Richelieu stop where there were underground restaurants called "caves." Each cave had its own specialty. One would have salads and appetizers. Some would have more formal entrées, and others specialized in deserts. A person could go from cave to cave in order to have a complete meal. The third and last restaurant we entered had an Israeli singer as entertainment. She was a pretty, well-built woman with long dark hair, who was wearing a blouse that showed ample cleavage. She wore a gold necklace with a large six-pointed star which rested comfortably within her exposed bosom. She did her own accompaniment on a guitar and would take requests if accompanied by a tip. B. gave her a fr.10 note and asked her to play the "Hatikvah" which is the Israeli national anthem. This "cave" was populated by many Muslims. The singer asked B. if he was seriously requesting this song. B. said he was, and so she played and sang the Hatikvah. It is a beautiful and haunting song. When we left the cave, two Muslims followed us out of the restaurant. One of them tried to come between B. and myself. B., without looking or taking a second thought, jammed his elbow into the intruder's chest. The man fell immediately to the side-walk and lay there in an unconscious state. I looked back and the fallen man was being attended to by his companion. B. told me to walk on and not look back. Later, B. told me that he gave that man a "solar plexus shot" which he learned in the martial arts class that was part of his Air Force training. The whole incident really shook me up. I asked him why he would ask that singer to play the Hatikvah. His answer was simple: "I really love that song, and I was sure that she could sing it properly." This incident was important to me. It crystallized what I had to do. I could spend a summer with B., but not a lifetime. I am not cut out to live on the edge. I need security. I need normalcy in my life. I always knew that it would be difficult to separate myself from B. Now it would be less so, especially if I am pregnant and I think I am!

Aug 3: I saw the gynecologist today, and she confirmed that I am pregnant. She told me if I wanted to keep the baby that I would require a major amount of rest. So, I left her office, returned to my hotel room and made arrangements to leave on August 5. I called Stephen and let him know the wonderful news. He was as excited as I was. I told him I couldn't wait to get home. Then we could be married immediately so as to make our baby legitimate. Stephen told me that we would go to Las Vegas on the weekend of August 10 to get married there. We would do a large formal wedding at a later date. I was ecstatic.

Aug 4: This evening, B. and I went to *Le Gentilly* for the last supper that I would have in Paris. B. and I joined a large group of regular customers. It was beautiful and it was melancholy. About ten o'clock that evening, we returned to B.'s room for the last time. The lovemaking was the most intense sexual experience of my life. In the morning he told me that I literally passed out after having sex. He was worried until he heard me breathing regularly. B. took off his t-shirt and showed me his back. Apparently, I dug my nails into him so deeply that there were six very red scratches that were so deep it took a while for the bleeding to stop. I was appalled. I did that!? Apparently so, although I have no memory of it. He laughed and told me not to worry about it and that last night was what Hemingway called, "having the Earth move beneath you!" That morning, B. took me back to my hotel. He thanked me for bringing him back to life and for sharing the summer with him. He would always be grateful. I reminded him of his oath, and he assured me that he would keep his word. He told me that he was looking forward to returning to flying status and resuming his Air Force career. He would miss me regardless of whatever happens in the future. B., wearing a smile, quoted Humphrey Bogart from the movie 'Casablanca': "At least we will always have Paris." We shared a long kiss goodbye. Then he turned and walked away. That was the last time I ever laid eyes on him. I am pretty sure that he was going to be sent to Vietnam. At least he thought so. May God watch over him.

Aug 5: This is my last entry in this diary. I am writing this on the airplane going home. Earlier, I called Stephen and told him when and where I would arrive back in Boston. Looking back on this summer, I have no regrets. I shared my time and my life with a wonderful man whom I will miss. I have something that I can look back on in my dotage and smile in reminiscence. I will see my doctors immediately as the pregnancy is very draining on me. I am not very strong physically. I do so want to see and have this baby. I just hope that he or she will be born healthy. Nothing is more important to me than the advent of this child. I do so want, above all things, to be a very good mother. God's will be done.

Anna finished reading her mother's diary and without words, she handed the small book to Mark so that he could read it. She watched him start to read as she quietly concentrated on what was on her mind. It was a strange and different place for her intellectually. She'd never thought of her mother as a sexual person. Obviously, she was. Who knew? After taking several more minutes to digest what she had read, it further dawned upon her that her mother was about the same age as she was now when all of these events occurred. She placed her hand on her bulging midsection, comforting the life now forming within her, and felt closer to her mother than she had in a long time.

1

INTRODUCTION

My name is Norris Blakeman. Now what kind of name is Norris? I don't know. But my mother liked it, and so I got stuck with it. My friends, all my life, just called me Blake.

I was born in 1942 during World War II. Both my parents were children of Jewish immigrants from Europe. Both were the youngest child in their respective families, and both were fluent in Yiddish. In fact, when they wanted to have a conversation that my brother, sister or I could not understand, they spoke in that language. I am the eldest of three siblings. We were raised in Brooklyn. When I was about seven years old, we moved to Long Island. In both my father and mother's extended families, my paternal grandfather and I were the only blonde-haired, blue-eyed and left-handed persons. Upon achieving adulthood, I stood 68 inches tall and weighed 153 pounds. I so resembled my father's father that I quickly became Grandma's favorite grandson. Grandpa died when I was quite young. Yet as I grew older, I quickly discovered that much of my character, as well as my physical being, came from him.

When Grandma and Grandpa were very young, they lived in a small shtetl (town) on the Russian Polish border. When Grandma, then the prettiest girl in the village, turned fifteen years old, her father arranged a marriage to the wealthiest bachelor available. Grandma, however, was in love with a sixteen-year-old, blonde-haired, blue-eyed, spirited youth. Grandma gave her father an offer he could not refuse, i.e., she would not go to her wedding bed a virgin unless she would be allowed to marry the love of her life. My great-grandfather loved his daughter very much and acceded to her wishes even though the man she was going to marry was dirt poor. Grandma and Grandpa got married at the ages of fifteen and sixteen respectively. Grandpa may have been poor, but he could read in several languages, and he was good with numbers. Their married life together was very difficult. Several of their children died of starvation due to the unrelenting prejudice against Jewish people in Eastern Europe.

To free his family from the overwhelming poverty and persecution which was pervasive in Tsarist Russia, Grandpa passed as a Christian and joined the Russian Army and rode with the Cossacks. He progressed quickly through the enlisted ranks, as he could read, write and do arithmetic. Grandpa eventually earned a place in the quartermaster section. Part of his duties was passing out and recording the pay given to other soldiers. In that position, he stole enough money to smuggle his wife and two remaining children out of the country and immigrate to the United States. My father was their youngest child and one of the four children who eventually survived. When I was four years old, Grandpa died at the age of eighty-six. Grandma and Grandpa were together for seventy years. Of all the grandchildren, I was the one who resembled Grandpa both in physicality and in personality.

It was apparent to the entire extended family that I was Grandma's favorite. Indeed, when Grandma visited with us, or we visited with her, she would not allow Mom or Dad to punish me, even when justly deserved! When Grandma would pass out gifts, I always received more than any other grandchild. Grandma died when I was eleven years old.

My father, Meyer Blakeman, was a very successful businessman. He married my mother, Lillian Schultz, about five years prior to World War II. He never served in the armed forces as he was past the draft age for World War II. Because he was so successful, he moved the family to Long Island. Basically, I grew up in Syosset, a very affluent suburb of New York City.

My father grew up in poverty. Financial success was the driving force in his life. When I was young, he had very little time for his children. He was a good and kind man who took his responsibility as the breadwinner of the family extremely seriously. He possessed a wonderful sense of humor, a dry wit, and he was well read and self-educated. He left almost all of the child rearing decisions to my mother. Looking back, I think he missed out on enjoying the best part of living because he did not fully participate in the lives of his children. The extreme poverty of his early youth adversely influenced his value system. Financial success, which he achieved, became an overarching goal of his life. That is until his last few years when he started to appreciate his children. I believe that before he died, he regretted some of his life decisions that caused him to miss sharing the normal ups and downs of family life. For example, I played four years of varsity soccer and two years of international soccer, and my father never saw a single game.

My mother basically raised all three of us. Mom, the youngest of three siblings, was denied any education beyond high school because she was a female. In the first half of the 20th century, Jewish women were not normally permitted to attend college. The expectation in the traditional role of Jewish life at that time was marriage, keeping a kosher home, and providing children for their husbands and for the community. Mom's particular problem was that God gave her a magnificent brain and then placed her in early 20th century society which basically confined her to the kitchen and the home. Doing housework and raising children, particularly after all her children started school, made her very frustrated. Combining that frustration with a very strong, almost virulent, temper sometimes caused Mom to be downright irrational. I was very much her child: God blessed me with a first-rate brain and cursed me with a similar temper.

When I was thirteen years old, Mom received a job offer to edit a local newspaper. She was not only fluent in four languages, but she was also "instant spell check" and "grammar check" without using a computer. Mom would do the *New York Times* crossword puzzle in ink and in less than 20 minutes. My father was appalled that she wanted to work. In one of the few times that he put his foot down, he forbade her from working outside of the home. Mom, who loved my father very much, acceded to his wishes. Hence, she took up the card game "bridge" where in less than two years she became a "life master." I learned how to play bridge in college, and I became a first-rate player. I played in some of the top-rated clubs in the New York area and even won some local championships. But in all my days, I never saw her equal. Simply put, my mother was far and away, absolutely the best bridge player who I have ever encountered.

Mom's abilities were extensive. She could read people like they were an open book. Her "personal radar" was unmatched. Part of that first-rate intellect that God both blessed and inflicted upon her was her ability to quickly, adroitly and completely understand any person who came into her orbit. A quick example will suffice. During my college years, my cousin Joan who was the daughter of my mother's sister, suffered a miscarriage after carrying her baby for 8 1/2 months. That miscarriage also caused my cousin to lose her ability to procreate. My family, all five of us, were driving to my cousin's house in order to sit "shiva" with her. Mom and Dad were in the front seat, and the three siblings occupied the back. Mom said to Dad, "I hope that Stan's sisters do not come sit "shiva" with Joan." Stan was Joan's husband.

Dad responded to Mom's surprising statement, "Why would you want that?"

Mom replied, "Because they both just gave birth to healthy babies and when they get there that's the first thing that will come out of their mouths . . . and that will devastate Joan! That's why!"

Dad: "No one could be that insensitive, period!"

Mom: "Just watch. You'll see."

Dad continued driving in silence and after a while we talked about other things. We got to Joan's home where we were welcomed by Mom's sister, my Aunt Bea. Joan was crying while sitting on the sofa. She got up when she saw my family enter. She hugged each of us, and all of us tried to comfort her in whatever way we could. I then sat down next to Joan. She asked me how college was treating me, and I told her all about my ups and downs with the coeds of my school. She really got into my personal peccadilloes and that gave her some relief from the unrelenting sadness of her reality. Sure enough, after we were there about a half-hour, one of Stan's sisters entered the room and, just as Mom predicted, started talking about her healthy newborn child. The effects, again as Mom predicted, were devastating. Joan sobbed uncontrollably for about 20 minutes before she finally regained some sense of control.

About ten minutes after she stopped crying, Stan's second sister came into the room and again, as Mom predicted, started to talk about her healthy baby. The results were the same. Joan was left sobbing again. This time it took almost an hour before she would regain control of herself. As usual, Mom "called the shots".

My mother had red hair and green eyes. She was about 5'3" and weighed about 130 pounds. Her features were very attractive except for a hook in her nose. When I was in junior high school, Mom had a "nose-job." The operation fixed the only flaw in her face. In one fell swoop, Dad got his trophy wife and his original wife in the same package. What I would later call a win-win situation. Mom, when she wanted, could, and did, dominate a meeting or some kind of social gathering. She was a blend of grace, beauty and intelligence. It was only in my later life that I came to realize the depths of her mind and the dead-on instincts created by the brilliant mind that God gave her. I often wonder what her life would have been had she been born some 50 years later. Her suffering caused by the social roles that ladies of her age were forced to endure made me devoutly support the cause of equal opportunities for women.

Mom and Dad made a very good couple. Where Mom was fiery and intense; Dad was temperate and slow to burn. Both were incessant readers and basically self-educated. When Mom got interested in any subject, she focused like a laser beam. Dad had a more general informational approach. His interests were widespread and extremely varied. As a result, Dad had an informed opinion on almost any subject that was brought to his attention.

Dad was 5' 7" and weighed about 205 pounds. He carried his wide girth well. In his youth he played baseball which was the only sport, besides golf, that he cared to play or to follow. He had a round face, brown eyes and a goatee. When he smiled, his whole face sort of "joined in." He was a successful businessman. He started as a truck driver and eventually came to own a small fleet of trucks.

When he hired other drivers, he went to the Teamsters Union and insisted that all his drivers be members of the local chapter. When issues of pay and benefits would arise, he told the union leader that his men would receive the same package as the bigger fleets and, if there was a strike, his men would receive the new pay and benefits from the first day of the strike retroactively. Over the years, many of his route assigners were also the shop stewards. In a few instances where there was a dispute, he took it to the union bosses who decided the issue. The respect for him was so deep that he won every time.

When I turned seventeen, I needed summer employment for my college years. Dad asked the leader of the union local to obtain a job for me. He provided an assembly line job bottling Pepsi-Cola. Of course, Dad and the union leader insisted that I join the union which I did. Dad believed, as I do today, that a man's labor is not just another commodity but the support of a family and the basis of a person's self-worth. It was worthy and deserving of common protection.

When my father wanted to expand the business, about the time I was seven or eight years old, he went to see his father-in-law, a well-connected, Orthodox Jewish man. Grandpa was not rich, but he knew many wealthy German Jews. He arranged a loan for my father without the normal collateral. What secured the loan for Dad was Grandpa's assertion that "Meyer Blakeman was a good man . . . a mensch!" His collateral was his reputation. The loan was to be paid back in a 10-year period. Dad completely satisfied the principal and interest in less than five years.

My father was a very generous man who lived his life in the present tense. When his father-in-law reached the age of eighty-three, Dad paid for a second Bar Mitzvah for Grandpa. In the Orthodox Jewish tradition, a lifetime is considered seventy years of age. So, Granddad was in his second life and celebrated his second Bar Mitzvah. My father gladly paid for this lavish celebration. It was Dad's way of saying thank you and showing respect.

Dad paid all my expenses through college. When I graduated, he told me that I was on my own financially which was fine with me. He provided me with a first-rate education, and that's what I needed to make my way in this world.

My father usually acceded to my mother's wishes. He was calm while she was fiery. Many times, Mom would react in anger or with some other emotion. Dad was as cool as the proverbial cucumber. He almost never lost his temper which is a trait I wish that I had more from him than of her. Unfortunately for our family, both Mom and I shared the same temper. This combination made it very difficult for us to find a common emotional agreement. When Mom and I would get into our usual arguments, my father would invariably side with his wife, and I would hear about a million times, "She's right because she is your mother!" This constant battling between my mother and me was ameliorated by the fact that I went away to college. In this case, absence, indeed, did make the heart grow fonder.

The one exception is informative. As I indicated before, Dad and the union got me a job on the assembly line bottling Pepsi-Cola. I worked there for four summers. During that time, I spent so much time working and being with my friends that there was little time left to interact with my immediate family. That also helped to reduce the friction. The third summer I worked there was one of the hottest in the recorded history of Long Island. During a particularly elongated hot spell, the main bottling line broke down, and the company was forced to use the second line around the clock for eight days until repairs were completed. That meant that senior workers worked from 6:00 AM to 4:00 PM. Junior workers like I was had to work from 4 PM to 6 AM every day for the eight days that the main line was down.

During this time, my mother's menopause was reaching critical mass. Her physical discomfort, mixed with her fiery disposition, made living with her unbearable, even for my father who loved her very much. Dad told me if I could avoid having an argument with my mother during this hot summer, he would buy me a car and pay for the automobile insurance during my last two years in college. All I had to do, for that summer, was **not** get into an argument with my mother. The long hours I worked because the main line was down helped in this cause. I missed almost all of her temper tantrums because I was working fourteen to sixteen hours a day doing backbreaking work in a factory that stayed between 80 and 90°F. By the time I got home, I would shower, sleep, eat something and go back to work. There was no time for friends or for fun, or for anything else, including arguing with Mom. After my eighth day working the elongated shifts, I arrived home at nine o'clock in the morning and took my usual shower. I was so tired that I left my soiled clothes in a pile in the middle of the bedroom which my brother and I shared. About an hour after I went to bed, my mother came into my room and picked up my dirty and sweaty clothes. Normally Mom would understand the situation and go with it but not this time. She lost her temper and started yelling at me. I was so tired that I didn't hear her, even though she was very loud. Finally, in desperation to be heard, she threw me out of my bed. Now, as tired as I was, I lost my temper. Car or no car, I didn't care. At that point, all I felt was anger. My father, hearing the commotion, came into the room.

Normally my calm-cool dad was anything but. He was as angry as I have ever seen him in my lifetime. He came into the room because Mom and I were yelling at each other. And neither one of us was listening to the other. In a loud, booming voice, Dad demanded, "SILENCE! Both of you!" Both Mom and I immediately stopped shouting and looked at my dad. The anger on his face was palpable. I was expecting to hear again as I've heard millions of times before, "She's right, because she's your mother!" But that is not what I heard. Indeed, my father turned to his wife and said, "Lillian, he gets the car. I don't care if he commits several felonies, he gets the car. DO YOU UNDERSTAND?!" My mother, realizing that she had gone too far, nodded. Then Dad told my Mom to go to her room . . . and she meekly did! That's when I knew that my father, who would give Mom almost anything that she desired, had his limits and that he would stand up to her if the issue was important enough.

Mom's anger, fueled in-part by her frustration, caused psychological damage to all three of her children. I know that my personal interaction with my mother affected my relationships with women all the rest of my life. It made it difficult for me to connect emotionally with any woman, even those whom I came to love.

After a reasonably normal upbringing, I went off to college. And that's where the story begins.

2

THE COLLEGE YEARS

Just after my 18th birthday, I attended Marietta College located in southern Ohio at the intersection of the Muskegon and Ohio Rivers. This school, at one time, was a Baptist oriented institution. Several years before I got there, the administration wanted to expand its pool of potential applicants and therefore became a secular rather than a religious institution. Being Jewish did not deter them from accepting my application. The school itself was a small liberal arts college with enrollment of about 1,200 students in total. I personally liked the warmth and intimacy of a small campus. Looking back, I can tell you without a doubt that I really enjoyed the four years I spent there.

In my first month attending Marietta College, I rushed several fraternities and was accepted into Tau Epsilon Phi. This fraternity, which I joined in my first semester, was a milder version of the one portrayed in *National Lampoon's Animal House*. We partied pretty hard, but most of the members were fairly studious in regard to their academic efforts. For my own part, I was more of a partier than an academic. I studied just enough to get by.

Most of the friends I made on campus were my fraternity brothers. In my sophomore year, I became very close with two of them in particular. Both became my roommates when we moved into a three-bedroom reconstructed, off-campus residence which was originally built sometime just after the Civil War. We stayed there until we graduated in June of 1964 because the rent was affordable. It was located on a hill overlooking the campus. We three were the only students in the neighborhood which was comprised of hard-working, blue-collar families who had numerous children and dogs. Our neighbors were upset, at first, when they found out that college students were going to be living in their neighborhood. However, they soon realized that we kept reasonable hours, and we behaved in a normal fashion. As a result, that resentment quickly turned into acceptance, and we became an integral part of the neighborhood . . . but more about that later.

My two best friends and roommates were Jared "JG" Gladon and Luigi "Lou" Cesore Cevenni. JG came from Great Neck, Long Island. He was several inches taller than I and weighed about 10 to 15 pounds more than he should have. JG had blonde hair, a round face filled with freckles and blue eyes that were set close together. He supported a small mustache which accentuated his rather smallish mouth. JG, also a Long Island Jew, possessed a sharp wit and keen mind. He had the ability to "read" people quickly. Often, we would share the same opinion of a person, but in almost every case he would get there first. His father was a very successful CPA whose accounting practice generated more than a comfortable income. Like my father, Mr. Gladon worked long hours and had little time for his children. And like my father, Mr. Gladon was too young to fight in World War I and too old to be drafted in World War II. JG had a definitive love-hate relationship with his father. He resented the fact that he never had a kind word to say about anything that JG did, yet getting the old man's approval became one of the main driving forces in JG's life. JG's mom died when he was in high school, so I never got to meet her. He was raised by his older sister, Susan, with whom he was very close. Susan left home right after JG left for college in order to start her own life away from her dominating dad. In the summertime, when we were not in school, JG would spend a lot of time with my family. We gave him the space he needed when the usual arguments started with his father. Besides, my dad was not a very judgmental person. In fact, he was just the opposite. Dad was warm, accepting, and possessed a wonderful sense of humor. My mother really liked JG, and she did her best to include him in much of what we did as a family. JG found acceptance and affection without conflict in my family's environment. JG became my de facto brother besides being my fraternity brother and best friend.

My other roommate, Lou, was born and raised in western Connecticut. His parents were both Italian immigrants. He had four brothers and sisters and was raised in a warm loving family environment. His father was a master carpenter whose moderate income was the sole financial support of the family. His mother was a stay-at-home mom who was deeply involved in all her children's lives and ambitions. His dad, Luigi Sr., helped with the children as much as he could after working long hours. Lou and his dad shared an abiding love for music. Lou was a superb trumpeter and saxophone player which he learned from his musically gifted father. In fact, by his senior year in high school, both Lou and his dad earned extra income by playing in the same jazz band.

Their home was modest and inviting. It was always filled with the smell of simmering tomato sauce (which his family called "gravy") emanating from the kitchen. Lou had black hair and wide-set, dark brown eyes. He was an inch short of six-foot with a lean, muscular body. He was a perfect example of something that my father taught me over the years. Dad used to say that there was no correlation between intelligence and wisdom. I could hear his deep voice, even now: "Norris, I know men who were very smart and constantly made poor life decisions. And I know others, not so smart, who always made good life decisions. Intelligence is a fine trait, but wisdom is more valuable!" Lou was the personification of this concept. He had to work harder than anybody in our fraternity in order to maintain a decent average.

But none of my fraternity brothers made better life decisions than Lou. When he was a freshman in high school, Lou was involved in a very serious automobile accident. He was a passenger in a car driven by his high school friend's mother when a drunk driver suddenly veered into oncoming traffic resulting in a head-on collision. Lou was the only survivor but just barely. He was in a coma for over a month. When he awoke, he was blind. It took the doctors four operations over the next two years to help him recover some eyesight. As result of this accident, Lou was forced to wear very thick glasses and, even with the optical corrections, his eyesight never got better than 20-50. During that recovery time, Lou honed his musical skills. The loss of eyesight sharpened his ability to differentiate musical notes. By his senior year in high school, he was a better artist than his gifted father. As a result, he was getting offers from well-established jazz bands all over the country. Lou made sufficient income from his musical gigs to completely fund his own education.

It took Lou several years to get over his survivor guilt as he was the only one to come out alive from that horrific crash. But in time, he came to realize that what had happened wasn't his fault. His innate wisdom drove his efforts to get on with his life. He witnessed the example set by his parents as to how a person should live his life. He cherished the love he received from his parents and siblings. When he went on numerous music gigs around the country, he saw many different kinds of people who possessed many more material items in their lives than the rather meager possessions that he and his family owned. He was never jealous of them. Indeed, he felt sorry for people who had things and not relationships. Unlike the rest of his hormone-driven fraternity brothers, Lou was not looking just to get "laid." He was looking for a deep and meaningful relationship. The accident, the ensuing recovery time, and the threat of potentially being permanently blind ended his adolescence. Unlike the rest of us, when Lou entered college, he was already a man.

In the spring semester of our sophomore year, both JG and Lou met their life partners. JG first met Constance Hope Thompson in an introductory psychology course. She really disliked her first name and preferred to use her middle name, Hope. JG struck up a conversation with Hope after the initial class. She appreciated his quick mind and sharp biting humor, so Hope accepted his invitation to have coffee together in the student union where they continued the conversation that was started in class. Hope was a 5'4" slender girl with light brown, shoulder-length hair and light blue eyes. She had a wide, generous mouth which produced an absolutely radiant smile when she was happy. Overall, a very attractive young lady. JG was immediately and strongly attracted to her. They quickly started dating and within a month they were a solid couple. Hope's family came from Virginia, and they were old line Presbyterians with very deep roots in their native Roanoke. As the relationship deepened, Hope's family had problems dealing with her choice of involvement with a Jewish man. Her father, the head of the family, argued vehemently against this budding relationship. The harder he pushed; the more Hope wanted to be with JG.

By their senior year, Hope and JG knew that they were going to get married after graduation.

My other roommate, Lou, met Nancy Lee Jordan in an American history class. For him, it was love at first sight. Her light blonde hair cascaded past her shoulders and fell to the middle of her back. Like Lou, she wore rather thick glasses, as her vision was poor without them. Her light blue eyes were widely separated and when she took off her glasses, I could see how pretty they were. She was, at 5'9", taller than I and two inches shorter than Lou. Nancy possessed long legs and generous curves. It was easy for me to understand why Lou was so attracted to her. Nancy's family came from Alabama where her father was a Baptist minister who believed in the literal Word. The Baptist background of Marietta College was the reason that her dad let her attend this particular institution of higher learning. Nancy was a shy girl with limited experience in dating. Lou chatted with her after every class for a month before he finally got the nerve to ask her out. Their first date was a movie followed by a trip to the "Fat Boy" restaurant for strawberry pie and coffee. Lou finally got to kiss her good night on the third date. He respected her traditional values. Indeed, he found them appealing and enhanced the love he felt for this wide-eyed, innocent young woman. Lou never pressured Nancy for sex or sexual contact. He sensed that Nancy was her dad's daughter. She was a born-again Christian who wanted to go to her wedding bed as a virgin. Lou, the most grown-up of all the students that I knew, not only appreciated her faith, but loved her for it. He was willing to abide by her wishes. By the middle of our junior year, Lou and Nancy were totally committed to a future together after graduation. During spring break of that year, Lou accompanied Nancy to her Alabama home. He later told me that her father grilled him "up one side and down another." When the old man was satisfied that Lou would respect his religion and respect her traditional values, he allowed the relationship to continue. When the pastor determined just how much Lou loved his little girl and the fact that he was truly a man in every sense of the word, the pastor gave both of them his blessing.

The girlfriends spent a great deal of time at our home. It was customary in the early '60s that college girls had a hard curfew: 10:00 PM on Sunday through Thursday; and 1:00 AM on Friday and Saturday nights. We normally made supper for ourselves and spent the evening quietly studying. During the weekend, I attended the parties which sprouted up around campus while my two roommates and their girl-friends would go see a movie and spend the remainder of the evening watching TV at our house. Unlike my roommates, I never established a steady relationship with any of the girls I dated.

In the spring, JG and I would go to the common area just behind our house and practice for the upcoming softball season. At Marietta College, the intramural softball games drew more fans than the var-sity baseball team. JG was the pitcher, and I was the centerfielder for our fraternity softball team. The children from the neighborhood were naturally curious, so they watched us as we played catch. After a while, JG and I set up bases and let the children play "running bases" with us which we all enjoyed. Just about every afternoon from the middle of March until finals started in the middle of May, JG and I would be out there playing running bases with the kids in our neighborhood. Of course, all the dogs in the neighborhood would join in. As a result, we found ourselves babysitting about a dozen kids whose ages varied from 3 to 12 years old. One of our neighbors was an elderly couple who babysat their daughter's two girls, aged five and three years old respectively. Their mother worked, as the children's father was out of the picture. We turned out to be a godsend for our elderly neighbors, as both had difficulty moving around.

Another neighbor was a young couple with an eight-year-old daughter. The mother was a twenty-five-year-old woman who had to work part time in order to help support the family. She told us that she used to be a catcher on her high school softball team. One day, she asked me if I would mind if she warmed up JG's arm. I told her that would be fine with me. She went to her house and came back wearing a T-shirt and very tight-fitting shorts. JG started pitching to her. One of his pitches went low and wide, and when the young lady bent down to catch the low pitch, lo and behold, her very tight shorts (which she wore when she was in high school) split from the top of the zipper all way back to just below the belt. She quickly rose and saw that she was basically standing outside in her underwear. She immediately turned beet red and ran back to her house. Being the "sensitive" guys that we were, we started calling her "Yogi" after the famous Hall of Fame catcher, Yogi Berra. Within two days, all my neighbors, including her husband, started calling this delightful young lady "Yogi." As far as I know, she is still being called by that name to this day.

Generally, around 5:30 in the afternoon, somebody in the neighborhood would start a charcoal barbecue. (This was the '60s and gas grills were not prevalent.) The other neighbors would go to the property of whomever started the initial fire and take their turns cooking whatever meat their family would eat that evening. The neighborhood was generally very noisy, because everybody, except us three college students, had children and dogs who loved to play outside until the sun went down and it was too dark to see. What amazed me was that a week before midterms and finals, all the kids and dogs were kept in the house. Our neighbors made it easier for us to study. We really appreciated the quiet.

At the start of our junior year, we acquired a female puppy. We decided to call her Arthur for two reasons. First, with her sad brown eyes and canine snout, she looked like one of our fraternity brothers named Arthur. Secondly, we figured that if we gave her a male name, she would be confused and not seek a male dog for sex when she went into heat. That did not work out as planned. By the end of our junior year, Arthur got herself knocked up. But being the good dog that she was, she gave birth to only one puppy. Arthur was a small white and brown dog that was mostly beagle. She had the run of our neighborhood and was more than welcome in any classroom or venue that belonged to Marietta College. She would visit the various fraternities and sororities, and pick up more than enough food . . . so much so that we rarely had to feed her. Everyone on campus knew her. For example, Lou and I took a course in statistics in the afternoon. Invariably, Arthur would meander into the classroom and sit between Lou and me. The professor, a dog lover himself, just smiled and appreciated her presence. In the spring evenings, when my softball team was not scheduled, I would umpire the other intramural softball games. Many a time, Arthur would come down from the hill and watch as I called balls and strikes. In between innings, she would come out to home plate to get her ears rubbed and then retreat behind the backstop.

Arthur became our living "alarm clock." From Monday through Saturday, Arthur would wake all three of us up by 7:30 in the morning as we generally had eight o'clock classes. On Sunday, however, Arthur let us sleep as long as we wanted. I don't know how she knew what day of the week it was, but she knew. Arthur slept in my bed, so I was always the first to get up. When she knew that I was up, she went on to Lou and licked his face until he awoke and patted her ears. Then she went on to JG's bed and did the same with him. Generally, we didn't talk until we got to the student union and had our first cup of coffee of the day and a small bite to eat. Then we said our "good mornings" to each other.

Arthur was never leashed while we were in college. She had the full run of the neighborhood and of the college grounds. We took turns taking Arthur to one of our respective homes during vacation periods. During spring break of our junior year, JG went home with Hope to meet her parents, and Lou went home with Nancy to meet her family. Generally, JG and I would take my car in order to return to Long Island where both our families lived. I advertised on campus for others who wanted a ride to the New York City area for spring break. I drove a small, beetle-shaped Saab that could hold four people. Three coeds responded to my advertisement and I agreed to take all of them to the New York City area. Since my roommates were going to their girlfriends' homes, it was decided among the three of us that I would take Arthur for spring break. Arthur was put on a leash for these trips as I generally stopped about three times at busy truck stops before reaching home. During this particular trip, I gave one of the coeds, a very pretty girl named Carol, the leash and asked her to walk my dog so that she could do her "business," and I could refuel my car. I watched this process in order to ensure that the proper amount of oil was mixed with the gasoline because my Saab was a two-cycle engine. About five minutes after I gave Carol the leash, she returned to the car holding both hands away from her body and crying. I asked what happened. It seemed that Arthur found a dead critter and started eating it. Carol tried to take it away from her, so she had part of a carcass on her hands. She handed me the leash and immediately ran to the bathroom to clean up. I really did forget to tell her about Arthur's proclivity to eat dead things.

It usually took about twelve hours to go between Marietta and the New York City area. This trip took 16 hours with three girl passengers. I think we stopped at about every possible bathroom between Ohio and New York! On the return trip back to Marietta, I told the girls that we would make three stops, and the last one would be Marietta College. I never saw any car empty as quickly as mine did when those girls left my car to use the bathroom during each stop! I made JG promise me after that particular spring break that he would never abandon me to travel with three girls again. He laughed and told me that "he would have my back."

Arthur was treated like a member of the family in each of our respective homes. She was a very friendly dog who loved people. Even JG's dad, usually a very dour person, warmed up to this loving dog. But the family that was best suited for her was Lou's family as he had several younger siblings. When Arthur had her puppy, Lou's family adopted him. After graduation, we decided that Arthur would go home with Lou's family.

During my four years at Marietta College, I never got serious with those whom I dated. I had a great deal of difficulty even talking with a girl, as I was extremely shy. That problem was helped by a strange confluence of events. After my sophomore year was over, there was a three-week strike at the Pepsi-Cola plant where I worked during the summer. I had some free time as I was not working on the assembly line. One of my fraternity brothers, *Ron Holfman,* knew that I was extraordinarily bashful around girls. He extended an invitation to spend a week with him and his family. Ron lived in Rockaway Beach which is part of New York City. His home was literally a stone's throw from a white sandy beach. Ron was a natural leader and athlete. He was the starting quarterback on his high school football team during all four years. As well, he was the starting catcher on the varsity baseball team. By his junior year in high school, he captained both squads. Upon first meeting him, he would not impress. He had average looks, light sandy hair, blue eyes and a slender build which gave no indication of what was inside. But, quite simply, he was one of the most natural and gifted leaders who I have ever encountered. He told me that if I spent a week with him and his family, he would help me overcome my shyness. I agreed.

His home was about an hour away from where I lived in Syosset, Long Island. I arrived on Saturday morning in early July. I met his parents and his younger sister. They made me feel right at home. That afternoon Ron took me to the beach where I would meet his high school friends and his girlfriend *Dana*. The prospect of meeting all these strangers made me very uneasy. Ron told me two things. First, be myself. And secondly, if Dana liked me, I would be accepted by the entire group. That afternoon, Ron and I made our way onto the beach. We carried nothing as the girls would bring the blankets, drinks and food. (Again, this was the 1960s!)

Ron's social group consisted of about 10 boys and 10 girls. The boys were the athletes who attended or graduated from Rockaway High School, and the girls were their cheerleaders. Thirty minutes after Ron introduced me to his friends, I figured out the social structure of the group. It was apparent to me that Ron, at 5'10" and the smallest male of the group was the unquestioned leader. The girls were pretty, but Ron's girlfriend, Dana, was easily the best looking of all of them. Each of the young ladies wore modest two-piece bathing suits, and the boys wore bathing trunks. Dana, a 5'6" brunette beauty with startling blue eyes was the leader of the girls. The best metaphor I could use to describe the social dynamics among the group was to compare it with the structure of a wolf pack. I clearly perceived that Ron and Dana were the alpha pair of the group. The rest of them took their cues from them.

Ron was two years older than Dana. They had started to date when she entered high school. Neither, since they first became a couple, dated anybody else. After I was introduced to all of them, Dana took me aside, and I spent the next hour and a half in a deep conversation with this very intelligent young lady. I'm not sure how she did it, but she got me to relax, and I found that I could really enjoy just talking with her. I spent the next week on the beach during the day talking with members of the group and playing football with the other guys. I'm a good athlete with exceptional speed, so I did pretty well. I was completely accepted by all of them and, after that week was over, I found it was easier for me to be myself with any young lady. As a result, I dated a half-dozen different coeds in my last two years at Marietta College, but none seriously.

My academic life at Marietta College was a mixed bag. When I first attended classes, my goal was to become a physician. The first year I got mostly A's and B's in the beginning academic courses. My sophomore year, my grades fell dramatically, as I found myself taking courses that I really did not enjoy. A perfect example of this was the vertebrate anatomy course which was taught by Prof. Silas. The most important part of the grade structure was the weekly labs. My average was about 15 out of 100 which meant that I was failing. However, Prof. Silas did have the following policy: He kept a small black book in the lower drawer of his desk. In this book he recorded humorous answers provided to him by the students who attended his class. If you made the 'book' you passed the course regardless of the merit of your grades. The trick, of course, was to make the 'book' which was the only way I was going to pass that course. During a lecture one morning, Dr. Silas asked the class, "What is a teat?" When no one volunteered, the professor asked one particular coed to answer the question. The young lady rose, turned very red, and finally stammered, "It is a nipple." Prof. Silas then asked another coed, "What is a nipple?" That young lady, got out of her seat, also blushing furiously, and finally answered, "A nipple is an enlarged sweat gland found on the breast." The professor then turned to me and asked, "Mr. Blakeman, what is a breast?" I stood up and said in a loud clear voice, "That's easy, sir. The breast is the white meat of the chicken!" Everyone laughed, including the professor. I saw him reach down to the lower left drawer, retrieve his black book, and make the entry. I never attended another class or lab after that, but I did pass the course!

In my junior year, I discovered economics. I took the introductory course and found that I really enjoyed the class and the professor who taught the subject. I started taking other various courses offered in economics and my grades improved dramatically. By my senior year, I was receiving all A's. I also noticed that my abilities to comprehend and retain knowledge were dramatically improving. I don't know why this occurred; I just know that it did. By my senior year, I retained more than 90% of what I read. My ability to do math also improved. It was like someone turned on a light in my head, and things that were difficult for me to retain or comprehend now became easy. When I took the GRE's (Graduate Record Exam), I scored in the top 5% both in math and economics and in the top 10% in language arts. When the grades were posted, my fraternity brothers (except JG) were astounded by my elevated results.

About a week before we graduated, JG, Lou and I decided to throw one humdinger of a party at our house. We not only invited all our fraternity brothers and all our campus friends, but we also invited the men in our neighborhood to attend, and they did. That was the only wild party that we had in the almost three years that we lived in that neighborhood. The music was very loud. We provided plenty of food, booze and beer. Thank God it was a warm evening because many of the invitees, including some of our neighborhood men, fell asleep on the grass. I guess we had a great time, but frankly I don't remember much of what happened! I do know, however, that the next morning there were some angry wives yelling at their drunken and sheepish husbands as they returned to their homes.

My parents came for graduation. Mom and Dad met all my neighbors. When the youngest granddaughter of the elderly couple who lived next to us presented me with a pressed flower, my mother was literally moved to tears. We had become part of the neighborhood, and I saw firsthand the real strength of our great country. It was these middle-class, hard-working men and women who provided the basic morality of our society. Their belief in the one God and in the Ten Commandments combined with their keeping faith with their country, their state, their neighborhood and with each other, created this moral backbone. When the politicians took this country to war, it was these people who provided the men and women who defended our country and our Constitution.

After graduation, both JG and Lou married their college sweethearts. Lou was the first to marry. JG and I drove down to a small town just outside of Birmingham, Alabama. Both of us were somewhat nervous, as we were Jews in the Deep South, and both of us opposed segregation. I wasn't sure what to expect during that weekend in late June. JG and I arrived Friday evening in time to attend the wedding rehearsal and dinner which followed. There we met Nancy's family. Her mother, Mrs. Jordan, was a tall, slender, blonde-haired woman who, nearing 50 years of age, still retained her feminine attractiveness. She was a very gracious person who made JG and me feel right at home. I met Nancy's brother and sister. It was easy to determine that all three siblings had the same parents. The center of the family revolved around Pastor Jordan. At 6'3", with thinning white hair and a booming voice, he was not only the head of his family, he was clearly the leader of his church and of the small town in which he resided. The pastor, unlike many of his white Alabama fellow citizens, did not approve or condone segregation. As a born-again Christian who believed in the absolute interpretation of the Word, he warmly accepted us as part of the wedding party.

During the weekend that we were there, both JG and I had a chance to talk with the pastor and discuss matters of faith. I found his interpretation of the last book in the New Testament, the Book of Revelation, both interesting and informative. He believed that those people and/or countries who turned against God's chosen people (the Jews) would be damned for all eternity. I found him, like myself, to be a strong supporter of the state of Israel. His discussion and interpretation of the Book of Revelation was very intriguing. So much so, that during the weekend I was there, I read this chapter from the New Testament in the Bible that was placed in the hotel room JG and I shared. After that weekend, I found that I had become comfortable in the company of born-again Christians.

The wedding was very traditional. The church held about one hundred fifty people. Every pew was filled. The pastor married his daughter to Lou in a quiet and dignified ceremony. I found it very moving. Afterwards, there was a wedding reception in the hall which housed the local VFW chapter. The food was ample and well prepared. Of course, there was no alcohol of any kind. The music provided by a five-piece band was traditional and not overly loud. The highlight of the afternoon occurred when Lou played his trombone for several numbers with the band. Everyone really enjoyed hearing him play as he was a superb musician. When Lou departed with his bride to parts unknown, JG and I started the long drive back to New York. On the way home, JG and I discussed how well we were received. Frankly, it surprised both of us.

A month later, I drove down to Roanoke and participated in JG's wedding. Unlike Nancy's family, Hope's parents were not particularly happy with their daughter's choice of a mate because she was marrying a person of the Jewish faith. Their ceremony was performed in Hope's family home. The entire wedding party consisted of 17 people: Hope's mother, father and sister; her aunt and uncle; JG's dad and sister; two sorority sisters of Hope; Lou and Nancy; three of her local friends; and of course, JG, Hope and me. The ceremony itself was very brief and performed by a local justice of the peace. The wedding reception, such as it was, was also in the family home. The food was sparse and not particularly appetizing. There was no music. Hope and JG left about two hours after being married.

However, it was great seeing both Lou and Nancy again. They had flown into Roanoke that morning to attend the wedding. All three of us left in my car just after JG and Hope departed for their honeymoon. We went to a local Denny's where we had a real meal and talked for several hours. I found out that Lou was accepted for graduate work at Auburn University and was going to start in the fall semester. Nancy had a job teaching elementary school. They would have sufficient funds to get by with her income enhanced by Lou's occasional musical gigs. Money would be tight, but they would get by. Besides, sharing this struggle only enhanced their relationship. It was great visiting with them. I drove them to the airport around six that evening and after hugs and kisses, we said our goodbyes. I was "alone with my thoughts" as I drove back to Long Island.

3

THE WASTED YEARS

During our senior year at Marietta College, JG and I had many conversations about our future. My personal inclination was to enlist in the Air Force, enroll in the Officer Training School (OTS) program, and eventually become a pilot. Many a night, JG and I would discuss that option. He said many times to me that an advanced degree was requisite in the work force that we were about to enter. JG was relentless in advising that I attend graduate school. Since my graduate record exam (GRE) scores were so high, I had obtained acceptances from three universities. I really wanted to join the military and fly, but JG's continuous warnings about the ability "to afford steak, rather than hamburger" mixed with my parents' advice and desire for me to attend graduate school pushed me to make a decision that I came to regret. Frankly, I allowed the people I loved and who loved me to make my decision.

After graduation, I returned to my Syosset home where I spent the summer. Instead of working as a Teamster for the Pepsi-Cola bottling company, I decided to take a job as a counselor in a day camp.

I loved kids, and I missed the ones that we used to take care of when we were living in Marietta. While working on Long Island, I met a lady counselor, Ellen. She was about three inches shorter than I with short dark curly hair, a round freckled face, large sad brown eyes and a full figure. Ellen possessed a superbly keen mind. She was fluent, at 18 years old, in four languages and conversant in three others. After knowing her for about a week, I asked her out on a date.

Ellen's parents were well into their 60s. They were both survivors of the Holocaust. Ellen was the only child that her mother would be able to bear, and she was born while both parents were about 45 years old. They absolutely lavished affection upon her. Ellen became the absolute center of the universe for two entire families as she was the only child able to survive after the Holocaust. In the fall, she would attend Cornell University. It was easy for me to understand why she was accepted into an Ivy League school. She possessed both a first-rate mind and the intellectual hunger for knowledge. Our conversations would last well into the night, and I found myself being attracted to the person within rather than just the normal physical attributes associated with the fair sex. Ellen's background caused me to treat her differently from any other girl I had dated before. After steadily seeing her for a month, I knew she was ready for a sexual relationship. Much to my surprise, I found that I would not go the distance with her unless it was under the auspices of marriage. I could not in any shape or fashion take advantage of her. Her family had tasted too much of the world's bitterness. I would not add to the misery that they had already endured. For the first time in my life, my limits were sharper and more defined than those of the young lady I was dating!

My life that summer was spread over three competing interests. My parents wanted to spend some family time together as I had been away for the past four years. JG and Hope found an apartment in

Queens and set up household there. JG was going to attend Brooklyn Law School in the fall, and Hope found a job as a psychiatric social worker. I would try and spend several nights a week with my fellow Marietta alumni. And, of course, I wanted to spend time with Ellen.

After dating Ellen for about a month, I felt it was time for her to meet my family and my best friend and his wife. Several times a week, JG, Hope, Ellen and I would go out for dinner and a movie. Hope liked Helen very much, but JG was always somewhat reluctant to fully embrace her as a friend. I noticed this, and I asked JG why this was so. He told me, after I pressed him for an answer, "I sense something amiss, but I don't know what it is." I know my limits. I eventually figure people out, but it takes me a long time to do so. I do not rely on first impressions because my track record frankly is hit and miss. I filed JG's misgivings away and pressed on with my relationship with Ellen. I really enjoyed her company, and since we had such different outlooks on life and tastes, we opened each other to different experiences. For example, she read Theodore Sorensen's The Making of the President, 1960 after I recommended it to her. Ellen was not normally interested in politics, but she really enjoyed that book. As for her influence on me, Ellen treated me to the Broadway production of *Fiddler on the Roof* for my birthday. I did not know that I would enjoy a musical as much as I did. That production was fabulous and touched me to my core as my family of Ashkenazy Jews came from the very area portrayed in that musical drama.

My parents really enjoyed having Ellen around. They enjoyed her quick mind and her thoughtful ideas. Mom never said much to me, but I sensed that she wanted Ellen as a daughter-in-law. Ellen's parents were always accepting of me. They trusted me with their most precious possession: their daughter. I think they knew that I would never take advantage of her or cause her any pain.

The summer of 1964 was a very pleasant time for me, but the world's troubles were like the dark thick clouds that gather before experiencing a major thunderstorm. First was the assassination of President Kennedy in November 1963. Then came the emergence of Vietnam as a political issue in the upcoming presidential election of 1964. Virtually all my family, JG and Hope, Ellen and her family, and almost everyone I knew were born and raised as Democrats. Indeed, growing up in my Jewish family there were the big three: God, Moses and Pres. Franklin Roosevelt! Very typical of a New York Jewish family. I also admired and respected Gen. Douglas MacArthur's warning, "not to get involved in a land war in Asia." As Vietnam became more and more a war rather than a police action, the potential to be drafted became the central and overwhelming factor in every young American man's life's decisions. By September 1964, when I left to go to Ohio State University in Columbus, Ohio, the United States had not fully committed to enlarging our presence in Southeast Asia.

I spent the next two years attending classes at OSU. As a result, I received a 2-S draft status which kept me out of the military. Personally, being deferred made me feel very uncomfortable. I am not the kind of person who wants others to do for me what I should be doing for myself. In the spring of 1965, President Johnson vastly increased our presence in Vietnam. I voted for him on the basis that he would not do so, for I believed then, as I do now, that a limited war is unjustifiable. If war is necessary, then fight it to win. We were not doing that. As a consequence, I opposed our commitment to South Vietnam.

For the next two years, my family, JG, and Hope constantly advised me to stay in school. When I went home for summer vacations over the next two years, I dated Ellen exclusively. She agreed with those closest to me and argued that I should continue my education. But my conscience was gnawing at me. Because I was blessed with a first-rate mind and a family who would support me, I would not have to fight.

The summer of 1967 was the pivotal year for me and my other two roommates from Marietta College. I had stayed in communication with Lou and Nancy. They were expecting their first child, and since Lou had all his medical problems emanating from the accident which occurred in his freshman year in high school, he was definitely 4-F draft status. He could not serve if he wanted to or volunteered to do so. For him, Vietnam was not much of a personal conundrum. But the opposite was true for both JG and me.

Since JG was in law school, he received a deferment. Both he and Hope were ardently against the war. They begged me to stay in school and continue my 2-S draft status. That summer, they decided that Hope would try to become pregnant, in part, to continue his deferment. JG was scheduled to graduate law school in June of 1968. Hope became pregnant in the fall of 1967. She was due to deliver her first baby around July or August of 1968. By this time, Hope's relationship with her Virginia family was asunder. The final blow came when she decided to convert to Judaism about a year before she became pregnant. That conversion and her anti-war views were the final straws which proverbially "broke" the camel's back. She would have nothing to do with her mother or father, or they with her.

The war influenced my relationship with Ellen. I did not want to keep her from dating while she was in college. I wanted her to enjoy the experience of attending a great university and not be limited by my desires. During the summer we did date exclusively, but during the year she could see who she wanted. I found that I did not want to possess her; I wanted to share time with her. Ellen became part of the anti-war movement. More and more, this involvement started to overshadow the rest of her personal life. In June of 1967, I retook the written exam for aviation in the United States Air Force Officers Training School (OTS) program. In September of that year, I received instructions to take a physical at Wright Patterson Air Force Base Medical Center located in Dayton, Ohio. The last weekend of August of that year, I took Ellen out for a final date. We went to a really fine restaurant and after the meal was over, I took her to the boardwalk area of Long Beach. It was a beautiful summer night with the stars plentiful in the sky. We walked hand-in-hand for a while until I found a bench where we could sit. I turned and faced her. I looked into her deep dark brown eyes and said, "You know how I feel about you?"

Ellen responded, "I want you to say the words. Tell me exactly how you feel about me."

I saw the tears forming in her eyes as I said, "I love you . . . I suspect that I always will."

"Then why are you not staying in school? Why are you giving up your deferment?"

"Because I must. I just can't turn away from what I feel is my responsibility. I am a free man in a free country who is obligated to take up arms when his country goes to war. To do anything else would make it impossible for me to live with myself and respect any kind of person who I would become. If I can't meet this obligation, then I would not be much of a person."

"But you don't believe in this war! So why go?"

"Because a majority of my fellow citizens voted for this present government which was legitimately elected. It is not for me to withhold my services because I think our leaders are wrong, especially when others are fighting and dying because their country needs their service. Part of being a citizen in a democracy is abiding by the decisions made by the electorate if arrived at in a legitimate fashion. My father never served because he was too young for the First World War and too old for the Second World War. My family has been in this country for three generations, and it's time that at least one of us helps to fight its battles. If I skip out on this responsibility, I would not be able to live with myself."

"I love you. I want to spend my life with you . . . please don't do this."

Ellen was sobbing. I held her tightly while she cried herself out. I was in my own personal hell. If I did what she wanted, I would never respect myself. If I did what I wanted and needed to do, I would hurt her grievously. Finally, she said to me, "Blake, please take me home." We drove to her home in silence, and when I kissed her goodnight, it was also goodbye. The summer of 1967 was the last summer which we shared together.

4

FIRST TOUR

On January 2, 1968, I officially entered the United States Air Force when I took the initial oath of office. Air Force personnel put a group of us on an aircraft that took us to Randolph Air Force Base located in San Antonio, Texas. It was there that I underwent basic training and Officer Training School (OTS) which lasted more than three months. That training gave the cadets the minimum knowledge needed in order to successfully serve in a military environment. The OTS program also made sure that we were in excellent physical shape by the time we graduated.

From there, I went to Laredo Air Force Base for pilot training. I did successfully solo several different types of aircraft, but my air work was not particularly good. As result, I washed out of pilot training. A month later, I received orders to attend Undergraduate Navigator Training (UNT) at Mather Air Force Base located near Sacramento, California. I arrived there in late September 1968. I was assigned as a student to a training squadron and given a room in a three-bedroom house that I shared with two other UNT trainees. The first of my housemates was Second Lieutenant Albert Kasner. I lived in the same house with this man for almost three months, and I can honestly tell you that I know little more about him than when I first met him. Physically, he was two inches past six foot with a slender build, dark hair and dark eyes. He kept to himself and that was okay with me. My other roommate, Andrew "Andy" Stone, was the total opposite.

Andy was about 5'10" tall and weighed about 165 pounds. He had red hair and light blue eyes. Andy was a world-class athlete who lettered in three sports in college. He was a handsome man with a continuous smile on his face. He loved life and embraced every experience with gusto. Also, Andy washed out of pilot training. This shared experience of failing at something that we really wanted helped bring us together. Andy is the kind of person who grows on you. After a lifetime of experiences, he is without a doubt, one of the kindest persons who I've ever met. He almost never cursed and never had a bad thing to say about anybody. He had the ability to accept people as they were, not as he wanted them to be. The more you knew him, the more you cared about him.

The UNT program lasted about 11 months from start to finish. All students were members of the training wing which was divided into three training squadrons. Each squadron had three classes with sixty students per class. About every nine weeks, a new class arrived to start training. Each class was broken down into three flights with twenty students per flight. The squadron that graduated the last class picked up the new one, and it rotated like that every year. My class was 69-03, or the 3rd class of fiscal year 1969. Each trading squadron had about 180 students and about 25 instructors.

The training was split into different phases of navigation. First phase was a dead reckoning or DR. This phase included classes on how maps or charts were constructed, how to read them, and how to measure a course and distance upon them. Dead reckoning, or DR itself, is both the science and the art of using whatever means available to guess an aircraft's position now and in the future. This phase had a great deal of theory and math and was basically taught using classrooms and flight simulators.

The next phase of training was map reading which taught the students how to use a chart to position an airborne aircraft. The training for this phase consisted of class work and the use of flight simulators. Most importantly, the student actually got into an aircraft to practice positioning an airplane, keeping a "Nav" log, tracking fuel consumption, and altering the heading of the aircraft in order to maintain a specified track.

The third phase was radar training. Basically, this was using radar which reflected what occurred on the surface of the earth under and ahead of the aircraft onto a scope. For all practical purposes, this phase taught a student how to use radar as a form of electronic map reading. This phase was taught both in the classroom and while airborne.

The fourth phase of training was celestial navigation. This was the single most difficult aspect of learning to become a reliable Air Force navigator. This phase was broken down into three sections: the first was pure theory, dealing with how and why the stars, the moon, the planets and the sun could inform a navigator as to exactly where he was over the surface of the earth; the second section, day celestial techniques, emphasized using those celestial bodies found in our solar system; the last section, night celestial techniques, the navigator would use stars and constellations to determine the position of the aircraft he was flying. This overall phase was so difficult that it resulted in about 25% of our students failing the course. Celestial navigation training separated the men from the boys.

The fifth phase of training was "over water" navigation. Here the student learned how to use the LORAN (long-range navigation system) to navigate huge distances while crossing the seven major oceans of the world. Again, classroom, flight simulators, and most importantly, actual flights over the Pacific Ocean was where the training really occurred. The student learned how to incorporate all navigation aids in order to position an aircraft with an emphasis on the use of the LORAN system.

The sixth phase of training was "grid" navigation. This particular navigational technique is used in or near both Polar regions of the earth. In these areas, the magnetic variation is so great that reliance upon a compass becomes untrustworthy. Before an aircraft enters these areas, the navigator aligns a free-running Gyro to an assumed grid north. Using that as a reference point, he then alters the aircraft's grid heading in order to maintain a specified track over the surface of the earth. This phase included extensive classroom and flight simulator exercises in conjunction with use in actual aircraft in-flight training. When a student passed his grid navigation check ride, he was assured of graduation and the receipt of his silver navigator wings.

The last phase of training was kind of an overview of the different aircraft to which a student might be assigned after graduation, what their missions were, and what would be expected of the navigator assigned to these different aircraft. It was in this phase that a student would go on a cross-country trip to any destination in continental United States, or in other words, this was a reward for doing a good job. The phases overlapped. The student would undergo classroom work for the next stage of training while flying and completing his current phase.

The aircraft that we used for our training was the T-29. This was a relatively small airliner powered by twin piston, propeller-driven engines. It had a maximum service altitude of 25,000 feet and a cruising speed of 190 knots. The normal crew compliment was twelve students, three instructors, and two pilots. Each student navigator had his own desk and instrumentation. The training wing assigned a partner to each student alphabetically. In my case, my flying partner was a second lieutenant Archibald "Arch" Bennet. Since my last name also began with the letter B, Arch and I were always assigned together, and it stayed that way for the entire course.

Arch's wife was a petite, brown haired, brown eyed woman named Judy. They lived in married quarters on the base which entitled them to a small, three-bedroom ranch house. They had two children, both boys, aged two and four years. Since Arch was a second lieutenant as I was, the family budget was tight. They could only afford one car. I agreed that I would always drive the two of us together for our training and evaluation flights. This was easy to do, as Arch and I were always scheduled together for the entire program. This freed up their family car for Judy's use. My normal routine was to stop by Arch and Judy's home to pick up my flying mate. In every case, Judy always had a superb meal prepared for both of us. The girl was a fabulous cook and took good care of her husband and her two boys. When she was in school at Nebraska University, her Jewish roommate taught her how to make challah which is a wonderful egg-rich loaf of soft delicious bread. Judy would make two loaves every month and give one of them to me. Let me assure you, I was the most overpaid chauffeur in the history of California!

In the beginning of November, 1968, I formally started the program of undergraduate navigator training. By the middle of December that year, I completed the first academic phase and was undergoing classroom training in the second phase. This was also the time that we started our flying training, usually concentrating on map reading and keeping a Nav log. In the fourth week of December through the first week of January, 1969, we were given leave to visit our families. I flew home commercially, and my father picked me up at LaGuardia Airport and drove me home.

During those two weeks, I visited JG and Hope almost every night. JG was "up to his eyebrows" completing work in his classes at Brooklyn Law School. He was doing well, but the big news belonged to Hope. When I first entered the door of their Queens apartment, it was evident to me that my best friend's wife was pregnant with their first child. I was thrilled for the both of them. But I must admit, the first time that one of your closest friends is about to become a parent, that fact changes your whole perspective on life. It is the passing of one of life's nexus points, and it is irrevocable. Hope was absolutely radiant. I knew, without a single doubt, that she would make a superb parent. She also informed me that she was undergoing conversion training in order to become Jewish. Hope did this because that is what she wanted. Hope told me that JG never asked her to do this; it was strictly her idea. I was ecstatic for both of them. JG asked me to be the baby's godfather, and I readily accepted.

Near the end of my leave, JG and I, after eating a wonderful meal prepared by Hope, sat and talked about our futures and what was happening to us. Hope was in the kitchen putting away the uneaten food and cleaning up the area. JG sat on one end of the sofa and I on the other. I asked JG how it was going with his dad and how his money was holding out.

"Well, Blake, it's like this," he answered. "Dad was angry with me because I married outside the faith. But when he got to meet Hope and see what a fine person she is, Dad, to my astonishment, not only accepted her, but welcomed her into the family. For the first time in my life, I think my father is really proud of me. So much so, that he has helped us enormously with tuition and rent. In fact, Blake, when he found out that Hope was pregnant with his first grandchild, he insisted that she quit her job and that he would make up the lost income. Can you believe that?! He really came up big."

"How is Hope's family taking the news?" I asked.

"Not well. Hope doesn't talk with her family anymore. The only exception is her younger sister. I know they've been talking over the phone together since we got married."

"Is she okay with this?" I asked.

"I think so. In fact, I think that my father is so smitten with her and so accepting, that she feels right at home here with me and my family. My sister Susan is crazy about her and that just makes it better. All in all, I can't complain. I love my wife, and I am really enjoying studying the law."

"Man, you're about to become a father. If it were me, I'd be scared shitless!"

"Well, I always wanted to become a father, but perhaps not this soon. Frankly, I'm excited and maybe a little scared. But as they say, the die is cast!"

After Hope completed her kitchen duties, she joined us. They had one large overstuffed chair which her pregnancy gave her absolute squatter's rights to use. She curled up on the chair and the three of us talked into the night about was happening to each of us. They were interested in the kind of training that I was undertaking at Mather Air Force Base. I filled them in about what life in the military was like. We also talked about current events. The topic that permeated almost all conversations from the latter half of the 1960s through the first three years of the 1970s was Vietnam. What was left unsaid was the poignant fact of my training: When completed, chances were at least

90% that I would be assigned to an aircraft that flew in that war zone. Both JG and Hope were glad that JG would retain his draft deferment and with the onset of parenthood, probably would keep his deferment indefinitely. But they were concerned about the fate that awaited me. The tears I saw forming in Hope's eyes affected me deeply. I loved both JG and her, and those tears showed to me that my affection was reciprocated. I hugged both of them goodbye as I went home to spend my last days of leave with my parents.

On January 3, my father drove me back to LaGuardia Airport where I caught a flight to Columbus, Ohio. I stopped there for one night to visit some people I had met during my time at Ohio State University. That was the year that OSU and the "miracle sophomores" defeated the Southern Cal Trojans (with O.J. Simpson) in the Rose Bowl and won the national championship of college football. While I was there, I picked up about a dozen posters celebrating this victory. The next day, I got on an airplane that took me into the Sacramento airport. I only hoped that I would return before Andy came back from visiting his girlfriend. I put my luggage in the car and drove as fast as I could back to our base house which I shared with Andy and Albert. I was in luck as I was the first to return. I retrieved those dozen posters celebrating OSU and proceeded to "wallpaper" Andy's room.

Andy was a different type of person—the kind that you do not run into every day. He was a native-born Californian and, of course, he rooted for the local teams, especially Southern Cal. Before we left on leave, we had spirited discussions about the upcoming Rose Bowl. Andy's family came and settled in Northern California. His father was a logger all his life. He taught his son how to live, and indeed, prosper in the wild forests that were the main part of the lower to middle Sierras mountain range located in eastern and northern California. Andy was easily the best outdoorsman and fishermen who I have ever met in my life. As I got to know him and his family, I found myself sharing some of his deep and abiding love and respect for the great outdoors, the mountain streams, the wildlife, and the magnificent skies and sunsets that made this relatively unpopulated area so attractive. Andy was an environmentalist long before it was ever a movement.

I was in my room when I heard Andy enter our house. He was accompanied by his fiancée, Heather, who was a native Californian blonde beauty. She was as tall as Andy with ideal features. Blue eyes, long legs, and a graceful figure made her a tremendous success as a fashion model. They had met the year before on the ski slopes near Tahoe. Heather was an excellent skier, but still no match for Andy. His adroitness on the slopes accompanied by his gentle manner and kind disposition, deeply attracted her. When Andy joined the Air Force and was sent off to pilot training school in Oklahoma, she returned to her native California to attend college at UC Berkeley. Her parents were more than well-to-do, but she continued to model in order to make some extra money. When Andy got his orders to attend UNT at Mather Air Force Base, he was very excited. Berkeley was only a two-hour ride. Every weekend, either Andy would travel to see Heather, or she would spend the time with him in Sacramento.

I heard them enter Andy's room. He yelled, "What in the world!?" And then he proceeded to my room, and he was laughing. "Where did you get those posters?"

"I stopped in Columbus, Ohio and picked them up. I just thought your room needed sprucing up. Hope you like them."

"Only you would do something like that. Actually, they are pretty nice posters."

With that, we laughed about it. Andy, a very gentle soul, was very slow to anger. He loved and appreciated a good joke, especially this one, as the posters came off easily and nobody was hurt.

"Well, I got news for you, Blake," he replied. "Heather has agreed to marry me this summer after she graduates Berkeley."

Heather was right behind Andy. She showed me her diamond engagement ring, and I passed on my congratulations to the both of them. I shook his hand. Heather stayed back a bit and my reading of her body language would not allow me to make physical contact with her. I perceived a reticence when it came to any of Andy's military friends, not just me. So, I kept my distance because to do otherwise would have invaded her personal space. It's one of my personality quirks: I will not go to someplace or be with someone that does not want my company. I'd much rather be alone. But Andy was happy and that's all that mattered to me. Later that day, Heather returned to Berkeley and the next day, Andy and I were back in class.

5

SANDY

Andy and I were classmates and part of the same flight. We were in the process of taking the classroom instruction dealing with radar. I was the only Jewish student in the flight, and I was also the only student from New York. A week after returning from Christmas leave, my classmates were riding me hard about the upcoming Super Bowl III. The overwhelming favorite was the Baltimore Colts of the National Football League who were a seventeen-point favorite to beat the New York Jets from the AFL. Now, normally I am a Giant fan, but since I was the only New Yorker, I had to root for the Jets. On Sunday, January 13, my entire flight came to our three-bedroom on-base house in order to watch the Colts take apart the Jets. Out of the 20 guys there, I was the only one rooting for the New York team. As the game unfolded, and the Jets won, I gave my classmates a truly well-deserved hazing. I have to admit; they took it like men. After the game, Andy and I laughed at how disappointed they were because the favored Colts lost.

Many of my classmates told me during the following week that they richly deserved all the hazing I was giving them.

By the end of January, Andy and I were close to passing the second phase. That meant we could look for off-base housing. Our other roommate, Albert, was in a different flight, and he wanted to live with some of his mates from the other group. That was fine with both Andy and me. After living together for one month, Andy and I knew that we wanted to continue being roommates. The policy at Mather Air Force Base regarding bachelor officers allowed Undergraduate Navigator Training (UNT) students to live off base in civilian housing once the second month of training was finished. The whole program took almost a year to complete.

California, at that time and maybe still today, was the epicenter of the sexual revolution. Being stationed there was like being a kid in a candy store. I grew up in a sexually repressed household and environment. In high school, I barely dated and when I did date, dating never resulted in anything more than petting. When I attended Marietta College, with its strong Baptist roots, there was very little gratuitous sex. At Ohio State, pretty much more of the same, as the Columbus area was solidly part of the Bible belt. When I went to Laredo Texas, I was too busy, and most of the available women spoke only Spanish. When I arrived in California, I was in a new world. When one of my classmates, Derek Evans, who most women would call a "stud muffin," endeavored to organize our collective social lives, he almost never failed. Tall, very good looking, and with absolutely smooth opening lines, he generally got what he wanted. He organized a party every Saturday night at one of the class member's abode. As he put it, he wanted to create a "target rich environment," and I don't remember his ever failing to do so. Derek went to the local colleges, the girl's dorms in particular, and posted the location and time of the next party. All of us would contribute about 10 bucks apiece in order to pay for the food and booze, and the host would provide the music. Lo and behold, every Saturday night, like clockwork, literally 30 to 40 girls would attend these parties. And believe me, they did come to party. These girls were serious students who wanted a good time and no commitments. Well, the navigator students fit their needs ideally. We were absolutely physically fit; we all had college degrees; and because Vietnam loomed in the distance, we were not craving any long-term commitments. Frankly, it was an unusual weekend in which a person didn't get laid. Being a red-blooded young man, who was hardwired to desire and appreciate the female body, I did take full advantage. As I said, a kid in the candy store!

In early February, Andy and I went looking for an apartment. The base housing office gave us a list of approved off-base housing. It was the second apartment that we looked at when lightning struck. The complex consisted of six identical four-plex buildings in which each unit contained four identical apartments, two upper and two lower. Each apartment contained two bedrooms, a family room, a small kitchen, one bathroom and approximately 900 square feet of living space. All the units came furnished with well-used but comfortable furniture. Each unit also contained a laundry room, located in the rear of the individual apartment building, which contained a washer-dryer set that was available to the people living in that unit.

The unit closest to the street had a sign indicating that the manager of the apartment complex lived on the first-floor apartment of that unit. When Andy and I did something together, I usually did the talking. Generally, I was brasher and had a New York point of view which went very nicely with my Brooklyn accent. We walked up to the door and knocked. After several moments, the door opened, and I was totally struck mute. I found myself staring at a beautiful girl who'd just answered the door. She had shoulder-length black hair, a beautiful oval face, sparkling brown eyes, olive skin and a beautifully proportioned body. She was wearing her gym clothes, which consisted of a T-shirt, shorts and sneakers. I was so stricken with her that I could not even speak. Finally, after an awkward silence, Andy stepped in front of me and asked, "Is there an apartment available?"

The girl smiled and said, "My mom is the manager for this complex. Right now, she's at work, but I can show you the one unit we have available here if that's okay with you?"

Her smile radiated beauty like a beacon, and as I was still struck mute, Andy continued the conversation. He told her that we were navigator students and that we needed a furnished apartment as soon as possible. She told us to wait by the door and that she would get the key to the available apartment. When she returned, Andy introduced both of us to her. She smiled and said, "My name is Sandra Caliprizzo, but everyone calls me Sandy."

After the introductions, she passed between Andy and myself and said to us that we should follow her. That was not only easy to do, but enjoyable to watch. The apartment she showed us was the one directly above the one that she and her family occupied. She opened the door to the vacant apartment, and it was clean and decently appointed. She led us to the rear of the building and showed us the available laundry room. She then led us to the rear of the complex where there was a swimming pool and lounge chairs available to all the tenants. Sandy showed us where the available parking was located and then took us back to her apartment. By this time, my voice had returned, and I said to her, "We'll take it." Andy, knowing how smitten I was, smiled and just nodded his head in agreement. Besides, the rent was well within our budget, and it was less than a mile to the main entrance gate of

Mather Air Force Base. That weekend, Andy and I moved into our new "digs."

During the next eight weeks, Andy and I were extremely busy flying radar training flights and starting the course work for celestial navigation. During this time, I would speak to Sandy almost every day. She was, at the time, seventeen years old and a junior in high school. Unlike any other girl that I'd met to that point, she was easily the most grown-up. Her father deserted the family when she was eleven years old. She helped raise her younger sister as her mom had to work full-time. She also did part-time work in a local department store and was used extensively by several mothers in the area as a babysitter. Even though she was very young, Sandy was already dealing with adult responsibilities. One day, during this time, I encountered her outside with two children who she was babysitting. Both were about three years old. I was chatting with her about the children when another mother approached us. This newly arrived mom was carrying an infant in her arms. She stopped by to ask Sandy about the possibly of her babysitting next Saturday night. During the conversation, the baby started crying. Sandy, without saying a word, put her hand on the baby's chest and almost like magic, the baby ceased his crying. When the mom carrying the child left us, I asked Sandy about this apparent "gift." She laughed and said, "It's just something I do. I don't know why it works, but it does." Seeing that "gift" of hers made me desire her even more, if that was possible.

During the weekends, I attended the parties Derek organized. I had little problem securing a date and spending the night with a different girl each time. What I did not know until later was that Sandy's bedroom was directly below mine. When I got lucky, usually every weekend, she would hear the pounding of the bed. At the time, I did not know if she felt the same way about me as I did about her. What was perfectly apparent to me, each and every time I encountered her, was that a palpable sexual tension existed between the both of us. Because of her age, I was very reluctant to pursue a deeper relationship.

This changed on Thursday in the middle of April, 1969. That morning Arch, my flying mate, and I were scheduled for a 5:00 AM briefing for a radar training flight which required us to be at base ops at 4:15 in the morning. That is what we who fly call an "O-dark thirty" briefing time! That meant that I'd be awakened at 3 AM by my very loud alarm clock. I would get dressed, go to Arch's home, eat a wonderful breakfast prepared by Judy, take Arch and myself to the flight line, receive a briefing, complete a flight plan, fly the mission, get debriefed by our instructors, take Arch home and finally, get to return to my apartment. By the time I arrived home, it was just past three in the afternoon. The weather was unusually hot, so as soon as I entered my apartment, I removed my sweaty "bag", otherwise known as a one-piece flying suit. I immediately changed into a bathing suit and sandals. The pool was empty, and I immediately dove into the water. After swimming for a few minutes, I got out of the pool and laid down on the lounge chair. I'd slept for about thirty minutes when I heard the noise created by Sandy and her sister swimming and splashing in the pool. The afternoon heat caused me to be covered with sweat. I dove into the water to cool down and when I came up, I was facing Sandy with about six inches of water separating us. Without thinking, we both reached for the other and immediately fell into a deep, passionate kiss and embrace. I knew at that moment that Sandy felt the same way about me as I did her. After a few moments, which allowed us to catch our breath, we kissed again.

"I wanted to do that from the first moment we met," I said to her.

"I know. I could see your reaction to my gym clothes and to me," she said laughingly.

"Well, I would like to take you on a date as soon as possible, but I think we need to ask your mom's approval before we do. I don't want to do anything behind her back."

"Then we'll ask her this evening when she gets home from work."

"Is that usually about five?" I asked.

"More like 5:30. Why don't you come down to our apartment about 7:30. I'll make sure that Mom has a good meal and, after we finish eating, we can ask her together." Sandy did most of the cooking and cleaning for her mother and her sister. She was, at seventeen years of age, more responsible and grown-up than the college girls I was dating while undergoing the UNT program. I agreed to her suggestion.

At 7:30 PM I went down to the manager's apartment and knocked on the door. Sandy's fourteen-year-old sister, Maggie, answered the door. Mrs. Caliprizzo, sitting on a sofa in the family room, saw me enter. Sandy was sitting on the other end of the sofa. I sat on a chair facing them. I then told Mrs. Caliprizzo that I really liked Sandy and wished to date her. I also told her that I would not do this behind her back. "The only way this is going to happen is for you to give me permission to do so period," I concluded.

Mrs. Caliprizzo told me that she would talk with her daughter and then give Sandy and me her decision the next evening. She wanted to think about it. That was the longest twenty-four hours of my life to that point. Finally, the next evening around 7:30 again, I went to Sandy's apartment. I sat down next to her as Mrs. Caliprizzo took the chair facing the sofa. "I will allow you to see my daughter under the following conditions. First, 11:00 PM curfew every night except Friday and Saturday. Those days I will allow a 1:00 AM curfew. Secondly, no drinking. Finally, Sandy must have time to complete all her schoolwork." I quickly agreed to all. After chatting for some 20 minutes,

I asked Sandy if she would like to take a walk for about an hour. I had to study for my celestial theory exams, so my time was limited. Sandy looked at her mother, who nodded her assent, and we left the apartment hand-in-hand. I was soaring. I don't think my toes touched the ground.

As soon as we were clear of the apartment, we turned, faced each other, and passionately kissed. Then holding her hand, we took an hour walk. I initiated the conversation by asking her how she got her mom's permission. She smiled and said, "Mom knows me. She knows that I am a very responsible person, and she feels that you are trustworthy. She really appreciated the fact that we would not do this behind her back." We continued to walk, and I asked her to accompany me to a class party which was scheduled next Saturday. Sandy readily agreed. I told her that I would pick her up about six, and we would go out for dinner and then on to the party.

Saturday finally came. Sandy was waiting for me at the door as I approached. She was wearing a simple white dress, absolutely no jewelry and black low-cut shoes. As I came to know later, the girl never put on any kind of makeup. Her skin was flawless. She needed makeup like most of us need a hole drilled in our head. We were late getting to the party as we spent over three hours in a restaurant eating and talking. She told me how tough it was when her father deserted the family. For almost two years, she cried herself to sleep every night. What helped bring her out of the depression that almost overwhelmed her was helping her mom cope. She, her mother, and her sister were very close. Sandy was the child who physically resembled her father and Maggie, her mother. Both Mrs. Caliprizzo and Maggie were taller than Sandy. Both possessed blond hair and blue eyes emanating from their Irish background, and both were very attractive.

By the time we reached the party, it was almost ten. I introduced Sandy to my classmates. Earlier, some of them, knowing that she was 17 years old, teased me about her age. I didn't say much in response, as I figured when they got to see and talk to her, they would see what I saw. It didn't take long. Inside of two hours, she enthralled each of them and easily won them over. After that first encounter, none of my classmates ever kidded me about her age . . . actually, I think most of them were envious. During the weeks and months that followed, Sandy was my constant companion. My classmates gave her a new nickname: "Foxy." It really fit her. After that date, Sandy was the only girl I wanted to see. I returned her to the apartment just before 1:00 AM, as I'd promised her mom.

During the week, Sandy and I would accompany Andy, with or without Heather, to dinner. Most of the time we would study together, take walks, and occasionally see a movie on the base. When Sandy and I were alone, we kissed passionately and after two weeks, I was allowed to explore all of her above the waist. I always respected her limits. I figured when it was the right time, she would let me know. This went on for about two months.

A breakthrough in our relationship occurred during the classroom portion covering night celestial techniques. As per usual, I was invited to a class party which was scheduled at one of my classmate's apartment located across the street from where Derek Evans had his off-base housing. Derek got a really good deal on a case of Seagram Seven, my drink of choice. I gave him the money needed to cover the cost of one bottle. Since the party was across the street from where Derek lived, he just told me to label one bottle as mine and use it as needed. Sandy and I arrived at the party about nine. I excused myself and walked across the street to make a drink. I only made one, as I kept my word to Mrs. Caliprizzo. A few minutes later, I returned, drink in hand, to the party. The music was loud and exclusively rock 'n roll. The music generated in the latter half of the 1960s, in my opinion, is the best rock ever conceived and performed. Sandy and I started dancing. The host had a reel-to-reel tape machine hooked up to the latest stereo equipment. Each tape would take about two hours before it ran out and had to be changed. About a half-hour into the tape that was playing, the Rolling Stones started with their hit song, "*I Can't Get No Satisfaction*" which given Sandy's limits on how far we could go absolutely applied to me. So, I started singing the words at the top of my lungs. My classmates laughed and continued dancing. Sandy turned beet red! I didn't think much of it at the time as to me it was just a humorous episode. My drink was running low, and I told Sandy that I would return shortly once I refilled my drink.

She looked up at me and said, "I want to go with you."

"Sure. I would love your company," I replied. We walked hand-in-hand into Derek's apartment. The door was never locked, and we just walked into the main room where Derek had established a bar. There was a bottle of Seagram's Seven located on the bar. It had my name on it. I made a drink and was getting ready to escort Sandy across the street in order to return to the party. Instead, she went to the sofa and patted the seat adjacent to her. I sat down next to her and she reached to kiss me. I responded passionately. She repositioned her body underneath mine. Without saying a word, she took my hand and placed it under her panties and between her legs. She was already wet with anticipation. I looked into her dark brown eyes. I got up and locked the front door. Then we quickly undressed and made passionate love on Derek's brand-new sofa. We continued our lovemaking for almost two hours. It was like experiencing a volcanic eruption, especially since I had been without any sexual relief for two months and, more importantly, because I wanted her so badly. Around midnight,

Sandy and I got dressed and returned to the party which was still going strong. I figured we could dance for another twenty minutes or so before I had to return her home in time in order to make her curfew. Wouldn't you know it? What was playing again was the Rolling Stones *"I Can't Get No Satisfaction."* Sandy and I started dancing, and now, instead of shouting the lyrics, I was whispering them. Sandy turned beet red again. From that moment on, until I breathe no more, that song will have more meaning for me than any other!

That evening changed our relationship forever. I was within two weeks of entering the night celestial flying phase. For the next three months, classes for the next two phases, which included LORAN/over-water techniques and grid navigation training, would only occur in the late afternoon in order to accommodate the rest requirements as stated in Air Force Regulation 60-16. That meant our flight briefing times would also be scheduled in the early evening which resulted in my not getting home until three or four o'clock in the morning.

Sandy and I became inseparable. I normally awoke around 2:00 PM. Sandy returned from school about a half-hour later. She would come into my apartment, undress and share my bed with me. I loved watching her do this as her body was magnificent. Every time she got near me, I physically got excited. What I really appreciated was the snuggling after making love. She put her head on my chest with her arm extended across my body. I loved the look of her, the way she smelled, how comfortably she fit in my arms, and the quiet peace and tranquility that I felt every time I held her.

During the weekends, Heather would drive up to spend time with Andy. Many times, instead of going to the class parties usually organized by Derek, the four of us would drive east to El Dorado, California. This was a small town about fifty miles east of Sacramento and located in the lower to middle Sierras. The only attraction in this town was a restaurant called *"Poor Reds"* which was a bar and grill established in 1849 during the gold rush era. It was built to service the miners who populated that area at that time. It was old, dilapidated, and filled with the smells of one hundred twenty years' worth of booze, beer and smoke. After entering, one encountered a seventy-five foot-long bar that was 15 feet wide with bar stools all around this rectangular structure. The restaurant part of Poor Red's, located in the rear of the building, was a 15' x 20' room with a large vertical barbecue pit built into the rear wall. It held approximately six tables and twenty-four chairs. The menu consisted of four possible entrées served with a baked potato and a small tossed salad. What everybody ordered, almost exclusively, was the barbecued ribs. All four entrées on the menu were barbecued using mesquite wood exclusively. That fuel which cooked the meat was flown in from Texas. All entrées were cooked in the large open-faced barbeque pit. The food was so good that it attracted customers from all over the Northwestern states and Southern California. Many a time when Sandy and I were there, we would talk to strangers whom we would meet while waiting to be served. We met people as far away as the state of Washington and others who would drive in from San Francisco. The people at the bar would be dressed in clothing that varied from torn jeans and a T-shirt to tuxedos and formal dresses. After entering, a patron placed his name on a list and waited at the bar until his name was called. This usually took anywhere from two to four hours. On Friday and Saturday nights, there were two hundred to three hundred people waiting either to enter the bar or the restaurant area. Frankly, Poor Reds served the best barbecue I've ever tasted. Everybody was friendly, and it was like going to a "come as you go" party which lasted the entire weekend. We never failed to have a good time there. In the last four months of my tour in Sacramento, Sandy, Andy, Heather and I became regulars. My favorite drink there was the Solid Gold

Cadillac. I'm not sure what was in this drink, but it was delicious . . . and potent. Either Andy or I would be the "designated driver" which meant no more than one Solid Gold Cadillac for the night.

During the week, Sandy would accompany Andy and me for supper if she could. She still had her duties and responsibilities associated with her family and the children who were in her care. Many evenings after supper we would go back to my apartment and study. All of us, after all, were still students. Sometimes Sandy would accompany Andy and me to the night celestial practice rack. This was a structure located on base that allowed the student navigator to hook his hand-held sextant to a Plexiglas dome which was the same one used in actual flights on the T-29 trainer. Every student was issued his own personal sextant. This equipment allowed a student navigator to practice finding usable Nav stars, then measuring the height of these celestial bodies above the celestial horizon and finally, obtaining both a true position and an accurate sextant error.

Sometimes, Sandy and I would drive in my car to the rest areas just off US Highway 50 in the middle to high Sierra's. I would park my car, a 1967 Camaro convertible painted yellow with black trim. I had the top down in order to practice my star identification. Sandy and I would make out for about an hour, and I'd redo the star identification again. By the time I started flying my night celestial missions, both Sandy and I became very familiar with the constellations and the navigational stars contained within them. The time span from initial intimacy to graduation was the singular happiest time of my life. It passed so quickly that it was almost like a dream.

During the month of May, I passed both the day celestial and night celestial check rides. These were actual flights where we used a sextant to fix (position) the aircraft. During day missions, we measured the angular distance of the sun above the celestial horizon. In the night version, we used the stars, planets and the moon's angular distance above the celestial horizon in order to fix the position of the aircraft over a point on the earth. The night celestial check ride, which I took in the latter part of May, started when we briefed at eight that evening. By the time we took off, it was past 11:00 PM. We were delayed due to some mechanical problems with the aircraft. We were taking the Over Land North route toward the state of Washington and over some fairly high mountain ranges that existed below. We climbed to our service ceiling altitude of 25,000 feet. The sky was absolutely clear of any clouds. When it was my turn to use my handheld sexton, I climbed into the Plexiglas bubble on the top of the T-29 aircraft. I hooked the sexton to the top of the bubble and looked around. I could see the stars as I have never seen them before. At that altitude, we were past approximately 70% of the Earth's atmosphere. It was now midnight and the constellation above was, appropriately enough, the Navigator's Triangle. It took me maybe another minute to identify the usable stars in that constellation, and for the first time in my life, I realized that the Navigator's Triangle was immersed, in its entirety, in the Milky Way constellation. At this altitude, many of the stars contained in the Milky Way were visible, and you could see all the swirls of stars normally hidden by the Earth's atmosphere. It was so beautiful it literally took my breath away. After 15 minutes, the instructor navigator patted me on my back and asked, "Are you having problems identifying stars?"

"No sir," I responded and immediately proceeded to show him where all the available navigational stars were located. He laughed and said, "Maybe you might want to fix the airplane!" I agreed and took my fix. It was a scramble for me to catch up with the aircraft, but I did. However, my grade was lowered significantly as I did not do well on the "pacing block" of the formal evaluation. Pacing was the student's ability to use his time properly. It was a fair grade as I lost quite a bit of time admiring the stars. Still, looking back, it is one of most beautiful sights I have ever seen in my lifetime and definitely worth losing some grade point average.

All throughout the UNT program, the Air Force stressed physical training. Every day, Monday through Friday, we had either two hours of formal PT training or two hours to practice the sport that we enjoyed as individuals. The formal PT training was usually single combat techniques emphasizing a mixture of the recognized martial arts. The trainer for this part of the program was Master Sergeant Williams. This NCO was about 5'6" tall, weighed about 145 pounds, and had reflexes which made a sidewinder rattlesnake look slow. Nobody, and I mean nobody, fucked with this guy. He was quick as lightning and possessed black belts in four separate martial arts. Several times a week, he would take over our class and teach us individual combative techniques. Much to my surprise, later in my life, I actually put some of these to use. When it wasn't formal PT training, I gravitated to the handball courts. I found that I loved the game. I developed good techniques and learned how to move on the court. As a result, I became a very competent player which helped me stay in top shape.

I took Sandy to every squadron function that wives and loved ones were invited. All my classmates liked her as she was such a sweet person besides being physically beautiful. She enjoyed the attention of my classmates during these functions. For my part, I was really proud to be the one who she chose. I realized, by the time we graduated and obtained our silver navigation wings that I wanted to spend the rest of my life with her.

I passed my last check ride in the second week of August. The only flying that was left was the mandatory cross-country flight. The Air Force generally recommended one day out and one day back. But I wanted to go home to Long Island. I needed three other students who wanted to go and at least one instructor in order to obtain permission for the extended flight. I asked Andy, who readily agreed. I found two more classmates who were willing to go. It took me about a week to get all the signatures necessary. I wanted to see my parents as they were taking a trip to Japan and would not be available for the graduation ceremonies. I asked my celestial instructor, Major Dylan Forster, if he would accompany us and supervise the trip. He agreed to do so. Major Forster was a wonderful instructor and one of the most handsome men that I have ever encountered in this lifetime. He was six feet tall with jet black hair and blue eyes. His smile was contagious and everyone, male or female, seemed to enjoy his company. He was a charismatic leader who possessed a marvelous sense of humor which he used extensively when teaching celestial navigation in the classroom. He was easily my favorite instructor.

During the third week of August, the crew consisting of four students, one instructor and two pilots, climbed aboard our T-29 trainer. We were scheduled for a five-day mission. We were given one day to fly out to our destination, Floyd-Bennet Field, located in Brooklyn. The first scheduled stop was Scott Air Force Base located in southern Illinois. We would refuel and proceed on to New York. We could fly this distance on the first day because of the prevailing westerly winds which would increase our ground speed and keep our crew duty day to something less than 16 hours. We would spend two days in New York and return on the fourth day using two days to complete the trip.

We took off at 6:00 AM on the first day. Everything was going well until we approached Western Kansas. It was my turn to navigate. I was using radar, and based on the returns that I saw in the scope, I knew exactly where we were. However, I saw this gigantic return approximately 35 miles ahead of the aircraft. I did not know what it was. I called Maj. Forster on the intercom and asked him to come to my scope. When he arrived at my position, I showed him three cities on the map and where they corresponded to what I was seeing on the scope. I wanted him to know that I knew exactly where we were. "So, what is it you want to know?" he asked.

"Well, sir, why is Kansas City, which should be in the eastern part of the state, located in central Kansas and appears to be coming toward us?" He lowered his head and took a close look at my scope. He cranked up the radar dish so it would reflect returns that were airborne and not on the ground. He immediately mashed his main intercom button and called the pilots. He told them to look at their radar scope, declare a weather emergency, and request landing at the first base possible.

I asked what was wrong. He told me that what we were seeing was a level VI thunderstorm, a ferocious beast of the air. UNT policy at Mather Air Force Base dictated that the T-29 aircraft were never, ever, scheduled to fly on any route that possibly contained convective weather. This was my first encounter seeing what a thunderstorm looked like on the radar scope. This one was the biggest I have ever encountered in my life. Air traffic control was notified by the pilots who did declare an airborne emergency due to weather. We were directed to Richards-Gabaur Air Force Base, which everyone in the Air Force humorously referred to as "Dickie Goober" Airport. About 20 minutes later, we landed and parked the aircraft. A bus took us to base ops, where I got to see the ground-based weather radar. The width of this one cloud was over eighty nautical miles wide and the altitude finding radar showed that the top of precipitation was in excess of 88,000 feet. Just after we got to base ops, we experienced softball-sized hail. We stayed in base ops for over an hour until the storm passed. That ended our first day of flying. A bus took us to officer housing, and we all got rooms for the night.

Around six o'clock that evening, we went to the officer's club for something to eat and after dining, we retired to the bar. A celebration was going on. It seemed that a class of F-105 Thunderchief pilots were graduating and receiving their certification to fly that particular aircraft. This fighter was called "The Thud" because so many had "dinged in" before the Air Force finally figured out how to fly that aircraft in a reasonably safe mode.

A white-haired gentleman wearing a military tuxedo with first lieutenant bars seemed to be in control. Next to him, there was a very dashing young man whose military tuxedo contained the full colonel insignia and many medals and ribbons. It didn't take long for me to figure out that for this celebration, the senior man changed jackets with the most junior man. I sidled up to a seat next to the white-haired gentleman. He looked at my patches and said, "Do navigators drink?"

"At least as well as pilots!" I responded.

The colonel smiled at my response and then snapped his fingers. Immediately, a bartender was standing in front of us. "What do navigators drink?" he asked.

"Seagram's Seven and soda, sir".

"Bartender, set this man up with 10 drinks a row . . . and make them Seagram's Seven and soda."

"Yes sir, Colonel."

I was finished with my fourth drink when Major Forster came up by my side. He looked at the colonel and said, "This student doesn't know that he has a 4:00 AM briefing time, sir. I think he needs to leave now."

The colonel laughed and told us to be on our way. I never did get in trouble for that breach of Air Force Regulation 60-16! Next morning, we awoke, ate breakfast, and flight planned the remaining part of our trip to Floyd-Bennett Field. After we completed our flight plan, and before we got on the aircraft, I called my father and told him what our ETA was to Brooklyn. He could pick us up at base ops. Dad understood and said he would be there.

We arrived around three o'clock in the afternoon. Dad was there, and Andy and I climbed into his car. The others went their separate ways. We were scheduled to meet two days later at base ops for the return flight. Dad took Andy and me to his country club located in Syosset, New York. My father was a very successful businessman. He took us to his golf club which was designed and operated for men only. Wives, including my mother, had limited privileges in the club. Remember, this was 1969 not 1999, and the world was different. Mom was waiting for us at a table in a lavishly appointed dining room. I gave Mom a hug and kiss and introduced her to Andy. Both of us were still in our "bags," otherwise known as flying suits. Once Andy got over his awe at being in such an affluent environment, he relaxed and the four of us enjoyed a wonderful meal and excellent conversation. I told my parents that I was serious about a young lady who I wanted them to meet. That's when they reminded me that they were going to Japan for three weeks. The trip was paid for, and they would not be available until the middle of September. They would arrange a trip to meet her, or she could arrange to come to Long Island and they would get to know her there. That seemed reasonable to me and after answering a lot of questions about her, Mom asked what we wanted to do for the next two days. I told her that I'd like to show Andy what New York was really like and to spend time with JG and Hope. After the meal was over, Dad drove us home. Andy used the guest room and for the first time in years, I slept in my old bed.

The next morning, I took Andy on an extended tour of the north shore of Long Island. In those years, the island was beautiful, and I really enjoyed showing him the sights. After lunch, I called Hope and told her that I would like her to meet my roommate, and she agreed. In the late afternoon, I drove to JG and Hope's apartment. We arrived around 5:30 PM. Andy and I went to the door and Hope answered our knock. The girl was radiant. I introduced her to Andy and said, "Where is my godson?"

Hope laughed and said, "He's taking his afternoon nap. He should be up in about a half-hour, and that's when JG should come home from work." I knew JG had recently graduated Brooklyn Law School and was preparing to pass the New York bar exam. He was working as an intern in an established law firm. His boss, who really liked him, made sure that he had sufficient time to study for the bar as part of his normal duties. Now that he was a daddy, Hope told me that he was very diligent in applying his time. Once he passed the bar, his boss was going to offer a major, full-time position with a direct path to partnership.

About a half-hour after we arrived, JG came home. As soon as he saw me, he came right up to me, and we hugged. After we both asked how each other was doing, I stepped back and introduced JG and Andy to each other. They shook hands and after a few minutes of conversation, I heard JG's son's cry coming from the bedroom. Hope immediately left our company and went to the bedroom. There she breast-fed her two-month-old son, Daniel Thompson Gladon. After about 15-20 minutes had passed, Hope, cradling the infant child in her arms, returned to the dining room. JG took little Daniel and showed off his beautiful son to me and Andy. He put a small towel over his shoulder and proceeded to "burp" his son. We continued conversing while JG took care of his fatherly duties. In the meantime, Hope was making final preparations to serve the meal. About a half-hour later, JG put his son in a nearby cradle, and we sat at the dining room table where we had a delightful meal. I complimented Hope on her recently acquired culinary skills to which JG responded with a smile," Who knew?" Hope, keeping with the light spirit, feigned anger and gave JG a light tap on the shoulder. Hope and JG were very curious about the Nav program in which Andy and I were on the verge of completing.

Then Andy took delight in describing my first encounter with Sandy. Everyone at the table had a good laugh at my expense. In particular, JG said that he would pay any amount to see me struck mute! In all the years that he knew me, he had never witnessed such an event. For the next two hours, we ate and conversed. Daniel, recently fed, was content to listen to the nearby conversation.

After the meal, Hope cleaned up and JG, Andy and I went into the living room where we could light up, sit back and continue the conversation. JG told me that Brooklyn Law graduates had the highest passing percentage of any school in the country as it pertained to the New York bar. He and his boss got along wonderfully. He was completely comfortable in the firm, and he was reasonably confident that he would pass on his first try. Brooklyn Law offered a pre-bar exam course that helped recently graduated law students prepare for this last hurdle. His boss not only gave JG the preparatory time needed, he also paid for the course. I asked what kind of law JG would pursue once he passed.

"I'm pretty sure that I want to practice general law with an emphasis on both family court and criminal court. That's what I find interesting. Corporate law is so boring that it makes watching grass grow look exciting. My particular skills are reading people and situations quickly and accurately. That's exactly what you need to practice family law. Besides, I get a feeling on how people react and I'm usually right. That makes me valuable in situations where a decision must be rendered by a jury. The boss knows that I can be useful in accepting or rejecting a potential juror. Those are the kind of skills that you can't teach. I know I have them and so does my boss." My long experience with JG confirmed what he had just said.

Hope joined us after she completed the cleanup chores and fed Daniel. She wanted to know more about Sandy. I readily answered all her questions. She was concerned about Sandy's age, and I told her that Sandy was more mature than any woman I've ever dated. When Andy, without any prodding from me, joined in a full-throated agreement to that statement, I could see that Hope's concerns were assuaged. Hope asked when she would meet her, and I responded that I would bring her back east before going on to my final destination, whatever that was.

That caused JG to ask, "What would your assignments be after graduating Nav School?" I told him that in about 10 days we would get our gaining commands and aircraft assignments. JG asked how this was done. I told him that the class would meet as an entire group which meant all three flights together in a single venue. All the potential assignments would be listed on the board. The man with the highest overall grade average would pick his assignment. The succeeding students would pick in order of class ranking. The lowest ranked student in the class would be left with the last assignment. JG asked about my class standing. I told him about my lack of pacing in taking the night celestial check ride. That enthrallment with the beauty of the Milky Way caused me to lose at least twenty spots on class standing. I smiled and told the three of them that what I saw was so beautiful it was worth it!

What was left unspoken was everyone's concerns about our being ordered into combat in Southeast Asia. The war was the unsaid gloom and the unwanted background of a truly delightful social encounter. Even when it wasn't being discussed, the war in Vietnam hung like a cloud affecting almost every citizen of the United States. Strongly held opinions varied from those who wholeheartedly supported our efforts to keep Vietnam and the surrounding countries free from the scourge of communism to those whose outright and militaristic opposition to the war led to civil disobedience, terrorist acts, desertion from duty, and flight to nearby Canada. Very few people were in the middle of this great divide. The divisive nature of such an unpopular war permeated every aspect of human interaction within the United States. When the time came for Andy to leave JG and Hope's company, the war was never discussed. We all unconsciously tabled that discussion. Instead, we emphasized topics where we had some measure of control in determining what our future would be. By ten o'clock that evening, Andy and I departed.

We returned to my home and Andy and I spent an hour or so with my parents. We went to bed in order to get up early enough so that I could take Andy on a sightseeing tour of New York City. The next day, we visited tourist sites such as the Empire State Building, the Staten Island ferry, and the great museums. We ate in the ethnic restaurants which populated the entire area. Finally, we went to *The Village Gate* which was one of my favorite venues. Both Andy and I really enjoyed the folk music played there. Sadly, we had to leave by 10 PM as we were going to be briefed early the next morning at Floyd Bennett Field.

We got up the next morning, and Dad took us to an all-night Greek diner where we had a superb breakfast. Then Dad drove us to Floyd Bennett Field base ops, and after saying our goodbyes, we entered the building as my father departed. There we met the other crewmembers. After completing the flight plan, we climbed aboard the aircraft and left to return to California. It took us two days to complete the return flight. I was anxious to see and hold Sandy again. Andy felt the same in regard to Heather.

We returned about 2:00 AM on Monday. Later that morning, about 8:30, Sandy came upstairs and joined me in bed. Her mother had just left for work, and she had no babysitting duties scheduled for the day. The classes I still needed to attend would not start until one. That left us about four hours of alone time, and we did not waste a minute of it. Having her in my arms was almost as necessary as breathing. Afterwards, I was ravenous and so I took her to a nearby restaurant for breakfast. I told her about the trip and that my parents wanted to meet her. That really is what she wanted to hear. The next week, the class assembled in order to pick assignments. This was held in a large hall. Each student was able to invite his wife and other loved ones to this ritual. I invited Sandy and she quickly accepted. This decision would be decisive for both of us.

On Thursday, August 28 at 1:00 PM, the entire class assembled in a large briefing hall. The class now numbered fifty-two after drop-outs and failures. With the invited guests and interested instructors, the total seated in the hall numbered about 200. Our leadership group was on stage and consisted of the wing commander, the squadron commander and about a half dozen enlisted men who were personnel specialists. After a congratulatory speech from the wing commander and a shorter one from the squadron commander, the choosing process commenced. I ranked 44th in my class of 52. By the time it came my turn to choose, the pickings were sparse. My choice became one of flying a tactical aircraft, the AC-119G gunship, or flying the B-52 bomber as a table navigator. I chose the AC-119G assignment because it only lasted about a year and a half, and once I was out of Southeast Asia, I would have my choice of assignments after completing a combat tour. Common knowledge: the choice to fly the B-52 resulted in a lifetime assignment. This was especially true regarding the navigator position. The B-52 was the main manned weapon system of the Strategic Air

Command (SAC). Frankly, given my personality, I felt that I would be best suited for either tactical or training commands. Andy, who had two places higher than I, chose to be a table navigator on a C-130 Hercules, otherwise known as a "trash hauler." Once a student made his choice, he received an envelope from one of the personnel specialists on stage. They entered the student's name on the orders, and some additional forms were filled out. After the last man was given his assignment, the assembly was called to attention and then formally dismissed.

Andy, Heather, Sandy and I returned to our apartment. There Andy and I opened our envelopes which contained our orders. Both of us were to report to basic survival training conducted at Fairchild Air Force Base located near Spokane, Washington. Our reporting time was Sunday, September 13, no later than (NLT) 1800 hrs. Classes would start on Monday morning, September 14. This training would extend for eleven days which included an eight-day trek in the mountain-ous area of central Washington. After September 25, I was ordered to Homestead Air Force Base in Florida, for water survival training school. My reporting time was Sunday, October 5, NLT 1800 hrs. That school was scheduled for five days. Andy had to report at Pope Air Force Base in North Carolina before he attended water survival training so he would be in a later class.

After water survival training, I had to report for basic C-119 school, located in Wilmington, Ohio. My reporting date was Monday, October 20, NLT 1800 hours at the Clinton County Airport oper-ations area. Located within that airport was an Air National Guard squadron which had the responsibility of conducting training on the basic, trash hauling C-119. I had to qualify as a basic navigator for that aircraft before I would be allowed to train as a sensor operator on the AC-119G gunship. After qualifying as a table Nav for the basic aircraft, I was then ordered to Lockbourne Air Force Base (now called

Rickenbacker Air Force Base) in Columbus, Ohio. I was to report on Sunday, November 16, NLT 1800 hours to base ops. On November 17, I would commence the last training I would receive stateside before getting orders to join the combat squadron located in Vietnam. This training was to be completed by December 23. I would be authorized a minimum of 14 days of leave starting on December 24. I was ordered to report for deployment at McGuire Air Force Base, New Jersey, on Friday, January 9, 1970 at 1300 hrs. I would receive jungle survival training at Clark Air Base, located on Luzon Island, which was part of the Philippines. After that school, I would be flown to Nha Trang Air Base to fly combat missions for the next year. My orders also contained the authority to arrange off-base housing during the times I was scheduled to be stationed at Clinton County Airport and at Lockbourne Air Force Base. Included in the envelope containing my orders was a list of acceptable hotels and motels in both areas and their contact numbers.

After much excited discussion, the four of us went to our local steakhouse and discussed what the future would hold for all of us. The happiest among us was Heather. As part of the student body of the University of California at Berkeley, she was a committed activist against the war. The fact that Andy would not have to participate in combat provided her an enormous sense of relief. She still had one year of school left to complete before graduating. Heather would join Andy a couple of months after he completed training on the C-130 Hercules. They would marry in March 1970 during Heather's spring break.

Sandy was unusually quiet and thoughtful during this meal. I was pretty sure I knew what was going through her mind. After we finished eating, we drove back to the apartment. I asked Sandy to walk with me. After we said our goodbyes to Andy and Heather, Sandy and I walked toward the American River and the park that was located on its south shore. We followed a walking path which paralleled the water.

That path had the river on one side and groves of large trees on the other. It was peaceful and serene. The red sun was low on the western horizon and the air temperature was rapidly dropping to very comfortable levels. Perfect walking weather. We were holding hands. We walked in silence. I finally spoke.

"I'm in love with you. I want you with me as much as possible and for as long as possible. Do you feel the same?"

"Oh God. Of course, I do. I knew the first time we kissed."

I stopped with her left hand cupped by both of mine, knelt and said, "Will you marry me?"

Sandy couldn't speak. She nodded her assent as her eyes filled with tears. She gently pulled me up and kissed me passionately for over a minute. Finally, she said, "Of course I will. It's exactly what I want. When do you think we can get married?"

The dates on my orders were emblazoned in my mind. I pondered for several moments and responded, "I think the best time would be sometime after Christmas. You have your Christmas break, and I would get my pre-deployment leave . . . both would occur at the same time. You could fly to New York for Thanksgiving to meet my family and be back in Sacramento to continue school. How does that time sound to you?"

"I think it fits."

"What about your mom? How would she take this?"

"I'm not sure, but I think she likes and trusts you, so I really believe that she will be okay."

We started walking again in silence. The river's movement across the embedded rapids provided a soft almost musical background punctuated by the occasional bird calls and high-pitched sounds emanating from the insects which inhabit the river bank. I could smell the moisture in the air. I was both happy and at total peace with myself. I pondered the situation and then broke the silence again. "I think the time to tell your mother of our intentions is when I return from survival training. That should be September 26. From that time until I must report at Homestead Air Force Base is some nine days later. I'll come back here, and you and I will ask her together."

"What if she says no?" Sandy asked.

"That's easy. You turn 18 on December 2. Then it would be your decision."

"You're right. I didn't think of that."

"Look," I told her, "I really want to do this the right way. And if your mom agrees, then I'll make sure you have a plane ticket to New York and back. There you can meet my family, my best friend, his wife and my godson. If we act behind her back, she will always resent me. I don't want that. I want our families to combine as harmoniously as possible. If we are patient now, we will have better relations with both families." A very happy Sandy gave me another wonderful, long passionate kiss. We headed back on the trail toward our apartment house.

The next nine days flew by. Our graduation was scheduled for September 6, 1969. The ceremonies started at 10:00 AM in the large assembly hall. The room was packed with soon-to-be graduating navigators, their families, instructor navigators, squadron personnel and wing staff including the wing commander and the base commander. Sandy, wearing a conservative white dress and white gloves, accompanied me into the hall. Her jet-black hair was gleaming and her dark brown eyes glistening with pride. I wore my dark blue formal uniform. In August, I was promoted to first lieutenant, so my shoulders bore the single silver bars. The ceremony lasted about two hours. Finally, I received my silver navigator wings and formal orders stating that I was now a "rated" officer. When the ceremonies were over, I gave Sandy the wings and asked her to pin them on me. She did so gleefully.

We spent the next week together as much as possible. Sandy started school and was only available to me in the afternoon and evenings. Friday evening was the last night that we could be together before I had to leave. Finally, early Saturday morning, September 13, Andy and I said our goodbyes to Heather and Sandy. We drove together in my Camaro toward Fairchild Air Force Base. We arrived late in the evening of the same day. We signed into the bachelor officer quarters (BOQ) where Andy and I shared a room together.

Monday morning we started our classroom training. After lunch, we had several more hours of instruction followed by four hours of hard physical training. The instruction generally centered on learning techniques that would teach us how to live off the land. We were taught about those indigenous plants which could be used for medicinal purposes. The afternoon PT sessions were designed to build up physical stamina so that a student would be able to successfully accomplish the eight-day trek. During one of these PT training sessions, I sustained a fall which left a pretty good lump on my head. I was taken to the flight surgeon where I was treated. Since I was a rated officer, I had to be seen as soon as possible. Besides, I wanted to get back to school as soon as I could. I did not wait long before seeing a doctor. The flight surgeon examined my head and used a bandage to close a small wound. While he was treating me, the doctor noticed a growth on the left side of my neck. He asked me how long this bulge had existed. I told him that I had noticed this for the last several months. He asked me what my orders were once I finished school. I told him what my itinerary was between now and the end of the year.

"When you get to Lockbourne Air Force Base, I want you to see the flight surgeon there. That bulge in your neck must be looked at before you go overseas. I want your word that you will see the flight surgeon before you take your pre-departure leave. Do you understand, Lieutenant?"

"Yes sir!" I replied.

"Then I have your word as an officer that you will comply with this request?"

"Absolutely, sir."

When the doctor was done with me, I rejoined my class. I didn't think much of it then, but that turned out to be a major turning point in my life.

After the mandatory three days of classroom instruction and PT were completed, we were ready for the dreaded eight-day trek through some of the most mountainous areas in the state of Washington. We had 84 students in our class divided into six flights containing 14 students each. Andy and I were in the second flight. For the next eight days and seven nights, each flight was given an old parachute to share among its members, and every individual flight member received 1,500 calories of food rations. We were put on several buses and driven to the starting point. From there we broke out into our separate flights with each flight led by an NCO survival instructor. We went our six separate ways. The first day, we had to trek five miles, mostly uphill, to the first base camp area. There we learned to make our shelter from parachute parts. These handmade shelters would have to last the entire seven nights of the trek.

Each day we had to find the next assembly point using only a map and a compass. We were further divided into pairs so that each pair would have to take a certain route while passing certain checkpoints and come to the assembly area for the evening. Andy and I stayed together the whole time. Frankly, being a navigator really helped make these chores much easier to accomplish. Besides, no instructor there, and I mean none, knew more about mountain survival than my roommate. Andy was the son of a logger, and he'd spent his whole life growing up in the sparsely populated mountainous area of the great Northwest.

One example should illustrate the whole experience. We were tasked to make fishing gear out of a parachute pack. My flight, using these techniques, caught sixteen small trout in some of the streams we encountered. I caught one and Andy caught 14! We did share our bounty with the others.

The last day, we had a three-hour march to the final assembly area. There we met up with the entire class. We loaded onto three buses and returned to Fairchild Air Force Base. Before the final dismissal, our instructors passed out our individual certificates of completion which in this case indicated that the individual duly named had successfully completed basic survival training. We were told that we were to place these certificates in the training folders we carried and that they would stay in our possession until we could turn them into the personnel office of our final gaining squadron. Every time we completed one of these mandatory schools, we received a blue certificate of completion. By the time a rated officer got to his first command, he would have accumulated at least four of these blue certificates of completion. This was my first.

It was late afternoon on September 25. Andy and I decided we would get a decent night's sleep and leave the next morning early. We expected to roll into Sacramento around supper time the next day. That's what we did. And that's when I found my world changed forever.

6

LOSS

Andy and I went to sleep early on Thursday, September 25. We were both so tired from the trek that by six o'clock that evening we were both asleep. I awoke about 11 hours later. I was anxious to see Sandy and hold her in my arms again. About a half-hour later, we went to a local restaurant for breakfast. We ate our fill and went back to the base, loaded the car, and signed out of the BOQ. By 0700 that morning, we were on the road.

I probably was driving somewhat faster than I normally would. Both of us were anxious to see our women again. We made the normally thirteen-hour drive in 11 1/2 hours. When we stopped at a roadside eatery, I tried to call Sandy's home number. There was no answer. That left me a little edgy, and I told Andy how I was feeling. He laughed and said that Sandy was probably out shopping with her mother or sister. "You're probably right. It's just . . . I have this weird feeling and I can't seem to shake it."

As we approached our old apartment house, my sense of dread increased dramatically. When I finally pulled into a nearby parking spot, I saw that the manager's apartment was unlit. Andy and I got out of my car and walked to the entrance of Sandy's apartment. On the door was a phone number to call if anyone was interested in renting the apartments in this particular building. I copied the phone number, and Andy and I went to a nearby gas station. While the attendant filled up my tank with gas, I found a nearby phone booth and called the number that I'd just copied. After a few rings, an elderly man answered the phone.

After a formal greeting in which I learned that his name was Mr. Henderson who owned the entire rental complex I asked where the Caliprizzo family was.

"Who are you exactly? What is your relationship to the family?" he asked.

"My name is Lieut. Blakeman, and I rented the apartment above the Caliprizzo family. During my stay there, we became very close."

"Well son, there's no easy way to say this, so I will just come out with it. There was a terrible accident on Route 50. Some drunk crossed six lanes of traffic and ran into Mrs. Caliprizzo's car. It was a high-speed, dead on collision. The cops reported this drunken son-of-a-bitch was doing in excess of one hundred miles an hour. Mrs. Caliprizzo was driving with both her daughters. They didn't stand a chance."

His words hit me like a strong kick to the stomach. I asked him when the funeral would be. He told me that the accident occurred some ten days ago. The family was taken down to the Fresno area where Sandy's father still resided. It was the past Sunday that all three were laid to rest. I thanked him for the information and quietly hung up the phone.

Andy, standing by my car, saw me as I approached. "What happened?" he asked with concern in his voice. I told him what Mr. Henderson related to me. It took maybe twenty seconds for the information to register with Andy. He asked where I wanted to go. I told him, "Let's take a walk by the river."

We drove my car to the park's entrance and found a nearby parking spot. We got out walked in silence for least a half hour on the path which paralleled the American River toward the very spot at which I asked Sandy to marry me. We found an exposed boulder, and we sat side-by-side, just quietly listening to the sounds of the river. We sat that way for almost 20 minutes when I finally spoke.

"This is the place where I asked Sandy to marry me. We were keeping it secret until today when I was going to ask her mother for her hand in marriage."

"I knew you guys were close. I was sure you loved her. I didn't know that it had gotten that far."

"I was in love for the first time in my life. Andy, I think I knew it the first time we met her. You know what she was wearing?"

"I remember. I remember also how hard it was for you to even talk . . . you were completely enthralled by her. I have never seen anybody fall so hard and so fast in my life as you did that day."

"God. I can't imagine what life is going to be without her. I feel like my guts just got kicked out. You know what's even harder for me is that we never got to say goodbye. I still feel that she's around, and I will see her again. I know that doesn't make sense . . . it's just the way I feel."

Andy put his hand on my shoulder and said to me, "Whatever you need. Just ask and you will never have to ask twice!" I silently nodded. A little while later, we decided to leave the area. It was painful for me to stay . . . too many memories.

We walked back and I drove Andy to his car, a yellow 1968 GTO. We got out and hugged each other. Andy was going to Berkeley to see Heather. I wished him well and told him to give her my best. When he drove off, I went to the BOQ at Mather Air Force Base and spent the night there.

The next morning, I started the long lonely drive to Homestead Air Force Base. I took my time driving across the country. I found that driving in silence was for me somewhat cathartic. Sandy was gone, and I knew intellectually that I would never see her again. But the heart wants what the heart wants. Some part of me still believed that she was still alive and that I would see her again. It was irrational, but that thought kept me going.

I arrived at Homestead Air Force Base two days early. After signing in at the BOQ, I finally called my parents and JG and Hope. They all were devastated by the horrible news. They'd never met Sandy, but they did remember Andy's wonderful description of her and how she affected me. They loved me, so the hard part was knowing a loved one is hurting and being helpless to alleviate the loss and pain. When I spoke to my mother, and she heard the loss in my voice, she started to weep. I told them, in separate phone calls, that I would be in New York for Thanksgiving if my training allowed. If not, then I would return for my pre-departure leave at the end of December.

I successfully completed the five-day water survival training. On the last day, I received my blue certificate of completion and left the next day for Wilmington, Ohio. I arrived and signed into the motel where I had made a reservation shortly after receiving my orders. There I had met three other classmates from UNT including Derek Evans. We got together and went out for dinner at a local restaurant and then proceeded to the motel's bar. All of us made reservations at the same location. They did not know what had happened to Sandy and her family. They were devastated by the news and asked me how I was doing. They asked me how I found out about this, and I told them about my conversation with Mr. Henderson.

"I can't believe that somebody in the Air Force would not have told you what actually happened!" Derek stated.

"I thought about this a lot when I was driving down here. The problem was that she was not formally my wife yet, so the Air Force could not know we were that close. I needed to change my notification information so that the service would know. I just didn't think that was necessary at the time. How could anybody?" I asked rhetorically.

After a couple rounds of liquid commiseration, Derek insisted that all four of us should see some college and professional football. Derek informed all of us that the University of Kentucky Wildcats were playing at home during the Saturdays that we were not scheduled to fly. And since we were all scheduled to be in the Ohio area through the third week of December, we should see the Cincinnati Bengals play whenever possible. I really didn't want to do this, but the peer pressure provided by my classmates prodded me into doing so.

Our classes started on Monday, October 20. They lasted four days. We had the weekend off and so the four of us went to Lexington, Kentucky and saw the University of Kentucky Wildcats play some Southeast Conference football. The next day, we went to Cincinnati and saw the Bengals play. The games we attended were exciting and spending time with my classmates helped me to keep my mind from dwelling on the past. In the next two months, we spent almost every weekend driving down to Lexington and Cincinnati to see the available football games. Now, my compadres all had "good luck" with the young ladies, particularly those coeds we met in Lexington. I was not interested and opted not to pursue even a casual relationship. I still felt that Sandy was alive somewhere in this world, and I did not want another partner. It wasn't rational. It just was. This feeling would dominate my very being for almost the next two years.

We flew out of Wilmington on Monday, October 27. We stayed at various Air Force and Navy bases that were located near the Atlantic Ocean or the Gulf of Mexico. We all received six training flights, and the last flight was a checkout for your crew position. All of us passed without problems. From there we returned to Clinton County Airport in Wilmington, Ohio. There we received our third certificate of completion, and we all drove to Lockbourne Air Force Base in Columbus, Ohio. We all signed in at the same hotel and awaited the beginning of our training in the AC-119G gunship.

On Monday, November 10, we started a three-day ground school. On the last day, we finally got to meet the gunship version of the C-119G. It was refitted for use in the Vietnam War. The lowly troop-carrying C-119 took on a tactical offensive role which its designers never could have foreseen. In its *AC-119G "Shadow"* variant, it was fitted with four six-barrel, 7.62-mm mini-guns, armor plating, flare-launchers, night-capable low-light television targeting scope LLTV), and a rear mounted, two million candle power search light. It was so powerful that in emergency situations in-country, field doctors used this light in order to perform operations during the night in order to save wounded soldiers. The gray paint was replaced by a dull black finish. The forward crew entrance door was blocked by the LLTV sensor whose shape resembled a water cooled, 50-caliber machine gun. That sensor was connected to a Plexiglas aiming device just left of the pilot's seat. When the sensor operator moved the barrel-shaped LLTV device to track a target, it would show that change on the Plexiglas aiming device. The pilot would fly the aircraft so that the fixed "piper" would be superimposed upon the moving piper which aimed the guns on to whatever the LLTV was targeting. Sitting amidships, just aft of the forward crew entrance door, was an enclosed jet engine whose sole purpose was to act as a generator in order to power the advanced avionics and especially the two million candle power search light.

Since I was a really junior navigator, I was only trained as a sensor operator. It was not particularly difficult. I had to learn how to estimate the speed of a moving target, to keep crosshairs on the target without much movement, and to discern different potential targets. We flew our first training flight on the evening of Monday, November 17. All flights were at night, as this aircraft was designed and assigned to fly almost all its combat missions after the sun went down. Since the door remained open, the cabin could not be pressurized nor heated. The fall of 1969 was one of the coldest on record in the Columbus, Ohio area. I was issued an arctic flying suit, because as a sensor operator I would be in the slipstream when operating the LLTV sensor. It was so cold for the next 4 1/2 weeks that I was stationed there, I would eat over 6,000 calories a day just to maintain weight. Some evenings, the wind-chill factor at my position was around 60 below Fahrenheit. Whenever I was not needed in the scope, I was permitted to place my rear up against the cowling which contained the jet engine and for me, frankly, was an enlarged fanny warmer!

We were required to complete twelve missions. The last one was to be the final check ride before going overseas. The training crew to which I was assigned needed sixteen flights in order to accomplish all required training. The need for the added sorties was caused by the fact that the C-119 was not designed for cold weather. And that fall and early winter we experienced near Arctic conditions. By early December, it was not unusual for the evening temperature to go well below zero degrees Fahrenheit. Because of the extreme cold weather, the engines and hydraulic systems did not operate properly. The result was that in sixteen takeoffs I experienced in that aircraft, four of them resulted in "MAYDAYs" or declared in-flight emergencies. We managed to walk away from all of them, but it gave me little confidence in the air worthiness of this weapon system.

After our flight on November 24, my training crew was offered a week's leave for Thanksgiving. I readily accepted. My copilot, Lt. William Fuller, whose nickname was Wild Bill, was also from Long Island, so we decided to drive together. Bill drove a luxury Oldsmobile powered by a 440 cubic-inch engine. Bill was a big dude, at least two inches past six feet and weighing close to 220 pounds. His light sandy hair and blue eyes, mixed with an almost constant smile, made him a success with young ladies. His gregarious nature and pure enjoyment of the moment made him a very popular crewmember. We decided to use his car, as it could hold more than my Camaro. We shared the driving and the expenses to make it easier on our lieutenant's pay. We left the morning of the 25th, and Bill dropped me off at my home in Syosset that evening. He would pick me up on Sunday the 30th so that we could return and be prepared to fly on December 1.

I spent that first evening with my parents, my brother and my sister. Of course, they wanted to know how I was doing. I tried to explain to them the enormity of the loss that I felt. Not too much later, we started discussing the normal family business. As usual, my family did not like to discuss deep personal feelings. I don't know why it was that way, but it was. Still, it was comforting being with them.

The next afternoon, Mom let me use her car, and I drove to JG and Hope's residence. I got there about three o'clock in the afternoon. After ringing the door bell, Hope opened the door and gave me a big hug. I must have held her tight for at least two minutes. When I finally let loose, I saw the tears in her eyes. "I'm so sorry. I know there's nothing anybody can say or do. Just know that both JG and I love you."

"That means the world to me. Now, tell me about my godson!" Daniel, at this time, was doing what most infants do . . . he was sleeping. Hope was beaming as she told me about the time he sat up and how he recognized both of his parent's voices. I asked her how she liked being a mom. Hope loved what she was doing. It seems that JG's dad wanted her to stay at home for as long as possible, so he augmented his son's income to allow this. I knew how strict the old man was after listening to JG complain about him over the years. Obviously, the old boy was taken with his new daughter-in-law and most especially his new and only grandson. I found out that JG passed the bar exam on the first try. Hearing that did not surprise me at all.

Now that JG was a practicing lawyer, he received a huge increase in pay, so much so that he and Hope would be looking in the spring for a three-bedroom house out on Long Island, probably near the border between Nassau and Suffolk Counties. I was really happy to hear that they were doing so well. I was closer to JG than any other living human.

I was there about an hour and a half when JG entered his home dressed in a suit and tie. After we hugged, I told him basically what I had said to Hope. He excused himself for ten minutes, as he wanted to change clothes. I was sitting on the sofa when he reappeared wearing a beat-up Marietta College sweatshirt over loose jeans and sneakers. I noticed that JG was about 15 pounds heavier than when I saw him last August. I couldn't help but rib him about the expanded waistline. He laughed and told me that it was Hope's fault, because "she became a damned good cook!" With that comment, we all laughed and the noise woke up my godson. Hope immediately got up, gathered her son in her arms and brought him into the living room. She placed a privacy towel over his head as she provided a breast for him to suckle. She told me that she would not normally do that, but since I was regarded as family, she had no qualms. I'd never seen a mother breast-feeding her baby before. Frankly, I found the whole process peaceful and restorative.

When Hope was done, she handed me the baby. She put a towel over my shoulder and showed me how to burp Daniel. It took me about ten minutes before he finally gave out the last burp. I pulled him down into my arms and his little blue eyes were looking right at me. He was not nervous at all and after rocking him for about five minutes, his little eyes closed and shortly after that, he was fast asleep.

"Now what do I do?" I asked.

JG got up, smiled, and gathered his son into his arms. He placed Daniel in his cradle. We then all retired to the dining room where Hope would serve the meal. JG was right. The girl had become a great cook. After we ate our fill, JG and I went outside to light up a cigarette or even two. At this time, both of us were heavy smokers. Since Hope didn't smoke and she didn't want Daniel exposed to it, JG agreed to only smoke outside the house. I just complied with house rules!

About 15 minutes later, Hope told JG that she would do the dishes in the morning because she wanted to spend time talking with the both of us. We retired to the living room. Hope, being the psychiatric social worker that she was, asked me how I was coping. I told them both that for me it was still unreal. "I never saw her dead body with my own eyes. I still believe for no rational reason that Sandy is still in the world. I still believe that I will see her again. I know it's crazy. It's just what I believe."

"It's not crazy," Hope replied. "It's the first stage of grief which is denial. For you, this will take longer than for most people because there was no physical closure. I don't know when it will hit, but when it does, just remember that JG and I will be available to you at any time or place. The denial you feel is a coping mechanism, and you're going to need it, especially if you enter combat."

"You're probably right. I feel like I am treading water. I have no desire to be with another woman. I so wanted both of you to meet her. She was such a sweet person. I don't think I will ever love another woman the way I loved her."

"That's true," Hope responded. "You may fall in love again, but it will be different. Maybe not as intense, but having value in its own right. This might not make sense now, but someday I think it will."

JG chimed in, "How's your training going?" I told him how tough basic survival was. I related to them an incident that occurred in the next-to-last day of trek. We just had completed a twelve-mile leg over extremely rough terrain from one checkpoint to another. Andy and I were the first trainees to arrive at the second checkpoint. The survival instructor told us to go over to a dried creek bed and take a rest. His final admonition to us was the following which I quoted exactly to JG and Hope: "Never stand when you can sit; never sit when you can lay down; and never lay down when you can sleep!" I was so tired that as soon as my head hit the smooth stones at the base of the dried creek, I fell into a deep sleep! The instructor awakened me several hours later when the last pair came into base camp. I also told JG and Hope some entertaining antidotes regarding water survival.

The conversation became much heavier. It was now more than a year past the infamous Tet Offensive. The war in Vietnam was becoming more and more unpopular and divisive. I stated, "If the weapon system on which I trained was available, the Tet Offensive would've ended much earlier. Gunships provide extremely accurate and immense firepower in a very short time. It was important to the grunts on the ground as it bettered their chances of survival by providing this airpower. That was enough for me. I wanted to be able to do my part by helping them. Whether the war was right or wrong, the guys fighting it needed to be supported."

JG and Hope sat quietly on the sofa. There was no answer to this declarative statement, so I changed the subject. "Tell me about the house that you are looking to buy."

JG told me that he was doing quite well. After he stated that he received a significant raise by passing the bar, he continued, "The boss really appreciates my work and my abilities. I just finished working second chair to him on some of our biggest cases. In one of them, I insisted that we keep one juror when everybody else on our side wanted to excuse this juror. It turned out that my boss followed my suggestion and lo and behold, the jury was hung. The prosecution requested that the jury be polled. It turned out that there was only one vote for acquittal, and that was the juror I told my boss to keep. The prosecution did not want to retry the case and so our client was released. That defendant was extremely wealthy and brought not only this criminal case to our firm, but some other major legal work. In about a year or two, my boss wants to open a satellite office somewhere in eastern Nassau County. He hopes to develop a strong family court branch in that area. I'm not sure, but I have the feeling that he wants me to head it."

"JG, given what I know about your ability to read people and situations, I would bet on it. That's one trait you share with my mother. The two of you can read people like nobody else I know." Frankly, playing poker with either one of them was a losing proposition.

We then talked about possible locations for both the office and where JG and Hope could find an affordable house. Since I was very familiar with Long Island, I could, and did, offer some advice regarding both locations. The area that interested Hope the most was the western portion of Suffolk County. Taxes were not as high, and the education offered to children was quite good. This location, especially if JG's job moved to Long Island, would be ideal for both purposes.

I asked JG when it would be possible for him to purchase a new home and to move his family into it. He laughed and said, "If we are frugal, maybe three years. Then I should have saved enough for a significant down payment and money for the move." We talked for a couple more hours, and I could see that Hope was getting tired. I hugged both of them goodbye.

The next two days I spent with my family. Dad took time off from work, and we visited with some of my relatives. Everyone was curious about life in the military. I was the only one on both sides of the family who was actively involved in one of the services. In fact, I spent Thanksgiving Day with my mother's sister and her family. Aunt Bea was a superb cook, and we had a very nice time. We left late Thanksgiving night and when we got home, we went straight to bed. I slept until about eleven o'clock in the morning when my mother woke me up because I had a phone call. It was Bill Fuller calling.

"Hey Blake, how are you doing?"

"I'm okay, Wild Bill. What's up?"

"I know we were supposed to leave on Sunday morning, but I just got off the phone with the weather service. There is a real bad storm brewing, and if we wait until Sunday, we may not be back in time to get proper crew rest before flying on Monday."

"When do you want to leave?"

"How about tomorrow? Say about ten o'clock in the morning. I'll swing by your place and pick you up."

"Sounds good. See you then."

I hung up the phone and told my parents that I was leaving the next morning. They were disappointed, but they understood the reason I had to leave early. Bill showed up on time and I said my final goodbyes to my family. I rode "shotgun" in Bill's car. By 10:15, we were on the road. Because of road conditions, we did not arrive at our motel in Columbus, Ohio until three o'clock Sunday morning. Even Bill's heavy Oldsmobile had trouble keeping on the road. In the span along Route 22 between New Jersey and Pennsylvania, our maximum speed was twenty miles an hour due to the icy roads.

On Monday, December 1, my training crew started flying again. Because of weather delays, maintenance problems and four in-flight declared emergencies, it took the next 17 days to accomplish the twelve required training flights. The last of these flights occurred on December 18. We took off at 10:00 PM and finished at 3:00 AM on the morning of the 19th. This last flight was my check ride which I easily passed. By the time we debriefed and received our blue certificates of completion, it was just past 4:30 AM.

A couple days earlier, I had seen the flight surgeon stationed at Lockbourne Air Force Base. When he saw the lump in my throat, he said that it had to be looked at by the doctors at the medical center located in Wright-Patterson Air Force Base. He scheduled a consult for me at 11:00 AM on December 19th. After receiving my last blue certificate, I was on the road to the Dayton area where Wright-Patterson Air Force Base is located. I already signed out of the motel, and all my personal and professional clothing and equipment were secured in my car's trunk.

I rolled into Wright-Patterson Air Force Base about 09:30 in the morning. I was directed to the medical center and parked my car in the long-term parking area. I entered the main hall and noticed the information desk. I was still dressed in my flying gear. I was scheduled to see *Dr. Frank Coyle* who was a top-notch surgeon. The lady at the desk directed me to the third floor. A few minutes past ten, I entered Dr. Coyle's office and walked up to the NCO who was sitting behind a desk. "Can I help you, Lieutenant?" he asked.

"Yes Sergeant. My name is Lt. Norris Blakeman. I've an appointment with Dr. Coyle."

He looked over his clipboard. He found my name and said, "Please be seated, sir. Dr. Coyle will see you in a few minutes."

I thanked him and took a seat. About 15 minutes later, the inner office door opened and a white-haired gentleman called out, "Lt. Blakeman, please follow me." My life would never be the same after that moment.

7

ADJUSTMENT

It was quiet, very quiet when I first woke up. I was in pain. It hurt me to move, even to breathe. The blue pajamas, standard issue at all Air Force hospitals, was thoroughly soaked with my perspiration. As painful as it was, I sat up and looked around. My movement was further restricted by the plastic tubes stuck in my right arm which fed me both food and medicine.

It was a large ward which contained approximately 30 hospital beds. My bed was located about 30 feet from a desk near the entrance to the ward. I observed a corpsman and a nurse sitting at the desk drinking coffee. My mouth was very dry and I wanted some water.

"Corpsman!" I rasped. The young airman dressed in hospital whites got up and came over to my bed.

"Good morning, Lieutenant. What can I do for you?" he responded.

"Could I have some water?" I asked.

"Certainly Lieutenant." I observed the corpsman with my eyes as it was too painful to turn my neck. He quietly whispered something to the nurse as he returned to my bedside with a flask of water and a bent glass straw protruding from the top.

"Drink this slowly," suggested the corpsman. I complied. It took me almost a minute to finish sipping a few ounces of water.

"Where am I . . . I mean what ward am I in?" I asked.

"You are in the ICU, the intensive care unit, sir."

"How long was I out?"

"About twelve hours, sir."

Just then the nurse, carrying a needle, came over to my bed. "Good morning, Colonel Coyle wants you to sleep for several more hours. This will help you go back to sleep. She brushed my arm with some alcohol and injected me with a sedative. A few moments later, I muttered goodnight and was again fast asleep.

The early morning light was streaming in from the windows as I awakened to the sounds of agony. I sat up with a great deal of effort and pain and looked for the source of the screaming. The sound came from a woman across the aisle. She was being tended by a corpsman and a nurse, different from the ones I'd encountered during the night. The corpsman was restraining the thrashing woman while the nurse injected her with some kind of painkiller. My eyes, in the light of day, took in the entirety of the ward. I saw another corpsman, a staff sergeant, sitting near the desk. I called to him, and the sergeant stood up and started coming toward my direction. But before going directly to my bed, the sergeant went over to a crib and checked its contents and then made his way to my bedside. "What can I do for you, Lieutenant?" asked the sergeant.

My mouth felt like sandpaper and my throat was sore. "May I have some water please?"

"Certainly, sir," responded the sergeant as he went to get some water for me. Shortly, he returned with a beaker containing a glass straw and gave it to me. I slowly sipped the water. In between sips, I asked the sergeant what happened to the woman who was screaming in pain.

"She was in a car accident. I don't think she will last the day. All we can do is make her as comfortable as possible."

"How about the crib over there?" I asked.

"That sir, is Captain Manson's daughter. She is only three years old, and she had an operation today to repair a heart valve. It is touch and go with her, but we are optimistic and very hopeful that she will make it."

"I hope you are right, Sergeant. Do you know how long before I can return to the surgery ward?"

"Dr. Coyle should be here within a half-hour to look you over. When you leave here is his decision."

I thanked the corpsman and just like everybody else, he checked the crib before returning to his station. About a half-hour later, I looked up and saw Dr. Coyle approaching my bed. "How are you doing, young man?" he asked.

"Well, my neck hurts a lot, but otherwise it's not too bad. I'd like to get back to the surgery ward as soon as possible. I really don't like this ICU."

Dr. Coyle laughed and listened to my heart while the corpsman accompanying him measured my temperature, blood pressure and heart rate. He looked at me with his soft kind eyes and said, "You are doing remarkably well . . . much better than I even hoped for. If your vitals stay stable, then I suspect you'll be out of here by day's end." I thanked the doctor, and he smiled in response. The doctor departed, and left me alone with my thoughts.

I started thinking about the series of events that brought me to this point. I finished my last check ride very early on Friday, December 19. I remember driving down to Wright-Patterson Air Force Base Medical Center. I saw Dr. Coyle that morning for the first time. After examining my neck, he determined that I needed the bulge (called a goiter) removed and biopsied. He was concerned so he scheduled surgery for that afternoon. That was basically a fairly simple procedure, and I was sent to the surgery ward after the operation was completed. Since I was an officer, I had my own private room. Dr. Coyle came in that evening and told me that he had sent the neck tissue to the Ohio State University Medical Center for an evaluation as to whether or not it was cancerous. He would have the results the next day.

The next evening, Dr. Coyle came into my room, and I could see by the expression on his face that the news was not good. He told me that I had both follicular and medullary cancer. Time was of the essence, so he scheduled surgery on Monday, December 22. I would be the first case, and probably the only case, that he would handle that day. He was going to do a complete thyroidectomy and a radical neck operation. I was devastated. Not only did I lose the woman I loved, but I would not be able to do what I trained for these past months. Throwing my whole being into flying helped me cope with the loss of Sandy. Now that was not possible. I got out of my bed, wearing the blue pajamas, and walked to the window. The sun was shining as I looked out over the wide expanse that formed this Air Force base. I was numb and the doctor waited as I sifted through thoughts running through my mind. Finally, I turned and said, "Que sera, sera!" (What will be, will be!) The doctor wished me well and said that he would see me bright and early Monday morning. Before he left, I asked Dr. Coyle to call my parents and explain to them what was going to be done and why. I told him that it was better if he explained it firsthand rather than my trying to tell them what was told to me. The doctor readily agreed and took my parents' phone number. Dr. Coyle, true to his word, performed the operation on December 22, 1969.

Every hour on the hour for the next four hours, the corpsman came and took my vitals. They were all strong. After the last visit, the corpsman said, "Dr. Coyle told the nurse that you will leave here by late afternoon and be returned to the surgery ward. All your vital signs are remarkably stable. He was surprised how rapidly you have recovered from six hours on the operating table."

I was still in pain, but I smiled at Coyle's surprise. I was always proud of my physical prowess and stamina. I believed in my heart that I would survive this. "Thanks for the information, Sergeant."

"You're welcome, sir." With that, the sergeant turned and went to the crib, checked its precious contents and returned to his desk. During the remainder of my stay in the ICU, I noticed that all the corpsmen and nurses made it a point to stop by the crib on their way to doing other things that had to be done in the ICU. Even when the girl's mother and father were by her crib, the ICU personnel still made their way over there. I thought to myself, with some pride, *when it comes to taking care of children, the Air Force definitively takes care of its own*!

I carefully and painfully returned to a sleeping position. I was still doped up and quickly fell asleep. When I awoke, I was back in the surgery ward. A little while later, Dr. Coyle came into the room accompanied by my parents. They had a solemn look on both their faces. Dr. Coyle explained to the three of us that the surgery went extremely well. He was absolutely sure that he removed all the cancer. He did a radical neck to assure that no stray cancer cells would get into the accompanying lymphatic system. The gouge on the left side of my neck and a lot of muscle tissue on my left shoulder would eventually fill in, so it would not look as grotesque as it did now. Mom was softly crying, but her spirits lifted when Dr. Coyle said that my prognosis was excellent. I would survive this. He ordered two radioactive iodine treatments in order to kill any thyroid and cancerous tissue that possibly still remained. I would stay in the hospital for at least the next two to three months. Dr. Coyle also informed me that I would have to take thyroid supplements for the rest of my life. My flying days were over before they got started.

Mom and Dad stayed with me for a week. Their spirits lifted when they saw that I was physically doing quite well. I was ahead of schedule. They wanted to know what I was going to do with the rest of my life. Frankly, I did not know. I told them that I would return home when the Air Force released me. We spent every day from morning until early evening together during that week. The only break was when I received physical therapy training in order to learn how to use my neck and the left side of my body which was now severely weakened. That was really hard on me as I am left-handed. I did manage to accompany my parents to the mess hall where we would share three meals each day. Dad was pleasantly surprised with the high quality of food served in this particular hospital. Finally, two days past New Year's Eve, my parents returned home. They felt better because I was definitely on the mend.

For the next three and a half months, I received all the treatment promised by Dr. Coyle. It all went without any unforeseen hitches. The latter part of March, I received my outgoing orders. I was to be placed on the Temporary Disability Retirement List (TDRL). That meant I would receive 100% of my base pay for the rest of my life as a fully retired officer. The Air Force ruled that my service was honorable and that the cancer that had stricken me was service related. On April 7, 1970, I received my final briefing and was given all my records, both operational and medical, and an honorable discharge. In addition, I was permitted to keep my regular flying suits and jackets, as they were going to be replaced by the new ones which would be manufactured using the newly developed Nomex material. The old flying gear was comfortable, but did not protect the wearer in case of high heat and/or fire. The new Nomex material was uncomfortable, but considerably safer. I left the base about 10:30 in the morning on my way to return home. Around eight o'clock that evening on April 7, I arrived at my Syosset family home.

After about a week of visiting with JG, Hope and my family, I knew I had to do something with my life. When I attended Marietta College, I took only a few math courses, as that department in my alma mater was not particularly good. I personally felt that my lack of a decent mathematical background really hampered what I would be capable of doing in any career path that I opted to pursue. I signed up as a part-time student at the CW Post campus (part of Long Island University) in order to take the first two courses of calculus during the summer. But those classes were not scheduled to start for almost two months. I needed something else to do. I needed to repair my body. I asked my father to give me a job as a "loader" in his truck yard. He readily agreed. I would work under his foreman, Isaac "Ike" Holtzman. Ike was a former marine who served during the Korean conflict. He saw 20 months of combat. He was a big man with about 250 pounds on a six feet three-inch frame. He had thin, blond hair and a large forehead, and a loud booming voice. I had known Ike since I was nine years old. He started out as a loader, then became a driver and finally, given his natural leadership, was promoted to foreman.

When my father told Ike that I was going to work as a loader, he nodded his agreement while looking directly at me, and in my dad's presence said, "Don't expect any favors from me. You're the boss's son, and I'm going to work you harder than any other man on the loading dock. Any questions?" I didn't have any, so I was told to report to the dock the next morning, attired properly, ready to work. And that's just what I did. Dad and I would get up early every morning and drive to work together for the next four months.

Ike, true to his word, worked me like a "broke-dick" mule. The first two weeks were almost pure agony, as my body, particularly my left side, had to stretch the scar tissue and reacquire strength. Ike pushed as hard as he could. He knew that I was not a slacker. Sometimes, particularly after a tough load, he would give me an extra 15 minutes rest. As my body started to respond to physical labor, I needed less time between loads to recover. Looking back on it, I think Ike had it just about right; he pushed as hard as he could, but without endangering my recovery. In the four months that I worked for my father, I recovered almost all my strength, thanks, in large part, to Ike.

While I was working for my dad, I kept an eye on the job listings in *Newsday*, the paper of record for all of Long Island. Finally, in late May, I read an advertisement seeking a math teacher for seventh and eighth grades in a local, privately owned military academy. I called and arranged an interview. Several days later, I met the headmaster, and I was exactly what he was seeking. My military background mixed with my desire to teach made me an ideal candidate for the position. After chatting with him for about a half-hour, he offered me the job and I accepted. I would move to an apartment located on campus by the end of August. My classes would start the first day after Labor Day, 1970.

In the meantime, I continued to work for my dad during the day and, after Memorial Day, I started taking courses in calculus at night. The first two weeks were brutal. I had not looked at a mathematics book in eight years. I would read and reread the sections covered in class. It wasn't coming easily. Finally, one night I couldn't sleep because I could not solve one particular problem assigned for homework. I kept dreaming about it. About 2:30 in the morning, the solution popped into my head. I immediately got out of my bed and went to my desk. I took out the problem and solved it in fifteen minutes. From that point on, although the math became more difficult for most in my class, for me, it became easier. It was like a dam breaking. All of a sudden, I was absorbing every concept that the instructor taught. Over the next year, during night classes, I received the highest grade in the class in my four calculus and integral courses. In one of my integral courses, we were responsible for knowing seventy-five formulas "cold." The night before the exam, using flashcards, I found that I already knew seventy-four of them without further study. For the one I couldn't remember, it took me about fifteen minutes, using pencil and paper, to derive the proper formulation. Something happened to my cognitive abilities that I cannot explain. Concepts that used to be difficult for me were now very easy for me to absorb and use. I don't know why this change occurred; I just know that it did.

During this time when I was transitioning from an Air Force navigator to a teacher, I got to spend a fair amount of time with JG and Hope. My time was limited because I was so tired from the combination of working for my father while attending night school. I would usually see them during the weekends. JG's ambition, combined with his innate abilities, drove him to work long hours, particularly during the regular week. Those long hours paid dividends as JG was placed on a quick path to partnership. He felt that he would be able to move his family and establish a new practice on Long Island for his firm within the next two years. Daniel was a little over a year old and getting into everything that was available for a toddler who was just learning how to crawl. Over the summer, the little guy started to walk. One very cute baby. Hope was as happy as I have ever seen her. She loved being a mom, and she was damned good at it. JG, remembering how his father ignored him when he was growing up, was careful to spend as much quality time with his son as he could. I was very happy for my friend and his wife. But my own life, at this time, was bleak.

They asked if I was seeing anybody. I told them I was not. I had no desire. It was so bad that when JG and I went out for a drink one night, we encountered some really pretty girls in the bar. JG enjoyed watching them. They did not distract or entice me one iota. My libido was just about nonexistent. I know both of them worried about me. They also knew that I had to work through this myself. Keeping the long hours working and studying helped me cope. I also received some help in this regard from a peculiar source.

Just before school started, my brother and I got into an argument about what made a great book. I argued all the mundane things that I was taught in college. He said it is style that was the most significant factor. He made a bet with me after he gave me his copy of J.R.R. Tolkien's The Hobbit and The Lord of The Rings trilogy. The bet was simple: I would read these two novels and determine if he was right or if I was. We wagered five dollars, and he left it to me to be the final and only arbiter. I readily agreed. Over the next ten days, I read all four volumes. When I was done, I paid him his five dollars. Now nobody, especially me, likes to lose a bet to his brother. But when he was right, he was right! Then I purchased my own copy of both novels after I returned the ones I read.

I found Tolkien's work to be the best fiction that I have ever read. Prior to this point in my life, I never appreciated poetry in any form. I not only enjoyed the beauty of his prose, but found myself captivated by the different lays so prominently featured in all three volumes of The Lord of the Rings. J.R.R. Tolkien is one of the very few authors who can make a world that doesn't exist extraordinarily real to the reader. The ring is a metaphor for the evil that results when trying to accomplish a good deed by using something inherently evil. The moral of the three volumes, in other words, is that the ends do *not* justify the means. During that summer, I experienced the lowest ebb of my life. What helped bring me out of my depressive state was reading and rereading Tolkien's trilogy. When I read his works, I was no longer in this world but happily in Middle Earth. For me it was like using drugs, but without any physical side-effects. It was total escapism and helped keep me sane.

August 21 was the last day that I worked for my dad. It was also the day that I finished my second course in calculus at Long Island University. I wanted to have about two weeks to prepare my lesson plans. Both my father and Ike were very understanding. By this time, I was doing more work than any other loader on the dock and felt that my physical strength was almost completely back.

My headmaster gave me the texts used for both the seventh and eighth grades. I integrated the required material with set theory which I acquired from my calculus textbook. I created a mimeographed 12-page guide on how to understand and use set theory to explain mathematical concepts. I gave a copy of this guide to every student in all six classes that I taught. Each student would use his guide over the course of the entire academic year. Once a week, I would devote about a half-hour of lecture time in order to deal with some part of set theory. I would continuously build upon that foundation. By the end of the school year, all my students would know how to use set theory in order to understand the mathematical underpinnings of algebra, ratios, and almost every other endeavor related to this field. Once a student understood this theory, it would be easier to absorb and use the more advanced mathematical formulae. That was the approach that I applied to my teaching techniques.

After working a solid week of writing lesson plans, I decided I needed a break. JG and his family went on vacation to Vermont, and my parents went away to the Jewish Alps (Catskills Mountains) for a weekend getaway. I was not in the mood for either one, so I stayed in my home and was quite alone. That Saturday, August 29, I decided to drive down to Jones Beach on the southern shore of Long Island. It was a pristine beach and on this particular night, there was an absolutely cloudless sky above. I arrived about nine o'clock in the evening and walked the beach by myself. I looked up and could see the Navigator's Triangle constellation which was formed by three first magnitude stars: Vega, Deneb and Altair. I could even see the outline of the Milky Way. My mind was suddenly thrown back to a year ago, almost to the day. I could sense in some unknowing way Sandy walking with me and holding my hand. For the first time since she died, I finally came to accept the fact of it. Alone on the beach, I dropped to my knees and wept like I have never done before or after. Not cancer, nor the loss of my ability to crew an airplane, devastated me as much as this moment in time when I finally realized the enormity of my loss. I could not go back and change time. I could only go forward. Fate is the tidal wave of events which pushes all of us in directions we might not otherwise travel. I could not go forward with my life until I accepted the salient fact that I would never see her again. That made this night on the beach decisive for me. At this point, I opted to make the best of whatever life remained granted by the one living God. I would become the best teacher I could. At least in a classroom, there would be an environment that I could control and accomplish some good.

The next day I moved my meager belongings to the military academy and made my small room my home for the next academic year. On Wednesday, September 3, I met all six of my classes, three of which were seventh graders and three who were in the eighth grade. From that time, until the middle of May 1971, those kids became the focus of my life. On the first day of class, I gave each child a copy of the twelve-page set theory guide. They did moan and bitch, but, when I explained that they had the whole year to absorb this information, they became more agreeable to the idea, especially when I told them that 20% of their grade would be based upon that information!

My life over the course of that academic year was one basically devoted to improving both my teaching skills and physical abilities. In order to accomplish this, I continued to study integral calculus at Long Island University where I took night courses during the fall and spring semesters. In both classes, I received the top grade in virtually every test I took. I improved my classroom presentation and instructional techniques. Nothing teaches faster than trial and error. By Christmastime, I was regarded as the best teacher in the facility.

To enhance my physical skills, I joined a fitness club which offered racquetball courts as one of the main attractions. I could no longer play handball because I could not lift my left arm much higher than my shoulder. One could overcome this handicap in racquetball, but not in handball. By the end of the year, I became a B-level racquetball player in my club. I would play at least three times a week and generally the sessions lasted more than two hours. Racquetball is, in my opinion, one of the finest ways to acquire strength, speed, faster reaction time, and most importantly, stamina! It also teaches a player who achieves a high level of skill to think quickly on his feet. When a ball is traveling well over one hundred miles an hour in a relatively small court, it is essential to anticipate and react quickly in order to achieve any kind of success at all. Some weekends, I would spend six hours on a racquetball court playing any and all comers. I won most of the time, but even when I lost, I was regaining the stamina that I had before the operation.

During this time, I started to correspond with my old college roommate Lou and my Air Force roommate, Andy. Lou received his Masters' degree in history from Auburn University and now was teaching in a high school located forty-five miles south of Memphis, Tennessee. On the weekends, he would play music gigs in New Orleans. He was becoming a highly regarded musician who earned more money from these weekend gigs than he did in the classroom. However, he enjoyed teaching as he loved being a positive influence on the children entrusted to his care. He and Nancy had two daughters, and he was very happy. He was truly sad when I told him how I loved and lost my Sandy. But I was really happy for him. He was a very wise man who turned a massive tragedy in his own life into a springboard for accomplishing his lifetime goals. The accident which almost killed him and almost left him blind, not only made him stronger but wiser. With all my other male friends, the war in Vietnam hung like a dark, unwanted storm which menaced the rest of their lives, whether they served or not. All of us, who were physically able, had to decide a basic question: Do I have what it takes? Frankly, all the rest is bullshit. That question forms the innermost core of an adult male, especially in times of war when his country needs him. The rest is window dressing. In Lou's case, there was no quandary. No service would accept him, even if he wanted to go. He was physically unable to become a soldier or a member of any service. Once the decision was taken away from him, he was free to pursue his own happiness. After he survived a horrific tragedy and emerged as a fully developed man, both physically and morally, no one, including himself, could doubt that he had what it took. Lou earned his happiness, and I was delighted for him and Nancy. Couldn't happen to nicer people.

While I was recovering in the hospital, Andy and Heather got married in a small civil ceremony in March 1970. He was now stationed at Pope Air Force Base in North Carolina, and Heather joined him there. In August, I received a letter from him when he told me that he was going to be stationed for a year in Germany. He really enjoyed flying 'trash hauling' C-130s. He especially enjoyed executing the parachute drops. While he was going overseas, Heather planned a return to the San Francisco area to be with her parents and do some modeling. She was making more money doing that than he made flying for the Air Force. That income disparity was not important to Andy. He had a very healthy ego, and the fact that Heather made more money than he did was not bothersome to him in the least.

In October, 1970, I received a letter from Andy airmailed from Frankfurt, Germany. He informed me that he heard rumors that the Air Force was looking to reinstate rated officers who were surviving cancer patients. He didn't know if the rumors were true or not, but he thought I would want to know this information. If I was truly interested in returning, he suggested that I should call down to the Surgeon General's office located at Randolph Air Force Base, Texas. I wrote to him that I was indeed very interested and that I would do as he suggested.

In early November of that year, after talking to three of four intervening people, I was directed to the office of Col. Ryan Nelson, the director of the program to which Andy referred. I called Colonel Nelson and to my surprise, he took my call immediately. I found out from him that the rumors were actually true. He asked about my background, what kind of cancer struck me, and how was I doing now. I answered all his questions as honestly as I could. He asked me if I would give him permission to examine my complete record. I readily agreed, and he told me that he would mail the necessary forms in order to make that happen. He would get back to me once he reviewed my entire record. True to his word, the next week, I received a large envelope filled with a half dozen forms and a self-addressed envelope that I would use after they were filled out. I started working on the forms immediately. It took me several hours to complete all of them. By late afternoon, I mailed the completed forms.

Just before Christmas 1970, I received a letter signed by Col. Nelson. In this correspondence, he informed me that I was a viable candidate for this experimental program. He also informed me that the program had not yet received its final approval from the Pentagon and possibly, from the President of the United States, who might be required to sign off on this experiment. As soon as a decision was rendered by the necessary authority, he would notify me of the results. I wrote a simple note of thanks and told him I would wait until he had an answer. I did all I could do, so I did not give it another thought. I just continued doing what I was doing, i.e., teaching, taking mathematics instruction at night, and increasing my physical stamina and strength.

During the Christmas break, I heard from Ellen. Apparently, one of our common friends informed her that I was no longer in the United States Air Force and that I was medically retired. She called my parents and Mom gave her my phone number at the academy where I was living and teaching. Out of the blue, she called me, and I was surprised to hear her voice. Ellen told me that she graduated Cornell, summa cum laude, and now was working in New York City in an advertising agency. She loved her job and was living in an upscale apartment in the posh east side of the city. We agreed to meet on the Saturday before

Christmas. I would drive to the city, as she did not own a car. Where she was living, cars were not necessary.

That Saturday night, I was lucky to find a parking space not too far from where she resided. There was a doorman at her residence who informed Ellen that I was there. She told him to let me up. She was living on the eighth floor of a twenty-story building. Her one-bedroom apartment was very comfortable and very well appointed. It had a great view of the city.

Ellen was no longer the girl that I knew. She was a completely sophisticated and outwardly self-assured woman. Her hair was cut to a page boy look which emphasized her large and expressive brown eyes. She wore an expensive, tailored, chic outfit which was highlighted, by what appeared to me, very expensive jewelry. She really took delight in showing me her new digs. She loved the lifestyle that the "East Side" of New York City offered. We left her place and went to one of the local bistros in the area. There we ate and talked for about three hours. She told me that she was engaged to be married but that she called off the wedding about a month before it was scheduled to occur. I asked her why. She told me that the man she was going to marry had joined the United States Army and was going to ship over to Vietnam as an infantry officer. She was totally and completely invested in the peace movement. She loved him, but she could not be part of the war.

In her new environment, she found many on the East Side who shared her outlook regarding the war. All her friends were active in the anti-war movement. The men that she most admired were those who fled to Canada. Frankly, I was astounded by her views. Her own parents were rescued in the Holocaust by the fathers of those men who now defended our country. Ellen was an extremely intelligent woman who got caught up in an environment where only one type of thought process was tolerated. I listened to her for about three hours. I did not do much talking. It dawned on me how deep the chasm of values was which separated the woman she became from the man I was becoming. I took her back to her apartment and said my goodbyes. From time to time, over the next six months, she would call me and we would talk. She generally called about two times a month when she was depressed. She needed me to listen to some of her deepest thoughts, and she knew that I would never, ever use them against her. I know she trusted me implicitly and required the vocal outlet that I provided, but I can't tell you why. Sometimes I would try to give her another view and see if I could break through. I guess that's the optimist in me. What I knew was that I answered her phone calls because I once deeply cared for her, and because I never gave up hope that she would acquire wisdom somewhere in her life. As my daddy always told me, "Son, there is no correlation between intelligence and wisdom!" Ellen was a perfect example of what my daddy preached.

That year Hanukkah and Christmas occurred on the same day. I spent that first evening with JG and Hope. JG was right. The girl was becoming a fine cook. Hope prepared a traditional Hanukkah feast which included latkes and beef brisket. We said the prayers and lit the candles before sitting down to eat. JG was up past 190 pounds and, after tasting how well the food was prepared, I understood perfectly why this happened. The physical work I did for my father plus the time I was spending on a racquetball court really helped keep my weight down. After I left the Air Force, my weight was approaching 180 pounds, but now I was well below 155 pounds. I kidded JG about his new "spare tire." He laughed and said that come this spring, he was going to join a tennis club. He was always a good tennis player before he got married. Now he wanted to devote more time to this endeavor because it would be one way of keeping his weight down while doing something he enjoyed. Hope encouraged this approach. She felt that it was worth the time that JG would have to give up with his family in order to keep him healthy. This was typical of Hope's persona; she always put JG and Daniel ahead of her own personal needs.

I think, looking back on the situation, that JG's and my choice of what sport to play was informative. I loved racquetball because it required a very fast reaction time, intuitive feel for where the ball would be and more power than guile. When a really good racquetball player hits a kill shot coming off the back wall, he can generate a speed that approaches 150 mph. When the small blue racquetball hits the wall at that speed, it generates an almost euphoric mood in the striker as the sound reverberates loudly in that small room echoing like a gunshot. Racquetball is power and speed mixed with some guile. Tennis uses a much bigger court at a slower speed, allowing more time to react and plan ahead. Tennis is as much guile as power. JG, being a wonderful reader of people and situations, naturally took to tennis. To me, tennis was boring. I loved the speed, the power and even the danger of being on a small court with other people swinging a racket. My skills were intuitive and fast moving which suited racquetball perfectly. JG was very good at reading situations and reacting to them both strategically and tactically. Tennis required those kinds of skills and, as a result, he became a very good tennis player.

During the meal, JG informed me that he was worried about his dad's health. His father who just recently celebrated his 64th birthday suffered a very serious heart attack about two weeks earlier. The old man was convalescing in a hospital. JG, Hope and Daniel planned to visit him the next day. I related to them how comforting it was that my parents were there for me right after my operation. I was worried for my best friend. His relationship with his father dramatically improved when Hope entered his life, and with the advent of Daniel's arrival, the barriers that existed between father and son melted away. I asked JG to pass on my regards to his father, and he agreed to do so. The mood was kind of somber, so I asked them if they would like to hear a brief humorous story of what happened to me during my stay at Wright-Patterson Air Force Base Medical Center. They enthusiastically agreed.

"Well, when I first entered the surgery ward for my initial consultation, I passed a 2nd Lt. Nurse named Rigsby chewing out a one-legged patient who was supporting himself using crutches. I found out later the patient was an NCO or sergeant. I just came in from flying my check ride so I was still wearing my flight suit. I took one look at the situation and suggested to Lt. Rigsby that she might want to let the guy sit down first before chewing him out. He thanked me and proceeded to hobble over to a chair where he was able to sit down. She was annoyed with me, but I didn't care. At any rate, after my second surgery, I was put back in the surgery ward. Because I was an officer, I was given my own room. I had a lot of difficulty sleeping immediately following my second operation. I was in a lot of pain and I didn't want to take narcotics. I would get up at night and visit with the night nurse. Her name was Betty Jo, and she was a beautiful, kind and thoughtful person. I just enjoyed talking with her. After two weeks, I asked if she wanted to join me for dinner at the officers' club. She agreed. It was not a date in reality, just two friends having dinner together. In order to do this, I needed permission from the Patient Squadron Commander which was some ground pounding lieutenant who had a small office on the first floor of the medical center. I went to see him in my pajamas and supporting a two-week growth on my face. I told him that I needed a permission slip to take out a nurse. He asked me if I was a rated officer. I answered in the affirmative. He just nodded, then sighed, and said, "You guys are all alike," and then he signed the necessary paperwork. Saturday night came around, and I was getting cleaned up and putting on my dress blues for the first time in over a month. Then nurse Rigsby tells me that I cannot leave the floor. At first, I was angry, but then I knew she did not have the authority to prevent me from doing this. I was going to consult with Dr. Coyle to get his ruling. After spending as much time as I did in the nurses' station with Betty Jo, I knew where the doctors' phone numbers were kept. I started to reach for them when Rigsby grabbed the list from me and said that she would call Dr. Coyle. She did this while I was standing there in the nurses' station. The conversation started with Nurse Rigsby explaining to Dr. Coyle that I wanted to go to the officer's club that evening to spend some time with Betty Jo and that she would not allow it. I knew the doctor already knew what I was planning as he verbally gave me the okay several days before. I then witnessed one half of the finest chewing out I have ever seen to that point in my life. All Rigsby could say were many, 'yes sirs' and 'no sirs' and finally, one truly emphatic, "Never again, sir!' During the conversation, Rigsby turned beet red and immediately signed the permission slip after hanging up.

"About a week later, she attempted revenge. They moved me from my private room to the open ward supposedly because of reduced holiday manning. The policy in the open ward was that every patient must be dressed in both top and bottom pajamas. I knew the chief nurse inspected the open ward every Tuesday and Thursday morning at nine, so I arranged, with the willing assistance from the ambulatory ward patients, that every man assigned to our ward had their pajama tops removed. When the chief nurse opened the door to the ward, all she saw was that every patient was bare-chested, including those poor guys who were immobile. The chief nurse took about fifteen seconds to take in this bare-chested scene, her eyes bulged, and she shouted, '**Rigsby . . . my office . . . now**!' She slammed the door closed and proceeded to chew Rigsby out so loudly that we could hear her in the open ward. Needless to say, Rigsby was not sorry to see me go!"

All three of us were laughing as I finished my story. We talked for a couple more hours when I took my leave. Instead of returning to the academy, I went home and spent the last week of 1970 with my parents.

8

RECOVERY

1971 was a pivotal year in my life. In mid-April, I received a letter from Colonel Nelson indicating that his experimental program was receiving a favorable response from the Pentagon and had the backing of the President of the United States. He informed me that within two weeks he would have confirmation of this fact, and he wanted to know if I was still interested. I immediately called the number indicated in his correspondence. I informed the person answering the phone who I was, and I was immediately put through to Col. Nelson.

"Good afternoon, Lt. Blakeman. I presume you've read my letter."

"Yes sir!" I replied. "I am still very interested in resuming my flying career."

"What aircraft would you be interested in flying? I'm not sure, but I think you'll have your choice."

"That's easy, sir. I was qualified in the AC-119G gunship. I really want to go to the upgraded version, the AC-130 gunship."

"I don't know, Lt. Blakeman. You have to take thyroid supplements for the rest of your life. That fact may disqualify you from flying combat."

"Sir, I can carry a plastic container that could hold 1,000 thyroid pills. I don't want to be a half navigator. Either I am fully rated, or I will stay retired."

"Is there any give to that position, Lieutenant?"

"No sir. I will not take another man's position away from a non-combat assignment. If I don't take the same chances as any other rated officer . . . well to me, it wouldn't be right. No sir . . . no give at all!"

"This may take longer than I thought. If I'm able to obtain a slot for you, it's going to take at least several more months to get further approval. Also, if you accept these orders, then you will lose your 100% disability. You do understand that, Lieutenant?"

"Yes sir. The timing works for me as I am both teaching during the day and taking math courses at night. All my classes will be over by the end of the third week in May. At least, that will allow me time to finish everything. If it takes longer than that, I want you to know that I signed up for a summer excursion to Europe. I am going to leave at the end of May, and I will be spending most of my time in Paris. If you need me, please call my parents, so they can get in touch with me through the American Express office in Paris. Also, you can send any written orders to the American Embassy. I will check every week that I am there. My ticket to return stateside is open-ended. When you need me, I should be able to be back home within no more than 10 days from when you first notify my parents or send orders to the American embassy. Will that do, sir?"

"Yes, Lieutenant that will do nicely. I want you to know that I admire your attitude. I also want you to know that I will do everything in my power to accommodate your wishes. You should hear from me somewhere between the third week of July in the second week of August. I don't have to tell you that bureaucracies move at their own pace."

"Thank you, sir! Will that be all?"

"Yes, Lieutenant, you can expect to hear from me in several months. Have a good day."

I returned the sentiment and hung up the phone. I'd heard the optimism in the colonel's voice. For the first time since that awful night on Jones Beach when I finally accepted that I would no longer have Sandy, I felt some optimism that I would be able to return to flight status. This was something I needed to do, and now I felt it could happen.

That evening I had dinner with my parents. I related the entire conversation that I'd had with Col. Nelson. My father was very quiet. I think he understood the conflict within me. My mother was upset. She liked having me around, and a career in teaching was something that she understood. My mother did not like flying in any way shape or form. This was really hard on her, but she also knew that I needed to do this. They both promised me that when the communication came from Col. Nelson, they would relay the information to me through the American Express office in Paris.

The only people I told about my possible return to active duty were my parents, JG, Hope, Andy and Lou. The next day after I informed my parents of the possibility of returning to flying status, I visited with JG and Hope. I went to their place and had dinner with the family. During the meal, I told them about the entire conversation I had with Col. Nelson. JG was very upset. He really liked having me close by, and he wasn't in favor of the Vietnam War. It was easier for Hope as she correctly perceived that this was a path I needed to travel in order for me to regain some sense of self-worth. It was during this meal that Hope shared some news of her own. She had been to her gynecologist who confirmed that she was indeed pregnant with her second child. It was great news to me, and I asked her when she was due. She told me that the doctor thought somewhere around the middle of August. Hope was absolutely radiant. An obviously elated JG was ecstatic that he would be a father for the second time.

They knew I was thinking about spending a summer in Paris. I discussed the choice I had to make. On the one hand, I could continue my education at Long Island University by taking more advanced math courses, or I could just take the summer off and do something that I'd always wanted to do my whole life. It was a tough choice, but I chose the latter. JG thought that I would be better off advancing my education, but with the possibility of flying combat within the year, JG understood that doing something that I've always wanted to do took precedence. Where I might be going, life could be very short.

I communicated my choice with Andy and Lou via air mail and both wrote encouraging responses. In fact, I received a second letter from Andy around the middle of May. In it, he informed me that he had just received orders to fly the AC-130 gunship. He would be in-country around the middle of June, 1971. It looked like we might get to see each other again sooner than either of us thought.

In the meantime, I continued to teach my courses, and my students did really well. The academy wanted me to return, and I told them that if the Air Force accepted me that I would go back into the service. But if the Air Force did not want me, then I would be happy to return to teaching. The headmaster asked me to inform him as soon as I knew. I was proud of the job my students did on the New York

State standardized exams as almost all of them tested at least two years over their present grade level. One of the main things I took from this experience was the importance of teaching students *why* things worked as well as *how* they worked. The fact that the vast majority of my students grasped set theory concepts enabled them to understand not only the work at their grade level but also the higher levels of mathematics that were in their future. My students, by the end of the academic year, almost to a person, had an understanding of set theory that would take them all way through the upper levels of collegiate mathematics.

During this time, Ellen would call me at night. Sometimes those conversations went well past midnight. Most of the time, I just listened as she went on about the men she was seeing and what was occurring in her job. None of it was memorable and frankly, I think she needed a sounding board. I think I provided that role for her, because I still harbored the hope that someday she would return to the person I first met. I know it was foolish, but, ever the optimist, it's what I thought. In the middle of May, I told Ellen that I was going to spend the summer in Paris. At first, she was stunned. After 15 seconds of silence, she asked when I would return. I told her most likely between the middle to the end of August. She wished me a safe trip and made me promise to call her when I got back. I did not tell her about returning to active duty. I would not say anything about this possibility, other than to the ones I'd already told, until it was a reality. My last day of teaching was on Friday, May 21. My evening integral course ended two days before. Early on Saturday morning, May 22, I took a flight over to Europe.

My first stop was Frankfurt, Germany. One of my classmates from UNT was stationed there, and he had a motorcycle that he wanted to sell. I saw his advertisement in *The Air Force Times*. I wrote to him, and we agreed on a price. I told him when my flight would arrive, and he met me at the airport. I went back to his place where I gave him a check, strapped my small knapsack on the back of the bike, and drove my new motorcycle westbound toward Paris. The motorcycle was a four-year-old, 900 cc Harley-Davidson roadster. It was in good condition, and after the first half-hour on the bike, I found that it was easy for me to operate.

By my first night in Europe, I made it to Metz, France. I arrived about 9:00 PM local time. There I rented a hotel room and spent the night. I got up early on Sunday the 23rd and from there drove into Paris. When I was accepted for the language course at the Sorbonne, I made arrangements to stay at the student dormitories in the *Citee Universitaire* complex located in the southern part of the city. I arrived at 3:00 PM and signed up for my room. Accommodations were rather sparse, but my room was both clean and comfortable. There were only a few students in the entire complex, as the majority of the students took the summer off. In fact, I had the only occupied room on my floor.

The next day, using a map and my knowledge of determining direction using celestial bodies, including the sun, I navigated my way to class rather easily. Paris is laid out like a wheel with concentric spokes emanating from the center and with the Seine River dividing it in the middle from east to west. I gave myself plenty of time to find where my class would be held. I arrived about a half-hour earlier than the required start time. The room that my class was assigned comfortably held 40 student positions. There were only 15 students the first day. The class had ten women and five men. The women were college-age to about thirty years old and generally very attractive.

I was hoping to put my past behind me and strike out again. I had been celibate for twenty-one months. The thought of being with somebody other than Sandy just left me cold. For the first time since I had lost her, I felt my libido starting to come to life. I waited that first day. I wanted to get a sense of what the women in my classroom were like and what kind of person they were before I asked one of them out on a date.

The next day, I was sitting in my seat when a beautiful blonde girl entered the classroom. She was not there for the first day of class. She passed a piece of paper to the instructor and, in a very soft voice, explained that her flight was delayed from Boston because of weather. She was no more than five feet tall, slender and very feminine. Her long soft blond hair fell well past her shoulder blades. She had an oval face, widely spaced green eyes, and a small petite nose. Something inside of me screamed that she was the one. It was the first time in almost two years that I felt a desire stirring within me . . . my libido was awakening . . . at last! As soon as the teacher called for a break, I went over and introduced myself.

Her name was Joan. I asked if she would have coffee with me. I told her that I found a place that served excellent coffee and some wonderful pastries. She smiled and said that she would be delighted. It took us about five minutes to walk to the coffee shop. I'm not sure I know why, but we really got along . . . even though we were a contrast in styles. Joan was dressed impeccably in a designer dress and very tastefully appointed jewelry. I, on the other hand, wore a T-shirt, leather vest, blue jeans and motorcycle boots. I think what broke the ice was the fact that we were both teachers. Joan said that she taught art appreciation and art history at a private high school near Boston. I told her that I taught math at a military academy. We shared stories about some of our students, and the time passed so quickly that before I knew it, we were both late in returning to class. The instructor, a Frenchwoman about forty-five years old, smiled and told us to keep better track of our time! After class was over, I asked Joan if she would like to accompany me for dinner that evening. She agreed, and I was elated. I asked her if she had ever ridden on a motorcycle. She had not. I asked her if she would mind and she smiled and said, "I think I'm really looking forward to it!"

"Do you have a pair of blue jeans?" I asked.

"No. But by this evening, I will."

I laughed at her response and found out where she was staying. She would meet me in the lobby of her hotel at six. When I arrived that evening, Joan was true to her word . . . she was dressed in a modest, long-sleeved blouse and blue jeans. Her hair was tied up in a ponytail and she looked particularly adorable. I climbed on the bike, and she straddled the seat behind me with her hands locked around my waist. I told her just to lean with me when I made turns. I took the bike out and immediately got into the traffic flow. I was getting used to the bike and how it responded. I was used to the aggressive driving habits of my native New York, so Paris was just a continuation of the same driving mentality. Joan got the feel of how to lean into a turn. Ten minutes into the drive, she became almost an extension of my own body. About twenty minutes later, we arrived at a restaurant that my brother recommended to me. He'd been in Paris several years earlier. I parked the bike. Joan got off first and then I dismounted. I could see the excitement in her face and in her voice when she said, "I really enjoyed that. We have to do more of that!"

I laughed and said, "Let's eat first!" Joan laughed at my response.

The restaurant was a moderately priced establishment which catered mostly to the French middle class. The menus were strictly in French. With my handy English-French dictionary which both Joan and I used, we placed our orders. Since I was driving, I limited myself to one glass of wine for the entire evening. After about twenty minutes of general conversation, we started delving into very personal topics.

I told her about Sandy, the cancer I had suffered, and the possibility of my return to active duty. It was important to me that she knew up front all the personal baggage I was carrying. She was a very sympathetic listener. When I told her about the August night, almost a year ago, when I finally was able to accept the complete loss of my fiancée, I could see her starting to tear up. To lighten the mood, I told Joan the same humorous story I told JG and Hope regarding my experiences as a patient at Wright-Patterson Air Force Base Medical Center. Her reaction was the same . . . full rich laughter.

I think my openness and a desire for an honest relationship was attractive to her. For her part, she responded by relating to me some of her innermost feelings and thoughts. Joan told me that she was engaged to marry a man more than twenty years her senior. She loved him, but she told him that she wanted an exciting summer before she settled down. She told me that she came from a very repressive and conservative Boston family whose roots went back to pre-revolutionary Massachusetts. She wanted to experience an adventurous life for a little while before she had to settle down into a rigid family and community life which awaited her. Joan's education and background emanated from a family of wealth and public service. She made it clear to me that if we continue dating it would be only for this summer.

She looked me directly in the eye and said, "Let me be very clear regarding this. If you and I continue to see each other, and no matter how strong the relationship develops between us, it must end when we leave Paris. Is that understood?"

I continued the eye-to-eye contact and said, "I will respect your wishes. When we leave Paris, the relationship will be over. You have my word as an officer and a gentleman."

"Do you also promise never to attempt to find me once we leave Paris?"

"I do. Again, you have my word on it."

She smiled at me while squeezing my right hand as she said, "I believe you."

We continued talking into the evening. We were so lost in conversation that about one o'clock in the morning, the waiter came to the table and said that they were closing shortly. The time had gone by so fast that we were both amazed it was that late. I quickly paid the bill, leaving a very large tip. We went back to my motorcycle, and I drove to her hotel. I kissed her goodnight and asked if she wanted to do this again tomorrow. She quickly agreed.

When I first arrived at the Citee, I looked around for a restaurant and found one that really suited me. It was located only two or three blocks from where I was billeted. The food was great, and I found, from the first day I was there, a group of very intelligent and thoughtful people who populated this particular restaurant. Its name was *Le Gentilly Cafe*. I ate there Sunday afternoon and evening when I first arrived, and breakfast and supper on Monday after the first day of class. The place was a haven for some of the intellectual elite of Paris. Among the regulars were several high officials of the national unions, some college professors, an elite mathematician and a French naval intelligence officer. The conversation there was always interesting and provocative. I felt right at home.

I took Joan to *Le Gentilly Cafe* for the first time on our second date. She loved the place and the conversation. The food was wonderful and since she was going to spend the night with me, I did not have to drive her back to her hotel. Therefore, when it came time to eat, I had a superb wine with my meal. We left *Le Gentilly* around eleven that evening. We held hands as we walked back to my dormitory room. We were both nervous, as I was only the second person that she would physically love in her life. For me, this was my first time in almost two years. Joan was not a strong physical person. She weighed less than ninety-five pounds. I was extremely gentle with her, and she responded to that gentleness. That, in turn, aroused me further and the experience in joining together was beautiful. When we finished, she quickly fell asleep in my arms.

Thus commenced the best summer of my life. We attended classes together, explored the city together and on weekends, we took long rides on my motorcycle while enjoying perfect summer weather which just added to the overall enjoyment that we both felt. Joan loved art, and I wanted to accommodate her desire to see some of the great artworks located in Paris and in particular the Louvre. One afternoon I took her to that great and wonderful museum, and I found it mildly interesting until we entered the hall which housed the great works of the French neo-classicists. When we entered this humongous room with its 30-foot ceilings and the dimensions of a high school basketball court, I was struck dumb. I'd never seen such superb art which resonated within my very soul. I asked Joan if she would mind if we stayed there awhile. She smiled and said it was perfectly okay with her. I think she got a kick out of seeing me really appreciate some great art. After that day, we visited the Louvre for at least the next six or seven afternoons. It was the best museum I've ever seen.

One of the highlights of that magnificent summer occurred in the middle of June. Joan and I visited the English bookstore located on Rue de Rivoli. Joan got excited when she saw an English version of The Little Prince. I purchased a copy for each of us. We took a stroll westward toward the Arch de Triumph. The weather was absolutely perfect: A cloudless sky, soft breezes and temperatures in the low

70s Fahrenheit. We walked on a widely paved sidewalk located on the north bank of the Seine River. After roughly two miles, we found a park with very lush green grass surrounding very large oak and maple trees. Joan was tiring, so I led her toward an enormous maple tree. I invited her to sit with her back against the trunk of the tree. In the shade it was a bit chilly for her. I removed my flight jacket and placed it over her shoulders to keep her warm and to protect her back from the bark of the tree. I laid down on the grass with my head in her lap. She proceeded to read The Little Prince in its entirety. I closed my eyes and just concentrated on her very soft reading voice. She read for almost three hours. It seemed like 15 minutes to me. Her voice gave life to the words of the author and transported me to the world in which he created. It was almost an "out of body" experience. For that brief interlude, time stood still. When Joan finished the book, we walked back to the Metro. We took the train back to the Citee and spent the rest of the afternoon and early evening making love. One of the truly great days of my life.

The whole summer passed so quickly. I was alive again with my libido fully intact. Every day in Paris, we explored something new and exciting. Every week, I did check with the American Express office. On July 26, there was a message from my mother stating that orders were waiting for me at the American embassy. Joan and I immediately got directions to the embassy's location.

The embassy was a large gated building protected by uniformed military; in this case, United States Marine Corps personnel. When I approached the main door, a marine sergeant asked to see my identification. I took out my billfold and showed him my military ID. He immediately came to attention and saluted. For the first time in over a year and a half, I returned a salute. Joan was a little taken back as I think this was her first experience with any kind of military service.

The guard directed me to the information desk. After telling the person behind the desk what my business was and why I was there, I was directed to another office. There I received an envelope from the Surgeon General's office, and in particular, Col. Nelson. I was directed to take a class-2 physical on Wednesday, August 18 at 10:00 AM at McGuire Air Force Base located in central New Jersey. Joan and I walked back to the American Express office where we both made reservations to return stateside. Joan was to leave on August 5, and I would leave on Saturday, August 7. We had a little more than a week together which intensified every moment for both of us.

On August 3, we had our last dinner together at *Le Gentilly Café*. That was the last night that they would be open, as they started their four-week vacation the next day. Because of that, all the regulars were there. Joan and I got there around six o'clock in the evening. We stayed until around eleven. After saying our goodbyes, Joan and I walked back hand-in-hand to my dormitory room. Joan, knowing this was our last time to be together, really let herself go. When we climaxed together, she dug her nails deeply into my naked back, drawing six scratches of which four bled and two which did not. As soon as she came, she literally passed out. I was alarmed at first, but when I saw her breathing regularly in a very, very deep sleep, I knew she was okay. Joan was a fragile person. I always took care never to put her in any physical danger or harm. Normally, she regulated her behavior to the limits of her weakened body. That night, she experienced unbridled, wanton pleasure for the only time in her life. Her reaction taught me that evening why some poets and authors call an extremely intense orgasm the "little death!"

The next morning, Joan awoke around ten o'clock. I showed her my back and she was totally aghast. "I did that? I can't believe it!" she uttered while turning beet red. "Are you okay?"

I laughed and said, "I never felt better. You were an absolute tiger last night."

"Oh my God! I never knew I had *that* in me."

After we got dressed, I drove her to a restaurant near her hotel. There we shared our last meal together. We walked back to the hotel. There by the entrance, she said to me, "This is the last time we'll see each other. I'm going to be married shortly after my return home. I hope you will keep your word."

I looked deeply into her lovely green eyes and said, "You have reawakened my desire to live again. For the first time in almost two years, I not only enjoy the present, but I am looking forward to living the rest of my life. You did that. I will always be grateful. And I will *always* keep my word." With that, I smiled as a thought occurred to me. I reached out and held her for the last time, and I paraphrased Bogart from the movie 'Casablanca': "I guess we will always have Paris." She smiled and I kissed her for the last time. We separated, and I turned and walked back to where my bike was parked. I never looked back. As long as I live, I will keep my word to her. But I will always be grateful too.

That afternoon, I arranged for my motorcycle to be shipped back to my home address in Syosset, New York. I knew that my parents would keep it for me for as long as necessary until I could retrieve it and take it to wherever I was living.

Saturday morning, I left Paris and flew back to New York. My parents picked me up at JFK Airport late Saturday afternoon. That evening, my whole family gathered together at one of our favorite restaurants, and I shared some of the events and experiences of this past summer. I also called JG and Hope and arranged to see them on Monday, August 9. I told Hope that I would be there about 9:00 AM, and we could spend some time talking before JG returned from work. She was really looking forward to it and so was I.

On Monday, I drove into Queens where JG and Hope lived. I arrived about nine. Hope let me in and I was appalled at how she looked. She was due to deliver her second child within a week. Daniel, like any normal three-year-old, was running around and Hope was exhausted in trying to oversee his activities while doing some of her normal household duties. The bags under her eyes were deep, dark and profound. She was the most tired individual that I have ever seen in my life. I was talking to her while she tried to make the bed that she shared with JG. I said to her, "Damn it, girl! You go to sleep now . . . I'll take care of Daniel. And I mean now!"

Hope nodded her assent and literally fell on her side on top of the bed. She was snoring before her head hit the pillow! Now I had the responsibility of taking care of a very active and curious three-year-old. I gathered him up and took him to my car, and I drove to my quarters in the academy. The school had WW II tanks and artillery pieces on display—perfect "toys" for this active child to use. He climbed over all the old weapon systems. I also gave Daniel a tour of the academy which included all the pictures and materials on display. We played and toured there for about 2 1/2 hours when Daniel announced that he was hungry. I wasn't sure what to feed a three-year-old, but I knew somebody who did. So, like any other red-blooded, American man, I returned home to my mama. I knew she would know. Mom loved children, especially boys. Daniel was not only very cute, but he was also extremely precocious. Mom enjoyed doting on him. She fed him. She played games with him and about 3:30 in the afternoon, I decided to take Daniel back to his home. I arrived around 4:30. I rang the doorbell and a refreshed Hope immediately opened the door. Daniel ran into her arms and she turned and said to me, "Blake, I think you may have saved my life. I do not remember ever being that exhausted."

"Girl, you fell asleep before your head hit the pillow . . . literally, before your head hit the pillow! You were the most tired person I've ever seen. How do you feel now?"

"Much better, thank you."

"Good. Now I need a nap!"

Hope laughed and said, "Go ahead and use the couch. I'll wake you when JG comes home." And that's what I did.

At six, JG came home and we were eating a half-hour later. He thanked me profusely for "literally, saving his wife's life!"

I laughed and said, "I'm an Air Force officer, and your three-year-old son just tired me out completely. I never knew being a parent could be so exhausting. Hell, I think it is harder than boot camp!" Everybody laughed in response.

I gave them a pretty complete synopsis of the past summer. They both were overjoyed in the change in my demeanor. I was starting to live again, and the change was very apparent to both of them.

Before I left, I asked Hope, as big as she was, how much she weighed. I came home weighing 147 pounds . . . I was two pounds lighter than Hope. I must admit some guilty pleasure in teasing her. I left a little before eleven at night. It was wonderful spending time with the three of them . . . soon to be four. Two days later, Hope gave birth to a healthy baby girl, Elizabeth Mae Gladon.

On August 18, I drove down to McGuire Air Force Base. I passed my Class-2 physical with flying colors. Three days later, I drove to visit JG and his newly-expanded family. I got to meet his new daughter whom the family called Mae. She weighed only seven pounds and was very, very cute. I was nervous holding this little bundle of life, but Hope walked me through the process of supporting her neck in order to hold her in my arms. This little tyke was as adorable as she could be. I spent much of the day with the entire family and for me, it was like being in my second home. They asked me about the physical, and I told them what the doc told me. I was in great shape and, except for taking thyroid supplements, I could still pass a Class A physical. Therefore, I was expecting orders any day now because of the doctor's findings. During the two months that followed before I received special orders, I spent almost all my time with both families: my birth family, and my adopted family.

During this time, JG informed me that sometime between Christmas and Easter, he would be offered a partnership. When this happened, he would be able to afford a home in Suffolk County somewhere near the Nassau County border. The new office which he would head would be located in Huntington, Long Island. That office would be a general practice office with emphasis on domestic family issues. JG's duties would also include some work in the main offices of the firm. When he worked in the city, JG would assist in some high-profile criminal and tort cases where his expertise in reading people would help in the process of selecting a jury. His personal radar was uncanny. The only person I ever met in my life who could equal him or even be a little bit better was my mom.

JG, at this time, was also involving himself in politics. He started with some volunteer work and donations to the Democratic Party of Long Island and of New York City. He did not support our efforts in Vietnam and was working to end the national commitment to that country. This was a bone of contention between us. I refused to let politics interfere with my personal relationship with my best friend. By the fall of 1971, JG was just a small cog in a large political machine.

My own personal feelings about the war were somewhat ambivalent at that time. I am a student of history, and I believed that if the United States, in 1956, allowed a national plebiscite election in Vietnam as agreed to in the Geneva Accords of 1954, Ho Chi Minh would have won by a large margin. Having said that, I also believed that Ho would have become the "Tito of Asia" and his innate nationalism would have altered, and probably stopped, the drive to convert all of Southeast Asia to communism. Much of the moral and legal justification for the war was just plainly false. This came out with the "Pentagon Papers" which were published in 1971.

Vietnam, at this time to me, was not a black-and-white issue. I did not like how we got into the war. I especially resented the lies that Pres. Johnson used to justify the expansion of the war. Having said that, the past was the past. It cannot be undone. In 1971, our nation's choice was going on and finishing what should not have been started or just leaving. At that point, it was my opinion then, as it is now, that the only moral thing to do was to press on and finish the job. Unfortunately, not only for our country, but also for Vietnam and its neighboring countries, history proved me correct.

I also called my headmaster the day after I took my physical. I told him that chances were better than 90% that I would be returning to extended active duty with the United States Air Force. He told me that he and my students would miss me. They would pray for me to stay safe while serving overseas, and he wished me well. I thanked him for the opportunity to teach that year. The experiences emanating from that year would shape the rest of my life.

On Sunday, August 22, I called Lou and Nancy Lee. It was great hearing their voices again. Nancy Lee was pregnant with their third child. Lou was really enjoying teaching and playing in a highly regarded jazz band on the weekends. Of all the people that I have come to know, he had the most enjoyable of existences. He was at peace with himself and his life. His early trauma gave him the wisdom to enjoy the present. That's what Lou did. I told both of them that I would probably be returning to flight status and should be getting orders within the next month or two. They were happy as they knew how important flying was to me.

Later that same day, I called Ellen and told her the same thing I told Lou. She was very successful in her advertising business and like JG, Ellen was becoming involved with the antiwar movement in New York City and the local Democratic Party. She also told me that she met a man that she really liked and that this relationship was becoming serious. Ellen told me that she met him while volunteering in the Democratic Party. She wanted me to meet him, and I told her that I would like to do just that. She was going on an extended business trip to New Orleans and later to San Francisco. She was going to return around the third week of October. She would call me then and we would get together when I could meet her new man. I said that would be fine, and I was looking forward to seeing her again. With that decided, we said our goodbyes and ended the phone call.

The next six weeks following Labor Day, I worked for my dad on the loading dock. Ike, the foreman, knew I was going back into the service, and so he took it fairly easy on me. The hard work helped me stay in shape while waiting for orders. In addition, I augmented my physical activity with as much racquetball as I could play. I wanted to be in peak condition before going to war. I also spent as much time as I could with both of my families. I do believe that little Elizabeth Mae could discern my voice before I finally left.

On October 21, 1971, I received special orders directly from the Pentagon, dated 15 October 71. These orders were signed by the Chief of Staff, United States Air Force, at the direction of the President of the

United States. I was assigned to the 16th Special Operations Squadron (SOS). I was promoted to the rank of captain. I was to return to extended active duty, including flying status, on November 10, 1971. I had to report to Lowry Air Force Base located in Denver, Colorado, no later than November 24, 1971 for sensor operator and interpretation school which lasted two weeks. I was then ordered to Hurlburt Field which was part of Eglin Air Force Base located in the panhandle of Florida. I was to report no later than December 15, 1971 for flight training in the AC-130A gunship. Upon completion of that training, I was to report no later than February 13, 1972 to Homestead Air Force Base in Florida for water survival training. From there, I was to fly to Travis Air Force Base where I would obtain transportation to Clark Air Base in the Philippines. There I would undergo jungle survival school for four days and when that was completed, I would be transported to Ubon Royal Thai Air Base in Thailand where I would join the 16th SOS. The target date for my arrival at Ubon was 7 March 1972.

After receiving my orders, I told my father that I would work until the end of the month. I would use the next ten days as personal time before I had to be sworn in again as an officer in the United States Air Force. Some of my classmates from UNT were navigators flying out of McGuire Air Force Base in New Jersey. I visited these guys and while I was there, I picked up the insignia I needed for my uniform, as I was no longer a lieutenant, but a recently promoted captain.

Also, during this time, I got a call from Ellen. She told me that she was now engaged to be married to the man she was seeing. His name was Matthew (Matt) Isaacson, and he was a school administrator in the New York City education system. Ellen told me that Matt graduated NYU in 1965 and took a job teaching in the city. In four years, he obtained both a Masters' in education and a PhD in educational administration. He was deeply involved in the Democratic Party, the teacher's union and the antiwar movement. He was recently promoted to assistant principal in one of the larger high schools in the city. Ellen wanted me to meet him, and I agreed. She gave me the name of a restaurant on the posh East side of the city. We would meet there at 7:00 PM on Saturday, November 6. When I entered the restaurant, I found Ellen and a man I assumed to be Matt at the bar waiting on me. I approached the couple and Ellen got up and gave me a hug. She then introduced me to Matt. He was an attractive man who was tall and thin and who wore glasses. His dark hair was almost long enough to reach his shoulders. He reached out and offered me his hand. His grip was firm, and he looked me in the eyes when he said hello. After the introductions were complete, we proceeded to our table. The waitress came and we placed our orders. The happy couple informed me that they were to be married at the beginning of the year. I offered my congratulations and asked if they had set a hard date. The answer to that question became the subject of the table talk for the next two hours.

It seemed that they were to move into Matt's apartment. The situation was complicated by the fact that Matt had a roommate. The apartment was originally rented to that roommate who allowed Matt to share it with him. He graciously gave up any claim on that apartment so that Matt and Ellen could redecorate it to their tastes. For the next two hours, I watched and listened in total fascination as they discussed whether to get married at the beginning of February or March of next year. The crux of the problem was when to kick out the roommate. The longer he stayed meant also that he would contribute half the rent and utilities until he vacated the premises. But if they kicked him out earlier, they would have more time to redecorate the apartment in their own tastes. For the next two hours, I listened in silence as they went back and forth on what was more important: the money or the time. I literally did not utter a word. I was waiting for one of them to be concerned regarding how their actions affected Matt's roommate. I might as well have waited until hell froze over. They were so involved in their own lives that there literally was no room for others. What I witnessed was totally self-absorbed, narcissistic behavior with each of them feeding off the other. After supper was over, I again offered my congratulations and best wishes and departed as soon as I could.

As I walked to my car, I felt this feeling of unbelievable relief. Their behavior was so repugnant to me that it literally killed whatever residual feelings I had for Ellen. It also taught me that JG was right, as usual. He sensed in Ellen something it took me years to finally acknowledge. When I left that restaurant, I was one totally happy dude. That poor shit could've been me. The best part for me was my unavailability when they got married. Combat gave me the best of all possible excuses not to attend. Call it a small, unintended perk.

On the morning of November 10, my father and I drove to a small naval outlet located in St. Albans, New York. I wore my dress blues for the first time in about a year and a half. It felt good to wear my country's uniform again. I took a copy of my orders and presented it to a naval officer at that facility. In front of my father, I retook the oath of office as an officer in the United States Air Force. I spent that night with my family and on November 11, I drove out to Lowry Air Force Base located in Denver, Colorado. I stopped at Columbus, Ohio to visit some of my friends there and let them know I was back on active duty again. I spent a couple days there and then proceeded to drive directly to my first assignment. I arrived on Monday, November 22. That's always a sad day for me as it was a day eight years before when Pres. Kennedy was assassinated.

My class consisted of fifteen men. All of us were rated officers, i.e., either pilots or navigators. When we signed into the bachelor officers' quarters (BOQ), we were told that we were not allowed, under any circumstances, to go to downtown Denver in an Air Force uniform. Because of the anti-war feeling that was so prevalent in that city, we could not wear the uniform of our own country. I found that situation appalling. At any rate, all the men in my group were trained to be replacements for established crews who were already in country.

I was scheduled to be an infrared operator (IR). However, my interests lay more in fire control than as a sensor operator. I asked the instructors if I could take both courses and both exams. They smiled with some amusement, but they allowed me to do so. During the two weeks I was there, I passed both exams handily. I received two blue certificates of training to add to my growing collection. From Lowry Air Force Base, I drove directly to Eglin Air Force Base arriving on December 15. Housing authority directed me to the nearest BOQ to Eglin Field number nine which was called Hurlburt Field. We lovingly refer to this field as "love potion number nine!"

It was there that I got my first look at the AC-130A gunship. She was all black. She was a high wing aircraft with four turboprop engines. Unlike any other C-130 model, the propellers were three bladed and huge—all other C-130 models have smaller, high altitude, four bladed props. The A-model nose was replaced by the rounder, D-model nose in order to accommodate the updated radar system. The AADS-7, infrared sensing system, was contained in a semi-spherical cover which was nearly 2 1/2 feet in diameter and located on the port side just aft of the radar nose and forward of the crew entrance door. Inside the AADS-7 infrared system was the movable sensing plate which was cooled to within 15° of absolute zero. It literally could detect minute temperature differentials from as much as twenty miles away. The display presented to the infrared operator (IR) was so acute that he could discern the upper and lower limbs of a human body at a slant range of 10,000 feet. In fact, if the individual being observed decided to urinate, the sensor screen displayed the stream leaving the body! The AADS-7 infrared presentation was like watching a photographic negative come to life. Targets which possessed radiant energy were seen as bright returns on the screen. Those returns that have little radiant energy were displayed as darker returns. The IR operator manipulated the movable sensing plate by using a joystick located at his crew position.

Just aft of the crew entrance door were the two 20mm Vulcan cannons. Each cannon had six barrels and could fire up to 6,000 rounds of 20mm shells per minute. Generally, the combined rate of fire of both cannons was reduced to 1200 rounds per minute in order to save ammunition. Every sixth round fired was a tracer which showed a red trail from the gun barrel to the ground. When the crew fired the Vulcan cannons, the rate of fire was so intense that it appeared as a steady red stream departing the left side of the aircraft all the way to the ground. Behind each Vulcan cannon was a canister approximately three feet wide and six feet high containing the ammunition used by this weapon system. Each 20 mm shell was approximately seven inches long, about the width of a quarter, and contained an explosive head. The cartridge, after firing, was expelled onto the floor in the middle of the airplane. After the mission was over, the gun crew had to pick up the expended cartridges by literally shoveling the spent shell casings into large barrels which were strapped to the floor of the aircraft. These casings would be reused.

Just below the crew entrance door and a little aft was the low light television system (LLTV). This was your basic light sensitive television camera. It literally magnified star light and the reflected light of the moon by a factor approaching one million times. The presentation that the TV operator (TV) saw, given a light environment of anything more than a quarter-moon phase, was equivalent to daylight using a normal camera.

On the underside of the aircraft was the Black Crow sensor system whose purpose was detection of the electric emanations coming from any kind of internal-combustion engine. The system could pick up the electric signature of a truck from a distance exceeding twenty miles. It was operated by a navigator who had undergone special training to become an Electronic Warfare Operator (EWO). The AC-130 gunships had the same electronic warfare countermeasure package as the B-52D model. We designated the Black Crow operator as BC even though he also operated the entire electronic warfare package.

The BC, LLTV and AADS-7 infrared systems were placed on movable platforms which contained sensors that related the positions of these sensors relative to the three axes of the aircraft. This information was fed directly into the main analog computer which kept track of each system. It would allow any of these systems and the Inertial Navigation System (INS) to be made primary and fed directly to the pilot's targeting screen located just to his left. On the screen was a fixed piper (resembles a sniper's crosshairs) which represented the aircraft, and a movable piper, which was the computer's representation of the target's location derived from information received from the sensor designated as primary. The pilot's job when firing was to fly the fixed piper (aircraft) onto the movable piper (target) by superimposing the two crosshairs.

Just aft of the wings and on the left side of the aircraft were two 40mm cannons capable of firing up to160 rounds per minute. They were top loaded in clips of four shells each. A 40mm cannon shell was approximately 20 inches long and about 1.5 inches wide. The actual warhead that each shell contained weighed about 2.2 pounds and was either filled with high explosive (HE) or an incendiary agent (MESH) which created a ball of fire fifteen feet wide whose interior temperature was so hot that it was measured literally in thousands of degrees and would immediately incinerate any person who was caught within that ball of fire.

Sitting amidships, in the interior of the aircraft, was the "booth." This was literally a closed room that was strapped to the floor of the aircraft. It measured approximately 8' wide, 7' high and 10' long. It had its own air conditioning system in order to protect the computers and delicate avionic systems contained within its walls. In the front of the booth sat the IR on the left and the BC on the right. Just aft of them sat the Fire Control Officer (FCO) on the left and the TV sensor operator on the right. Both the TV and IR positions had two screens: a large one sitting in the middle of their display panel and a small one in the upper part of the panel. The smaller one is used by each sensor operator to monitor what the other sensor operator was observing. The main computer allowed any of the sensors to "slave" to another sensor. In other words, it allowed one sensor to be directed to what another sensor was observing.

The FCO's job was to coordinate the efforts of the entire crew while in the offensive operational mode. There was a large screen at his position where he viewed what the TV or IR was showing on their respective screen. During normal operations, the FCO kept IR on his screen and looked just to his right in order to see the TV's presentation. The aisle separating left and right sides was approximately two feet wide, so it was easy for the FCO to see the TV's screen. The FCO also controlled the Inertial Navigation System (INS). This system used three free-running gyros to compute the aircraft's position. The INS had nine waypoints and each of these could be used to store targeting information. The main fire control computer was capable of taking information from the INS and treating it as a sensor in its own right. If the crew wanted, it literally could fire at a target generated by the INS. The FCO also had a VHS taping system which recorded everything that the FCO heard through his headset and whatever sensor he placed on his viewing screen. The FCO, the pilot (AC), and the BC were the only ones on the crew who heard all the returns from the electronic warfare detection devices. However, only the FCO and the AC heard every intercom system on the aircraft. The FCO determined windage and gun line errors. He did this by placing on a movable "Calc Board" the results of three shots and then determine the wind vector and gun line error. He informed the table navigator (TN) of the correction and then the TN placed this information into the main computing system. The FCO's other main job was to coordinate the entire attack. The FCO determined which sensor was "hot," what the other sensor would track, which weapon to use and the type of ammo that would be loaded into it. He determined the order of battle, and he had at his position, a "kill" switch which would immediately stop any firing from any weapon system. In a few words, when the aircraft rolled left into the attack mode, the FCO controlled the entire crew.

Just aft of the booth, on the starboard side of the aircraft, were two 40mm ammo racks. These racks were approximately 3' x 7' each and contained four shell clips. Some shells clips were HE (high explosive), and the others were mesh metal ammo. Aft of the guns and on the port side, was the same search light that was found on the AC-119 gunship. The main difference is that AC-130 engines develop so much power that it was easy to operate the system using nothing but the electricity generated by the four massive engines that powered the entire aircraft. And near the rear door on the starboard side was a flare dispenser which the illuminator operator (IO) controlled. It would dispense a flare connected to a parachute system which gave off more than two million candle power. With LLTV capabilities and that much light, it made what was on the ground as visible to TV as if it was during high noon on a sunny day.

However, the main purpose of the IO was defensive in nature. The C-130 aft doors opened up and down, not left to right nor right to left. The top door opened from the middle of a closed position and raised up to the open position. The bottom door, when raised, was in a closed position and lowered into the open position. Our normal flying configuration was to have the upper door in the open position (raised) and the lower door in a closed position (raised).

The IO would attach himself to the aircraft and with his body prone on the lower door, he would stick his head outside the airplane to see if any approaching threat was visible. The enemy, when firing at one of our gunships, had to use tracers in order to see where his fire was going to in relationship to the aircraft he was targeting. If the enemy gunners did not use tracers, they could not correct for the wind vector or gun line error. Their problem was a moving target, and they had the benefit of being stationary when they were shooting. Our problem was the reverse. We had the advantage of being a moving target, but that made it more difficult to effectively aim at a ground-based target. Whatever the enemy fired at us, whether it was cannon fire, otherwise known as AAA (pronounced Triple-A), or whether with missiles, the projectile would be visible to the naked eye. It was the IO's responsibility to detect the threat, determine the safest path for the aircraft and her crew, and then inform the pilot of what adjustments he had to make in order to assure survival and safety. The IO's interphone was set six decibels higher than all other intercoms or radios. Survival literally depended upon the IO's judgment and the pilot's ability to hear and react quickly to the IO's directions.

After I reported to the main headquarters of the 16th Special Operations Squadron, I asked that my training in both the infrared operator (IR) and the fire control officer (FCO) positions be continued. Since I'd passed both exams while at Lowry AFB, and since the need for new FCO's was glaring, the brass granted my request. Unlike anybody else who trained there, I became qualified in two crew positions.

What I did not know at this time was that every training report on each of us was being forwarded, on a daily basis, to the overseas combat squadron headquarters located in Ubon, Thailand. Normally, the Air Force wanted only senior navigators to be assigned as fire control officers (FCOs) because when the aircraft was in the offensive mode, the FCO controlled the entire crew, including the pilot. Normally, the 1st Special Operations Wing (1st SOW) command structure would not have granted my request because of my lack of both rank and experience. But the reality of war altered the normal protocol. It was difficult to find men who could competently perform FCO duties. Need drove the search. I did really well in both crew positions. There were many competent IRs, and few competent FCOs. I was allowed to cross-train, and by mid-February 1972, I passed my flight evaluations for both crew positions. I also found out well after I went to Southeast Asia that my daily training reports were scrutinized by the overseas combat flight examiner pilot, *Major Conrad Story.* His very able crew (Crew No. 1), was put in more danger because they had an inept FCO. They had to suffer extended exposure over a target area because his FCO could not quickly and accurately determine the order of battle, windage and gun line error. Maj. Story read my daily training reports and told the operations officer that he wanted me, Capt. Blakeman, as his crew's FCO. Since he was the flight examiner pilot and regarded as the best AC in the squadron, the operations officer, who was second in command, readily agreed to his request. Unbeknownst to me at the time, I was assigned to Crew No. 1 well before I departed CONUS on my way to Southeast Asia.

9

THE RABBI OF THE BOOTH

The weather in the panhandle of Florida during the first six weeks of 1972 was particularly good. All I needed was six weeks of flying in order to get all the required training completed. On February 10, 1972, I flew my evaluation ride. I checked out in both the IR and FCO positions. Before I departed, my orders were amended. When they were first written, the people in the Pentagon did not realize that I'd already completed both basic and water survival within the last two years. I did not have to attend those schools again. I needed jungle survival school, and the squadron desperately needed more qualified fire control officers. As a result, my orders were amended to reflect both needs.

I was given a week's leave before I departed on a commercial flight to Travis Air Force Base in California. I drove up to New York after my check ride and spent that week visiting my parents and JG and his family. Everybody was healthy, and I had a chance to say goodbye to both of my families. JG and Hope knew that I was flying a combat aircraft. I did not want my parents, particularly Mom, worrying too much about me. They knew that I was flying a C-130. I intentionally left off the AC part of the aircraft I was flying.

Saturday, February 19, I departed Travis Air Force Base on a troop-carrying DC-8. The aircraft was destined to Clark Air Base in the Philippines with a fuel stop in Hawaii. In the military, we called these DC-8s "cattle cars" as they carried well over 200 military personnel, and except for the crew, no civilians. They are certainly not the lap of luxury! I arrived in the Philippines on February 20.

The next day, I attended Jungle Survival School which was a very unique experience. The first two days were spent in a classroom learning how to survive in a jungle environment. The next two days, the Air Force bussed all the trainees and their instructors into the jungle occupied by a tribe of people called the "Negritos." We were divided into elements with 14 trainees and one instructor per element. Each element had a Negrito tribesman as an additional instructor.

The Negritos are an aborigine tribe. The men are small in stature, usually less than five feet tall. They are thin and wiry. They have curly black hair and are very dark skinned. They also possess one of the strongest ethical codes of any people whom I have ever encountered. They are not to be underestimated because of their small stature. The men are warriors in every sense of the word. They will keep whatever promise they make. They mean what they say and say what they mean. They will not steal, and they will not take charity. Each Negrito instructor earned a 100-pound bag of rice as payment for instructing an element.

When the Japanese occupied the Philippines during WWII, they never controlled the Valley of the Negritos. The Japanese soldiers, who were generally considered excellent jungle fighters, attempted to annihilate the Negrito tribes. When they encountered the Negritos, they more than met their match. After spending two days and one night in the Negrito jungle, I believe with all my heart that there is no better jungle fighter in the world than the Negrito warrior.

One example will serve. We went deep into the jungle where the Air Force instructor told us to wait 15 minutes before entering a clearing which was approximately two hundred square feet in area. There were 14 of us in the element. We were told that a Negrito warrior, our instructor, was hiding in that clearing. We spent thirty minutes searching for him, and we couldn't find him. After the allotted time, the Air Force instructor called to our Negrito instructor and told him to come out of hiding. A wooden log came to life as a man. We were stepping over him, on him and around him without realizing that he was a living man. If I hadn't seen it with my own eyes, I would not have believed it.

Clark Air Base hired many Filipinos to fill in as civilian personnel. One of the problems that the Air Force faced was the unbelievable amount of material that was stolen annually which was euphemistically called "shrinkage." A couple of years before I arrived, the Negrito chief asked the base commander to have a no-notice inspection of all his security police (SP) in the morning before they changed shifts. The base commander complied, and lo and behold all the SP's had a white stripe painted on the back of their boots without their knowing it. The chief then asked that his men be paid to guard Air Force materiel, and the base commander agreed. The shrinkage problem disappeared overnight, as well as some Filipinos! However, the indigenous community depended upon a certain amount of theft from the Americans in order to survive. They complained to their government, and the Air Force was forced to end the agreement they had with the Negrito chief.

The Air Force had excellent relations with the Negritos. Frankly, both groups followed the officer's code: "I will not lie, cheat or steal, nor tolerate those who do." The Negritos didn't name it, they just lived it. Their tribal leader was given the rank and privileges of a full colonel. When he came onto the base, he was given a driver and a car. In payment for helping train all the combat crews flying in Southeast Asia, the tribe members were given the privilege of a free education if they so desired. The chief's son got a college education because of this earned benefit.

Japanese-American aviators who entered the Valley of the Negritos would not come out alive. The Negritos, at least at the time when I trained with them, would kill any person possessing recognizable Japanese traits without a second thought. A Japanese-American member of the United States Air Force did jungle survival training in Panama or some other place, but never, and I mean never, at Clark Air Base in the Philippines.

I completed jungle survival school on Friday, February 25, 1972. On the following Monday, I departed Clark Air Base on a C-141 aircraft bound for Ubon Airbase in Thailand. After the plane landed and taxied to an area near base ops, the ground personnel brought a staircase on wheels to the entrance of the aircraft. We then deplaned. I went immediately from an air conditioned, dimly lit aircraft to unbelievably bright sunshine and a temperature approaching 115°F with a relative humidity approaching 100%. Besides the immediate heat and extraordinarily bright sunshine, my senses were attacked by a horrific smell, which was the combination of moisture, insecticides and burning excrement. I do not have the words to describe the pervasive odor of Ubon Airbase. I will say that after a week or so, I hardly noticed it. But it did take some time.

After I took four steps into that environment, my uniform was soaking wet with my own sweat. Those of us going to the 16th Special Operations Squadron (16 SOS) were met by Captain Young, who took us via a base car to our squadron headquarters. This was a large, all white building with the following displayed over the entrance:

THE FABULOUS FOUR ENGINE
FIGHTER OF THE WOLFPACK

When I entered squadron headquarters, the first thing I noticed was a large white board called the 'Frag Board' which displayed every scheduled mission (frag). The frag board was set up like a matrix. The crews were listed vertically by numbers on the left side of the board. From there, moving toward the right, the board listed the date that a crew was scheduled, the time of departure and the frag number. Each frag was a particular mission assigned to the 16th SOS. The aircraft commander was given a frag sheet which corresponded to the number posted and contained all the mission parameters assigned to his crew. These included such things as the target area, the type of mission (search and destroy or support troops in contact), the time over target, any contact information with ground forces or airborne command-and-control, and the assigned call sign. All our aircraft used the call sign, "Spectre." The frag order gave the crew the last two digits of the call sign. For example, the frag order for Spectre 18 was a support mission in II Corps starting at 1900 hours local. The crew that flew that particular mission would then use the call sign Specter 18, even if operations substituted another crew and/or aircraft. Call signs were randomly selected and stayed with the particular mission assigned by the frag order.

Captain Young took us to a briefing room after showing us all the different offices located in the squadron headquarters. He started a three-day orientation program that was required before flying a first mission. We learned where things were, how to record ground training requirements, and just day-to-day things needed to function properly in this tropical climate. For example, before I left Florida, I was told to bring as many of my old cotton flying suits as I possessed. I did so. Capt. Young told us to take those cotton flying suits and bring them to a small building on base which housed women who would cut down the sleeves and embroider a Spectre emblem, our wings, our names and our ranks on these old flying suits. They were comfortable and easy to wash. More importantly, they were accepted as proper uniforms on Ubon Royal Thai Air Force Base. The orientation classes started at one o'clock in the afternoon and ended by nine o'clock in the evening. The reason they started so late was that everybody flew at night. The object was to get a new crew member adjusted to operating at night and sleeping during the day.

By the end of the first day of orientation, I was assigned to my crew quarters which were called "hooches." Each hooch was an elongated building containing six bedrooms and a small covered porch area which was about four feet wide and ran the length of the hooch. Each bedroom was a 12 x 14 room which contained two beds, two portable closets, two small desks and one large window which opened to the front of the hooch. All the windows, however, were darkened in order to keep out the sunlight. Each room had its own air conditioner which kept the temperature at 70° constant. The reason we had air conditioning was due to the fact that we flew at night and had to sleep during the day. Rank was not a consideration as the enlisted men who flew with us also enjoyed air-conditioned quarters. My roommate, Capt. Green, was a maintenance officer. His hours were from six in the morning to six in the evening and, as a result, we hardly ever saw each other. It was a good deal for both of us as it was like having your own room. Once I was established there and flying, I rarely went to bed before 9 AM and usually I was up by four or five o'clock in the afternoon. Adjacent to each hooch was an outdoor shower. My routine, once I started flying, was showering in the morning before going to sleep. In Thailand, one had to make sure that before entering the shower stalls, one carefully examined the stall to ensure that it was free of cobra snakes trying to escape the morning heat. Let's say that salient fact added an unwanted bit of excitement to a daily chore.

Part of the initial orientation was meeting our commanding officer. I had the great fortune to serve with the best officer I have ever met in my lifetime, *Col. Harry C. Canham.* Our commander was an imposing figure of a man. He stood just over six feet, was somewhat barrel chested, had light blue eyes and grayish blond crew-cut hair which was rapidly turning all gray. He possessed a very deep voice. Col. Canham welcomed all his newcomers personally. He flew almost as much as any other pilot in the squadron. He would not put anyone in danger that he himself would not face. Indeed, as I would come to learn, all commanders, from wing commander all the way down to virtually all operational squadron commanders, embraced this leadership philosophy. Our wing, the 8th Tactical Fighter Wing (8th TFW), also known as "*The Wolfpack,*" was the most decorated unit which participated in the Vietnam War. Our commanders, all of them, were leaders, not managers. They led by example and none better than Col. Canham.

The second day of my stay in Ubon, I ran into Capt. Andy Stone, my old roommate from UNT school. He was always thin, but now he was approaching appallingly gaunt status. Andy was the first company grade officer to be checked out as a FCO. When we saw each other at the O' Club (officers' club), we both got excited about seeing the other. After the usual greetings, I asked Andy how things were going with him. His demeanor took a definitive turn for the worse, and it didn't take a psychoanalyst to determine that he had a major problem. We were both with other groups, and we excused ourselves and found a table where we could talk quietly and privately.

Andy hated the killing, as he was a believer in the sanctity of life. He was the most junior of all the FCOs, yet he was considered one of the best. He did his job well and that fact helped keep his crew alive. The conundrum for him was that the better he did his job; the more people were killed. It was the nature of war and especially true when one was a Fire Control Officer on a gunship. What exacerbated his problem even more was that his wife, Heather, was actively participating in the anti-war movement. After he got his orders to fly gunships, Heather returned to her roots and her family in Berkeley, California. Two months before I arrived at Ubon, he received a letter from Heather demanding that he stop flying combat or she would leave him. Some of his friends, who knew both of them, wrote to Andy that Heather was now sleeping with other men who were deeply involved in the anti-war movement. He was torn between his love for his wife, his anger over her reported infidelity, and his duty to his country. Andy, to his credit, never sought to be with the numerous and pretty Thai women who worked on base. He was always faithful to Heather.

I encouraged him to do his duty. He was highly regarded in our squadron as a very able FCO. His ability to do his job competently while being fired upon helped keep safe the crews who flew with him. I asked him, "What is that worth?"

He answered, "It's worth a lot."

"Then hold onto it. I'm not a great philosopher or psychologist, but I do know that walking away from your crew, your country and your duty, means walking away forever from who you are. By doing that, it may not be possible to ever find your way back. Andy, I make this promise to you. If we both make it back to the world, someday you will thank me for this conversation. You are one of the best people I have ever met in my life, and you deserve a woman who will really appreciate you. I can't be the only person who can see what a wonderful human being you are . . . just hang in there!"

Andy thanked me, and I could see that he was starting to feel better about himself. He told me that he had been there for over eight months and was due to leave by the first week of June of this year. I told him that if a relationship between him and Heather could be salvaged, then it would be. In around four months, he would find out, one way or the other. For the next three months, we would talk whenever he was feeling blue regarding his wayward wife or the missions we were sworn to complete. Andy did finish his year with exemplary service to his crew, our squadron and our country.

After completing three days of ground school, I started flying. I was issued four Nomex flight suits, my own parachute, survival vest and a Smith & Wesson 38 caliber combat special pistol. After the first mission, I realized that my body was too short for a shoulder holster. I decided to "John Wayne" it . . . in other words, I strapped on my pistol using a Western-style holster. The next 10 days after ground school, I completed my six training rides in actual combat.

My seventh ride, which occurred in the first week of March, was also my check ride. It was the first time that I flew with my assigned crew. *Major Conrad Story* was my aircraft commander and this was the first time I met him. He was a tall thinly-built man, well above six feet, with grayish blue eyes and a very serious countenance. The co-pilot, *Capt. Ken Barth*, was a stocky blonde-haired gentleman and stood about six feet tall. The flight engineer was *MSgt. Bob Turek*, who had dark thinning hair, dark eyes and a crooked smile. The infrared operator was *Maj. Dave Gordon,* the most senior officer in the booth. The TV operator was *Maj. George Hatvany,* who was also a very senior navigator. The Black Crow operator was *Capt. Ken Newman,* and *Capt. Claude Cox* was the table navigator; both were very senior captains. The gunners were *Ron Simmen, Al Rogers, Ron Fritts, George Wallace*, and the lead gunner was *Army Armstrong.* The illuminator operator was *Phil Lucero.* This was crew number one, and I was its FCO. The check ride started out as a truck hunting mission along the Ho Chi Minh Trail that passed through southern Laos. We found a convoy of four trucks and without much delay or wasted actions, we destroyed all four. We started hunting more trucks when a call came in from Hill Top which was one of the call signs used by airborne command-and-control aircraft. We were directed to a firefight in II core. I directed the attack that helped save a forward outpost fairly deep in enemy territory. I easily passed my check ride.

The next day, I flew with my crew without an instructor or flight examiner. We were scheduled for an early frag and our briefing time was 4:30 in the afternoon. The briefing rooms were located in the squadron building. Major Story stood at the front of the room. He told us what the mission was and some of the parameters issued in the frag. He then asked me which aircraft was assigned to our crew. It was my job, as the crew's FCO, to inform them as to any known maintenance problems with the assigned aircraft. It was then that Maj. Story said how happy he was to have me as his fire control officer and looking directly at the other three members of the booth (TV, IR and BC), he said in his deep gravelly slow Alabama drawl, "The only voice that I want to hear from the booth is Blake's. Everybody understand that!?" The other three members of the booth all nodded in agreement. In essence, the booth was mine to direct even though I was far and away the most junior officer stationed within its walls. That was not a problem for any of my crew members because they really appreciated my ability to quickly and adroitly do my job. Besides, they were a very strong crew that needed a competent FCO to make them a truly great crew. I fit the bill.

Once the report detailing our aircraft's maintenance record was completed, I left the briefing room while the rest of my crew was still there. My job then was to be driven to the flight line where I would enter through the aircraft's rear door and power up the Inertial Navigation System (INS) which had to be done using an outside power source. While this process was going on, I was the only one allowed aboard the aircraft. I had to sit quietly in my seat until the gyros in the INS were up to speed and set. The system was so delicate in the warm-up stage that if I walked on the floor of the cargo section, I could induce an error in the INS. The onboard auxiliary power unit (APU) could not be used for the same reason, as the vibrations would adversely affect the gyros that are contained within the INS. It usually took around 45 minutes to properly align the INS. Once the system was in the green and running, I would call out to the crew chief and have them power up the APU. I looked forward to seeing that light in the green, as once the APU was turned on, I would also get air conditioning for the booth. Usually, during the early frags, the temperature inside the all-black airplane could exceed 145°F. By the time I got the INS up, my flight suit was thoroughly soaked with sweat. And nobody, not even the crew chief, could enter the plane until the INS was up and running. That is why I always carried two extra water bottles in my flight suit. Once the APU was on, I would drink at least one of them in order to replenish my body's hydration.

During the first six weeks after I checked out, I generally flew about every other day. When the mission was over or if I was not flying, I would generally go to the Spectre Hooch which was a small square building that contained one 30' x 30' room. Usually, there was a continuous running poker game and a twenty-four-hour well-equipped bar. I was a regular at that poker game, and I usually averaged winning $50 per night. My days usually started between three and five o'clock in the afternoon when I would awaken. I would then go to the officers' club where I ate most of my meals. If I was flying, I would go to the squadron building for a briefing. If not, I worked on some ground jobs that were assigned to me. Also, when I was not flying, I would go on to the racquetball courts which were kept open 24 hours a day because of the different flight schedules of the various squadrons which made up the 8th TFW. I usually played about three hours per session of racquetball. It really helped keep me in shape.

My crew readily accepted me. After I joined them, we became much more effective. They appreciated my ability to quickly comprehend the tactical situations that we encountered. I made good decisions in very little time. They appreciated my instinctive hunches which inevitably proved to be accurate, although I could not explain them. Our firing accuracy was second to none which meant less time over target and less time exposed to enemy fire.

To my knowledge, I was the only Jewish person in the squadron. I flew every mission with a red ski cap which I wore under my headset. I wore a gold, six-pointed star (the Magen David) attached to my dog tags. My crew called me "The Rabbi of the Booth!" I liked the name. I felt totally accepted by my fellow crewmembers. All of us, to a man, trusted each other implicitly and without hesitation. We even developed unspoken communication with each other. For example, I would see how Dave (IR) was holding onto an area that he was scanning and I knew, without his saying a word, whether or not he thought he had a valid target.

The best hunting time to track and destroy trucks along the Ho Chi Minh Trail was during the dry season which in Southeast Asia was from November to the end of March. Once the rainy season started, the cloud cover was so thick that it obscured a lot of target traffic from us. In addition, it was so rainy that the enemy had trouble moving their trucks along the trails because of all the mud they had to encounter and overcome due to the heavy rainfall. Around the middle of March, our frag orders started to alter our hunting area from the trails to barges found on the Mekong River running from north to south. One mission comes to mind as an example of this change in orders.

On Thursday, March 23, we pulled second frag which briefed around 9 o'clock in the evening. Our orders were to search and destroy all traffic flowing along the Mekong River extending from Cambodia to Vietnam. We departed about eleven o'clock in the evening, and we were on station and searching for enemy shipping by midnight. About an hour later, we came across three powered boats. One of the boats was extremely large, measuring about 120 feet long and almost 30 feet wide at its thickest point. The other two boats were about a third of the size of the larger one. As soon as we started our left-hand orbit, which meant we were going into the offensive mode, the two smaller boats made for the shore. That left the bigger boat in the middle of the Mekong River, and judging by the amount of smoke emanating from its center located steam engine, doing so at full speed. This particular section of the Mekong River is over two miles wide especially as we were approaching the rainy season. I ordered the IR to track the smaller boats and told TV to track the larger. The moon was three-quarter phase and its light was more than sufficient for the TV to continuously track the larger boat.

I ordered the TV to be primary in the computer and that the number three gun loaded with HE shells be made ready. I then called for "Tweaking" procedure.

> AC: "In the sight." (This meant that the pilot was looking at the Plexiglas sighting device and he would fly the fixed piper onto the moving piper until they were superimposed. When that occurred, the pilot would fire a single round and state how close to superimposing the position of the pipers were at the time of fire.

> AC: The first round was fired. "One high." That meant the fixed piper was one "mil" higher than the moving piper.

> FE: "189 knots". The ideal speed is 190 kt. Part of my tweaking procedure is to account for any variance in airspeed.

> CP: "30." The copilot is reading the attitude indicator and stating the exact angle of bank that the aircraft experienced at the moment the cannon was fired. Again, as part of the tweak, I must account for any deviation from 30°.

> FCO: "Good shot. Next firing point is at 220°." This meant that in my opinion the shot was usable in determining windage and gun line error. The heading I gave the pilot is the

approximate heading the aircraft will be when he next shoots. I am looking for approximately 120° separation between shots. Three good shots on my tweak board will allow me to mathematically determine both the wind adjustment and the computer counts needed to offset gun line error.

AC: When we reached 200° heading, "In the Sight." A few moments later, "Super."

FE: "190."

CP: "29°."

FCO: "Good shot. Next heading 040°."

AC: At 020°, "In the Sight. One low."

FE: "190."

CP: "30°."

FCO: "Good shot." From there it took me about 10 to 15 seconds to determine windage and gun line error. "Wind: 172 at 6. Give me two up at three forward."

TN: "Wind and counts set."

FCO: "Clear to fire!"

AC: "In the Sight. Super." Major Story just fired four continuous rounds.

FE: "190."

CP: "30°."

Seven seconds later, at least two of the first four shells hit the large boat directly amidships. The explosion emanating from the destruction of that large boat was so great that it caused secondary explosions, more than a mile away, on both sides of the Mekong River and blanked out both the TV and IR for approximately one minute until they could reset themselves. Previously, I locked in the last known position of the two smaller boats into waypoints loaded into the INS. I stated, "IR, take INS guidance." Dave, my IR sensor, "slaved" his sensor to the INS.

When the IR returned to service about a minute later, Dave said, "I've got the targets."

FCO: "Take IR guidance."

TN: "IR is in the computer."

AC: "In the Sight." Fifteen seconds later, Maj. Story fired off another four rounds. "One high."

FE: "190."

CP: "30°."

Seven seconds later, a second boat took direct hits and was destroyed. The same procedure was employed and after another thirty seconds, the third and last boat was destroyed. Within the next two weeks, because the gunships were so effective, we literally stopped all traffic flowing south along the Mekong River between Laos and South Vietnam.

During this time, on the days I was not flying, I studied the briefing books which contained much of the mathematical theories upon which the gunship operated. I was interested in how the gun settings were derived and more particularly what assumptions were made in the computation for determining those settings. After about a month of flying without an instructor, I was appalled to see how high the computer counts were in order to correct gun line error. I came to the conclusion that one of the assumptions used by the engineers who computed those gun settings was that the aircraft was perfectly aligned in all three axes of flight. However, virtually every AC-130A aircraft that we flew experienced high G-turns in order to avoid AAA or missiles, or both. In my opinion, every A model gunship was "bent" in at least one or more of its axes and that the axes were continually changing due to the constant use of high G-turns in order to avoid enemy fire. So, I computed what the gun settings should be based on the computer corrections reported during the last five missions for each aircraft. I gave these new gun settings to the lead gunner and had him use those settings instead of the ones posted in the aircraft.

The results were astounding. My average circular error went from 2.5 mills to less than 1.2 mills. Each mil represented one thousandths of a degree which converted to a linear distance of approximately 10 feet. If my circular error was 1.5 mills, it meant that 90% of our fire would land within fifteen feet of the exact aim point. This is why it worked. When we cranked in a large correction into our analog computer in order to offset gun line errors, it resulted in making the pilot's job of flying geometry more difficult. High computer counts are similar to watching a dog try and chase his tail in a circular fashion and never catch up to it. Proper gun settings made achieving fire "geometry" much easier for the pilot, in both effort and, more importantly, reducing the time to achieve a proper orbit. My crew noticed the difference immediately. We were spending less time in determining a better "tweak." Also, our circular error was literally cut in half which reduced the time over target. The less time we spent over target reduced our overall exposure which bettered our odds for survival.

During the last week of March, we were getting Intel reports (confirmed by our BCs who were all qualified electronic warfare officers) that there was a possible SA-2 site located in Tchepone, Laos. That is a small town located in the Laotian Panhandle and is at the crossroads of several narrow truck routes which comprise part of the Ho Chi Minh Trail. The SA-2 is a Soviet surface-to-air missile (SAM) which is radar guided and carries a shaped warhead containing upwards of half a ton of high explosive material. This missile can exceed speeds of Mach 2 and altitudes higher than 75,000 feet. Every C-130 version is extremely vulnerable to this weapon system as our props make unusually large radar targets.

On the night of March 28, my crew was in the Spectre hooch. We had just completed an early mission, and we ran into the crew of Spectre 13 as they were getting ready to brief and depart for a late mission. It was about 11:30 at night, and I overheard the conversation that Major Story had with his counterpart, the aircraft commander of Spectre 13. They were arguing about the best altitude to fly in central and southern Laos. Major Story argued for the lower altitude which would give you a better chance to avoid the dreaded SA-2 SAM attack, but would make you more vulnerable to AAA (Automatic Anti-Aircraft or "flack") cannon fire. In the combat areas that we flew, almost all the AAA was either 37mm or 57mm. Both sizes contained a contact fuse which would ignite the shell when it hit the aircraft, and if contact was not made, the shells would explode at a preset altitude. Both of them were potentially deadly, but at least after sustaining a hit, there was a good chance to survive it. That was not true of a SA-2 strike which would result in almost certain total destruction of our aircraft. The other pilot was just as adamant in his belief that AAA, because it was so much more prevalent where we flew, was the greater threat. The last thing I heard him say to my pilot was that he would fly at a higher altitude. He departed about 11:45 that evening and was on station over Tchepone by 02:30 AM. Approximately one hour later, Spectre 13 sustained a direct hit by a SA-2 SAM. All 13 crewmembers perished that night. May God rest their souls. Unfortunately, and at great cost, the tragic loss of life definitively ended that argument.

10

SPRING OFFENSIVE OR SECOND TET

According to the history books, the North Vietnamese Second Tet or Spring Offensive started in the middle of March, 1972. It took the 7th Air Force about two weeks to get the 16th SOS involved. The reason for this is that the whole AC-130 gunship program was so classified that many operational commanders were unaware of our capabilities. A perfect example of this phenomena occurred in the winter months of 1971. The battle damage assessment (BDA) reported by my squadron was not believed by the various levels of command within the 7th Air Force. The Commander-in-Chief (CINC 7th AF), a four-star general, decided that he would ride along on a truck hunting mission over the Ho Chi Minh Trail. The crew placed the general on a folding seat in the rear of the booth located between the FCO and the TV. That night, the general witnessed the crew destroying 45 trucks. He was so impressed with the gunship's ability that when he got on the ground, he made MIG-Cap (protecting an airborne asset from being jumped by Soviet-made fighter aircraft) the primary mission of all the F-4s in country.

By the time the general rode with the crew, the AC-130 gunships had been in country for almost a year and a half. When the second offensive started, the overall commander of all forces in Southeast Asia, *Gen. Creighton Abrams*, was probably unaware of the gunship's capabilities. As with any bureaucracy, it took several weeks for the information to wind its way up to the higher commands.

At any rate, whatever the reason, it was April by the time we finally got involved in the Spring Offensive, and in particular, with the siege of An Loc, Vietnam, which is a small city north of Saigon and halfway between Saigon and the Cambodian border along Route 7. The enemy launched an overall attack at the end of March, 1972. Their goal was to capture the city and declare it the provisional capital of the southern half of Vietnam. The city was defended by a much smaller force of South Vietnamese Rangers and three American Forward Air Controllers (FACs). The reason that the enemy started his action in the latter part of March was due to the weather. This was the onset of the rainy season and, as a result, the cloud layer would be thick and based just above the surface which made using air support of ground troops only an intermittent option at best. It is precisely the same reason that Hitler attempted the Battle of the Bulge offensive in the middle of winter, during very poor flying conditions, in order to offset the huge advantage in air power that the Allies possessed. It is a remarkable coincidence, to me at least, that Gen. Creighton Abrams, our overall commander in Vietnam, was, at the time of the Battle of Bulge, a Lt. Col. and a tank battalion commander who was at the forefront of relieving the besieged city of Bastogne.

Another reason that the enemy started its offensive at the end of March 1972 was the scheduled refit of all our H-model gunships which would render them unfit to fly until completed. The updated version of the H-model gunships would include the following: replacing the analog computer with a new and more advanced digital computer; upgrading all four engines, and replacing the aft 40 mm cannon with a 105 mm howitzer which was mounted upon a movable, hydraulically-driven platform which allowed the howitzer to "slave" to the sensor tracking the target. This refit was scheduled to last until the end of August 1972. In the meantime, the squadron manned the H-models before manning the older version. As result of this decision, when the Spring Offensive began, the H-model crews were fully manned but couldn't fly and the A-model crews who could fly were only half manned resulting in my squadron having 25% of its capacity available for combat. I believe the enemy's knowledge of our lack of capacity during this time was a factor in their decision to initiate the Spring Offensive.

During April of 1972, I was one of 13 qualified FCOs available for all 26 A-model crews. The result was that I was scheduled to fly two or three "frags" every day during the month of April. Starting April 1st, I was flying between 14 to 18 hours of combat each day. I would fly one or two missions with my crew and fly a second or third with another. After 10 days of this, my body broke down. I notified base ops that I needed a night off which they gave me. I literally slept 24 hours and resumed my three-a-days till the end of the month. Major Story was aware of the physical toll that this was taking on me. Consequently, when we were returning from flying a combat mission either over the trails, supporting troops in South Vietnam or assisting the South Vietnamese Rangers at An Loc, he allowed me to sleep on the way home. When the siege of An Loc was finally broken, I was given a day off on April 30. I once again slept around the clock, this time for 26 straight hours. After I slept that long, I woke up in a totally disoriented state.

The first day we arrived over An Loc, we radioed Zippo 11 (pronounced Zippo One One), an Army Ranger who was the forward air controller who was stationed in the city. At first, he thought all we could do was drop flares. My table navigator informed him of our capabilities. He was dubious, so we gave him a demonstration. We first locked onto his exact location. He was in a small building in the southeast corner of the city. We then asked him to indicate to us a building where the enemy was already hiding. He told us that there was fire coming from a building 102 meters and bearing 045 degrees from his position. I entered that range and bearing in the computer and after tweaking the aircraft's weapon system, we fired for effect. We took out that one building and left the surrounding buildings intact. By the end of the night, he was directing fire as close as 10 meters from his position. That was the first night that we worked with Zippo 11. It would not be the last. I noticed that when he was under fire, his voice was as smooth as glass. When the pressure was relieved, he spoke with just a hint of a stutter. Our job was to get Zippo 11 stuttering! That first night, we enjoyed good weather. We really watered his eyes with our ability to bring enormously accurate fire onto a target. From that day on, the Spectre aircraft became Zippo 11's best friend.

Most of that month was a blur to me, but three missions stand out. The first one occurred during the second week of April. The enemy moved in a 37mm AAA cannon in order to shoot us down. This gun site was manned by a "nine level" crew which is Air Force jargon which means the highest skill level a person could obtain in regard to his or her occupation. Just before reaching An Loc, we did a quick orbit and a half in order to obtain the windage and gun line error. With our weapon system properly "tweaked", we proceeded on to the city where we took up our station. While we were contacting Zippo 11, we started taking on fire:

IO: "TRIPLE A...UNDERNEATH... BREAK RIGHT, BREAK RIGHT!" Pilot immediately turns right in a four G turn.

IO: "CLEAR!" Pilot reenters "geometry" or a circular orbit around the target.

FCO: "IR, can you track that gun?"

IR: "Roger, searching." After 15 seconds, "I got him!"

FCO: "Take IR guidance!" I ordered IR in the main computer and entered IR's position into waypoint 1 of the INS.

TN: "IR set."

FCO: "Give me number 4-gun, mesh metal!"

AG: "Number 4 gun is ready, with mesh!"

FCO: "Clear to fire."

AC: "Pilot in the sight." After a few moments, Major Story fired off a four-round burst and says, "Super".

FE: "190."

AC: "30."

IO: "AAA UNDERNEATH! BREAK LEFT... BREAK LEFT!" Pilot banks hard to left.

FCO: I see that IR lost the target and say, "IR slave to INS."

IR: "Roger." After two seconds, "Target reacquired." At that moment, we saw the result of the four round bursts just fired. I could see the first round actually hit the hot barrel of the 37mm AAA cannon. The barrel was very hot due to the recent firing and as a result, was very easy to see it on the AADS-7 IR screen.

When that mesh metal hit the gun barrel, it not only vaporized the enemy gun crew, but the heat was so intense that it also distorted the gun barrel itself. After that, we never received any more AAA firing while over An Loc.

The second mission came about a week later. Again, we were working with Zippo 11. The weather over An Loc was unbelievably bad, so we attained a proper tweak before taking up our station over the besieged town. The bases of the clouds were about 500 feet and there were several layers between the bases and the tops around 7,000 feet. The clouds were too thick for low LLTV to work and about every third or fourth orbit, the IR would be able to obtain a momentary picture of what was happening on the ground. We did manage to locate the hut where Zippo 11 was located. His voice was very steady and therefore, we knew he was in trouble.

ZIPPO 11: "Enemy fire coming from bearing 048, range 15 m."

TN: "Roger. We are looking for a hole."

ZIPPO 11: "I need help now!"

FCO: "Pilot, FCO request."

AC: "What do you suggest FCO?"

FCO: "I think we need to turn off our recorders."

AC: "All recorders off." I turned off my recorder and after 10 seconds, "What do you have in mind?"

FCO: "I want to fire using the INS. I've been tracking this system during the whole mission and it is unusually accurate." My suggestion was a clear violation of the rules of engagement (ROEs) because they (the ROEs) required visual acquisition of any target before firing, particularly in a populated area.

AC: "If anyone objects, say so now. If I don't hear in the next 60 seconds any objection from any crew member, I will follow FCO's suggestion." After one minute of silence, the pilot said simply, "Let's do it."

FCO: "Put INS in the computer. Range and bearing 048 at 15. Set site one mil, auto fire."

TN: "Set."

FCO: "Make number 3-gun primary with HE."

AG: "Number three gun set with HE."

AC: "Pilot in the sight."

From there, we started firing. The pilot did not have to fire the system, as the computer would fire off the rounds when all the set parameters of flight were met. About every third orbit, I updated the INS with Zippo11's position, visually using the IR. Two out of every three orbits we were virtually blind due to the clouds below us. Zippo 11 would give us range and bearing data regarding each target, and we updated our computer using his information. Occasionally, I would see one of our rounds hit, but for well over 90% of the firing we did that night, we did not have any visual confirmation of what we were hitting. We supported Zippo 11 in this manner for over three hours. In that time, not a single shot was misplaced. It was like the hand of

God directing the unseen fire onto the enemy in order to protect Zippo 11 and the men with him. It was truly miraculous! By the time we left the station, Zippo 11 had a slight stutter which meant that he was safe for the moment. That night, everyone on my crew put his career on the line because we knowingly violated the ROEs which was potentially a court-martial offense. It was the only way to save Zippo 11 and the South Vietnamese Rangers that he led. If given the same choice, frankly I would do it again. It also showed just how much faith my crew had in me as their FCO!

Looking back on that mission, I feel with some confidence that had we not made the choice to violate the ROEs, An Loc would have fallen that night. Without having eyes on the ground in the form of American forward air controllers, we would have been helpless assisting any remaining resistance to the North Vietnamese. We could not just blindly fire such deadly ordnance in a populated area without causing enormous collateral damage. The decision made by Major Story was the pivotal decision of the entire second Tet Offensive. The courage it took to risk his and his family's future in order to save the mission and one Army FAC reflects the true nature of this magnificent aircraft commander.

The third mission that stands out was the last one I flew over An Loc. It was April 29 and we were on station about nine o'clock that evening local time. At the start of the fourth week of April, the H-model gunships were coming back online. The Air Force realized the mistake that was made in refitting the H-models and brought enormous assets to Ubon airbase in order to correct the situation. On this night we were working with Tunnel 10A (pronounced Tunnel Ten Alpha) south of An Loc. Meanwhile, a newly refitted AC-130H was working north of the town along Route 7 between An Loc and the Cambodian border. Our target was a large number of enemy ground troops making their way northward toward An Loc. That night, we had over a 50-knot wind at altitude, and Major Story had a student pilot in the left seat. Because of the strength of the wind, the student pilot could not get into proper "geometry" which in essence is the prescribed orbit that we needed to fly around the target. Tunnel 10A was getting desperate.

Approximately 1100 to 1500 NVA soldiers were about ready to overrun his position. It was then that Major Story said, "I think I'll take left seat. You and I will switch." Now I have every interphone in my ear, and I can tell you that a cheer went up on each of them. With the old man in the left seat, we would soon be in firing geometry. Inside of one and a half orbits, I had the tweak set and cleared the pilot to open up. And open up he did. Inside of four orbits, the old man emptied the two Vulcan Gatlin cannons and fired off virtually every round of 40mm ammo. When we were done, there was not a single enemy soldier left alive. We departed for Saigon in order to rearm and refuel. We were back on station inside of two hours.

Meanwhile, the AC-130H, working north of the city, came across 25 T-54 Russian battle tanks making their way from the Cambodian border town toward An Loc along Route 7. This occurred at the very same time we were destroying an enemy battalion south of the city. The obvious intention of the enemy was to link up this battalion of tanks with the ground troops that we destroyed just south of An Loc. The crew determined wind vector using the 40mm cannon. They determined the gun line error in the first 105mm round they fired. In the next 25 howitzer shots they fired, they destroyed 25 tanks. After the gun line error was determined, virtually every shot found its mark. After that night, given the enormous losses suffered by the enemy, An Loc was never seriously threatened again. That night effectively ended the second Tet Offensive. History records that it was over some six weeks later, but history is wrong. That was the night that the enemy knew as long as there were gunships in and around Vietnam, Laos and Cambodia, if they ever came together en masse to create a large force, instead of having a military asset, they would create one large target. That was the last night I ever saw the enemy try to amass a large force. Gunships made that effort futile.

11

A GUNNER'S MOON

For the first time in five weeks, I enjoyed having two days off in a row. During the almost overwhelming number of flying hours I accumulated during the previous month, I perfected my "gun setting" sheet. When I flew with other crews, I used this new technique in order to determine the best gun settings for each aircraft. This new technique took into account the changes that occurred along the three axes of flight as each aircraft continued to fly combat and make high G-turns in order to avoid enemy fire. The gun settings I used were mathematically derived prior to each departure. For the past two months, I used my gun settings exclusively instead of the ones posted on the side of the booth. My crew was used to this new technique. However, the other crews were at first dubious but quickly accepted the new settings when they saw the results. I was getting a reputation as a top notch FCO.

On May 1, 1972, our frag ordered us into the A Shau Valley and to be over our target area at 0100 hrs. Our interdiction mission was basically to "search and destroy" all trucking that we found. In the previous two weeks, our BCs were getting "RHAH cuts" emanating from the A Shau Valley. These "cuts" were the electronic signals of the tracking radar used by SA-2 SAM (Surface-to-Air Missile) crews in order to aim their weapon system. That is the same SAM that destroyed Spectre 13 five weeks earlier over Tchepone, Laos.

We briefed at eleven o'clock local that evening. However, we were delayed for two and a half hours due to a serious maintenance problem. The aircraft assigned to us finally had to be scrapped, and the replacement aircraft was "Balls One-One." This A-model gunship's last three digits of its registration number were 0-1-1 which was painted in red on the nose of the aircraft. Balls One-One is my all-time favorite aircraft. This "puppy" just did not miss. My average tweak in this particular aircraft was less than a half a mil, or five feet. When we were assigned this aircraft, everybody on the crew had a smile. In the history of aviation, no aircraft in the world destroyed more trucks than this particular plane. In the dry season of 1971-72, this aircraft destroyed more than three thousand trucks. Another thing I liked about this particular airplane was the crew chief whose responsibility it was to ensure that the aircraft was ready to fly. When I would go out to the aircraft in order to bring up the INS, he would be there, sitting on the tail door, reading a well-used version of Tolkien's Lord of the Rings trilogy.

That night, we were two days past a complete full moon phase. Just before entering Balls 1-1, I looked up at the sky and saw a "Gunner's Moon." That is a condition which occurs when the sky is well lit because the moon is at or near full face, and there is a high thin overcast between that celestial body and the surface of the earth. That high thin overcast creates a lit background of a shiny, whitish gray sky. Our black airplane stands out like a sore, fucking thumb when flying under this well-lit overcast. We become more visible to the nine level gunners who were trying to shoot us down. A Gunner's Moon is both beautiful and deadly. It certainly made our mission a much more dangerous one to accomplish.

This angst was exacerbated by the fact that we were hunting in the A Shau. This valley, over the twelve-year history of the Vietnam conflict, was in allied hands for less than six months out of the entire time that the war persisted. We were almost three hours late by the time we got our new aircraft and finished all the preflight duties required. It was a little after 04:30 in the morning when we arrived on station. Within 15 minutes, BC picked up some "movers" or trucks.

BC: "Got Movers... possibly 10."

FCO: "Take BC guidance." Both the TV and IR slaved to BC without me saying a word.

IR: "I have a visual."

FCO: "Put IR in the computer." TV slaved to IR. I set waypoint One to IR. I have IR on my battle screen. He's in distant mode and I could see 10 trucks. The fourth truck is the largest truck I've ever seen or will ever see on the trails. "IR, lock onto truck number four."

IR: "Roger. Target in sight." I update the INS, waypoint One. TV slaves IR.

FCO: I see TV locked on target number 4. "Put TV in the computer." I update the INS.

TN: "TV is hot."

FCO: "Tweaking procedures. Number four gun, HE."

AG: "Number four gun set. HE."

AC: "Pilot in the sight." Pilot expends a round. "Super."

FE: "190."

CP: "29°."

FCO: "Next heading 190°."

AC: "Roger."

IO: "AAA UNDERNEATH! BREAK RIGHT! BREAK RIGHT!" The pilot violently turns the aircraft to the right. "AAA STARBOARD... BREAK LEFT!" Pilot turned aircraft left. After a few moments, "Clear."

FCO: "Slave to INS."

TV: "Target reacquired."

For the next two minutes, we went in and out of our shooting orbit in order to avoid the extremely accurate AAA that was being fired at us. Finally, after the second orbit, I had my tweak and gave the table navigator, the windage and gun line error computer corrections. I told the pilot to "fire away."

Major Story quickly got back into firing geometry and within 10 seconds shot off a four-round volley of 40mm cannon fire containing HE or high explosives. I saw the first two hit truck number four. This particular truck was over eighty feet long, the biggest truck I ever saw on the trails in my year there. Normally, our procedure was to destroy the first and last truck in a convoy. That traps the rest of them on the narrow trail. This time, I had a feeling that it was imperative to destroy this particular truck. I can't tell you why I felt this. All I can tell you is that some instinct within me was screaming, "Kill that truck!" When those two shells hit truck number four, the resulting explosion was so great that it rocked our aircraft and blanked out both the IR and the TV sensors for almost three minutes. The good news for us was that the explosion created so much light on the ground that we were now invisible to the enemy gunners below. All that light on the ground made the sky so dark that we were no longer visible, even with a Gunner's Moon.

While waiting for the sensors to return to an operational mode, our F-4 Phantom escort called us.

> Night Owl 21: "Spectre 15, Night Owl 21 requests permission to drop hard bombs on target area."

> FCO: "Pilot. That's okay by the booth. We'll be down for two more minutes."

> AC: "Roger," to me. Then over the radio, "Night Owl 21, Spectre 15. Permission to drop. Advise Clear."

> Night Owl 21: "Roger." Thirty seconds later, "I'm in." After another 30 seconds, "PULL UP! PULL UP!" Then to us, "Night Owl 21 is off target, resuming Mig-cap altitude."

> AC: "Night Owl 21, what happened?"

> Night Owl 21: "We had to pull up as we encountered pieces of that truck you destroyed at our puke (drop) altitude." That altitude was 6,000 feet above the ground!

After our sensors returned to the operational mode, we proceeded to destroy the remaining trucks. The trucks immediately before and after truck number four were already burning hulks. Spacing between trucks was approximately three hundred or four hundred meters. The explosion was so great that it took out the two trucks bracketing that very large truck. Since we did not encounter any more AAA and the tweak was so very good, we spent less than a quarter of an orbit for each of the remaining targets. When we left, the jungle trail was on fire for 2 1/2 to 3 km along the trail running through the A Shau Valley. The total time over target, including all the evasive maneuvers, was less than nine minutes. My average circular error was less than three feet. Just as we were pulling off this target area:

> BC called out, "I got twenty movers!" I immediately told the TN and the crew to take BC guidance.
>
> TN: "Belay that order. New heading 270°."
>
> FCO: "I got twenty movers. We're fucking driving nails!"
>
> TN: "Pilot, heading is 270°."
>
> AC: "Roger. 270 it is." The plane is turning due west.
>
> FCO: "Sir, I got 20 movers!"
>
> FE: "Hey FCO...open the fucking booth door and tell me what you see!"

I opened the booth door and looked at the large opening in the rear of the airplane. The upper cargo door is always open in our combat mode. I saw the sun literally positioned just over the closed, lower aft door. I was so into what I was doing that I had not realized that it was now past sunrise, and we were extremely visible to the enemy gunners. Needless to say, I received a lot of kidding about that incident from my crew. Looking back on it, it definitely was funny. But it's also informative in this sense. I call it "tunnel vision on steroids!"

Immediately after returning to our home base, the entire crew met at the BDA (Battle Damage Assessment) shack. Major Story purchased a case of beer for the entire crew, and they took my VHS tape and played it on a five-foot television screen. My entire crew plus our

Night Owl escorts met up in the BDA shack and knocked down a few "brewskys" each while watching the mission tape on the oversized screen. The enlarged view helped the personnel who worked in the BDA shack determine what was destroyed. When we saw that 80-foot truck on the big screen, it became apparent to all of us what it was. That truck contained four SA-2 missiles. I felt particularly good in destroying that target. That was our "payback" for the loss of Spectre 13. The Intelligence (Intel) NCO who ran the BDA shack told me that he was going to keep our entire tape intact and use it in its unedited form for the "Best of the Month" tapes that were put out each and every month. In addition, the Intel NCO also felt that it was a perfect training tape, and he would send a copy to our home base at Hulbert Field in Florida to be used for that purpose.

On the way back to the O' Club for some chow, Dave (my IR) asked me why I attacked that truck first. I told him that I normally would've hit the first truck and the last truck in order to trap the remaining vehicles along a narrow jungle trail. But my instinct, at some unconscious level, told me to attack that truck first. I told Dave that I was learning to appreciate that inexplicable, innate sense. It was something that would make me a better FCO and a better crewmember. I also knew that in me, it was very strong. Dave was almost twenty years older than I and was like an older brother to me. He smiled and confirmed my opinion. He told me that was one of the reasons I was among the very best FCOs in the squadron. He also told me that everyone on the crew really appreciated having me as their fire control officer. I felt really good about that. When I was with crew number one, I was home!

About two weeks later, my crew's gunners received a no-notice evaluation ride from the chief gunner, Chief Master Sgt. Hudson who stood 6'6" inches tall and weighed 265 pounds. His body fat had to be less than 1%. Sgt. Hudson was one of the strongest men who I have ever encountered in my life. He reported directly to Col. Canham. No one, and I mean no one, could give that man an order outside his flight duties except the commander himself. If there were discipline problems with his gunners, he took care of it. In the year I was there, I received absolutely perfect military courtesy, respect and obedience from virtually every gunner in the squadron. If you wore a black Spectre hat and were an officer who flew with the gunners, you received their best behavior and superb discipline. However, if you were not Spectre, it was wise never to order them around. The gunners as a group were among the toughest enlisted men in any service. Their loyalty to the officers who flew with them was unmatched in any other group that I've ever seen.

I wasn't sure why my gunners were getting a no notice check . . . until about a week later. The chief heard reports that I was using different gun settings. I guess he wanted to see for himself. As per usual, I gave my gunners the settings based upon calculations from FCO reports for the last five missions of that particular aircraft. In the AC-130A, only the pilot and the FCO have access to all the separate interphone systems used by the crew. I generally listened to all of them in order to know what was going on within the entire aircraft. I heard Chief Hudson complain that we were not using the posted gun settings. I heard Army Armstrong tell him not to worry: "FCO knows what he's doing." (FCO is pronounced phonetically as "foco")

After we were airborne, we went to a safe area in order to tweak the weapon system before going into a very hostile environment. The tweak took less than 1 1/2 orbits. Circular error was less than a mil or 10 feet. I heard my gunners telling the chief, "We told you that he knows what he's doing. We got the best damned FCO in the squadron!" We had a successful mission, and after it was over, Chief Hudson asked me how I came up with those numbers. I gave him a synopsis of the method I was using and the assumptions upon which they were based. I'm not sure he understood the math involved, but he did appreciate the results . . . faster tweaks and less time over target. That increased both the safety of the crew and their effectiveness in accomplishing the mission.

Three days later, I was offered the position of instructor FCO which I gladly accepted. At this time, I was the most junior A-model FCO in the squadron. Virtually all the new guys who I would instruct would outrank me. But in combat, ability and effectiveness trumps everything.

Early in the second week of June, 1972, two things happened that really affected me. The first was that my crew, except for me, were all getting two weeks of leave. I would be flying exclusively with other crews. I was used to doing this when we were trying to protect An Loc during the second Tet Offensive. This opportunity allowed me to demonstrate, to other crews, the effectiveness of the new way of determining gun settings. Virtually every pilot I served really appreciated how much easier it was to get in and maintain firing geometry (the perfect orbit around the target) when the computer counts needed to adjust gun line error was reduced to numbers less than 15 mils.

The second event that affected me was the departure of my old roommate, Andy Stone, who was "returning to the world" or otherwise, going home. He was relieved to be no longer involved in taking another life. He missed his home country, particularly the mountains in which he was raised. But he was depressed because of the letters he received from his wife Heather. She had become thoroughly entrenched in the anti-war movement, and she wanted a divorce. Some of the pretty Thai women who populated our base tried to tempt him and although he would kid around with them, he stayed faithful to Heather. She, on the other hand, made it clear that was not true for her part. Heather not only was unfaithful, she made sure that he knew of it. In my year there, I never saw anyone leave combat as depressed as Andy was when he departed. He was ordered to Mather Air Force Base as an instructor navigator. Once in California, he hoped to salvage his relationship with his wife.

My own opinion of her was that she was a spoiled brat. Heather was a product of wealth and privilege. She was used to getting her own way . . . sometimes with just a smile. She was an exceptionally pretty girl who used her good looks to obtain what she wanted. I was never impressed with her ability to think "outside the box." She took to the liberal orthodoxy with little thought. Heather wanted to be accepted by her friends at Berkeley more than she wanted a marriage with Andy. She was the perfect embodiment of her "good" intentions outweighing the consequences of her actions which obviously were not an import- ant consideration in determining her behavior. She made Andy miser- able and almost destroyed a very good man.

Andy was due home by the middle of June. The Air Force granted him a full month off before he had to start training to become an instructor navigator. That program took a full two months before he would become a fully qualified instructor. He told me, just before he left, that he was going to do his best in order to salvage the marriage . . . whatever the cost. He was, and still is, the kindest and most loving person imaginable. It was devastating to see him so depressed. I feared for him as I saw him get on the C-141 "freedom bird" on his way back home to the United States.

12

SPECTRE 11 GULF

June 18, 1972, started off like any other day. My regular crew was on their two-week leave and so I was flying with many other crews. I was excited because it would be the first time that I would fly with my hooch mate, *Capt. Paul Gilbert.* Paul was a quiet, introspective man. He stood about six feet tall, with a slender physique, dark slightly graying hair and dark brown eyes. He spoke with a slight Southwest Texas accent. I spent many evenings having philosophical discussions about music, history and political movements. I really enjoyed these talks as Paul was an intelligent, educated man. When he wasn't flying, he was either listening to classical music or reading some text or writing his fiancée, *Ms. Georgianna Burke.* I never met her, but judging by her portrait which was prominently displayed on his desk, she was a very attractive woman. Like Andy, Paul was absolutely faithful to his fiancée . . . even with all the temptations that were available on our air base.

We drew first frag, and our hunting area was the A Shau Valley. Our call sign was Spectre 11 (Spectre One One). We were to be on station no later than 8:00 PM local time. The moon was totally dark which meant that it would be harder for the enemy to track us with AAA fire. We arrived on station at the prescribed time. Within 15 minutes, BC picked up a target, and I requested that the TN put BC in the computer which he did. Shortly after that, IR had the target in sight. It was a single truck parked in the valley with its engine running. We started into the orbit to tweak the weapon system. On this ride, Paul was the instructor and had a student pilot in the left seat. The student, *Capt. Wilson*, got off the first shot, and I told him what the next heading should be. A moment later:

IO: "STRELLA UNDERNEATH...BREAK LEFT..BREAK LEFT!" [A "Strella" is a shoulder mounted, infrared seeking, surface-to-air missile (SAM).] Student pilot slowly breaks left. About five seconds later, I heard a thud sound on the right side of the airplane. "We're hit...direct hit on number three engine!" (That is the inborn engine on the right side.)

AC: Paul, who was sitting on the right side, sees the engine on fire. He says in a very calm voice, "I got it." He says to the flight engineer (FE), "Fire suppression number three." At this point, the IR and BC left their seats and both departed the booth, headed for the aft opening. The instructor IO, *SSgt. Bill Patterson*, jumps from the aft opening into the jungle below.

FE: "Roger." The BC and IR are now just clear of the booth door.

AC: "I'm going to dive the airplane... see if we can get this fire out." Paul puts the airplane in a steep, high-speed dive with the nose almost perpendicular to the ground. Not only does the fire not go out, it is now streaking more than 100 feet past the tail of the aircraft. "It's not working." Paul pulls up on the yoke, levels the airplane, rings the alarm bell, and says, "BAIL! BAIL! EVERYONE ABANDON SHIP!"

When we heard Paul's last order, both TV (*Lt. Vic Reid*) and I departed the booth. We headed for the aft opening. Just as we got five feet outside the booth door, the right wing broke off from the body of the airplane which put the aircraft into a high-speed, flat death spin. We experienced 11 to 13 G's due to the immense centrifugal force. That meant I no longer weighed 150 pounds, but closer to 1,800 pounds! I literally could not move a muscle. Both Vic and I were plastered against the 40mm ammo racks, located on the starboard side of the aircraft and more than 20 feet away from the aft opening. While my back was against the ammo rack, I could see the dark figures of the aft gunners also plastered against the skin of the aircraft. The plane was on fire and everything took on a dark, red haze. I felt enveloped by the heat surrounding me. I was protected by my Nomex flight suit. Even so, I remember distinctly feeling very warm. I could not escape in any way; I thought the end was near. I looked at the men with whom I was flying with and to whom I would share this final fate. I felt that no man could have better company facing the eternal abyss. I experienced a feeling of absolute peace at that precise moment . . . maybe for the only time in my life. My mind wandered into what I read in the last book of Tolkien's trilogy. After the ring goes into the fire, Frodo and Samwise stumble onto a rock in a sea of lava and Frodo says to Samwise, "I am glad you are with me here at the end of all things." That was absolutely my last conscious thought before the aircraft blew up.

I recalled that everything was reddish, then everything went white, and finally everything went black. When I regained consciousness, I felt much cooler. I looked around, and I was no longer in the airplane. The gunship had exploded into four or five pieces and expelled me like a ballistic missile. I had no sensation of falling, but I could see the trees, illuminated by the burning gunship, rapidly coming at me. I immediately pulled my "D" ring which activated my parachute. Less than five seconds after the parachute deployed, I hit the top of the trees, and using the tree penetration technique that I had learned in survival school, I slithered my way through the branches. I came to a stop. The light generated by the burning wreck gave me enough visibility to see clearly about 50 yards in every direction. I could see the ground was only three or four feet from the bottom of my boots. I hit the quick release and fell onto the floor of the jungle. I was on the ground alone in the A Shau Valley, the most dangerous place for American serviceman in all of South Vietnam.

I felt a great wave of fear which almost overcame me. I calmed myself down and remembered the training provided by the Negritos. I concentrated on that and compartmentalized my fear. First things first. I looked around and did not see any other living being. My first task was finding a place to hide. I found a gigantic tree with elevated roots. The Negritos taught us that at night, when hiding, it was important not to create any kind of silhouette I burrowed into an opening at the base of the tree below the root structure. The large tree that provided my cover was approximately 2/3 of the way from the base of the valley to the top of the hill. That was the perfect place to hide, according to the instructions I received from the Negritos, especially when the hill face had a very steep incline which this one did.

I was bleeding from a shrapnel wound on my neck. I used the camouflage stick to color my face and neck which also helped to close the wound because it contained a coagulant agent. I removed and pocketed my watch as the luminous dial would glow-in-the-dark. I then removed my UHF radio from my survival pack and turned it on. The radio came with an earbud which when attached to the radio would direct all sounds into a small speaker which fit in the user's ear. Only the user could hear the broadcasted communication.

My watch told me that it was 8:43 PM local time. I turned the radio on and dialed Channel A, the UHF emergency frequency, 243.0, and listened. I heard our escort, an F-4 Phantom whose call sign was Night Owl 23 (Night Owl two, three). He was calling on that frequency. "Any survivors of Spectre 11 come up guard."

I waited five seconds and answered, "Night Owl 23, Night Owl 23, Spectre 11 Gulf on guard, how copy?"

NO 23: "Spectre 11 Gulf, I read you loud and clear. Come up channel D." I tuned in channel D. on my radio.

Spec 11G: "This is Spectre 11 Gulf on channel D, how copy?"

NO 23: "I read you loud and clear. Are you in a safe hiding spot?"

Spec 11G: "Affirmative."

NO 23: "Stay on this frequency, and let me get a couple of cuts." He circled my position and used his direction finder to get three lines of position (LOPs). Where they intersected represented my position on the ground. To check the accuracy of his position, he went "Christmas tree" (turned on his lights) and told me to tell him when he was directly over my position.

Spec 11G: When he was directly over me, I told him, "Now!"

NO 23: "Come up in twenty minutes. This frequency."

Spec 11G: "Roger."

Twenty minutes later, I turned on my radio and listened. Night Owl 23 was working with Spectre 11D and Spectre 11P. I waited until they finished communicating and indicated I was on the frequency. Night Owl 23 told me to call this frequency on the hour (10:00 PM local). I told him I would.

By ten that evening, the light from the burning aircraft was almost extinguished. The area around me was darkening quickly. From the time I landed on the ground to this moment, I noticed that the jungle's noises slowly elevated and now were fairly loud. It was a cacophony created by insects and other small creatures. With that background noise, I turned on my radio and spoke softly into the microphone, "Spectre 11 Gulf on channel D, how copy?"

> NO 23: "I read you loud and clear... how is your hiding place?"

> Spec 11G: "It will serve until daylight, over."

> NO 23: "Roger. Come up in one hour... you'll be working with a Nail 44 (OV-10 Recon bird).

> Spec 11G: "Roger." I turned off my radio in order to preserve the batteries.

By eleven that evening, the light from the burning gunship was totally extinguished. The sky and the area where I was hiding was darker than a well digger's ass! Frankly, I now liked the dark. I turned on my radio.

> Spec 11G: "Nail 44 (Nail four, four) Spectre 11 Gulf, channel D, how copy?"

Nail 44: "Spectre 11G, I read you loud and clear. I'm going to over fly your position, going Christmas tree. Tell me when I'm directly over your position."

Spec 11G: "Roger." The Nail bird turned on his lights, and when he was directly over my position, I radioed, "Over!"

Nail 44: "I'll be with you for the next four hours. I want you to come up on the hour, every hour. How copy?"

Spec 11G: "Roger. Will do."

For the next four hours I stayed hidden under the elevated tree roots. The jungle was very noisy. It was filled with the sounds of insects, monkeys and animals whose name and type I did not know. About ten minutes before I was going to make my own 0200 radio call, the jungle suddenly became very quiet . . . and that disturbed me greatly. I made my call at 0200:

Spec 11 Gulf: "This is Spectre11 Gulf, channel D."

Sandy 01: "Spectre 11 Gulf, this is Sandy 01; I am the on-scene commander." (Sandy aircraft were A-1E Skyhawks which was a World War II naval attack aircraft that could loiter over a target for seven hours and was extremely accurate in providing covering fire for ground positions.) He, as did the other two birds, went "Christmas tree" over my position so that he knew exactly where I was hiding.

About 0220 (2:20 AM), I heard the enemy moving into my area. I could tell from their sounds that they were coming from the top of the hill toward the valley, and very close to my position. As the noise level of the jungle subsided, my fears increased proportionately. I took out my Smith & Wesson .38 Combat Special, made sure that all its cylinders had bullets, and placed it on my chest. My heart was pounding as I heard them move closer to my position. I then called Sandy 01. After I established that he was on frequency:

> Spec 11G: I whispered into my radio, "Enemy close... recommend fire my position."
>
> Sandy 01: "Are you well hidden?"
>
> Spec11G: "Affirmative."
>
> Sandy 01: "Maintain radio silence till they pass."
>
> Spec 11G: "Roger."

I gripped my pistol and pointed the barrel toward the opening in the root structure. If one of them stuck his nose into my hiding area, I was going to blow him away. The enemy used toy metal clickers in order to keep track of their comrades. I heard these clickers and their footsteps passed within a dozen feet of my position, both left and right of me, going down the hill toward the valley. About 20 minutes after I heard the last of the clickers and the enemy they represented, the jungle became noisy again. That noise was the most beautiful music I think I have ever heard! The jungle knows when a predator is making its way through its environment and reacts to the presence of predators with silence. When the predators pass, the jungle resumes its constant and loud refrain.

The enemy was unaware of Vic's (Spectre 11D) and my location because they never saw our parachutes deployed. This is true because our chutes opened so close to the treetops. The VC passed very close to both of us on their way to the other side of the valley. They did see Bill Patterson's (Spectre 11P) parachute as he left the airplane just after the missile hit. So, they went through Vic's and my positions on the way to where they guesstimated Bill was hiding. The jungle stayed noisy throughout the rest of the night.

At first light, around 5:00 AM I realized that my nighttime hiding spot was not adequate for open daylight. I found a wonderful hiding place not too far away. It was a briar bush that was near seven feet high and very thick. I worked my way into it. Its thorns were long and sharp. No sane person would stick his hand in that bush. I informed Sandy 01 of my new hiding spot. I told him it was about 50 meters toward the valley from my old position. He acknowledged my new position and informed me that rescue was going to be delayed for three or four hours so that the F-4s could put down enough ordinance to suppress any kind of major AAA threat.

I found out later that virtually every F-4 in country came into the A Shau and dropped numerous bombs, napalm and other incendiary devices into that valley. Their usual "puke" or drop altitude was 6,000 feet above the ground. That morning, I was approximately 1,500 to 2,000 feet above the valley floor. All the F-4s came screaming through the valley, and all were at an altitude well below my position and much lower than their usual drop altitude. I watched for 3 1/2 hours as the Phantoms decimated the enemy forces.

Finally, Sandy 01 called and told me, as well as the other two survivors, that a Super Jolly helicopter (HH-53) was going to pick us up. His call sign was Air Force Rescue 521. I saw the chopper pick up Vic who was injured and required assistance from a PJ who descended onto the ground and helped Vic into the chopper. Vic had a broken ankle, and that's why he needed assistance. I was next:

AFR 521: "Spectre 11G, AFR 521 channel D, how copy?"

Spec11G: "Loud and clear."

AFR 521: "Come out of your hiding spot and show yourself."

Spec 11G: "Roger."

I worked my way out of the bush and walked to the open spot about 20 meters uphill. When I was in the open, I unzipped the front of my flight suit toward the oncoming helicopter and showed them a lot of white skin. We did this so the chopper crew would know that we were Americans. It worked well if you were either white or if you were an African-American. Air Force Rescue had special identification procedures for Asian Americans.

The HH-53 Super Jolly was now over my position. He dropped a tree penetrator down to the ground about six feet from where I was standing. As soon as the penetrator reached the ground, I went up to it, opened a foldout seat, placed the wide strap around my waist and below my armpits, encircled the penetrator with my arms, and finally yanked the metal cord. Then the chopper slowly lifted me from the ground until I reached the top of the trees. We were receiving small arms fire and that's when I found out just how fast a Super Jolly can climb to 6,000 feet which is well above the danger area. Once we were at six thousand feet, the rescue crew slowly reeled me in while I was holding onto the tree penetrator. When I was even with the right-side door, the PJ (Para Rescue personnel) swung me and the tree penetrator away from the aircraft. When I swung back toward the entrance, the PJ released the lock on the metal cord holding the penetrator which allowed me to literally bounce in and along the floor of the helicopter. A small bouncing ball of a navigator . . . that was me. I think I bounced two or three times before I came to a stop on the floor of the chopper. The PJ closed the door and tapped my shoulder three times. That was the signal for me to release my death grip on the tree penetrator. When I got up, the PJ helped me out of the harness. When I was free of the tree penetrator and standing on my own feet, I put my arms around the PJ and kissed him on the cheek! I was one happy camper to be free of the A Shau Valley. Sometime later, I asked that PJ if I was the only one who ever kissed him. He told me about half the guys who were rescued did the same thing. That made me feel a little better knowing that I had company! The chopper went across the Valley, and with suppressing fire from Sandy and the Phantoms, they picked up Bill. Once all three of us were loaded into the HH-53C helicopter, we made a quick dash to the Da Nang Airbase located in eastern Vietnam.

Once we arrived at Da Nang, we were put in an ambulance and transported to the local hospital. There they removed everything we were wearing and placed them in large plastic bags . . . even my .38 Smith & Wesson combat special went into the bag. I was in the shower for over an hour trying to get clean. A medic gave me blue pajamas to wear. I had to see an army doctor so that he could remove the insects that burrowed into my armpits and groin area. That was not a lot of fun. The three of us were on adjacent beds, not knowing what was to come. Out of the 15 crew members of Spectre 11, including my good friend, hooch mate and pilot, Capt. Paul F. Gilbert, the three of us were the only survivors. We didn't know why us and not the others. There are some questions without answers.

Around noon local time, a two-star general came and visited with us. The general asked if we would like to return to Ubon Royal Thai Air Force Base. Bill and I immediately said yes. This was not possible for Vic as he had to be transported to Clark AB hospital in the Philippines for treatment. The general provided us with his T-39 aircraft which is basically a corporate Learjet that holds about a dozen people. His crew flew Bill and me back to Ubon. I would not see Vic again until some-time in September when he returned and was able to resume flying.

Upon arriving at Ubon, there were 300-400 men and all the wing brass, including the wing commander. They were there to welcome us back. Many asked if there was a possibility that others might have survived. I told them that the chances were very small, if at all. It meant a lot to both Bill and me that virtually all who could be there, were there. After a few minutes, they put us on an ambulance and took us to the base hospital. Both Bill and I stayed there overnight. I was grounded for 10 days, because they suspected I suffered a concussion after being blown out of the airplane.

The next morning, someone brought me a change of uniform, and I was allowed to leave the hospital. I would see the flight surgeon once a day for the next 10 days before he would clear me to fly. I asked my commander if I could fly my first frag with my own crew and he readily agreed. During this time off, I worked with *Lt. Col. Wilson*, an excellent pilot, reviewing all classified data on the SA-7 missile which is the one that shot Spectre 11 down. Col. Wilson and I came up with a way of reconfiguring all the gunships as well as the appropriate tactics which should be used to defeat that particular missile system. Our suggested changes were adopted by my squadron commander. This information was classified then, and probably remains classified today. Our squadron faced many more firings of this weapon system without sustaining a single hit.

I continued a practice which I started after I checked out as a fire control officer. After every mission, I would go to the main entrance of the base. Just outside the fenced-in area and along the main access road was the place where the beggars (most of them were leprosy sufferers) hung out. It is an absolutely horrible disease, and it was my practice to give one of the lepers a 500 Baht note (worth approximately five dollars in US currency) after every successful mission. That amount of money would feed that individual for a year.

Many times, I would walk through the town, do some light shopping, and see how the normal Thais lived. I observed that even the poorest American citizens have a much higher standard of living than the vast majority of the folks I saw living in Ubon.

On June 30, my crew was all assembled and I flew my first ride after being shot down. Dave, my IR, gently scolded me when he said, "We go on vacation and you get your ass shot down! What are we going to do with you?"

I answered him by saying, "That's easy . . . don't go on vacation!" He laughed. That was the start of 80 or more missions that I would fly before rotating out of Southeast Asia.

13

THE RAINY SEASON

It was the summer of 1972 which was the rainy season in Southeast Asia. Our mission load was vastly reduced as the rain was so intense that truck movement along the Ho Chi Ming Trail was nearly impossible. Besides, the inclement weather made visual acquisition of any target difficult even with the advanced infrared system. As a result, our mission load dropped off considerably to about one or two missions per week per crew. The squadron used this time to update all our aircraft with a reconfiguration that would allow us to defeat the SA-7 SAM. It also gave us time to train a new group of fire control officers particularly for the A-model system. Since I was the instructor FCO, I was flying about twice as many missions as the average squadron crewmember. By the middle of August, the flight examiner FCO and I completed the training of all the incoming FCOs. Now virtually every A-model crew had their own FCO. Col. Canham was very appreciative of the work that the flight examiner and I accomplished in order to get all crews up to speed and fully manned. By August 15, the flight examiner FCO was due to rotate stateside, and I was named as his replacement. I was also told that I would pick whomever I wanted as the next instructor FCO. The squadron wanted a name by the end of September in order to ensure a smooth continuity of change. Every time I flew with another FCO, I was looking not only to check his competence but also to evaluate his potential as an instructor and as a flight examiner.

After I checked out as the flight examiner, I went to see Col. Canham. I wanted all the A-model FCOs to use my technique in order to compute a more accurate gun setting. The colonel who had flown a half dozen missions with my crew understood the benefits of this change. I requested a two-day downtime for the all the A-models and their crews so that I could hold classes and instruct every A-model FCO. Col. Canham immediately agreed, and in the third week of August, I held two classes, and every A-model FCO attended. Virtually every one of them out ranked me, but they listened and learned.

I carefully monitored all the gun-setting forms over the next month. All the A-model FCOs used these forms and techniques. Even those who groused, and those who didn't, came up to me to tell me how much they and their crews liked the new gun setting procedures. As a result, the average circular error reported by all A-model crews was reduced from over 2.5 mils to less than 1.2 mils. It meant that crews were spending less time over targets and therefore reducing the amount of time they were exposed to enemy fire.

Another interesting result emanated from this change. The Air Force was contemplating getting rid of all the old A-models and replacing them with the updated H-models. After I made this change, the A-models were outperforming the H-models in every measurable parameter a flight. That ended the idea of replacing the A-models.

This change really improved the morale of every A-model crew. Col. Canham was very pleased with the results.

In late August, I started training a new FCO. His name was *Capt. Robert "Bob" Liles*. It was apparent to me from his first training ride until the time I checked him out that Bob was the best student I had in all the time that I was there at Ubon. I informed Col. Canham of that fact and requested that when Capt. Liles completed three months of combat, he be named the instructor and eventually, the flight examiner FCO. Col. Canham informed me that everybody was as impressed with Capt. Liles as I was, and he would follow my suggestion. By the end of December, he would be named as the new instructor FCO. At least that was the plan. Bob and I became good friends. He told me that he was married to a wonderful woman, and he had four beautiful daughters. Like Paul, he was totally faithful to his wife and family.

Most missions we flew during this time were combat support. Because of the overwhelming amount of rain that fell in Southeast Asia during this time, we did not do much in the way of truck hunting or interdiction as the trails were impassable. However, there was one standout mission.

Capt. Tom Watson was one of the many pilots whose crew needed a FCO, and I filled in until we could train one of the incoming navigators to fulfill that role. Capt. Watson, a very good-looking man, had an IQ approaching 200. He also had an absolutely photographic memory. He immediately saw the value of my new procedures as he completely understood the math and the assumptions behind it. Capt. Watson intimidated the members of his own crew because he knew more about each job than the person performing it making it difficult to serve under him. He was quick to question their decisions.

The first time I crewed with Capt. Watson, I had this problem. I was used to the policy that my crew employed . . . basically, I would run the crew in the offensive mode without having to explain myself. During that mission, Capt. Watson kept asking questions that frankly interfered with my ability to do my job as I saw it. The frag board indicated we were going to Cambodia to support an indigenous forward air controller (FAC) who had targets ready for us to destroy. His call sign was "Tiger Claw." We arrived over our operating area on time. This was during the rainy season and the weather was quite abysmal. What exacerbated our sensor problem was the fact that our AADS-7 infrared system was inoperative. Therefore, we relied solely on the LLTV.

Once we were in our assigned operating area, the TN radioed Tiger Claw by using the frequency listed in the frag. The person who answered had a distinct Asian accent which was understandable. He gave us the coordinates that he wanted targeted. There was something about him that bothered me. I was the only one on the crew who was completely and totally uneasy following the directions of this FAC. We put the coordinates into the INS and had TV slaved to that system. I looked at what was on the TV's screen and due to the extensive cloud cover, there was nothing definitive displayed on that particular sensor. My instincts were screaming; I hit the "kill" switch which prevented firing of any of our weapons. Capt. Watson was very angry with me and demanded to know why I did this. I told him, "I will not release the kill switch until he drops two flares." The flares that I asked to be dropped would provide approximately 2,000,000 candle power light from each flare. Reluctantly, Capt. Watson finally agreed to drop two flares. The IO called "Flares away!" Five seconds later, the flares lit and what I saw on TV appalled me. There was, for anybody to see, an entire village with their long huts lined up in rows. The Cambodian family unit usually put all family members in one hut, and as the family expanded, they enlarged the length of the hut. If we had fired, we would have destroyed every generation of every family within that small village. It would have been a catastrophic violation of the rules of engagement (ROEs). When I saw what this FAC (Tiger Claw) was targeting, I told Capt. Watson, "Under no circumstances will I permit fire!" Then I recommended that we go on to our secondary operating area. Since he couldn't fire, Capt. Watson reluctantly agreed. When we returned back to base, I asked Capt. Watson to accompany me to the BDA shack. He did so. It was there that I showed him what the TV displayed once we had the light from the flares. When he saw that, his mouth almost hit the floor. His eyes got as big as saucers and he asked me, "How did you know this? What was your first clue?"

I answered, "I had a bad feeling. I sensed something was really wrong with this guy, Tiger Claw. I can't tell you why . . . I just know that when I get these feelings, I listen to them. You can ask my crew. They absolutely trust my instincts."

Capt. Watson said, "If we had fired, we would have been court-martialed not only for violating the ROEs but possibly even for war crimes."

I answered, "You're right. That's why I hit the kill switch!"

Capt. Watson apologized profusely to me. I told him that he needed to be able to trust his crew more and if he did so, he would be a better aircraft commander. That night "watered" his eyes. From that time on, when I flew with him, he allowed me to run the crew as I did with Major Story. He also followed my advice by biting his tongue and allowing his crew to operate using their best judgment. As a result, he did become a much better aircraft commander. Many times, he asked me to join his crew, but no pilot was better than Major Story, and no crew better than Crew Number One! However, we did become very good friends as I could hold my own with him.

During this period of time from when I was shot down through to the end of October was a difficult time for me. About a week after I was recovered from the A Shau Valley, I received a letter from Ellen. She complained about Nixon's price fixing, the shortage of some consumer items, and then asked me, "Is combat really terrible?" I was appalled by her question. I was on a plane where twelve good and true men had just died. At that point, I just gave up on her. I know she was extraordinarily intelligent and could speak seven languages, but she just didn't have the wisdom to know what was important. Her letter was my last communication from her or to her. I just ignored her and went on with my life. I never heard from her again.

Also, during this time, I tried to write letters to the families of those men who did not return. Every time I did so, I experienced mind-bending nightmares. I endured one really bad, sleep ending, nightmare after writing to Paul's family. Both Vic and I survived because we followed Paul's directions until the end. He never stopped flying that airplane. He never put his survival ahead of improving his crew's chances to successfully exit that aircraft. I sent a letter to his family telling them how much I liked him, how much I respected him, and how much I would honor his memory. One letter was all my psyche could manage.

In the middle of September, Intel was warning us of a potential sapper (commando) attack from Laotian and/or North Vietnamese forces upon our base. After the second Tet Offensive, we knew that the gunships were the most feared weapon system in country. That made Ubon Royal Thai Air Force Base the most immediate and valuable target for the enemy. In Thailand, USAF managed all assistance to the people in the country-side, and, in return, they passed warnings to our intelligence personnel regarding enemy movements and potential threats.

On September 21, we had several hours warning that a fairly large company of heavily armed commandos were making their way toward Ubon from the Laotian border. About a week earlier, I had recommended to my operations officer, *Lt. Col. Tomassini* that we practice assault takeoffs and landings to prepare for an enemy attack either here at Ubon or at some other base. Lt. Col. Tomassini laughed and said that we would lose more airplanes than we would save as the pilots were completely out of practice doing those procedures. When the word about the possible attack reached wing headquarters, the brass decided to launch one A-model gunship. They picked my crew to defend the base. (After all, you might as well send the best.) We quickly scrambled onto an available aircraft. As we did so, the base came under attack. We had less than half of the runway to use. Normally, Major Story would let the copilot take off, but not this time. We helped defend the base for the next eight hours. That included two perfect assault takeoffs and two perfect assault landings. All the enemy commandos were killed. Two of them made it onto the flight line and passed a line of F-4 Phantoms. They did not stop for a moment in order to throw a single grenade at any of them . . . they were headed straight for the gunships. They were killed before they reached our birds. The next day, I saw Lt. Col. Tomassini, and I reminded him that, "We did two perfect assault takeoffs and two perfect assault landings, so what about my idea about practicing them again?"

He laughed and said, "Your pilot is Conrad Story. Because he can do it doesn't mean my other pilots could!" I just nodded my head in agreement.

On October 28, 1972, I flew my last mission with my regular crew. The officers were scheduled to rotate in 10 days and this was to be the last mission that we would fly together. This mission was like the first one I flew with them in that we started with hunting trucks in Laos and were called off to support some troops in trouble in Vietnam. In 4 1/2 hours, we completed a mission without a hitch. When we landed, the ground crew hosed the departing crewmembers with water. After our usual debrief, we assembled for a rousing party in the Spectre Hooch. We all got pretty well plastered, except of course, Major Story, who was not a drinker. I was scheduled to leave on my two-week vacation on October 30 and would not be back to Ubon until November 14. I was going to take a C-141 to Bangkok and there, I was going to catch a TWA flight to London, England, where I would meet my brother. By the time I returned, the officers of my crew would all have rotated back home, so I said goodbye to all of them. I had come to trust all of them implicitly and without hesitation. I would miss them very, very much.

The next day at squadron headquarters, Major Story was cleaning out his desk, as he was due to rotate stateside. Since we were both flight examiners, we shared the same office. He asked me to sit down by his desk. He then said to me, "You know, Blake, that before you came here, my crew was hampered by not having a competent FCO. I read your training reports from Eglin Air Force Base on a daily basis." He started smiling as he continued, "I read about this brash, young, inexperienced captain who insisted on becoming a fire control officer instead of a sensor operator. Your training reports were excellent. I used my position as the flight examiner pilot to secure your services as a fire control officer on my crew. It was one of my best decisions, as you were the missing piece. As it stands today, there is no better crew than ours . . . period!"

I think I turned a little red, and said, "Thank you, sir!"

"Blake, I have one more order for you. You will be getting a new pilot, navigator and sensor operators. My order is very simple: Make them a crew. Your new aircraft commander is a brash young pilot. He's good, but he needs seasoning. It will not be easy, but if anybody can do it, you can."

"I will do my best, sir." With that, we shook hands again and that was the last time I saw my favorite pilot. I left early the next morning for my vacation and when I returned, I met my new pilot and crew.

14

END OF TOUR

On November 1, I joined my brother in London where we spent five days touring the city. Then we departed for Paris for my last week of leave. I took my brother to *Le Gentilly Café,* and we spent a lot of our time there. I was welcomed back there like I was a long-lost family member. The conversation and food were as good as I remembered. Madame (co-owner) made sure that I had some Coquille St. Jacques for dinner before I left. I had four pictures of the AC-130 gunship that my commander preapproved, and I gave several to the owners of the café and one to a French intelligence officer. I enjoyed meeting some of the friends who I made in the summer of 1971. When my week was up, I flew back to Ubon and arrived back on station by Monday morning, November 13, 1972.

Later that same afternoon, I met my new crew. My new pilot, Capt. Mark Mayhew, was just as Conrad Story described him. He was a few years short of thirty years old, a few inches taller than I. He had dark hair, brown eyes and an attitude that he was the best pilot around. His best friend, Lt. Steve Miller, was my new infrared operator (IR). Both of these men were very aggressive in their approach to flying combat. What worried me was that crewmembers who did not respect the enemy and his capabilities were the first to be shown the error of their ways. Unfortunately for those who fly with people like this, their attitude put others at risk besides themselves. These two in particular fed off each other which could lead to reckless actions. Needless to say, I was thoroughly alarmed.

Conflict arose on the first mission I flew with them. We were on a truck hunting mission in central Laos. The IR was transfixed on a hotspot in the road. It was not a truck but an opening in the jungle canopy that allowed the sun to heat that part of the road or trail. When I declared it was not a target, the IR argued with me over the interphone. The pilot sided with his best friend, and we shot up an empty part of the trail. I tried talking with my new pilot, but to little avail. I was growing frustrated.

The next conflict came three days later when we were sent to the A Shau Valley for an interdiction mission. We were up on first frag, so we were on station by 8:00 PM local time. BC picked up one truck sitting in the open with its engine running. IR then picked up the truck and had his crosshairs on it. My instincts kicked in, and I told the pilot to find another target. The pilot argued with me, and the table navigator, much to his credit, gave the pilot a new heading and would not put the IR in the computer. The pilot was really steamed by my reaction and said to me when we got back to base, "Blake, I know you were shot down, but you just can't ignore targets like that. The next time I am going to insist that we fire, period!"

It was about midnight after I had this conversation with my new pilot. I went to the O' Club where I met the crew who replaced us in the A Shau. I spoke with their FCO and asked him if he'd encountered that particular truck. He did indeed. They rolled in on the same truck and were almost shot down. It was a AAA trap, and they were very lucky to survive it. In fact, that incident and their survival was due to the most famous call ever made by an IO (Illuminator Operator). This crew which replaced us in the A Shau came across the very same truck that we encountered in the same location and assumed the normal geometry around the target. They were in the process of obtaining a "tweak" when they got hosed. What the IO saw was one wall of flak coming from the left crossing with another wall of flak coming from the right. It appeared to the IO that both volleys would meet at the airplane in which the crew was flying. This particular IO was a Black NCO who usually spoke perfect English when communicating; not a hint of the ghetto slang that was part of his early environment. The call went something like this: "TRIPLE A LEFT! TRIPLE A RIGHT! STOP THIS MOTHERFUCKER!" The quick-thinking pilot pulled back on the yoke, reduced the power, and performed a power-on stall procedure. The pilot watched in horror as one wall of flak crossed another wall of flak right before his eyes. They didn't know how they avoided getting hit. They barely escaped that trap. I spent the next three or four hours talking with other experienced crewmembers. I was getting ready to leave when the crew that had third frag over the A Shau came and told the same story as the crew that they relieved. I left the O' Club and headed straight for Capt. Mayhew's hooch. I was going to leave the crew. I did not want to fly with a pilot that did not allow me to do my job properly. I knocked on his door, and he opened it up and asked me inside. Before I could say a word, Capt. Mayhew said, "Blake, I think I know why you're here. You're not the first of the crew to see me tonight. The gun crew, the table navigator and the IO were here earlier. They told me that I better start listening to you or they would ask to leave the crew. I guess I owe you an apology."

I told him about the conversations I had with the crews that replaced us on station over the A Shau. When I called him off this target, I helped the crew avoid a AAA trap. I informed him of my last conversation that I had with Major Story who ordered me to make the replacement crewmembers a functioning crew. I continued, "If you do not listen to me and not allow me to run the offense, I will leave the crew. I have been approached by at least a half dozen other pilots who asked me to join their crews. The choice is yours!" Capt. Mayhew was momentarily taken aback by my vehemence. He promised me that situation would never happen again. We shook hands, and I told him that I would hold him to his promise.

Several days later, we were assigned third frag back into the A Shau. We were on station at our frag time of 0200 local. After an hour of searching the trails, I saw the IR puzzling over a potential target. I knew immediately it was a truck; it was part of a convoy that was parked, waiting for sunlight in order to move on. The engine had cooled to some extent, but there was enough heat for me to determine that it was a legitimate target.

FCO: "IR, hold that target."

IR: "But I'm not sure..."

FCO: "God dammit! Hold that fucking target!" On main interphone, "Put IR in the computer."

TN: "IR in the computer."

FCO: "TV slave IR." I see TV comply and I load waypoint one into the INS.

TV: "I think I can make out a truck."

FCO: "Put TV in the computer." On booth interphone, "IR search along the trail for other trucks." IR "rogered" my command on the booth interphone.

TN: "TV in."

FCO: "Tweak procedures. Number three gun, HE."

AG: "Number three gun set. HE."

AC: "Pilot in the sight." Capt. Mayhew fires the first shot. "One forward."

FE: "190."

CP: "30°"

IO: "TRIPLE-A UNDERNEATH! BREAK RIGHT! BREAK RIGHT!" Capt. Mayhew immediately initiates a hard turn to the right.

IO: "Clear."

FCO: "Take INS guidance."

TN: "INS in the computer." TV slaves INS.

TV: "Reacquired Target."

FCO: "Put TV in the computer. Next heading 130°."

TN: "TV in."

AC: "Pilot in the sight." Capt. Mayhew fires second round, heading 140°. "Super."

FE: "191."

CP: "30°."

FCO: "Next heading, 020."

AC: Pilot fires third round heading 010. "Super."

FE: "190."

CP: "30°."

IO: "TRIPLE-A RIGHT! BREAK LEFT! BREAK LEFT!" Pilot complies. After a few moments, "Clear!"

FCO: "Wind 110 at six, counts four forward and two down."

TN: "Computer set."

FCO: I see that TV has already reacquired target. "Clear to fire."

AC: "Pilot in the sight." Capt. Mayhew fires off a four-round burst. Seven seconds later, a direct hit on the targeted truck. The resulting fire blinds the AAA gunners on the ground.

I then directed the IR and TV to find other targets. With the light from the burning truck, TV picked up three more trucks which were destroyed in less than one half of an orbit. About 30 minutes later, BC picked up movers, and we did the same thing there. We were in and out avoiding Triple-A until that first truck was destroyed. And finally, in the last half-hour on station, we came across another small convoy. All in all, we destroyed 14 trucks in three target areas.

When we returned to base, Capt. Mayhew invited the entire crew into the BDA shack. The Intel personnel put my tape into the player and opened up the display on the ultra large screen. I started taping from the time that IR was indecisive as to whether or not he had a target. I did not say a word as I let the tape do my talking for me. Capt. Mayhew was very impressed with my work and from that moment on, I had no further problems working with him. The next time we briefed before a mission, Capt. Mayhew made the same statement that Major Story made to the booth personnel: "The only voice I want to hear from the booth, is Blake's!" I had no further problems with my new crew members and as result, they became a really good crew. I was happy to be able to fulfill the last order given to me by Major Story.

The first week of December, we pulled third frag into central Laos doing a truck hunting mission. The weather was not particularly good and neither BC nor IR were picking up any movers. Our operating area was in the Highlands of south-central Laos. IR picked up a strong return of some kind of heat emanating from a mountainside approximately 500 feet below the top of the mountain. I ordered TV to slave IR, and he complied. I looked over the TV and saw that he had no return whatsoever. We had a heat source of unknown origin. Again, my instincts kicked in. I ordered IR in the computer and we went into tweak mode. We could only get a return on IR for 130° of a 360° orbit. Therefore, I initiated a two-shot tweak at the beginning and the end of when the IR return was visible. I had the TN adjust the firing altitude to reflect the altitude of the target, not our altitude over the terrain below. By the second orbit, I had an acceptable tweak which the TN put in the computer. I gave the pilot his firing parameters. We would fire only in that part of the orbit where IR could still see the target. I ordered number four gun loaded with mesh metal and cleared the pilot to fire. In the approximately 1/3 of the orbit that IR had visual acquisition of the target, Capt. Mayhew fired off three bursts . . . each burst containing four shots. I could see on the IR that some of that Mesh metal actually hit that hot spot. We were coming to where the IR was going dark when all hell broke loose. The ensuing explosion was the biggest one I experienced in my year there. First, the shock wave emanating from the explosion pretty severely buffeted our aircraft. Next, the IO told the pilot to break right, as there were pieces of the mountain coming up near our position in the orbit. The pilot complied. It took a full three minutes or more after the explosion occurred for both the TV and IR to recover from being automatically shut down due to the combined excessive light and heat energy. When both sensors recovered, I asked the pilot to circle the explosion area so that we could get it on tape in order to provide more information to the Intel personnel in the BDA shack. Capt. Mayhew did not need computer guidance of any kind. It was easy enough for him to circle that burning mass visually. He gladly complied with my request.

When we got back to base, everyone, including our F-4 escort crews, hurried off to the BDA shack. We all wanted to see what in the world it was that we hit. Capt. Mayhew provided the beer (he was learning), and we all put our feet up and watched the entire sequence that I taped upon the ultra large screen. We went through the sequence twice. It became apparent to all of us that what we were seeing was a cave opening. The energy that IR picked up was the body heat from the enemy combatants who were holed up in the cave. Obviously, the enemy was using that cave as a storage area for their explosive ordnance. When our crew skipped in at least three or four rounds of mesh metal, we ignited a stash of ammo and ordnance. I was glad that we taped the results when we circled the mountain after the explosion died down. Intel estimated that we blew some 500 feet off the top of the mountain! I am not sure to this day what kind of ordinance would create such a big explosion.

On December 18, 1972, Pres. Nixon instituted Linebacker 2. This was an all-out operation which brought the B-52 bombers into the war to be used against strategic targets located in North Vietnam.

As result of this operation, the rules of engagement (ROEs) were drastically changed. The only target up north that was off-limits was the dikes and dams. Had we gone after them, particularly after the end of the wet season, we could have flooded and killed about 90% of the population of North Vietnam. The change in ROEs even filtered down to the war in the south. It was easier to obtain permission to fire in all instances. Our normal escorts of F-4 Phantoms were now directed up north for chafe drops and Mig Cap Missions in order to protect, as much as possible, the B-52's making their bombing runs against targets in Hanoi and Haiphong Harbor. We lost approximately 25 B-52's in the first three or four days of Linebacker 2. By the fourth day, the North had run out of missiles, and most of their Mig fighters were either shot down, or their airports were made inoperative by the constant bombing. Therefore, Mig Cap was unnecessary for us; besides, there were no spare jet fighters to go south.

The most dangerous flying time in the span covered by Linebacker 2 occurred during the first day when the enemy had all his defenses intact. Flying during the first day of Linebacker 2 also illustrated the leadership style of the 8th Tactical Fighter Wing. The first group of F-4s were led by the wing commander. The second group was led by the vice wing commander, and a third and last group was led by the commander of the 497th Tactical Fighter Squadron, also known as the *Night Owls*. At Ubon and the 8th TFW, leadership was by example!

On December 21, the fourth day of Linebacker 2, we were scheduled for a second frag for a combat support mission in South Vietnam. Our call sign was Spectre 15. We departed approximately 30 minutes late due to a minor maintenance problem. After we were airborne, we picked up a Mayday transmission from the Table Navigator (TN) aboard Spectre 17 on UHF 2. Our TN answered his call.

Spec 17 TN: "MAYDAY! MAYDAY! Spectre 17."

Spec 15 TN: "Spectre 17, Spectre 15, how copy? What is your condition and your location?"

Spec 17 TN: "Spectre 15, read you 5 x 5. We are 40 NNW of Pleiku, just inside the Laotian border. We took three 57mm rounds between the number two and number three engines."

Spec 15 TN: On interphone, "Pilot, heading 105°, max speed."

Spec 15 AC: "Roger."

Spec 15 TN: "Spectre 17, Spectre 15 is approximately 90 miles from your position. How is your fuel?"

Spec 17 TN: "We have 8,000 pounds, but we are using 20,000 pounds an hour."

Spec 15 TN: "Where is the fuel going?

Spec 17 TN: "It's leaking amidships. The FCO told me we have six inches of fuel on the floor of the cargo department."

Spec 15 TN: "You do not have enough fuel to make the fence (Mekong River). Get out of that airplane now! Do you understand? Get the fuck out of that airplane now! We are approximately 20 minutes from your position, and we will provide you cover. Get the fuck out of that airplane!"

Spec 17 TN: "The pilot has ordered everybody to stay in their seat. He's determined to fly back to Ubon."

Spec 15 TN: "I repeat. You do not have the fuel to make the fence. I don't care what the pilot said. Get the fuck out of that airplane NOW!"

Spec 17 TN: "I think..." That was their last transmission. Spectre 17 exploded and my pilot, copilot, flight engineer and navigator saw the massive explosion even though, at this time, we were 80 miles away.

Spec 15 AC: "Oh my God!

After Spectre 17 exploded, we were ordered to return to our original mission. The job of covering the wreckage area and looking for survivors was given to Spectre 07 which was closer to the wreck site. When we returned, we found out that fourteen out of the sixteen men aboard that aircraft lost their lives. Included in the group who did not survive were *Capt. Robert Lyles* and *First Lt. Delma Ernest "Ernie" Dickens*. Both of these men were really good friends of mine. Whenever I think back to these days and when I say Kaddish, the Jewish prayer for the dead, they come into my mind, as I pray that the one God will give them eternal rest.

The next day, the entire squadron assembled and was addressed by Col. Canham. The old man was both somber and extraordinarily angry. The loss of this gunship and its crew was obviously very hard for the colonel to take. I will remember his exact words as long as I live. The fact that the aircraft commander, *Capt. Harry Lagerwall*, ordered his men to stay in their seats when there was six inches of fuel on the floor of the cargo compartment was, according to Col. Canham, "A complete and total abuse of authority!" He went on, "In my opinion, this was a case of 13 murders and one suicide!" Col. Canham told us that from then on if any crew member felt, after some catastrophic event, that the plane was not flyable, "Then each of you have my permission to abandon ship. You do not have to wait for the pilot to give you the order." The colonel took his time and looked at each of us. He went on, "And pilots **will not** give such an order as 'to remain in your seats' in the future! NOT MY PILOTS . . . PERIOD!"

By the end of December, we were hearing rumors of an impending cease-fire. Because of that, our missions were held down to about one or two per week. I was scheduled to rotate home around the third week of February, 1973. In early January, I received my new orders. My next duty assignment would be as an instructor navigator at Mather AFB. I was very happy with this assignment because it meant that I would see Andy again. After receiving my orders, I had to arrange my whole baggage shipment back to the States and Mather Air Force Base in particular. This chore took me to a shack located approximately 50 feet off the main runway. I walked to the shack to arrange my shipment and, in particular, the date and time that the movers would come to my hooch to pack up my whole baggage. As I arrived at the shack entrance, I witnessed the departure of three flights of F-4 Phantoms. Each flight consisted of four F-4 Phantom jets with each carrying 18,000 pounds of ordnance. They were all flying northeast in order to bomb targets in North Viet Nam. They all revved up their engines to full afterburner power and departed together as one four-ship formation. The power generated by the eight jet engines of the flight literally shook the ground for hundreds of yards. I was by the shack and both the building and I were literally shaking as the ground moved below my feet. Seeing a full military powered four-ship departure was one of the most awesome sights that I can remember.

On January 26, 1973, I flew my last combat ride. After I landed, I walked around an AC-130 Gunship for the last time. I put my hand on the nose of the airplane and whispered to her, "I have 177 combat rides . . . and I still have trouble believing what you can do!" The AC-130A Spectre gunship is and was an awesome weapon system. Its first designation when it entered combat was the FC-130A, or fighter-cargo aircraft. That's why on the entrance of the 16th SOS building the following was etched in stone: "The Home of the Fabulous Four-Engine Fighter of the Wolfpack".

The A-model was the only Hercules aircraft that had no hydraulic control de-booster. If the pilot turned or pulled the control yoke, there was an instantaneous reaction to the aircraft control surfaces of 4,000 pounds per square inch. All other Hercules, and all other cargo aircraft for that matter, have de-boosters which slows the reaction caused by the pilot's movement of the control yoke. The de-boosters are placed in the aircraft to limit the possibility of the pilot's sudden yanking or turning the control yoke so hard that the maneuver will result in the aircraft experiencing more than three G's in any of the three axes of flight. In one instance, I was in the plane when Capt. Mayhew, in order to avoid a missile strike, made a 7 1/4 G. turn, and the plane still flew and avoided the missile. The A-model was the only cargo aircraft ever built that could withstand such a violent turn. Its wings were specially reinforced in order to accomplish all aerobatic maneuvers. It was the only model that had pressurized fuel supply so that the engines would receive fuel regardless of the attitude or the G loading of the aircraft. All other cargo planes, including other versions of the Hercules aircraft, had gravity fed fuel. These aircraft could not go inverted nor do aerobics, even if their wings could stand the excessive G forces, because they would stop flying due to fuel starvation. Our A-model gunships had the huge, three-bladed prop which were particularly responsive at lower altitudes, i.e., generally at or below 20,000 feet. Those big props gave the pilot at low altitudes an immediate acceleration response which was further enhanced by the fact that the engines were upgraded to the E model version. These E-model engines were designed for airplanes that weighed 50,000 pounds more than we did. The aircraft had an excessive amount of power going to the props at low altitudes which gave it an extraordinary mobility when airborne. In other words, if all other cargo aircraft were like SUVs, then the A-model gunship was like a Ferrari!

The next day was the formal cease-fire. I wasn't scheduled to leave until February 25. I was asked if I would spend three days at Clark AB in the Philippines to address the group of students at the Jungle Survival School while taking care of my unusual medical requirements. I readily agreed. From there, I was scheduled to take another DC 8 "cattle car" ride to Honolulu. From there I would fly to San Francisco. My month's leave would start upon my arrival stateside. I would have to report at Mather Air Force Base no later than April 1, 1973.

Having three weeks off the flight schedule was a mini vacation for me. The first day, I slept around the clock again. That was the third time I did that in the year I spent in Ubon. I enjoyed the company of my squadron mates. My new crew members really enjoyed playing racquetball, and we played a lot. However, the ones with whom I most wanted to share this time were either stateside or dead. In some ways, it was a very melancholy time for me. Saturday, February 18, I attended the last So-Wa-Dee party (good-bye party) at the Officer's Club before departing Ubon. I was expected to say a few words as I was one of the ones leaving. Unbeknownst to me, all the gunners came uninvited into the Officer's Club. They quietly bracketed the sides and the back of the room. After my speech, they quietly left the club. They were not supposed to be there, but there they were! The wing commander, to his credit, allowed them to show this token of respect. I was moved greatly by this gesture. I think they appreciated my ability as a FCO. Whenever we returned from a mission where we fired the Vulcan cannons, I always helped the gunners shovel the spent 20mm brass into large steel containers. I never asked them to do anything that I would not do myself. I have never met a more loyal group of men than the aerial gunners of Spectre!

One week later, I was on a C-141 as a passenger on my way to Clark Air Base. I spent the next three days as a guest of the Jungle Survival School personnel. There on the Wall of Fame, I found my name and the location of my shoot down. This Wall contained all the names of those crewmembers who successfully survived being shot down. I told my story to the present class of students and all the instructors assigned to the school. Afterwards, they asked questions which I answered as fully and honestly as I could. I also went to the hospital for a two-day check-up to make sure that my cancer was still fully in remission. Part of my personal responsibility was to complete an extensive annual physical in order to maintain my flying status. Clark AB had an advanced, well-developed hospital, so I "filled that square" while I was there.

On February 28, 1973, I departed on a DC-8 for my destination, Honolulu, Hawaii. When we landed, I was taken by the SP's (security police), because I had a sealed package of 1,000 pills. These were the thyroid pills which I carried when I flew as part of my personal survival package. While all the other passengers got a chance to see something of the island, I spent the next six hours in the SP area awaiting confirmation that I was carrying medicine and not drugs for sale in the States. This was my first, but not my last taste of what it was like to be a returning Vietnam combat veteran. And believe me when I tell you, it was not a good taste! Finally, I was allowed to board an aircraft bound for San Francisco. I never got a chance to look around and see something of Hawaii.

I arrived in San Francisco about one in the morning, local time. I could have spent some time there, but I was anxious to see my family. My mother and father, at their advanced age, were now spending winters in West Palm Beach, Florida. I went to the United Airlines ticket counter and asked for space available either to Miami or to West Palm Beach. The ticket agent had an opening for a flight leaving at 2:00 AM arriving in Miami at nine o'clock in the morning. I accepted that flight, and the agent added my name to the manifest. I was in my class-A uniform which made the flight free for me. When I was sure that I had a definite ticket, I called my parents in West Palm Beach and told them to meet me at Miami International Airport. They were very excited to hear my voice and said they would be there.

By the time I reached the gate, I saw my parents waiting just outside the passenger area. The first one to see me was my mother. She raced up to me and held me. Then she started to cry. For the next 15 minutes, I held her as she literally cried her eyes out. In that one moment, I knew with every fiber of my being how much I was loved. Dad waited his turn and when Mom finally let loose, he also gave me a big hug. It was great to see them again. They never did know what I did the year I flew combat. I did not want to worry them and the less they knew, the better they would sleep.

I spent the next week with my parents, but I was anxious to see JG and his newly expanded family. I called JG and told him that I would be going to New York the next morning. In the year I was gone, he had made partner and with his bonus money, he could afford to buy a new home in the Dublin Hills Estates, located in the western part of Suffolk County. He gave me his new address and some driving instructions to get there. I told him that I would be there around five o'clock the next day.

The next morning, Dad drove me to the West Palm Beach Airport where I boarded a plane for LaGuardia Airport. My brother, Marvin, who supervised my dad's business in his absence, met me there. He took me to the truck dock. Marvin would inherit the business as I was immersed with my Air Force career. Again, I traveled in my class-A's. When we arrived and parked near my dad's office, I got out of the car in order to look around and see the changes that were made. There was my old foreman, Ike. He took one look at the ribbons on my chest, just below my wings, and said, "Where the hell have you been?" I told Ike that my parents didn't know that I was in combat, and I wanted to keep it that way. He agreed to keep my secret. I visited with some of the men with whom I used to work, and it was very pleasant. By three o'clock in the afternoon, Marvin drove me to the family home. I put my stuff away and changed into civilian clothes. I had the use of my mother's car as they would not return until the end of April. I left the house about 4:30 that afternoon and drove to what I thought was JG's house.

As it turned out, I knocked on the door of JG's neighbor. These fancier homes did not have the house numbers prominently displayed, so I thought I was knocking on JG's door when a petite and very cute brunette wearing shorts and a halter top, opened the door and said, "Hello, can I help you?"

"Yes, you can. You can let me take you to dinner tomorrow night," I responded.

She laughed and said, "Do you always knock on strangers' doors looking for a date?"

"Well actually, I was looking for my best friend, JG, otherwise known as Jared Gladon. I know that he lives somewhere around here. In fact, I thought this was his house. But meeting you was a very fortunate accident."

"He lives in the next house," she said as she pointed to the house immediately to her right. "About tomorrow night, what do you have in mind?"

"I know a great restaurant in Oyster Bay that serves excellent seafood. My name is Blake, and JG and I have been best friends since we entered college together as freshmen. What's your name?"

She smiled and said, "My name is Lisa Stein."

We shook hands, and I said, "Lisa, it is a pleasure to meet you. How about six o'clock tomorrow evening? I promise, I don't bite!"

She had a firm grip, which I liked in a woman. "How should I dress? Is it a fancy restaurant or an informal eating establishment?"

"I'll be wearing a tie and jacket. You can take your cues from that. I'll be here at six."

We said our goodbyes, and I wandered next door to JG's house. I knocked on the door and was met with a hug and a kiss from Hope. Daniel came running up for me to pick him up and hug him. He was all excited to see his "Uncle Blake." A few moments later, JG entered. He'd already changed into a sweatshirt and blue jeans. We hugged each other for a long time. It was so great being with my second family again. I asked where Elizabeth Mae was. Hope told me that she was down for a nap and would be up in about a half-hour.

Hope wanted to show me her new house which I wanted to see, so I got the Cook's tour. It was a beautiful three-bedroom ranch. Hope did a great job decorating it. After the tour was over, we retired to the den. They had a lot of questions. I wanted to get to all of them, but I told them that we could talk after both children were put to bed. JG informed me at this time that he was a full partner, and he was running the office located in Huntington, Long Island. He had to travel to the city about three times a month unless there was a major case that needed his expertise. He had to work long hours, but his income was now six figures and regularly increasing. While I was away, JG's father passed away. What made it easier for him to accept that both his parents were no longer alive was the fact that he and his dad had completely reconciled. Hope and the children she bore really opened Mr. Gladon's eyes and softened his approach to his only son. I was sorry that I wasn't there for my best friend when his father passed.

Hope told me that she loved being a mom, but she still wanted to go back to school to earn her advanced psychiatric social worker degree allowing her to establish her own practice. She would wait for Elizabeth Mae to start kindergarten and with both children in school, she would go back to being a part-time student. It was then that I heard a crying sound coming from one of the back bedrooms. Hope got up and retrieved her daughter. About three or four minutes later, she came out holding Elizabeth Mae. The last time I saw her, she was a babe wrapped in some kind of blanket. Now she was on the brink of being a toddler, and she was absolutely adorable. Her blond hair was starting to fill in. She definitely had blue eyes and the cutest little smile. Hope let me hold her, and she started to feel my face and looked at me with some curiosity. The fact that I had a mustache really fascinated her. After a while, she wanted to return to her mom and made that wish abundantly clear. I handed her back to Hope and told her that her daughter was beautiful. I looked at JG and said, "Thank God she looks like her mom!" He laughed and nodded his head in agreement.

Hope took both children and fed them. In JG's home, the children did not eat with their parents until they were at least seven years old. That was the way he was raised, and that's what he was going to do also. It was almost eight o'clock by the time we sat down to eat. The food was superb. Hope had become a great cook. When she finished serving and could sit down and join the both of us, I told them of my conversation with their next-door neighbor. JG looked at me and said, "You son of a bitch! You've got a date with Lisa."

"I do. I learned in Southeast Asia to never pass up a target of opportunity!"

"What do you know about her?" JG asked.

"All I know is that she looks very cute in shorts and a halter top. Besides, I liked her smile."

Hope said, after hearing this banter, "I met her parents and they seem like good people to me. I've been over to their house several times. All I know about Lisa is that she was a student at Berkeley. She's home for just two weeks to visit her parents, and she will return to California where she is working."

After that, the conversation became quite serious. I related to both of them some of what happened to me in the year I was in-theatre. This was not easy. There is a barrier to communication between those who experience combat and those who never did. I did my best to tell them what it was like to be part of a gunship crew. What they could understand and interested them the most, in particular, was the night I was shot down. I related that whole experience in a great amount of detail to both of them. What I wanted them to understand, more than anything else, was the unbelievable feeling of peace that I felt when the wing broke off, and I was trapped in a burning airplane that was in the process of completing a death spiral. I think by trying to explain this feeling to them, I was also trying to understand what I had felt and why I'd felt that way.

We talked until midnight. I could see both Hope and JG getting tired so I told him that I had to go back home to rest. I told JG that I would let him know how the date went with Lisa. I returned to my Syosset home about one o'clock in the morning. I took a shower and fell into a troubled sleep. I suffered nightmares whenever I talked about that night in the jungle. That night was no exception. Finally, after getting up and reading some of Tolkien's poetry, I went back to sleep and awoke about eleven the next morning.

Later that day, I shaved and showered. The only suit that I had was my class-A uniform. All my other formal wear was in the baggage that was on its way to Mather Air Force Base. Besides, at 5'8" tall and weighing 152 pounds, I cut a trim figure. I went to Lisa's house and arrived precisely at 6:00 PM. I knocked on the door, and when Lisa opened it, she had a surprised look on her face. She was dressed in a chic, black dress which did a very competent job displaying her attractive figure. "I didn't know you were in the service."

"Yes ma'am. I had to wear this as all my other clothing is making its way to the Sacramento, California area. That's where I'll be stationed. And I might say, you look really good! I'm not one who notices clothing too much, but that dress you are wearing is outstanding. "

Lisa smiled as she made a complete turn in front of me in order to show me the entire dress. Then she said, "Thank you very much. You look very nice yourself! Where are we going?"

I greatly appreciated the 360° view as I responded, "To the Oyster Palace. It's one of my family's favorite places to eat. It's quite formal, but the food is superb. I think you'll enjoy it."

I escorted her to my mom's car and opened the door for her. She was not used to being treated like a lady. It was a change of pace for her. She gracefully sat in the passenger seat, and I gently closed the door after she was safely inside. I made reservations earlier that day, and we arrived about 10 minutes before the prescribed time. A valet took care of the car. The maître d' was dressed in a dark suit and tie. He saw my nametag on my uniform and said, "We have your table for two in the seaside dining room. Will that do, Capt. Blakeman?"

"That would be perfect," I answered. The room was well appointed and had a great view of the Long Island Sound. The maître d' led us to a table with two chairs which provided the customer a scenic view. He pulled the chair out for Lisa, and I sat in the chair opposite her. The server came over and took our order.

I told Lisa what JG and Hope said about her and her family. She told me that she'd graduated this past spring from Berkeley, and she really enjoyed the lifestyle in the Bay Area. She was working in an upscale boutique. She was tired of studying and wanted to take several years off before going back and getting her master's degree. Lisa was an only child, and she had promised her parents that she would go back to school after her 25th birthday. Her field was history, and eventually she wanted to teach high school. Her parents wanted Lisa to come east immediately. That led to a huge fight and the compromise that she would be allowed to do what she wanted before she turned 25. They accepted this accommodation, and that is why she decided to come home and visit, ". . . when this strange man accidentally knocked on my door!"

I laughed and asked her what period of history interested her the most. Lisa concentrated her efforts on American history, and in particular, the women's movement in our country. She gave me a general background covering the last one hundred and fifty years of American history, particularly as it pertained to the suffrage movement and the struggle women endured in order to achieve equality with their male counterparts.

I recounted to Lisa the struggle that my mother endured being a woman, blessed with a superb intellect, and forced by society into a subservient role. The resulting psychological toll suffered by my mother made me very receptive to the equal rights movement for women. Lisa, looking at the uniform I wore, said to me that a military man having such an enlightened opinion surprised her. She imagined that the service was male oriented. I laughed and told her she was right and that: "I live in the military society; I thrive in the military society; but I do have my own ideas."

We conversed for three hours over supper. I ordered a very nice, light white wine with the meal. I limited my intake to only two small glasses. Lisa finished off the rest of the bottle, and I ended with coffee, as I was driving and did not want to do so while being impaired in any way. I asked for the check and paid my bill with a good tip for the server.

After the meal was over, I escorted her to an area where we were able to walk parallel to the Long Island Sound. The sky was absolutely clear, and I pointed out to her the constellations that were overhead. We held hands as we walked and listened to the sounds of water lapping against the shore. I stopped, gathered her in my arms, and kissed her. She responded passionately.

"I don't want this night to end," I said.

"Neither do I. Do you have a place where we can go?"

"As a matter of fact, I do. I have my parents' house, and they will not return until the end of April. Would you care to see it?"

She smiled, and responded, "I would indeed!"

We walked back to the restaurant where I got my car from the valet and gave him a five-dollar tip. He opened the door for Lisa and we got in my mother's car and drove to my parents' house. We made love for the next three hours in my parents' bed! Now, this was the best homecoming I could ask for. It was almost five o'clock in the morning before I returned Lisa to her home. We kissed, and I asked her if she would like to go out the next day. She agreed.

Over the next two weeks, Lisa and I spent quite a bit of time together. I got to meet her parents. They were very nice and very supportive of Lisa and me spending a great deal of time together. We also double dated with JG and Hope on several occasions. One time, Lisa and I babysat for Daniel and Elizabeth Mae so that JG and Hope could have a night on the town to celebrate their anniversary. We spent a lot of time with my brother Marvin who was very taken by Lisa. The two weeks that Lisa and I spent together went by quickly. Even the sex got better as she learned that she could trust me, and as for my part, I was developing very strong feelings for her. I really enjoyed her company, and I was hoping we could develop a more lasting relationship.

I knew she was returning to the Bay Area. I would be stationed not far from there as it was not more than a two-hour drive from Sacramento to the San Francisco/Oakland area. I wanted to see her when I came out West. I sensed a reluctance on her part and I didn't know why. I knew we had an immensely strong attraction for each other. I knew that she liked and trusted me, and I also knew that something was on her mind that affected our relationship. It was my last night with her when I found out what it was.

We were in my parents' bed. We had just made love. I was on my back with Lisa resting her head on my right shoulder and her right arm sprayed over my torso. I could feel her erect nipples as they pressed into my chest. I was gently caressing her back. She was going to leave the following afternoon. Her parents were going to drive her to the airport. Lisa raised her head and gently kissed my lips. I could see tears forming in her eyes and I asked, "What's wrong?"

"I want to tell you, but I'm ashamed," she said.

"Just tell me. You'll feel better and we will deal with it . . . whatever it is."

"One the reasons I've not gone back to school is that I have a drug problem. I have been clean for six weeks now. The man that I loved before meeting you is still deeply involved with cocaine. He's the one that got me using. Being with you has been a breath of fresh air for me."

"I presume he lives in the Bay Area."

"Yes, he does."

"How do your parents feel?"

"They were thrilled when I met you," Lisa continued, "When they knew you were a serviceman and not involved with the counterculture, they were very happy. You're exactly what they want for me. That's why when we stayed out late, they did not object."

"The question is then, how do you feel about me?" I asked.

"I like you very much and if we continued, I could see us forming a very long-lasting relationship. Although, when I first saw you wearing a uniform, I was really taken aback. I was scared of any formal authority because I have been part of an alternative lifestyle for so long. The friends I have in California would absolutely freak if they met you."

"Lisa, I am enamored with you. I enjoyed being with you in every way, shape and form. But I am a career military officer. Drugs in my life and my environment are not tolerated. In this case, the Air Force and my personal feelings are one. Zero tolerance . . . period. If you decide you want to see me when I get to California, you have to be drug-free. It is absolutely my bottom line and a line that I will not cross."

"Then you are still interested in me?"

"God, yes. Absolutely!" With that, she kissed me passionately, and we made love one more time before I had to take her home.

The next day, Saturday, March 24, Lisa left for San Francisco. My flight was a week later and my destination was Sacramento. When I arrived, I called her San Francisco number. I was told by the woman named Susan who answered the phone that Lisa suffered an overdose and was hospitalized. Susan was one of Lisa's roommates and her best friend. She knew who I was as Lisa had spoken to her about me. I told her to wish Lisa my best with the rest of her life and hung up. To this day, I will never understand why people do drugs and why they wish to alter what could be a beautiful reality. I'm just a man, and I know I don't have all the answers.

15

BACK IN THE WORLD

On April 2, 1973, I started training at the Instructor Training School (ITS). This program would last two months. The first month, we learned classroom techniques and how the Air Force wanted its subject matter taught. The second month, we learned how to teach navigation while airborne and how to grade the students when giving them check rides after every phase. My instructor was Major Trevor Wilkinson.

Major Wilkinson was a tall and lean man. He was well-fit, and he spoke with a clear Alabama drawl. He interjected a great deal of humor and wisdom in his classroom. I heard rumors that he was quite the ladies' man, but I didn't know him on a social level. We always broke for lunch at the same time. We would go to the O' Club for the noon meal. The reason we always ate there was a waitress named Nannette who was one of the four or five most beautiful women I have ever seen. Major Wilkinson's humor was on display when he described Nannette in his slow, southern drawl, "Well, I know she ain't perfect, but for the life of me, I can't tell you why!"

This program gave a beginning instructor a better background for teaching students than anything I have seen in civilian life. When this course was completed, a graduate possessing some competence in the field being taught, would be totally prepared to teach. I know I was.

Shortly after I completed the ITS course, the Undergraduate Navigator Training (UNT) program underwent a major change. For the first nine months I was there as a qualified instructor, we trained under the old program using the T-29 aircraft as our main training aid. That was basically the same program that I underwent as a student. Frankly, speaking as a person who experienced both being a student and an instructor in that old system, I can make this declarative judgment. The educational system and the aircraft that replaced the T-29 produced a far inferior product than the one it replaced. The new aircraft was the T-43A, which is a modified Boeing 737. Both aircraft contained 12 student positions suited for in-flight instruction. The T-43A offered much better instrumentation and a modern digital computer to aid the student. The program was reduced from just under a year to nine months. What was removed was a great deal of theory of why certain navigational techniques work. This program emphasized teaching the student navigator how to operate systems . . . not really how to navigate. It was apparent to virtually every instructor that I knew, that the new system would deliver an inferior product. It took the Air Force some three years to recognize its mistake. What finally awakened them to the enormity of the problem was the fact that students who graduated from the new program in the first three years of its usage were failing to pass their initial check ride at a 70% rate when they arrived at their initial gaining commands. As a result, the operational commands had to provide the training that we did not deliver at the basic level.

Every instructor was faced with a dilemma after the start of the new program: Did you teach the syllabus as directed, or did you enhance your course work with sufficient theory to provide students with the knowledge as to why these procedures worked? My experience (as a middle school math teacher who taught all his students advanced set theory in order to expand their own understanding of numbers) made this dilemma particularly difficult for me. On the one hand, I was given orders to teach a certain syllabus. I do follow orders, even those I do not like. But combat taught me that sometimes, you can't. Judgment must apply to all orders. For example, the one time that my crew, at my request, ignored the ROEs in the battle for An Loc resulted in the strong probability that we saved the FAC, the men who served with him, and probably both the mission and the city itself. Also, if UNT instructors augmented the program, the Air Force would not get a true reading of how effective the new program was in fulfilling its mission.

I was convinced that we would turn out an inferior product. In the end, while the Air Force was experimenting, crews from the gaining commands were put at risk with navigators who could not navigate. Furthermore, the individual UNT graduate went into dangerous situations not properly prepared. Probably 80 or 90% of the instructors followed their orders to a T. I was part of the 10 or 20% who didn't. My specialty, particularly in classroom instruction, was celestial navigation. The first class I picked up as the platform instructor (i.e., the teacher who takes a section of a class all way through a phase to include all classroom work and time in a flight simulator) was not a problem, as it was still under the old program. It was my second section and all the ones that followed that I decided to augment the syllabus with theory so as to teach the student navigator why something worked, as well as how it worked. What amazed me at first, and later made sense to me, was this salient fact: The 10 or 20% of us who did not follow the prescribed syllabus and taught theory were almost all, if not all, experienced combat veterans.

I solved my problem this way. At the very end of the radar classroom phase and before the students were scheduled to start celestial instruction, I ordered my incoming section to attend a mandatory Saturday class that would last eight hours. In this additional class, I taught the students even more theory than what was taught in the old program. The amount of theory included in the old program was still not sufficient for marginal students who had difficulty in applying navigational principles. I expanded the theoretical background to be inclusive in every phase of celestial navigation. In the four years I taught celestial navigation at Mather Air Force Base, I only lost two students in Toto in every section I taught, and that happened with my first class when I realized that the theoretical base wasn't strong enough. After those two failed, I did not have another failure for the remainder of my four-year tour. Not only that, all my students passed their initial check ride in their gaining commands. When I was done with them, they were navigators. Moreover, I did this openly. I would never operate behind anyone's back. My squadron commander knew what I was doing and said nothing. It was his way of silently approving what I was doing without leaving a paper trail. Then again, my commander was a combat veteran!

I opened these extra Saturday classes by telling the students that from now on they would see the world as the ancient Polynesian seafarers did because they were the finest celestial navigators the world had ever seen. What were some of the assumptions of the Polynesian word view? First, the world was the center of the universe. Second, all celestial bodies, except the sun and the moon, were painted upon a celestial sphere which rotated around a stationary Earth. Third, the diameter of the celestial sphere was infinity. Lastly, this celestial sphere rotated from east to west every night, and revolved 1° every day, so as to change the sky presentation from night to night and season to season. This obviously is not correct astronomically, but when navigating over the surface of the earth, it works beautifully. Also, celestial computations are rather lengthy, and it is easy to make a computation or entry error. Knowing theory makes finding these errors and correcting them easier and less time-consuming to accomplish. When navigating, time is your enemy. That's why in a navigator's check ride, the largest individual graded item is "pacing" or answering these two questions: Is every required entry and/or task done in a timely manner? Does the student or navigator keep up with the airplane or fall behind? If the navigator is truly competent, he will be ahead of the aircraft. Knowing theory makes a navigator competent.

Within my first year there, I obtained a reputation as a hard, but fair instructor. In every section that I picked up as their platform instructor, I heard more complaining than any other instructor did. However, when the students were finished with me, they were very appreciative. While about a quarter of the students in other sections were washing out of the program due to an inability to successfully integrate celestial navigation in their repertoire, all my students flourished. They were not stupid. Usually by the second week that I had a section in class, they understood that my motivation was to make each of them a truly competent navigator, not a fucking systems operator! That was my driving force, and since they were the ones who benefited, they all came to appreciate me. I remember two instances which really pointed this out.

Capt. John Weiss and four of his classmates from a previous section I had taught, came into my room uninvited, just as my extra Saturday theory class was starting. Capt. Weiss, the leader of the class next scheduled to graduate, addressed the new class. He said, "Kiss your wives or sweethearts goodbye . . . when you are in Capt. Blakeman's class, you will not have time for them. But you will become navigators. We have a special presentation for Capt. Blakeman." With that, Capt. Weiss handed me a package which I opened in front of my new section. It was a Hawaiian grass skirt! The five members of my old section and I all laughed. Capt. Weiss then addressed the class by saying that all of them would become Polynesian navigators! Capt. Weiss and his four cohorts left shortly thereafter. I then proceeded to teach my new section all the theory that they would need.

The second instance was at a squadron party which had approximately three classes and nine sections of students. In this case, a section which I was about to pick up started saying some nasty things that they heard about me. That did not sit well with another section that was about to graduate. The argument got so heated that it actually led to a fight breaking out. After about two weeks with my new section, they understood what all the others knew. My motivation was not to unnecessarily make their lives miserable, but to teach them enough so that they could not only pass the celestial phase of navigation, but become truly competent navigators in their gaining commands. Once they understood this, all other problems dissipated.

During the time that I was checking out as an instructor, I looked to see if I could find Capt. Andy Stone. I knew he was assigned to the same training wing. I found out he was on leave and would not be back until sometime in May. I finally ran into him just before I passed my final check out and would become a certified UNT instructor. It was the third week of May, during lunch, I saw him at the O' Club. He was so gaunt that his uniform was baggy on him. He was always thin, but now he was approaching an emaciated state. We were happy to see each other and after hugs and a handshake, we sat down and ate together.

He told me that he was applying for a hardship separation from the service. Andy had to get out if he had any chance of saving his marriage. Heather, his wife, was now completely and totally anti-military.

I asked, "Will the Air Force let you do that?"

Andy answered, "Not so far, but I retained a lawyer and he thinks that they will. However, I'll get a general discharge, not an honorable one."

"That's terrible. I know how hard the past year of combat was on you. The Air Force should just let you go. You served your country well and deserve an honorable discharge if that's what you want! Andy, are you sure you want to give up flying? I know you really enjoyed your time with trash hauling C-130s."

Andy responded, "Blake, I can't do it anymore. I have trouble sleeping. I'm not eating and I'm depressed all the time."

I told him that he could call on me at any time, day or night, if he needed help or somebody with whom to talk. We talked about some of the guys who we knew in common and the shortcomings of the new program that was about to be unleashed at Mather Air Force Base. I tried my best to comfort him, but to little avail. I had to leave, as my classes were starting and I was required to be there. Besides, Andy had an appointment with the flight surgeon so he had to leave as well.

We said our goodbyes, and I didn't see him again until about two weeks later when he dropped by my room in temporary quarters. Andy was leaving the service that day with a general discharge. He came by my room to give me a trunk filled with his uniforms and other military paraphernalia. He told me to give it away or throw it away. He just didn't care anymore. I told him, just before he left, that I would hold onto them. "Someday, you are going to want this trunk back. I don't know when, but I promise you this: I will hold onto to it for as long as it takes. On that you have my word."

"You're more optimistic than I am, but I really appreciate it." I asked where he was going. He responded, "Two days ago, Heather served me with divorce papers. I have already signed them. She had no intention of keeping our marriage together whether I got out of the service or not. I still love her, but I don't think I will ever forgive her. I'm going to the mountains in Wyoming. I think I will go to the Grand Tetons. It is beautiful, and I know there are other Vietnam veterans living up there." I wished him well. Andy was another one of the 'walking wounded' left mentally scarred from that war. I would not see him again until more than two years had passed.

Just after Andy left, I received orders to personally attend Squadron Officers School (SOS) in Montgomery, Alabama. I would be gone for six weeks. I called Lisa to see if she wanted to come with me if she could stay clean of drugs. I wanted to give her one last shot because I really liked her. I thought if she could become drug-free, then we might have a future together, and I expressed those sentiments to her. She started crying over the phone. I knew she wanted to change her life; she just wasn't sure that she had the fortitude to do so. Hearing the pain and suffering in her voice really depressed me. But I knew, even then, that beating a drug addiction starts with the addict. If Lisa wanted my help, I would have been there for her, but it had to start with her. For the last time, I said goodbye to her and really meant it when I wished her well. It was the last time that I ever heard her voice. As I hung up the phone, I thought of some of the words to a Steppenwolf song called *The Pusher*:

> Ah, but the pusher is a monster,
> Good God, he's not a natural man,
> The dealer, for a nickel, Lord,

He'll sell you lots of sweet dreams,

Ah, but the pusher will ruin your body,

Lord, he'll leave, he'll leave your mind to scream.

God damn, the pusher,

God damn, God damn the pusher,

I said, "God damn, God, God damn the pusher man!"

When I returned from SOS, I looked for a place of my own. I made enough money playing poker at Ubon to make a decent down payment on a two-bedroom townhouse and furnish it. The complex I chose had about twenty fourplexes, each similarly designed. The two end apartments were two-bedroom townhouses and in the middle two were the larger three-bedroom townhouses.

The townhouse adjacent to my own was occupied by a family consisting of a husband, a wife and their four children who ranged in age from ten to twenty-one years old. I became interested in getting to know them, because the third child was a very pretty girl who was 18 years old. Her name was *Christie Lyons* and I found her to be a very nice person. I met her dad, *William "Bill " Lyons Senior; her mother, Gloria; her two older brothers, Bill Junior (whom we called Billy) and Tom; and finally, her younger brother, John.* I met all of them in the first week that I moved in to my new townhouse.

Bill was a large man standing 6'2" and weighing 245 pounds. He was a Korean War veteran who was fifteen to twenty years past my age. His thinning hair was gray, and he possessed very kind grayish blue eyes. He was a master carpenter which meant that he would be able to do virtually any kind of carpentry. He never went past high school, but like my dad, he was self-educated. He enjoyed reading various and sundry books, and he read the *Sacramento Bee* every day. His wife, Gloria, whose nickname was "Chickie" was a very attractive brunette with dark penetrating eyes. They had met when Bill was twenty-five, coming home from Korea, and Chickie when she was fifteen. It was love at first sight. Three days after he met her, Bill asked Chickie to marry him, and she agreed. They were married when she turned sixteen. By the time I met them, they had been married for more than a quarter century. The bond between the two of them was as strong as any that I have ever encountered in my life.

Bill Junior, or Billy as we called him, was a few inches taller than I, with blond hair, blue eyes and a devil-may-care smile. Tom was just over six foot, very blonde, and very good looking. Both boys did very well with the ladies. Christie had blonde hair, blue eyes, stood about 5'4" tall and had a trim athletic body. The youngest, who became my fishing buddy, was John, and he was very small for his age. He stood barely five-foot tall with blonde hair and blue eyes. I really enjoyed fishing the American River and other freshwater venues that were plentiful in northern California. At least once or twice a week, I would be fishing with one or more of the family members, but John was the one I spent the most time with when it involved going out on the water.

Inside the first month that I was living there, I became a member of the family. Over the four years I spent living in that townhouse, we shared everything. In July, I invited them to the awards ceremony where I was to receive the Distinguished Flying Cross awarded for valor in combat, the fourth highest medal that an Air Force member can earn. Bill, who was a marine, really appreciated the ceremony and being there to witness it. For my part, having the Lyons there was, in effect, having my own family present. Everything that happened to me over the next four years also involved the Lyons, and the reverse was also true. I was there for the good things as well as the bad, as they were for me. I can honestly say that there was nothing that we did not discuss as it pertained to the family to which I felt that I now belonged.

There was a fence which separated our patios in the rear. Bill built a door into that fence so that we could go back and forth from each other's townhouses without using the front door. I had the *Sacramento Union* delivered to my house. In the morning, Bill would put up twelve cups of coffee in his coffee maker, and I would put up twelve in mine. Then I would bring over my pot so the family would have twenty-four cups available each morning. Bill and I would swap papers, as the *Bee* was liberal and the *Union* was conservative. We talked about everything under the sun. I believe that having a family available to me and accepting me so totally was instrumental in my overcoming the psychological baggage I incurred from a year's worth of combat.

Bill and Chickie had a very large gray cat named *General Lee*. He was the biggest tomcat I had ever seen. General Lee, as a rule, did not like strangers. But when I came into the Lyons' home, he took to me immediately. Now when I sat down in one of Bill's chairs, the General would leap onto my lap where he would overlap my thighs by least six inches on either side. As I said, he was one huge cat. I once saw him jump from the ground to the top of the carport in a single leap. If I hadn't seen it with my own eyes, I would not have believed it. The fact that the General so readily accepted me accelerated my acceptance into the family. With the General living in my complex, we never had to worry about rodents or any other critters!

In August, 1973, I picked up my first section in the classroom. At that time, I was teaching using the old syllabus which did contain a fair amount of theory. I took to it like a duck takes to water. I loved it so. About three quarters of the way through the classroom presentations, my section decided to have a party. They decided to hold this event in an apartment complex just off base where most of the married students resided. They invited me, and I accepted. At this time, I was not seeing anybody in particular, so I came stag. I put on the clothes I wore when I was in Paris and drove my Harley to the event. The students admired the bike and the wives wanted to take a ride. So, I gave each wife, except the last one who rode with me, about a 10 to 15-minute ride where I kept the speed well under forty miles an hour, as I did not want to scare them. They all enjoyed it.

However, the last wife was special. Her name was Victoria Higgins, and she was married to 2nd Lt. Jack Higgins. She had jet black hair and sparkling, wide-set blue eyes. Her oval face, small nose and generous mouth made her look particularly appealing. She had given birth to a son who was, at that time, eight months old. Looking at her body, one would never know that she gave birth within the year. Her nickname was Tori, and she remains, even today, one of the sexiest women who I have ever met. I could tell that we had a connection on a visceral level. I put her on the back of my bike, and we went for a ride. I took that 'puppy' over a hundred miles an hour, and she loved it. We rode for just over forty-five minutes. I left the party about a half-hour later thinking about Tori and being sorry that there was nothing I could do about the way I felt.

It was the middle of October when 2nd Lt. Jack Higgins washed out of UNT. He failed on his last two check rides and that meant automatic expulsion from the program. I did my best to keep him enrolled, but I was not successful. He had orders to attend missile training school which was part of the Strategic Air Command. Frankly, I stayed in the background regarding both of them. That is until one day, about a month after he washed out and two weeks before he was scheduled to leave in order to attend missile training school, I received a phone call from a teary Tori Higgins. She told me that Jack was drinking too much and was becoming abusive. She was scared for herself and her son. She needed a place to hide while Jack sobered up. I asked where she was, and she told me that she was with one of her married friends, but there was not enough room in that small apartment for her and her son. I had an extra room in my townhouse and I asked her, "Do you want to stay with me for a while until this settles out?" Tori agreed and told me where she was staying. I drove my car to the address she gave me, and she was waiting outside. She only had a few things that she could quickly carry, as she had to leave before Jack became violent. It did not take me long to load her few belongings. We put her son in the baby car seat that she had with her, and I strapped it down in my back seat. We drove to my place.

I set up a spare bedroom for her. I used a small drawer filled with towels as a crib for the baby. The spare room had its own bed which Tori could use as long as she needed to do so. She fed the baby and put him to sleep. We stayed up most of the night talking. She and Jack met when they were students at the University of West Virginia. She was a cheerleader, and Jack was a safety on the football team. They married just after they graduated and just before Jack entered the United States Air Force as a second lieutenant. She wasn't sure that she wanted to marry him, but at the time, she was already two months pregnant.

About midnight, I went to bed. About a half-hour later, Tori knocked on my door and asked if she could come in. I told her she could, and then asked her what was wrong. She entered the bed and asked to be held. All she was wearing was a thin nightgown and panties. She came into my arms. She was trembling. I gently rubbed her back. Tori looked up at me, and I could feel myself drowning in her large luminous eyes. We kissed, gently at first, becoming more and more passionate. I released the ribbon that held her nightgown to her body. She watched me intently as I gazed upon her exposed breasts for the first time. They were small, but well formed, and they excited the hell out of me. I quickly took off her panties and entered her. Over the next two hours, I made love to her three times. Finally, she fell asleep in my arms.

The next morning, I made breakfast for both of us. Tori had small bottles of food for her son, Damien. We all ate greedily. I discussed the situation with Tori regarding her safety. I told her to see the squadron commander, as he would issue orders keeping Jack away from her and her son. She used my phone and called her parents who lived in Elkton, Delaware. She informed them of the situation between her and Jack. Both of her parents were greatly concerned for her safety and told her to come home as soon as possible. They would purchase a ticket for both of them. She wouldn't have to worry about any furniture or other belongings; they just wanted her home safely. She told them that she was leaving in two days.

She could have left that day, but she wanted to spend some more time with me. That was fine . . . hell, that was better than fine with me! She called the squadron commander who understood her plight. He would order Lt. Higgins not to come within 500 yards of his own wife. The Air Force did not look kindly on wife battering. He asked Tori if she has a place to stay. She said she did. I called the scheduling officer and asked for two days of emergency leave which was granted. We spent the next two days together. I purchased clothing for her and Damien so that she would not have to return to her apartment. She gave her parents my number so they could reach her at any time. They called back the next day and gave her the departure information for a flight from San Francisco Airport to the Philadelphia Airport where they would meet and take them home.

The next two days was like a honeymoon. I introduced Tori to Bill and his family. It really helped a lot, because Chickie had a stroller and other baby paraphernalia that she was saving for the time when she would become a grandmother. I drove Tori and Damien to the river where we used the borrowed stroller. We walked along the path which paralleled the American River. Later, when we returned to my townhouse, we used Chickie's crib to provide a better bed for Damien. Two days later, I drove them to the San Francisco Airport. I kissed her goodbye and told her that I would write.

About one week later, I received my first of many letters from Tori. She was safely ensconced with her parents, and she was immediately initiating divorce proceedings. She didn't care about the property settlement or any alimony. She only demanded minimum child-support for Damien. Tori was applying to Delaware University to obtain the credits she needed in order to teach. She would live with her parents until she could find a job and secure her own place. I wrote her back telling her how much I enjoyed her company and that I missed being with her. About once a week, I would run up my long-distance phone bill by talking to her directly.

This was the time that we were transitioning from the old program, using the T-29, into the new program using the T-43A. As luck would have it, the T-43A was equipped with LORAN C (long-range navigation), not LORAN A. The problem for the Air Force was a perfect example of a bureaucratic fuck up. Systems Command controlled how this new aircraft was to be configured. They, of course, decided that LORAN C was much more modern and used by most of the gaining commands. Therefore, they configured this new aircraft with LORAN C. Had they bothered to ask any instructor navigator on base, they would've found out that on the West Coast (where Mather Air Force Base is located) only had LORAN A available. The local fishermen, who were all equipped with LORAN A, did not want to spend thousands of dollars required to upgrade to the LORAN C system. It would take another two years for the Air Force to overcome the political opposition of the fishermen and get LORAN C installed on the West Coast. In order to do an overwater training ride, the syllabus required a four-day temporary duty (TDY) trip to Dover Air Force Base where the students were able to practice and eventually check out on using the LORAN C equipment.

All the squadrons asked for volunteers to take a group of students to Dover Air Force Base and practice their overwater procedures flying over the Atlantic Ocean. This was a lucky break for me as Tori lived about thirty minutes north of the base. I immediately volunteered for all available slots offered by the three UNT squadrons. The new program reached the initial overwater phase in February of 1974, so I got to see her about once or twice a month for the next fourteen months when I was not the primary instructor in the classroom. The wing wanted a cadre of instructors who were qualified to teach overwater navigation using Loran C and who were familiar with the different problems caused by flying into unfamiliar air traffic control zones. Because of my excellent reputation, I was immediately accepted into the initial cadre of overwater instructors. I generally flew these missions with the same group of instructors.

Everyone in this cadre knew why I wanted to fly to Dover Air Force Base. Even the pilots were generally the same ones that we used for every mission. Again, the wing wanted the personnel to be cognizant of the peculiar rules that one must endure when flying on the East Coast. Having experienced instructors and pilots made for fewer mistakes. By the fourth or fifth month of doing this, I had the procedures down pat. By the time we landed and taxied to our parking area at Dover Air Force Base, I had my students debriefed. When we went out for practice rides, I was always the last one aboard the airplane. The other instructors and pilots in the cadre always teased me that I would develop a steel blue 'hard on' the closer we got to Dover Air Force Base! In a word, my very own form of DF steer! They all saw that Tori was always there to meet me, and believe me when I tell you, she was **very** easy on the eyes.

During this time, I was content to keep things the way they were. I did not date others. The sex between us was phenomenal. It never got old because we could only see each other on such a limited basis. We wrote each other several letters a week and would spend an hour phone call about once a month. (Remember, this is before long-distance rates came down.) I found myself caring for Tori more and more. During my trips to Dover Air Force Base, Tori would stay with me in a nearby motel. Her parents would provide care for Damien, and we would spend three or four days together depending on the length of the mission.

On March 10, 1975, I was with Tori at our favorite motel in the Dover area. She was excited that day as she was completing the last of the additional courses required in order for her to receive a certificate to teach in an elementary school. She did very well with her practice teaching and as a result, Tori was offered a position in the Wilmington, Delaware school system starting next fall. I was happy for her and sad for myself as I knew that our regular meetings would cease when she took on a full-time job.

Later that night, after making love, I experienced a waking dream. I'd had them before, but this was the first one that Tori actually witnessed. A waking dream is one where your mind goes to someplace that your body is not. In my case, I was back in the A Shau Valley. Tori told me later that I was calling in "airstrikes to Sandy Zero One." She had no clue as to what I was saying, but seeing me reacting to something occurring only in my mind scared her. I concluded that I was reliving the time when the enemy was all around me, and I requested airstrikes on my position. She awakened me back to reality. I was sweaty and shaking. She held me tight until the shaking was under control. As the dream's effects subsided, I found her holding me started to arouse me. We made love again and I was able to fall asleep.

For the next two days that she was with me, I sensed a sadness in her. I asked Tori if experiencing a waking dream bothered her. She wouldn't answer me at first, and I didn't press it. Finally, the last day that we were together, Tori told me that I was right and that she needed time to work things out in her own mind. We had just finished eating our breakfast, and we were back on the flight line and in her car when Tori turned to me and smiled, "Give me some time to think things through, and I will write to you as to what is going on with me. I do love you."

I kissed her long and hard. I looked into those deep blue eyes and told her, "I love you very much. I would like to have a life with you." With tears in her eyes, we said goodbye. I got out of the car with my gear and boarded the waiting airplane. I didn't know it then, but it was the last time I would see Tori.

A week later, I received a letter from her. This is what it said:

Dear Blake,

I love you. I will always love you. I will always be grateful. You were there when I really needed you. After the horrible experience that I had with Jack, you taught me that there are men out there who can love and not be abusive. For that, I will always be grateful.

But it's just not me anymore. There is Damien to consider and his interests are the most paramount thing in my life. You live in the past. I can only imagine how horrific a year's worth of combat experience is and what it does to the psyche of the individual who goes through it. That waking dream you had really scared me. If it was just me, I could and would, deal with it. But Damien needs stability, and making a life with you on a full-time basis would not be fair to him.

I'm going to be teaching full time in the fall. This is something I've always wanted and now I'm getting a chance to do it. My mom is looking forward to spending quality time with her grandson when I'm away teaching. This is the only place that I can provide a loving environment for Damien to grow and mature without feeling guilty about leaving him.

You will always be in my prayers. I hope God looks out for you and that you find the happiness that you richly deserve. Please don't hate me.

Tori

I received her letter about a week after I saw her in Delaware. Frankly, I had a pretty strong premonition of what she was going to say, but it still hurt like hell. I went over to see Bill and Chickie. I showed them the letter, and we talked well into the night. I was very close to both of them and when they told me that there was merit in what Tori wrote, it made me think. They made me look at the world through her eyes and as a parent which they were and I was not. When I left the house, I was no longer angry. I will always miss her. I did love her. And I will always wish her well. We shared some absolutely beautiful times together . . . that's what I will remember while there is breath in my body. I did not write or call, or try to see her, as I will never go anyplace or be with any person who does not want to be with me. That is a personal anathema to me.

However, every time I hear the Eagles' "Witchy Woman," I think of Tori and her luminous blue eyes:

> Raven hair and ruby lips
>
> sparks fly from her finger tips
>
> Echoed voices in the night
>
> she's a restless spirit on an endless flight
>
> wooo hooo witchy woman, see how

high she flies

woo hoo witchy woman she got

the moon in her eye

She held me spellbound in the night

dancing shadows and firelight

crazy laughter in another

room and she drove herself to madness

with a silver spoon . . .

About three weeks later, Saigon fell to the North Vietnamese. Combining that fact with losing Tori put me in an absolutely deep and dark depression. I didn't know why at the time this event affected me so greatly, but it did. What helped keep me sane was the familial contact and inclusion that I received from Bill and his family. I found that fishing and being near the water was therapeutic. Bill's younger son, John, loved fishing, so he and I would fish all the through the mountainous areas of northern California, generally for trout. If I was not flying in the evenings, I would go over to Bill's house and the entire family (myself included) would watch TV together.

We were all totally involved with a PBS program called *The Discovery of the Nile*. It was a 15-part series that basically was a biographical story of Sir Richard Burton, the great 19th century humanist, author, explorer and philosopher. Every Sunday night we all gathered around the TV as none of us wanted to miss a minute of this show. During the last episode, after Sir Richard Burton dies, his widow, a devout Catholic, burns all his papers. All of us Lyons (both born and adopted) were aghast at the enormity of her crime against humanity. Her narrow-mindedness deprived all the generations to come of her husband's intellect, philosophy and general musings. It didn't matter that we were not very likely to read any of his material. However, we all felt the loss. This was a perfect example of what our combined family life was like.

About 10 days after Saigon fell, a friend of mine visited me. Her name was Casey Thornton. I'd met Casey over in Ubon, Thailand. She was visiting her husband, and I met her in the Spectre hooch. Casey was an attractive, vibrant, blond woman, thinly built with a quick wit and an acid tongue. She and I hit it off immediately. I was strongly attracted to her, and I felt that my feelings were reciprocated. I never acted on it because she was a wife of one of my squadron mates. When I returned stateside, I heard that Casey and her husband were finalizing their divorce.

When I returned from Squadron Officers School (SOS), Casey, who was visiting her father in Sacramento, heard that I was stationed at Mather Air Force Base. She called, and we got together. Casey was not a woman who was seeking a permanent relationship or husband. As she put it, "I tried captivity once . . . never again!" She enjoyed sex and since we were attracted to each other, Casey became my friend "with benefits." About every six months, she would come by the house and spend the weekend with me. Then she would go off to some other place. The amazing fact or coincidence is that she always showed up when I really needed her. This was one of those times after receiving a "Dear John" letter from Tori and after the fall of Saigon.

She knocked on the door and there she was. Seeing that it was Casey made me feel a lot better. I opened the door, and she asked, "Is this a good time?"

I opened my arms and she ran into them. I gave her a big hug and a kiss and said, "As per usual, your timing couldn't be better!"

She looked at me quizzically and I said, "Let me take you to dinner, and I will explain the whole thing to you." She agreed. We left for a great restaurant in the middle of Sacramento, and I told her how I'd met Tori, fell in love and then got dumped. After dinner, I drove to the parking area near the walking path adjacent to the American River. We walked hand-in-hand. It was easy to find our way as the moon was full with just a thin overcast above. I looked at her and said, "Hey Casey, it's a gunner's moon. Now I don't have to worry about it." Casey knew exactly what I was talking about as she had spent a month over in Ubon. She got to know almost all the men that flew with both her ex-husband and me. She was also familiar with the gunship vernacular. It was easy for me to communicate with her as she was over there when we lost Spectre 13 and all thirteen men who flew her.

I told Casey about the conversation I had with Bill and his family after I received Tori's "Dear John" letter. She thought what Bill and Chickie told me was sound advice. We walked in silence for a while with both of us enjoying the moonlit river and the sounds of the water rushing by. I asked Casey if she wanted to spend some time with me over the entire weekend. She replied, "Thought you'd never ask. I have all my stuff for the weekend in the back of my car. When we get back to your place, I'll get it and I'll stay until Sunday afternoon. I have to leave to return to Colorado because I'm finishing up my bachelors' degree." She brought in her suitcase and we went back to my place to enjoy those "benefits."

The next day, Saturday, we decided to go eat and see a movie. Casey wanted to see "American Graffiti." That movie had an excellent review, and it was playing in the base theater. We both enjoyed the movie and especially the music of the late '50s and early '60s. At the end of the film, before listing the credits, they flashed on the screen what happened to each character in the movie. The young, bi-speckled

Terry reminded me of my friend Lt. Ernie Dickens who was killed when Spectre 17 went down. Their outward appearance and personalities were quite similar. Terry's film fate was being killed at An Loc, Vietnam. I wasn't prepared for such an ending. I sat in my seat and quietly wept. I was lucky in one sense. Probably the only person whom I could date and would understand exactly what was going through my mind and emotions was sitting right next to me. Casey quietly held my hand until I was ready to leave. Part of the reason it affected me so deeply is that I was so utterly unprepared for the emotional upheaval created by that particular ending. Ernie and I flew many missions together over An Loc. That was the time period when I was flying with two different crews each night. I thought I was going to see a movie about life in the valley in the early 60's and the music that such an environment produced. I was looking forward to seeing a comedy and instead, I was faced with the enormity of loss, and I had no way to prepare for it.

Casey spent the weekend with me, and I was grateful that she did. She left Sunday, April 27. Six days later, I picked up a new section as its platform instructor. I loved this job more than any other single endeavor that I have ever tried. One of the great experiences of my life was helping a class absorb and then use the theory in order to navigate using celestial bodies. The celestial phase lasted 10 weeks. During that period, I was so busy instructing my section that I had little time to reflect on my own problems and what I felt regarding the tragic fall of Saigon.

After my section passed both the day and night celestial exams, they decided to have a pool party in the apartment complex where many of the married students resided. They invited me and I accepted. The bachelor students also invited some of the young ladies who lived in the apartment complex. This class was led by *Capt. John Weiss* who was the student class commander. John was married to a fine woman, Susan, who initially was very angry with me because I assigned so much homework. But when John and his section mates did so much better in their flight evaluations than anybody else in their class, Susan wasn't so mad at me anymore. She realized that the higher class rank that John achieved would result in his having a greater choice of assignments. Believe me when I tell you . . . Air Force wives were extremely interested in the assignments given their husbands! In the end, she was very grateful to me, as John was at the top of his class.

Susan had a friend whose husband just walked out on her, and she thought we would get along. She introduced me to her friend, Marianne Wilson, who was about two inches taller than I. She had light brown hair falling to just above her shoulders, grayish blue eyes, with a little hook in her nose, a small petite mouth and very long legs. Since this was a pool party, Marianne, dressed appropriately, was wearing a fairly modest two-piece bathing suit. I found her to be attractive as Marianne had a very nice figure to go along with her straightforward attitude. She was not an overly pretty woman, but she exuded an aura that I found compelling.

When I started talking with her, she flatly told me that her husband just walked out on her. One day he was there and the next day he wasn't. I asked how she felt about the situation. She answered, "That's his problem. I'm going to live my life, and I am never looking back." There was a firm conviction to her voice. She looked me in the eye when she said that and I, with every instinct in my body, believed that she was telling me exactly how she felt. I found her to be a very interesting person. She was entirely straightforward. The girl had no guile and that, to me, was seductive. Marianne would, if she wanted to answer a question put to her, do so completely and honestly. I found her openness very refreshing, and I asked her if she wanted to go out that evening for dinner. She quickly agreed.

Later that evening, I picked her up and took her to my favorite place which was "Poor Reds." She had never been there before. As per usual, we had to wait three hours to eat and while sitting in the bar, we talked to people who literally came from neighboring towns up to 700 miles away. This was a totally new experience for her. She had a quick wit, and she was very intelligent. She gave better than she took in the usual banter going back and forth. Marianne absolutely loved the place. When we finally got to eat, she attacked those ribs like a great white shark attacks a baby seal. She wasn't dainty; Marianne was absolutely real! She didn't just like Poor Reds, she absolutely adored the restaurant. We had a great time. When we were leaving, she said to me, "Could we do this again?" I told her, most definitely!

I took her back to her apartment which she was sharing with another woman. I kissed her goodnight, and it was like magic. I could feel that she felt the same way I did. All at once, we both started ripping off the other's clothes. We left a trail of garments from the living room into her bedroom. By the time we reached the bed, both of us were completely naked. She had small, well-formed breasts and legs that wouldn't quit. She wanted me to enter her right away, so I did. We made love for more than three hours. After we both climaxed, we would lay back on the pillows, and both of us would light up a cigarette, smoke and take a brief rest . . . and then start up again. Just before we went to sleep, Marianne said," It's been more than six months since the last time I had sex. Harry walked out on me about five months ago and he withheld sex from me for a month before he left. I still don't why he was so angry; he wouldn't talk to me. You're the only other man that has had me. Harry and I were high school sweethearts, and we were married right after we graduated. Before tonight, he was my only experience with sex."

I got up on my elbow, caressed her face and told her, while looking directly into her eyes, "Harry didn't know or did not appreciate what he had. You are far from being my first, and I can tell you, without any doubt, that you are phenomenal! With that, I kissed her, and we fell asleep in each other's arms. From that time on, I saw Marianne as often as my schedule would allow. Many weekends we would double with John Weiss and his wife.

One weekend Susan invited us to have a Saturday night dinner at the apartment she shared with John. They were both from Massachusetts and Susan was a superb New England chef. The first time we were there at their place, Susan made New England clam chowder. The absolute best I had ever tasted. It was so good that I had four portions. When it came time to serve the standing rib roast, I was too full to eat much of it. I certainly had no room for dessert. To remedy that situation, Susan invited the both of us again two weeks later. When I walked in the door, Susan handed me a sealed 64-ounce jar of her homemade New England chowder. Susan told me, in no uncertain terms, I was having one small bowl of New England chowder that evening so I would be able to enjoy the rest of the meal! "Yes ma'am!" I answered. We sat down and had an absolutely wonderful meal. The conversation was great, and I really enjoyed being with this particular group. Of all the students that came under my purview, Capt. John Weiss was easily my favorite.

I also took Marianne deep sea fishing. The first trip we took was to Monterey. We got aboard the *Monterey Queen* which was the largest party boat in that basin. While we were on the way to the fishing hole where we would drop our lines, I asked the Queen's captain if we could take a tour of the control cabin. He agreed and showed us all the instrumentation that he used to navigate and control his vessel. He had a LORAN A set up. I told him that I was an instructor navigator and showed him a way of putting his LORAN to better use. Doing what he used to do, he could get to within half a kilometer of a particular fishing spot. I showed him how to further tweak the system to cut that error by 90%. He was really appreciative. I thanked him for the tour. Then Marianne and I fished for three hours and caught our limit. Marianne had a great time. The girl loved fishing. When we returned, we passed out fresh fish to people in both our neighborhoods. We kept enough to invite John and Susan to my place for a fresh fish fry.

We became so regular together that it was important to me that Marianne meet my adopted family, the Lyons. After we had dated for several months, I invited Bill and Chickie to my place for supper and to meet her. They really took to her as she had no pretense. They enjoyed her quick wit and her native intelligence. When she slept over at my place and got up, she knew that coffee would be available next door in the Lyons' kitchen. Marianne had little trouble adapting.

The summer of 1975 was also another turning point for me due to several simultaneous occurrences. First, the Air Force wanted its officers to participate in community activities. This was essential after the debacle of Vietnam. I chose to officiate little league baseball. I had previous umpire experience in college, and I loved the sport. With my commander's permission, I signed up to be a little league umpire. This also kept me off the Dover TDY run as I had to be available three evenings a week in order to officiate. Since I was not seeing Tori anymore, this was a benefit and not a drawback. After my first month of doing this, I found that I liked one team in particular and asked the little league assigner to do all the *Rosemont Giants'* games. That worked out well for him as Rosemont was the furthest away from the other teams in the league.

The team players had the best-looking moms in the league, another benefit! I mean hands down, no lo contendere! One situation comes to mind. One of the players, a boy named *Kevin*, could not buy a hit for over a month. His mother was a professional model and a beautiful woman. One day, Kevin hit a tremendous shot in the gap for a legitimate triple. After he slid into third base and I called him safe, he got up and asked for a timeout. I didn't know why and I wanted to make sure that he was not hurt, so I allowed the timeout. Kevin got up and he immediately ran across the diamond into the stands and received a kiss from his mom. He then ran back to third base. Before I called the ball back in play, I walked over to the stands and faced the spectators. I took off my mask and chest protector, and threw them onto the ground. I stood with my hands on my hips facing the parents in the stands and yelled, "THERE WILL BE NO KISS BREAKS ALLOWED, UNLESS THE UMPIRE GETS HIS!" The parents broke out in wholesale laughter as I put my gear back on and called the ball back into play. After the season was over, I again signed up for the next year to be an umpire for the Rosemont Giants.

The second occurrence was my purchase of a log cabin on ten wooded acres in the middle Sierras, very near the Yuba River. The cabin was located about fifty feet from a year-round stream. The price was right, and I fell in love with how beautiful the land and the surrounding area were. I hired Bill and his son, at full union wages, to construct a roof and a floor for my new cabin. I went with Bill to purchase all the items and raw materials he needed to complete the job. He and Billy enjoyed camping, so for them it was like a working vacation. They spent a week in the cabin and completed the job. I can tell you with certainty that no cabin or structure anywhere in Yuba County had a better roof or floor than mine.

During the remainder of 1975, my life took on a comfortable consistency. Marianne and I would double on the weekends either with Bill and Chickie or John and Susan. We took several weekends to go to San Francisco after John graduated and moved on to his gaining command. One weekend in particular, we drove to Monterey where we spent one day fishing on the *Queen* and another day exploring the mouth of the Big Sur River which is one of the most beautiful spots on God's green earth.

I was generally pretty happy, but I still missed Tori. The sex that Marianne and I shared was unbelievable. Both of us fed on each other's appetite. Being with Marianne was the closest I have ever come to being addicted to some form of narcotic. For example, in the middle of October, I spent two weeks on leave visiting my parents and JG and Hope. When I returned to Sacramento, Marianne was there to give me a ride back to my place. As soon as we entered my townhouse, we were at each other like big cats in heat. We were both nude by the top of the steps. I enjoyed spending time with my parents and with JG and his new family, but I was edgy all the time. I didn't have my "Marianne fix!"

The last week of the year, Marianne went away for a week to visit her parents. I spent almost the whole week with Bill and his family. I asked Chickie for her permission to take John, now approaching his twelfth birthday, deep-sea fishing in Monterey. She agreed, and I scheduled us for the day before Christmas to go on a fishing charter. We had to leave before 2:00 AM in order to make the six o'clock departure. John had never been deep-sea fishing before. This was my Christmas present to him.

There was only a half dozen fishermen, so the captain used a smaller boat instead of the *Queen*. It took three hours to get to the fishing hole. We dropped our lines when told to do so by the captain.

John would fish right next to me where I could keep an eye on him. Sure enough, about fifteen minutes after we dropped our lines, Johnny got a huge hit. We were using multiple hooks on a single line. Johnny had two large cod fish take the baited hook at the same time. I saw his pole bend straight down and almost took him overboard. I grabbed the back of his belt and held him securely in the boat. I let John work his pole and his line. He was an experienced fisherman and knew how to 'play' the fish up to the surface. I called for the gaffe and one of the mates helped bring in two cod fish that weighed collectively around fifty pounds (John weighed less than eighty pounds, soaking wet). We spent three hours fishing, and everyone on the boat caught his or her limit. Then we spent the next three hours traveling back to port. The small boat had a wooden cover over the diesel engine. Johnny was the only one aboard who was small enough to curl up and go to sleep atop that cover. That's what he did. The mates cleaned the fish, then put the fillets in a plastic cooler and covered the fillets with ice during the three hours it took to return to port.

On the way home, we stopped at Denny's restaurant. Little Johnny out ate me, and I suspected that he was about to get a growth spurt . . . after all, his daddy was six foot two! We got home at nine o'clock in the evening on Christmas Eve. The family tradition included sitting around the dining room table and sharing a bottle of whiskey. I had no problem with this as none of us were going to drive after we left the table. As soon as we got home, Johnny explained what he had caught and then immediately went to bed. That's when Chickie said to me," I know he's going to be tired. He's always the first one up on Christmas morning."

I replied, "Chickie, there is no way he's getting up before noon tomorrow. That little guy just spent nine hours on the ocean in a small boat. He caught about two times his own weight in fish."

"Well, I know my son. He'll be up before six o'clock tomorrow morning!"

"Chickie, I know you know your son . . . what you don't know is what nine hours on a boat does to a person."

"I'll bet you I'm right!" Chickie said to me.

"I'll take that bet. And I'll make the time noon tomorrow."

"I'm so confident, I'll make the time six tomorrow morning!"

We went back and forth and finally decided on 10:00 AM. Chickie was famous for cooking a fabulous turkey dinner which she served on both the Thanksgiving and Christmas holidays. Our bet was simple. If she won the bet, I would take her and Bill to the best restaurant in Sacramento . . . my treat. But if I won, then Chickie would make another Thanksgiving/Christmas turkey dinner to be served in February for the entire family. Bill really enjoyed the back-and-forth between his best friend and his wife. Either way, he was a winner because he loved his wife's turkey dinners as much as I did. The next morning, Chickie had to wake up Little John well after noon because she wanted to see her youngest open his gifts. Even then he was cranky because he wanted more sleep! In February, I collected my bet, much to the delight of myself and Bill!

16

THE BEST JOB

The first two months of 1976 passed without any notable events. Marianne spent most evenings at my place even though she maintained her own residence. She was not in a hurry to get a divorce, and I never pushed her to do so. Chickie made good on the bet regarding her son. As a result, the Lyons family, myself and Marianne included, enjoyed another Thanksgiving turkey dinner. We all had a lot of laughs, generally at Chickie's expense, on how well she knew her son. I almost felt guilty, but then it was a truly great turkey dinner!

The first week of March, I had a surprise visitor. There was a knock on my door. I opened the door, and standing in front of me was a very large man who pushed by me and entered my house. I noticed immediately that there was a gun in his right hand. He had to be at least six foot four and 245 pounds. I asked, "Who are you, and why are you bringing a gun into my house?" I don't know why, but I did not feel that he was a true threat; the same instincts that kept me alive in Southeast Asia kicked in again.

"My name is Harry Wilson . . . I'm married to Marianne. I want to know what your intentions are."

"Give me the gun and I'll answer your question," I said. He hesitated at first, but then sheepishly handed over the weapon, and I asked that he sit down so we could talk. He sat down on the sofa, and I took the chair facing him.

"Is it serious between you and Marianne?"

"For my part, yes, but I'm not sure how committed Marianne is to me. I'll tell you what I know. First, Marianne has never, to my knowledge, sought a divorce from you. She does not want to give up her own apartment, although I asked her to move in with me. Frankly, I think she is still in love with you, but you really hurt her when you walked out and never told her why you did so. I can tell you this. If you had used a gun or gone after me, you would never have seen her again. I may not know her as well as you do, but she is one very independent-minded young lady."

Harry nodded his head and said, "You're right."

"Why the hell did you walk out on such a woman?"

"It's the dumbest fucking thing I've ever done in my life. We got into a huge fight, and I stormed out of the house. Just at that time, this cute girl at work made a play for me, and I started to fool around with her. I was going to show Marianne that I really didn't need her. Well, the joke's on me. I'm miserable, and I really miss her."

"If you really miss her and you really love her, you have to do three things." Harry raised his lowered head and looked directly at me. I continued, "First, you have to tell her how you feel. Don't worry about your ego. Secondly, do not, under any circumstances, try and box her in . . . that girl needs her space. She is an independent-minded person who absolutely hates to be told what to do. Besides, she is a very competent person and she knows it. Thirdly, never ever lie to her again. I can promise you that if she gives you another chance, it will be your last."

"Do you think she will?"

"Yes, I do. Frankly, I wish she wouldn't, but I can see in her eyes when she talks about you that she still cares. You were her only love up until the time that you walked out on her and were unfaithful to her. I think she wanted to know that she could be attractive to another person. I helped validate her persona, and I know that she cares for me, but it is you she truly loves."

"Are you going to tell her what happened today?"

"No . . . you are. If you're going to be honest with her, you had better start now."

He sat on the couch with a faraway look in his eyes. Finally, he arose and said, "I'll follow your advice."

I took the bullets out of the gun and handed him the weapon. He put it in his pocket. I walked to the door and opened it for him. He left without saying another word. When I saw that Harry had truly departed, I went next door and told Bill and Chickie everything that occurred.

Two weeks later, I got a phone call from my squadron commander. He told me to come to the office immediately. I was grading some check rides and it took me a while to clean up and get properly dressed. About forty minutes after receiving the phone call, I came to attention in front of my commander who asked me to sit down. He went on to say, "Blake, I have bad news. The American Red Cross just notified me that your mother is dying, and the family wants you home immediately. I am granting you emergency leave to go home as soon as possible. As of now, you are off the schedule until further notice. When you get home, give me a call and let me know the situation and how much time you'll need."

I was totally stunned. I heard from my family that Mom was sick, but I didn't know it was so serious. I thanked the commander for the leave and told him that I would call him as soon as I got home and knew what was going on. I got up to leave and the commander said, "If there's anything we can do, please let us know." I thanked him again, saluted and departed the office.

When I got back to my apartment, I immediately told Bill and Chick what was happening. Then I called Marianne and informed her about my mother's illness. I told her that I would call her from New York with some updates. Marianne wished me well, and I told her that I would miss her. Bill said that he would look after my place for me and that he would drive me to the airport. I thanked them both and went back to my apartment where I made arrangements to fly to New York. Later that evening, Bill drove me to the Sacramento Airport where I boarded a plane that took me to LaGuardia Airport, with a two-hour stopover delay in Chicago. That was the first flight I could grab. When I reached Chicago, I deplaned and made a phone call to my father to let him know when and where I was coming in. Dad said he would pick me up when my flight arrived.

By the time I arrived in New York, it was almost 5:00 AM local time. My father was waiting for me at the gate. On the way home, he told me that Mom had suffered from colon cancer which had spread dramatically and swiftly through her entire body. She was now in Sloan-Kettering Hospital, and the doctors told Dad that she had no more than two or three days at most to live. It had been about nine months since the last time I'd seen my mother. She told me that she wasn't feeling particularly well, but she still looked like Mom. I had no idea at the time just how seriously ill she was. My family was not known for our communication skills!

The next day, my family drove in Dad's car to the hospital. We went to my mother's room. What was left of my mother was a living skeleton. All she could do was moan. They gave her so many drugs to kill the pain that I don't believe she was even conscious or knew that we were there. This vibrant woman whose womb gave me life was being tortured by a ruthless disease, and there wasn't a damn thing I could do about it. Being helpless, for a man, is an intolerable situation. We are, by our nature, driven to find answers . . . solutions to problems . . . and here with my mother who I loved, I could do nothing for her. All we could do was help each other grieve. That's what we did. Mom died the next day.

I spent the next week with my family, JG, and Hope. After the funeral, Dad was going to live in West Palm Beach full-time. My brother would take over the business. He got one half of the business, and my father's brother Sam got the other half.

I called my commander and told him that I would be back in Sacramento by the end of the month. He told me that he'd arranged for me to pick up a new section and take these students through the celestial phase. I would start with my new class on Saturday, April 3. I thanked the commander, and he asked when the funeral would be. I told him, and he wished me well. On the day of the funeral, my family received a beautiful floral arrangement from the squadron. I was appreciative of his thoughtfulness.

Two days before I was scheduled to return to Sacramento, I called Marianne and asked her to pick me up at the airport. She agreed to do so and told me how sorry she was to hear of my mother's passing. I thanked her for her concern and said that seeing her would do me a world of good. I could almost see the crooked smile on her face as I said those words.

Marianne was true to her word. When I deplaned, she was there. I told her about the funeral and how hard it hit me, especially not being able to help my mom in her most desperate hour of need. We went back to my place and made love the entire night.

The next day, I made breakfast for both of us. I knew something was on her mind, and I would let her tell me in her own way and in her own time. After the meal was over, we both cleaned up the kitchen, and she asked me to go into the living room where we could talk. That's what we did.

"Something's on your mind. What is it?" I asked.

"Harry came by. He told me what happened and how you handled him. I want you to know how appreciative I am. You turned an ugly and dangerous situation into a manageable one. I am torn, because I love two men. I didn't know that was possible. I always thought that Harry was the only one for me. I loved my time with you. We're so compatible that it's frightening."

"You know that I want to make this permanent. I care deeply for you and when I do not have you next to me, I feel like part of me is missing."

"Blake, I know you care for me deeply, but Harry needs me even more. You have the ability to live without me. I don't think Harry can. He was my first love, and he will always be my deepest love. He wants me back, and I think he has taken what you said to him to heart. He told me that he will never try and order me around again or lie to me. He was miserable without me and he needs me back. I just can't say no to him. I wanted to tell you myself, face-to-face, because I respect your feelings and felt you deserved to hear this in person."

Marianne arose and said that she had to go. I thanked her for her honesty and said that I would miss her very much, but I also wished her well. I think part of me cared so much for her that I wanted her to be happy. I did not feel jealousy . . . I'm not sure why. I was always grateful for what time we shared together and even to this day; I still truly wish her well. We kissed for the last time, and she departed.

About 10 minutes after she left, I went next door and talked to Bill and Chickie. I tried to explain to them how I felt. At first, I was confused. But after talking with them for some time, it started to crystallize in my own mind why I felt the way I did. Marianne, to me, was almost like an addiction. Instead of a narcotic, it was having unbelievably great sex with her and enjoying her company. For the next several months, I went through a form of withdrawal. I have been with much prettier women in my life, but none of them could excite me as completely and thoroughly as Marianne did. I would miss her, but it would not be the devastating blow like the ones I'd suffered in the past. Part of my reaction was the realization that what she said to me was true. Harry needed her more than I did.

What also helped was the fact that I was picking up a class in less than a week. That always made me feel better regardless of what was going on in my personal life. Being a platform instructor teaching celestial navigation was the finest job that I ever had. I got to teach a class of eighteen young men, all college graduates, about the art and science of navigation. The ten weeks that I had the class always passed very quickly. I loved every minute of it. I always got to know the men in my class, and they understood that I wanted them to succeed when they went out into the field.

On Friday, April 2, the day before I was to pick up my new class, I got a surprise visit. I came home from the flight line after a day celestial mission. I no sooner got home and went to the refrigerator for a cold one, when I heard the doorbell ring. I opened the door and there was Andy Stone, accompanied by an attractive woman, standing on my doorstep. I immediately hugged Andy and after we said our hellos, I invited both of them inside the house. Andy introduced the woman who accompanied him. Her name was Emma Norstadt. She was five foot four, with very blonde hair, wide-set blue eyes, an attractive oval face, and a little on the heavy side. Emma wore absolutely no makeup. Her dress was simple and modest. As we started talking, I realized that she had an extraordinary intellect.

It had been almost three years since I'd last talked face-to-face with Andy. I asked both of them to stay over the weekend. We could use the time to catch up with each other. I had the spare room and invited Andy and Emma to use it. They agreed, and I showed them the townhouse. About fifteen minutes later, we were in a local restaurant and started telling our stories and sharing memories. I told Andy about Tori and Marianne and how I had a gun pulled on me. Andy, in turn, told me that two months after he left his gear with me, he received the final divorce papers from Heather. It was the lowest point in his life. He was living in the mountains near Jackson Hole, Wyoming. The first year, he basically stayed by himself. He lived off the land and became quite reclusive.

Later, he got a part-time job. That's where he met Emma as they were both part-time mountain guides. They started seeing each other and now were a solid couple. Emma had three children, each by a different father. Emma never married any of the fathers or anyone else for that matter. However, each of the fathers asked her to marry, but she declined. This woman had a Masters' degree in English and possessed one of the sharpest intellects that I had ever encountered. She lived by her own rules. Emma was a pacifist and a strict vegetarian. She was very feminine, yet she would never use guile to achieve an end. Her three children all lived in Jackson Hole with their respective fathers. She had joint custody with each of them. There was never any animosity with the men in her life as they put the children's welfare above any other consideration. Her three children, consisting of two boys and a girl, all graduated high school before their 16th birthday. Each got a full scholarship to college. The youngest was her daughter who was 14 years old at the time I first met Emma. At that tender age, she was already a junior in high school.

We spent the evening talking. I told Andy that I had an eight-hour class scheduled for the next day. He was surprised, as classes were never held on Saturdays. I related to him the problems with the new UNT program, especially the fact that students did not get any theoretical background in celestial navigation. I told them to make themselves comfortable and that we would go out together that Saturday night. They agreed. I took Andy and Emma to Poor Reds. I told them both about my cabin in the middle Sierras near the Yuba River. Both were excited when they heard about that so I asked if they wanted to go out to see the cabin.

The next day we drove about an hour northeast to the hidden logging road which was the entrance to my property. The cabin was approximately two miles off the paved road which paralleled the Yuba River. I showed Andy the specific markers which identified the entrance to the hidden logging road. We then took that logging road over a bridge and into a small valley that contained my cabin and the adjacent, year-round stream. Emma gave a shout of pure joy when she saw the cabin. Bill had put on a great roof and a solid floor. The cabin itself was 15 x 25 and tall enough to have an elevated loft above the main room. It had two windows with wooden shutters. It also contained a pot-belly stove with an exhaust pipe which allowed the smoke to exit above the roof.

Emma asked me how often I used the cabin. I told her that I had not yet spent a night there. She then asked if she and Andy could use it after her children finished school in early June. I told her that I would be very pleased to share my cabin with the both of them and that they could stay as long as they wanted. She was one happy camper! We drove back to my townhouse. Andy and Emma packed their gear and departed back to Jackson Hole. They would return in early June with all their meager belongings and move into the cabin at that time. I was very glad to be able to help my old friend and to have him around again; a classic win-win situation.

The next day, I started teaching celestial navigation to my section. The class proceeded in the usual fashion; my students did very well. One very interesting thing happened during the night celestial portion of the curriculum. The second week of May, I was scheduled to teach a two-hour lesson entitled: "Latitude by Polaris." Before the class started, a full colonel navigator entered my classroom. I called the class to attention. The colonel told us to carry on as he was there to evaluate my performance while teaching that particular lesson.

The first part of any lesson taught by an Air Force instructor is the attention/motivation step. This is the piece of information or story that will make the students eager to hear what is about to come. I used the story of the *Lady Be Good*, a World War II B-24 bomber, as my attention step. I heard about this particular aircraft when I was flying gunships. The crewman who told me about the *Lady* was an infrared operator. He was also the oldest flying navigator in the entire service at that particular time. This Lt. Colonel told me about his earliest experience as a second lieutenant navigator. He was in the same B-24 Liberator squadron as the crew of the *Lady Be Good* aircraft. They departed Soluch, Libya, on a night bombing mission over Naples, Italy. On the way back to Soluch, the crew was low on fuel and so they made directly for home base. The aircraft that made it back safely all used latitude by Polaris. The reason they used this method was due to an unusual and massive change in the jet stream. This high-altitude wind structure usually starts well above 25,000 feet, generally runs from west to east, with a speed normally well under 200 knots. That night, the jet stream ran north to south at altitudes at or above 10,000 feet and contained winds well in excess of 350 knots.

Latitude by Polaris is a technique that the navigator uses to determine latitude. He puts Polaris, also known as the North Star into the sexton and determines the height of that particular star above the celestial horizon. The latitude of the aircraft is equal to the angular distance of Polaris above this horizon. The aircraft that made it back safely all took up headings that put their aircraft far west of their destination while heading southward. Their navigators entered the dome with their sextons and when Polaris was at the right angular distance above the celestial horizon, they turned their aircraft due east. They stayed in the dome in order to continue using the North Star to determine the amount of "crab" into the wind that was required to maintain a straight easterly track.

The navigator of the *Lady Be Good* eschewed this technique. Their ground speed, due to the unusual jet stream winds, was in excess of 600 knots. When they finally ran out of fuel, they parachuted into what they thought was the Mediterranean Sea. Instead, they were 1,000 miles past their destination well into the heart of the Sahara Desert. The eight crewmembers who survived parachuting, all went north, as they assumed that they were just slightly south of their home field. None of them ever returned. They all died of exposure and extreme thirst. Had they gone in any other direction they would've survived. When the aircraft was found 15 years later, the recovery team took out all the navigation equipment and tested each of them. All worked. I ended my attention step by telling my class an old axiom: "They bury pilot errors. They can't find navigator errors!" I had their full attention. By the end of the first hour, every student knew how to employ this technique. During the second hour, we started working on the assignment that they would have to complete before class the next day. The colonel walked around the room and noted that all my students were doing the work properly. In all the years and all the classes that he monitored; he never saw an entire class performing this technique flawlessly . . . that is until this day when he monitored my class.

When the lesson was completed, he asked me questions regarding the amount of theory that the students obviously knew. He asked to see my personal syllabus. He saw that mine was quite different from the standard lesson plans. He asked if I wrote it, and I answered in the affirmative. Then the colonel looked me in the eye and said, "Presently, 70% of our navigator graduates in this new program are not passing their initial check rides in their gaining commands. However, all of your students did pass. That is why I'm in your class today. I wanted to know what you are doing differently and to see if we can incorporate your approach into the new program. It's been more than ten years since I monitored an instructor's performance in a classroom. I want you to know I really enjoyed your presentation."

I thanked him, and then we spent the next half-hour discussing the importance of theory in the teaching of celestial navigation. For once, a very senior officer in training command listened to me as I was a very experienced instructor. I told him that I emphasized theory so that a student would be able to do his assigned tasks quickly and efficiently. Knowing theory would also help them to recognize a mistake and quickly correct it. When he saw how easily my students absorbed the material in what is considered a fairly difficult lesson plan, he was duly impressed. He told me that the large numbers of our recent graduates had problems completing their initial check-out because of their inability to use celestial navigation. I received the highest rating he ever gave in this "no notice" evaluation.

I found out later, he went to both my wing commander and squadron commander and told them that he wanted all celestial instructors to follow a new syllabus that I would write. I was given a month off the schedule in order to comply with his request. I wrote the entire "day and night celestial syllabus" which included every lesson plan and, with the help of our support staff, created all the training aids that future celestial instructors would use in the classroom. I also wrote three versions of the final exams for both day and night celestial navigation. The wing accepted my entire syllabus without change. However, it still took nearly 3/4 of the year in order to fully adopt this new syllabus, as it required two more days of instruction. It also meant that my Saturday class would remain unchallenged until the extra days of instruction required to teach theory were included in the general curriculum.

In the month of June, I started to umpire little league games again. I asked my assigner to continue doing the Rosemont Giants games again and like the previous year, he agreed. One day I heard the parents talking about forming a new soccer team and how they needed a coach. I was a high school varsity soccer player with two years' experience in a semi-pro league (The Portuguese-Americans), and I knew how to teach the sport. I offered my services to the parents if my commanding officer would allow me to be off the schedule for Tuesday and Thursday afternoons after 2:30 PM and all day on Saturdays. The parents readily accepted my offer.

The next day I asked my squadron commander if I could have that time off the schedule. Under normal circumstances, that request would never have been granted, but this was in the wake of the most unpopular war in our country's history. Community relations moved up the priority list of missions, and as a result, the commander allowed me to be off the schedule. His decision was not an easy one because I was not only one of his best instructors, but I was also a check navigator. That meant I was one of the few instructors authorized to give and grade student evaluations. Only 10% of the instructors had this rating. The commander, fully aware of how valuable my time was to the squadron schedulers, walked with me to their office and told them that starting August 3, I would be off the schedule at the times I requested. This would continue until further notice. The schedulers were not a happy group, but I was ecstatic. This would give me the time to do a proper job coaching these kids.

I was a single captain on flying status with little or no experience with 10- and 11-year-old children. Frankly, I treated my charges like 'boots' in basic training. For five to six hours a day on Tuesdays and Thursdays, and nine hours on Saturday, I took a group of seventeen boys with no experience and taught them the game of soccer. Our first game was on September 4. That gave me five weeks to prepare them and mold them into a team. We relentlessly practiced basic skills for the first three weeks. Then I started adding position play and tactics. Every practice was also filled with conditioning training.

During that summer of 1976, Andy and Emma, who now resided in my cabin in Yuba County, would come down from the mountain to visit with me about once a month. Andy was a world-class soccer player and would help train some of the boys in our Saturday practices. Andy and Emma visited with me on the Friday before our first game. He wanted to see the newly-formed *Rosemont Rebels* play. I was duly nervous as I had no idea how well my boys stacked up against the competition. It was then Andy uttered these fateful words to me, "Blake, if they win, I will come down next week to see them play again, and I will keep coming until they lose." I told him I would hold him to his word! We won that first game 6-0 and that was only the start of what was to follow.

We were scheduled for a twelve-game season. We won all our games. In fact, we scored well over sixty goals that season with only two scored against us. The travel soccer association in California during those years divided teams into three categories: A teams had more than five years of playing together; B teams had two to five years of playing together; and C teams had less than two years together. We were obviously a C team. That year a B team dropped out, and since we had the best record in the C team league, we received the invitation to compete in the Northern California Championship Tournament. We readily accepted. For the next five weeks, we played all A teams. We won the first four of these games and made it all the way to the Championship game. In that last game, played on Sunday, the day after Christmas, the score remained a scoreless tie after regulation and two overtime periods. We lost the shoot-out 3-2. During that game in regular play, we had four shots bounce off the upper cross bar which was set at seven feet, not the eight-foot goals that my team always used prior to that game. That was very frustrating to my players, their parents and especially to me.

More important than the team's winning was what it accomplished for my good friend. Andy kept his word as I knew he would. For the next seventeen weeks, he and Emma spent their weekends at my place. I called members of Andy's family and told them that he would be spending weekends with me. They would call or even come to my townhouse to spend time with their son or brother. Their presence and love, combined with Emma's emotional support, helped this truly wonderful and gentle man come back to the world. It was as if God, in His infinite wisdom, provided this team to help heal one of

His best people. After all, how many 10- or 11-year-old boys can and would practice five to six hours on Tuesdays and Thursdays, and nine hours on Saturdays over a continuous twenty-two week stretch? Well, I had seventeen of them!

By the end of that run, Andy asked me to return his Air Force memorabilia which I gladly did. By the end of 1976, Andy asked Emma to marry him. She accepted. I think she did so because she so loved Andy and truly appreciated his beautiful and gentle soul and because he needed her more than any other partner she'd ever had. By the end of that year, Andy got a full-time job with US Forest Service outlet located near my Yuba River cabin. Joy had returned to my friend. Seeing him happy again really lifted my own spirits. It was a great way to end the year.

In November, I took the law boards. My scores placed me well into the top 10% tier of college graduates who took that exam. I applied to McGeorge School of Law in Sacramento, and in March, 1977, I received my acceptance. I put in my papers to leave the Air Force, and I was told that I had to remain in the service. Too many rated officers were leaving or had established Dates of Separation (DOS), and the Air Force was in jeopardy of not being able to accomplish its basic mission: the protection of the people and the Constitution of the United States. My request to separate was turned down. In its stead, I received orders to go to Air Force rescue with training commencing in July, 1977 at Kirkland AFB, New Mexico.

Just before I left Sacramento, I got a surprise visit from Casey. She recently graduated from college and was joining the United States Air Force. She was going to start her OTS program about the same time I was going to start my training for rescue HC-130 aircraft. We spent a memorable weekend together. Andy and Emma joined Bill and Chickie with Casey and me. We all went to Poor Reds for my last meal in the Sacramento area. We had a great time and didn't get home until well past two o'clock in the morning. Andy and Emma drove back separately. Casey left Sunday, July 10, and I left the next day. She lifted my spirits and helped me accept my continued service in the Air Force. That was our last time together.

17

33RD ARRS

I spent the first two weeks of September, 1977 in New York. I managed to spend a lot of time with JG, Hope, Daniel and Elizabeth Mae. The kids were growing fast. During the day, I accompanied Hope and the children to the Bronx Zoo. I had a blast watching the children's reaction to the various animals on display. They especially enjoyed the big cats and particularly one very large male lion. We watched as some adolescent girl was teasing this brute. It was just before feeding time, and the large male cat was restless while awaiting his food. The girl was throwing individual pieces of popcorn at the lion. The big cat roared loudly which made the girl stop momentarily in her attempt to torment the animal. After a brief pause, the girl continued again to throw pieces of popcorn at the caged lion. That's when I found out two things about a male lion that I never knew before. First, he can urinate in a direction opposite the one he is facing. Secondly, the stream of urine can travel in excess of twenty feet. The big cat hosed his tormentor with a strong stream of urine which hit directly in her face! The male lion not only got the girl to stop tormenting him but also received a standing ovation from the approximately two dozen onlookers who all felt that the girl got exactly what she deserved.

When we returned back to their home, the kids went to the den to watch TV while Hope prepared supper. We talked about the children and how quickly they were growing. For me it was truly astonishing, as I saw them about once or twice a year, so the normal changes associated with child development were accentuated and sudden, not gradual as one who sees them every day. Hope and I also discussed my disappointment in being blocked from attending law school. She understood how I felt and thought that the Air Force did not deal fairly with me.

Around 6:00 PM, JG came home. He kissed Hope and gave me a huge welcoming hug. He then went to his bedroom to quickly change from his suit to jeans and a T shirt. By then, Hope had dinner prepared, and we all sat down for a wonderful meal. I told JG about what Hope and I had discussed earlier. JG was particularly incensed with the service for not allowing me to leave active duty and attend law school. It was our dream to practice law together, and the Air Force would not let that happen. What made it especially difficult for me was that I did not have to return to flying status but did so of my own volition. JG counseled me that I must complete my new assignment, even though it meant another three-year commitment. If I ever wanted to pass the bar and practice law, I needed an honorable discharge. I could not take a general discharge like Andy did in order to save his marriage. Besides, that option was totally off the table as far as I was concerned.

After the meal was over, we all retired to the den where JG spent some quality time with his two children. He played with them together and individually. I knew he wanted to be a "hands on" dad. He was not going to repeat the mistakes of his father. I enjoyed watching this interaction between JG and his children. From their squeals of joy, they also appreciated their father's undivided attention.

When it was their bedtime, they gave me a hug and a kiss goodnight. Together, JG and Hope put them to bed. When they returned to the den, JG asked if I wanted to take a walk while Hope took care of the dishes. Hope told us to hit the road as we would be in her way. We went for a long walk around the beautiful neighborhood of upper-income housing in which Hope and JG now resided. We walked in silence for almost twenty minutes. I knew something was bothering my friend, and I waited for him to collect his thoughts so he could tell me what was on his mind. After all the years together, I knew that no one could hurry JG in speaking before he was ready, and he knew that I would wait until he was ready to unburden himself.

The last time I saw him in such a state was during our junior year at Marietta College. On that day too, we walked in silence for a while when JG finally told me of the possibility of his becoming a father. Hope had missed a period, and she thought she might be pregnant. He wanted my advice, and when we both agreed that if that was the case, he should marry Hope, and that I would be best man at their wedding. Until that time, I did not know how far their relationship had progressed. When our fraternity brothers asked me regarding their relationship (as they did from time to time), my standard answer to how far they went was ALWAYS: "JG was getting bare elbow!" Even when I knew differently, my answer to the usual inquiry remained unchanged. JG knew I could keep his secrets.

By this time, it was almost complete nightfall. The sun had retreated below the horizon and the moon was barely a quarter full, so it was pretty dark and I could not make out JG's expression. Finally, he said, "I took on a new client two months ago. Her name is Doris and she was seeking a divorce. She was married for ten years and her husband cheated on her. Doris is a particularly beautiful woman, and she was totally distressed and angry. While I was taking her information, she started crying. I went to comfort her and the next thing I knew, she started coming on to me."

"What did you do about it?" I asked.

"At first, she just wanted to be held, so I let her cry on my shoulder for a while. Somehow, that led to kissing. That turned us both on and led to having sex with her on my sofa in my office. Until that time, Hope was the only woman that I knew in a biblical way. We were both virgins when we made love together back in college. I feel terrible about what happened, but it was the most exciting sex I've ever experienced."

"How long has this been going on?"

"For about eight weeks now. Doris knows it is not serious. I still love my wife and I want to keep my family together, but the sex is spectacular and almost addictive. So, we keep seeing each other."

"I know how that can happen." I then recounted my history with Marianne who was married went we slept together. Based upon that experience, I told JG, "When it happened to me, I was single and had no one else in the equation. But you are not in the same place. When Marianne went back to her husband, it took me a long while to want other women again. It was like what I imagined a drug rehabilitation course to be like. It wasn't that I was in love with her; it was how good the sex made me feel and how physically debilitating it was when we were apart. When I had a steady diet of sex from Marianne, I had a constant need of more. When I would come home for a couple weeks of leave, all I could think of was getting back into her pants again."

"That's exactly what I'm going through." JG continued, "I feel so guilty, but the sex is so good and she makes me feel like Superman, not just a chubby middle-aged married guy!"

"Listen JG, you are risking your marriage and your career. I am no lawyer, but there may be sanctions applied to you regarding sleeping with a client. Besides, Hope is far from stupid. Eventually she will figure out that something is wrong. Hope is a beautiful person both inside and out, and she is one great mother to your children. End this thing before it destroys you."

I could almost sense JG nodding his assent. He then asked, "How long did it take to get over Marianne?"

"About three months. Then my libido finally returned to form. In fact, I just recently ran into Marianne about two months ago. I was getting ready to leave the Sacramento area when I ran into her at one of the local stores. We greeted each other warmly. She told me that she was pregnant and very happy about it. Her husband now treated her much better than he did before and they were both looking forward to the arrival of their child. For my part, I wished her well and felt nothing. I was finally over the addictive hold she had on me, and I could move on."

We continued in silence for the remainder of the walk. I wanted to give JG space and time to consider what I said. When we returned to his house, Hope greeted us warmly. The children were asleep, and we retired to the porch to continue the conversation started during supper. We talked about how well Lou and Nancy Lee were doing. Hope and Nancy stayed in constant contact with letters about every month. I asked how their neighbor, Lisa Stein, was doing. I had not heard from her in more than three years.

Hope turned from a light mood to a much darker countenance. "You know I finished my Masters' degree in psychiatric social work, thanks to my father-in-law, may God rest his soul. Well, I started a part-time private practice. About two years ago, Lisa died of a self-inflicted drug overdose. Edna Stein was devastated by the loss of her daughter. I helped her cope with her new reality, but I did so as a friend and neighbor, not as a professional. She was their only child and her death was difficult for her to accept. I have helped Edna to be able to come to terms with such a senseless loss."

"I am so sorry to hear this news. I really liked Lisa and I wanted to continue seeing her but only if she ditched the drugs. She didn't, and so I went my own way. I offered to help her in any way possible to kick her habit, but the addiction proved too difficult for her to free herself. What a Goddamned waste!" We talked together for several more hours. The subject turned to politics.

JG was becoming ensconced in the Democrat Party. His political connections were growing in both Nassau and Suffolk Counties. Both of us grew up in Jewish homes where God, Moses and FDR were revered . . . and sometimes not in that order! I personally worked in the JFK campaign of 1960 while I was a freshman at Marietta College. JG enthusiastically supported President Carter while I had my doubts. We both voted for him, but I was not sure that he was up to doing the job. Looking back on that conversation, I can see a perfect metaphor to illustrate the different ways that we perceived politics. I was not involved with politics (an officer is strictly forbidden to do so) as a matter of law and practice. I took the usual interest every two years when national elections were held. JG was personally involved with politics on almost a daily basis. I was astonished how much his children grew and changed between the times I saw them. In the same manner, I was also amazed at the political alteration that was taking over the Democrat Party. JG did not see it the same way, as the transformation was gradual to him; he lived with incremental change occurring on a daily basis, just as he was less amazed at his children's development because to him it was gradual. I told JG and Hope, to their utter astonishment, that I almost voted Republican and had that party nominated Ronald Reagan, I would have voted for him. A little while later, I said my good-byes. I would not see them again for the next eighteen months.

My orders were to proceed to Kadina Air Base, located in Okinawa, Japan, to fly the HC-130H aircraft. On Monday, September 26, 1977, I arrived at Kadina AB. En route, I spent three days at Fairchild AFB getting a refresher course in survival training. I reported to my direct boss, *Lt. Col. Frank Watkins* who was also the operations officer of the 33rd Aerospace Rescue and Recovery Squadron (33rd ARRS). Col. Watkins was the highest-ranking HC-130 pilot in the squadron. He was a tall man with dark curly hair and physically both fit and handsome. I would come to know later that he was also a very good, experienced pilot. He welcomed me to the 33rd ARRS. He told me that I was the most senior navigator in the squadron. Therefore, I would become the resource manager of that crew position. My ground job was to make sure that all the navigators in the squadron were up to date in maintaining their flying currency and that all other non-flying regulatory requirements were also up to date as well. He showed me where my desk was located, what forms I needed to fill out, and those I needed to track. It took me about a week on the job to appreciate all the various tasks that I had to perform in order to keep all my navigators both proficient and current.

I also had to maintain my own proficiency as a rescue navigator. I was assigned to *Capt. Gary Blokland's* crew. Gary would be my primary pilot for the next three years. He and I trained together at Kirkland AFB in obtaining our initial checkout in the HC-130 aircraft: Gary as the pilot and aircraft commander (AC) and me as the navigator (TN). Gary was just over six feet tall and a very good-looking man. He was a graduate of the Air Force Academy, and he was transitioning from copilot to pilot. Gary was the second-best pilot that I knew from my own experience. The only pilot I would rate above him was Maj. Conrad Story, my old AC from my gunship days. Gary had that perfect blend of self-assurance (without being cocky) and reliance on his crew to do their individual jobs. He not only had 'great hands' as a pilot, he also used excellent judgment in virtually every decision he made in dealing with the mission at hand. Gary also possessed a very dry, sharp wit. He loved to laugh, as he truly enjoyed people. The entire crew loved flying with him. He was easily the best pilot in my squadron.

Shortly after we checked out locally, our crew was assigned to a three-day training slot in the Philippines. We returned to Kadina about 4:00 PM local time in order to attend a reception for our new squadron commander, *Col. Ryland B. Dreibelbis.* By the time we debriefed and completed our post flight duties, it was close to five and the reception was well under way. Gary and I went from the flight line directly to the Officer's Club (O' club) to meet our new commander. We did not have time to change so we went in our flight suits (AKA as "bags"). We went to the bar in the reception area where we both ordered adult drinks. I looked around to see if any available "talent" (young ladies) were present. I immediately spotted an extraordinarily pretty woman who I guessed to be about thirty years old. I started to move in her direction when I felt my whole body being lifted by my pilot, who grabbed the top of my "bag" and literally held me about an inch above the floor.

I looked back over my shoulder and said to Gary, "What are you doing?"

He answered, "You're headed for that hammer (good-looking woman) over there. Am I right?"

"Yeah, Gary. I got a radar lock on her, and I want to see if I can get to know her better. She is easily the best-looking woman in the building!"

"Well, Blake, that is the COLONEL'S WIFE!"

"Can't be. I heard the colonel has two daughters who are both in their early twenties."

"That's true. It is also true that you are locked onto the colonel's wife."

"Okay, you can let me go now. I am not going anywhere!"

Later on, both Gary and I met both *Col. Ryland and Peg Dreibelbis.* That occurred when the colonel returned from his training flight and joined his wife. Col. Dreibelbis was a few inches taller than I. He was thin with some graying of his hair, and he possessed a strong grip as he shook my hand. He also was in his "bag" as he was an HH-53C Super Jolly (helicopter) pilot. He spoke softly, but firmly, as a man who was very secure in knowing who he was. I would come to know him as a superb commander who balanced the demands of the mission with the needs of the men who served under his leadership. His beautiful wife was every inch and in every sense a lady. She was also soft spoken, had a very keen wit, and was very loyal to her colonel and the men that served under him.

I personally experienced a perfect example of her sense of humor and her compassion. Somehow, and I can assure you not from me, Peg Dreibelbis found out that I was going to make my move to introduce myself to her before I knew she was the colonel's wife. Frankly, I thought she was a very pretty and young school teacher. I suspect that Gary might have mentioned my almost misadventure to her, but I can't prove it. At any rate, one day about a month later, I was scheduled to be the alert navigator, and I came to the headquarters building about forty-five minutes early in order to do some work and get my morning coffee. When I arrived at the office, I could not find my personal coffee cup. No cup, no coffee! The briefing was scheduled for 0730, and I was still frantically looking for my cup ten minutes past the briefing time when the phone rang at my desk. I picked up the phone and the voice in my ear said, "Where is the alert navigator?"

I angrily responded, "I am up here, and I can't find my fucking coffee cup. Who is this?"

The voice said, "It is the alert pilot, Col. Watkins . . . your boss. Get your ass down here now!" He hung up angrily. NOT my finest moment!

I went downstairs and received my briefing. After we broke to return to our respective desks, Col. Watkins told me to follow him into his office. I did and he told me to close the door behind me which I did. He then proceeded to give me the best chewing out that I ever received. Frankly, as we say in the Air Force, "He tore me a new asshole!" When he was done, I meekly left his office and returned to my desk to attempt to do my office work, although it was difficult for me to concentrate given the dressing down I had just and justly received.

The next day when I arrived at the headquarters building there was a perfectly wrapped gift box sitting on top of my desk. Attached to the top of the box was a small envelope. I opened the envelope and removed the card. It was written with an elegant penmanship and contained the following message:

> "Every young officer needs some insurance for his career. I hope you use and enjoy this small token.
> Peg Dreibelbis"

I removed the gift wrapping and opened the box. It contained six brand new coffee mugs! I laughed out loud. The lady made my day. In the eighteen months that I served in her husband's command, I came to know that her penmanship just reflected the elegant lady I knew her to be. I saw her at the O' Club the next day, and I thanked her for the gift. I told her that it really lifted my spirits. We talked for about fifteen minutes. She told me that she and the colonel had been married for twenty-five years and moved twenty-three times! Frankly, I was astonished. She looked as if she was thirty years old, and so I asked if she was a child bride. She laughed and with a smile said that she was twenty-one when she married Ryland. Looking back on my life, Peg Dreibelbis was as gracious a person as I have ever encountered!

About six months later, I had a chance to see Col. Dreibelbis' leadership first hand. The Air Force hierarchy decided that our main overwater navigation system (LORAN C) had to be replaced with the embryonic GPS or Global Positioning System. The only problem was that GPS depended upon a minimum number of satellites to be operational. In the Far East where we were stationed and flew the vast majority of our missions, the satellites required to give constant and reliable navigational information were not yet operationally ready. We were ordered to remove our LORAN receivers which worked most of the time and then replace them with the nascent GPS receiver that was constantly unreliable. I told Col. Watkins about my concerns, and he ordered me to come up with an acceptable solution.

I did my research, and found it was a simple matter of reconfiguring the navigator's station aboard the HC-130H aircraft. Col. Watkins accompanied me to the commander's office where I briefed Col. Dreibelbis regarding my suggested reconfiguration. He was not a fixed-wing pilot, but after a brief explanation, he understood the mission ramifications that the loss of LORAN C would produce. Over the vast expansion of water that is the Pacific Ocean, a navigator has to be able to determine Lines of Position (LOPs) in order to establish a true position. Without accurate LOPs, a navigator can only obtain a dead reckoning position (DR) which is basically a guess. If he can obtain one LOP or two LOPs that are almost parallel to each other, the navigator can obtain a Most Probable Position (MPP) which is basically an "educated" guess. But if the navigator can get two LOPs which are nearly perpendicular to each other or he can obtain three or more LOPs, then he could "fix" the aircraft's position accurately . . . no "guesstimating"! The commander was so impressed with my arguments that he went full bore to implement the suggested change to aircraft configuration. He even ordered our HC-130Hs reconfigured in anticipation that the Air Force (AF) would accept my proposal.

Four months later, the AF put my suggestion on abeyance and ordered our squadron to be configured as every other C-130 in the fleet. That led to many near disasters in the Eastern Pacific theatre and six months after that, the AF realized its mistake and ordered all C-130s to be configured as I had first suggested. The colonel never gave up. He saw solving that problem to a happy conclusion. I know all my fellow navigators appreciated his unflinching support to get the equipment we needed to do our jobs.

During that six-month time when we lost our LORAN C, my crew was ordered to fly to Anderson AFB in Guam. Before leaving Kadina AB, we were warned that there were several typhoons in the area between our departure and our destination. After takeoff, when Gary would first level out the aircraft, it was my practice to put up the sextant and get an immediate celestial LOP. I compared that to a radar position in order to determine the sextant error which applied to the sextant that I was using. That's what I did on this mission. But by the second "fix," we were totally engulfed in clouds because of the typhoons located along the route. The clouds produced by the storms were so thick that I could not see any celestial body, including the sun, in my sextant eye piece. Without LORAN C, I was reduced to using Doppler as my only usable aid. That situation resulted in my obtaining only DR positions over the next four hours of flight. Our problem was exacerbated by the ominous presence of humongous thunderstorms which lined our course. By the fifth hour of flight, I knew that we were at least 230 miles north of our preflight or planned course due to the really heavy thunderstorms which covered that track. I thought we were abeam our destination, and I kept looking for a hole to take us to the south. I was getting close to the point where we would have to risk thunderstorm penetration when I saw on my radar a significant break in the storms which opened toward the south.

I called to Gary, "Pilot, Nav. Do you see the hole opening at your one o'clock position?"

Gary answered, "Roger Nav, I see it."

"Good. Fly to the middle of that hole and take up a heading of 1-8-0."

Gary put us in the middle of that hole and established a heading of 1-8-0. The thunderstorms raged on both sides of our aircraft. They more than doubled our 25,000 feet of altitude. I called Gary: "Tune in Anderson VOR/DME frequency 111.7, channel 54, I-dent Uniform Alpha Mike. You should receive it in less than three minutes, and it should show us due north of destination."

"Roger Blake . . . I hope you guessed well!"

"That makes two of us!" I answered.

Two minutes later, Gary said, "We got a good lock—206 NM due north of Anderson. Good work, Blake!"

As we approached Guam, I saw on my radar scope that the island was surrounded by level four to level six thunderstorms. (Level six is the highest and most dangerous of these storms.) I used the radar's iso-echo function to find the "softest" approach into the island base.

"Pilot, Nav. Prepare for thunderstorm penetration procedures. Heading 1-4-0."

"Roger Nav. Airspeed 150 indicated, heading 1-4-0. Flaps set."

I directed the aircraft east of Anderson to allow Gary to pick up the ILS approach into 24L, a runway that was more than 11,000 feet long. There, along that approach, were the weakest of the encircling thunderstorms that literally surrounded the entire island. Those "weakest" were still level four "boomers" which are very heavy and still very dangerous storms. We entered the ring of boomers, and the turbulence we experienced was enormous. The surrounding rain was so intense it almost seemed as a body of water rather than rainfall. Gary's windshield wipers were useless in that maelstrom. His visibility was damn near zero. I felt as if we were riding atop of a raging bull, and that ride lasted for about ninety seconds . . . ninety very long seconds. We emerged from the storms, and the aircraft flight smoothed out dramatically. From there, Gary made an uneventful landing. When we touched down, I punched my interphone button and said, "Well, at least now we don't have to wash the aircraft!" Everyone laughed, which helped relieve the tension.

When we returned from Guam, I talked to Col. Watkins. I told him that I really needed LORAN C. I further informed him that the nascent GPS was "useless as tits on a boar hog!" I had to go over four hours in terrible weather conditions without any way to "fix" the aircraft's true position. Col. Watkins had me write up a formal hazard report which I did. Later, he had me meet with other resource managers and squadron commanders from all the C-130 squadrons stationed in the Pacific Theatre of Operations. The purpose of this gathering was to make a coordinated request that hopefully would focus AF leadership's attention to a very serious problem. This effort was spearheaded by Col. Dreibelbis who tirelessly pushed to have the

LORAN C navigation system reinstalled in every version of the C-130 that flew in the Far East. He may have been a helicopter pilot, but he did thoroughly understand our problem. Several months later, AF high command allowed us to modify our aircraft in accordance with my original proposal. Without the leadership and determination of Colonels Watkins and Dreibelbis, this necessary change would not have been possible.

The 33rd ARRS was an unusual unit. Most squadrons only fly one type of aircraft; we flew two: the HC-130H and the HH-53C Super Jolly helicopter. Our version of the Lockheed Hercules was configured for exceptional endurance, for high performance ranging from very low altitudes to 43,000 feet and everything in between, to provide in-flight refueling to our HH-53 helicopters and as a platform to deploy the "para-rescue" airmen who are referred throughout the Air Force as "PJs." Our fully loaded takeoff weight was 175,000 pounds which included up to 75,000 pounds of jet fuel. The crew consisted of the pilot or aircraft commander (AC), the copilot (CP), the navigator (TN), the flight engineer (FE), loadmaster (LM), two PJs, and on occasion, we also had a radio operator (RO).

The HH-53 aircraft is a twin-engine Sikorsky helicopter that is one of the largest and fastest of its genre ever built. Its gross weight was 44,500 pounds. It could obtain speeds in excess of 200 knots and altitudes over 12,000 feet, which is truly exceptional for a rotary wing aircraft. It was capable of being refueled in the air, even in instrumental metrological conditions (IMC) or in layman's terms, severely reduced visibility. The job of the HH-53 Super Jolly was to go where the fixed wing aircraft could not, whether in combat or peace-time rescue. Because it could be refueled, the HH-53 was an "ocean capable" aircraft. The rescue HC-130s would escort and refuel our helicopters across great expanses of ocean which is the prevalent environment of the Asian Pacific theatre. The crew consisted of AC, CP, FE and two or three PJS, depending upon mission requirements. In its combat role, it provided mountings for two 50-caliber machine guns and one 7.62 mm Gatling gun.

Both aircraft provided a platform to insert the PJs in a rescue mission. PJs are a breed apart. In the annals of warfare, and in Viet Nam in particular, they are the most decorated group of men in the Air Force and perhaps, even in the military as a whole. They are experienced paratroopers who can depart an airborne aircraft at any altitude, and they jump into every environment that our planet provides from the hottest jungle to the cold of Antarctica, from the highest mountains to the lowest valleys, and from wettest (oceans) to the driest (deserts). They are expert survivalists who are expected to jump and literally rescue those poor souls who are trapped within the worst of conditions. They must be certified in every survival school offered in the military. In addition, they are all certified as experts in scuba operations and martial arts. Their professional requirements also include medical training. A fully qualified PJ can do duties we now assign to nurse practitioners and can perform operations such as an appendectomy, bone resetting, and bullet removal in combat conditions. When not on a mission, they train about ten hours a day. They are the most physically fit airmen in the service, bar none. By the time an enlistee is a fully qualified PJ, the Air Force has invested at least $200,000 (in 1977 dollars) worth of training into that individual. They are also a lot of fun to "run" with when on a TDY (temporary duty) assignment in a location known to have a supply of pretty women available!

About one year into my tour at Kadina AB, we had a situation develop. A small, but populated, remote tropical island had an outbreak of some type of communicable disease. The state department wanted the indigenous folks to be inoculated. They needed a medically qualified person to administer the shots who could parachute onto that small island. That meant a PJ. The island was too far away and too isolated for a HH-53 mission. Our squadron used the HC-130H as the means to transport the sole PJ selected for this mission. He and his medical supplies were dropped successfully onto the island. The people who inhabited this tropical paradise do not have the same moral code that we experience in the States. The women go topless and are, by our standards, quite promiscuous. Even the female American Peace Corps representative went topless to better fit into the society in which she was trying to assist. Our PJ spent a week there. It finally took a Navy *submarine to reluctantly pry him from that island!*

In the eighteen months I spent in the Far East, there were two missions which really stood out. In the first week of November, 1977, I was assigned to a mixed crew doing combat rescue training in a large exercise conducted in the Philippines. My pilot for both missions that I wish to relate was *Capt. Randy Dill,* an Air Force Academy graduate and a wonderful pilot. Randy was a large gregarious man (6' 2" in height), and he was also the flight examiner pilot. On this first mission, several of our normal crew positions, including the FE and LM, were filled by higher headquarters personnel who wanted to evaluate our overall effectiveness. We were working with one of our squadron's HH-53 helicopters practicing the techniques that we would employ if called to support an active military operation. During the mission, my radar scope presented a "washed out" return which made it virtually unusable. I was going to "write it up" after the mission so that maintenance personnel could repair it before our next flight. We took-off about 2:00 PM local time, and we were scheduled for a four-hour flight. Just as we were getting ready to return to base (RTB), the Rescue Coordination Center (RCC) called us on our UHF radio informing both the HH-53 and us that we had a real combined rescue mission.

When that occurs, both aircraft change their call signs from "Jolly" (HH-53) and "King" (HC-130H) to Air Force Rescue and the last five digits of the aircraft number. Our call sign then became "Air Force Rescue 6-0-9-5-2" (AFR60952), and the Jolly's call sign became "Air Force Rescue 6-5-3-1-1" (AFR65311). This call sign change is necessary as it informs air traffic control and all neighboring aircraft that a real rescue mission with human life at stake is occurring. It also makes our requests to air traffic control go to the top of the priority list. After our call sign changed, I looked at my radar scope and to my utter amazement, I saw the best radar picture that I had ever experienced in over 3500 flight hours as a navigator . . . and I did nothing to bring this about! A true miracle.

We were ordered to depart the island of Luzon and fly 155 NM (nautical miles) over water to Bataan, a small, isolated island. We were tasked to accompany the HH-53 helicopter and provide navigational assistance and fuel as needed so that they could land on the island's soccer field and pick up a very pregnant lady who was suffering from a potentially fatal breech birth delivery. In order to save this woman and her unborn child, we needed to get her to the large hospital in Manila. Our problems in doing this mission were exacerbated by a huge weather front moving into the area and the fact that we had less than a full fuel load when we took off earlier in the day. By the time we reached Bataan, it was 8:05 PM local time, and the November sun was setting. The Jolly set down on the soccer field and attempted to load the pregnant lady aboard. Well, this woman had never seen an aircraft, let alone a Super Jolly. She thought the airplane was literally going to "eat" her, and she became hysterical. The native island leader finally ruled that her husband go on first and accompany her to Manila. The PJs helped the terrified man aboard and then loaded the reluctant and very pregnant lady onto the starboard gurney. They gave her husband a folding seat so he could hold his wife's hand during the flight. All that commotion took over half an hour to accomplish. We circled the soccer field until the Jolly took off on or about 8:40 that evening.

While we waited for the helicopter's departure from Bataan, the flight visibility steadily decreased, and we encountered heavy rain and widely spread layers of thick low-lying clouds. I had no trouble picking up the helicopter on my radar as it departed the island. The Jolly had to maintain a maximum altitude of 1,800 feet above mean sea level (MSL), as the patient would bleed from her vagina if the chopper went any higher due to the reduced ambient air pressure that accompanies higher altitude. About half way to Luzon, the main island of the Philippines and the place where Manila is located, the Jolly pilot informed us that he needed fuel, and he needed it quickly. Randy Dill, my AC, called for an IMC (Instrument Metrological Conditions) refueling procedures.

IMC refueling starts with me (TN) giving the AC headings to come five NM behind the Jolly at 1,600 feet (200 feet below the Jolly's altitude). I gave the Jolly crew, using Randy as an intermediate, a heading of 2-4-0 and told them to maintain heading and altitude. Using radar, I put us on a course behind the chopper. The helicopter radar return was plainly visible on my scope. I set the radar to relative heading display which used the longitudinal axis of the Hercules aircraft as the basis or zero angle. I called to my AC, "Five miles in trail."

AC: "Roger...No joy."

TN: "New heading 2-5-0."

AC: "Heading 2-5-0." After a few moments, "Established 2-5-0."

I waited until the chopper was just about to be running down the left side of my cursor and told the pilot, "New Heading, 2-4-0. Four miles in trail."

AC: "Roger...Established heading 2-4-0."

TN: "Course looking good." After another minute, "On course...three miles in trail."

AC: "Three miles, no joy (no visual sighting)."

TN: "On course...two miles in trail."

AC: "Two miles, still no joy." Our IMC minimum was one mile in trail and I can hear the anxiety in Randy's voice. We had higher headquarters personnel aboard and our mission was being monitored by major command officers in the RCC.

TN: On course...one mile in trail. Continue heading 2-4-0."

AC: "Heading 2-4-0. No JOY!"

TN: "I have a perfect radar lock, continue heading 2-4-0." About a half a minute later, "Half mile in trail, perfect position."

AC: Randy turns his head toward me and says with rising anxiety, "No JOY! Are you sure?"

TN: "Randy, just fly the fucking airplane...we are in perfect position...Quarter mile in trail...continue heading 2-4-0."

AC: "Roger."

TN: "Two hundred meters...One hundred meters!"

AC: "I got JOY. Perfect position!" Then on the UHF radio, "AFR 65311, this is AFR 60952, how copy?"

AFR311: "Loud and clear."

AFR952: "We are coming under your position right now...do you have joy on our position?"

AFR311: "Roger. We have you in sight. Your position is perfect! We will use the port drogue." The drogue is shaped like a bag mitten cone only it is about three feet in diameter and is attached to a four-inch refueling hose which is over 100 feet long and stored in the HH-130 on a roller located in the left wing.

Then the helicopter dropped down 200 feet to our altitude once it was safely behind our position. They reduced their air speed to match ours. His position was now approximately 100 feet in trail so the chopper can reach the extended port side drogue. The HH-53 pilot flew the large proboscis located on the front of his aircraft into the refueling drogue. When done correctly, the drogue female receptor locks on to the male end of the proboscis and then both aircraft receive a "green light" signal on their respective control panels.

AFR952: "We have a green light."

AFR311: "Roger. Green light confirmed."

AFR952: "Initiating fuel flow...Advise when full."

AFR311: "Roger, we have positive fuel flow."

A few minutes later, the Jolly informed us that they had full tanks. The FE released the lock and we retrieved our drogue. The AC accelerated our air speed to get well in front of the Jolly and then climbed to a higher altitude and come behind the chopper. From that position, we continued to provide the helicopter with navigational information. The entire procedure, from the time that the Jolly pilot called for refueling till the HH-53 finished sucking up 9,500 pounds of JP-4 fuel was less than 10 minutes! It was the best "refueling" that I had ever directed in the worst of conditions!

The next stage was directing the chopper to the main Manila airport. We had to fly to Luzon and enter the Lingayen Gulf which was the fastest way to transverse the island. Consequently, it was also the most dangerous way to fly to Manila especially when the helicopter's top altitude was restricted to 1,800 feet. That altitude was perilous because the high terrain on that island extended to just under 4,000 feet. In addition, the low cloud cover and rain were so intense that the pilots in the Jolly had zero visibility aloft. It was so bad that sometimes the chopper pilots could not see the flashing light on the end of the front mounted refueling proboscis. We did not have sufficient fuel in our combined effort to go around Luzon. As we entered the Lingayen Gulf from the north, I asked the AC for permission to talk directly to the chopper. It was too cumbersome for me to keep passing heading changes to the Jolly using the AC as an intermediate. Randy saw the wisdom of this request and quickly agreed to it. He told to me to use "Victor One" radio.

When we overflew the southern coast of the Lingayen Gulf, I called the chopper: "AFR311, AFR952, victor radio, how copy?"

AFR311: "We got you 5 by."

AFR952: "Turn left, heading of 1-9-2. Report established 1-9-2."

AFR311: "Roger. Turning left to 1-9-2." A few moments later, "Established 1-9-2."

This started the longest night of my life. I would use the radar to "fix" the Jolly's position. I then turned the Jolly aircraft to keep it away from the unseen, but deadly high terrain that was all around the helicopter. The chopper never went more than five minutes without a course change from me. They were flying "blind" in zero visibility and literally depended upon my ability to use radar to keep them from flying into a "stone-filled" cloud. Many times, before this mission, I would give helicopter pilots headings to fly, and they usually complained if the headings I gave were **not** rounded to the nearest five degrees but that was in visual metrological conditions (VMC). That night I gave them headings that were not only down to single digits, but on two occasions were literally down to the nearest 1/2 degree and the Jolly pilots never complained . . . they flew the headings I gave them!

Finally, after a little more than an hour of flying over land, we reached the southern coast of Luzon and entered the Bay of Manila. About twenty miles from the international airport, the chopper's destination, I "painted" the radar reflectors on the approach to the main runway. I placed the cursor over the extension of the runway and directed the Jolly to the extended runway projection. I asked if they wanted to be turned over to Manila approach. The helicopter pilots insisted on using my directions to the runway. Randy secured the permission from approach control, and I continued giving the chopper pilots headings to fly. I flew them to a position over my radar cursor which represented the extended runway. I kept turning the helicopter until the drift was "killed", and their course would take them directly over the runway. I was still using VHF radios to communicate with the Jolly aircraft:

AFR932: "A-R-A procedures...fly heading 0-7-0, maintain 1,800 feet." ARA stood for Airborne Radar Approach.

AFR311: "Established heading 0-7-0 and 1800 feet."

AFR932: The chopper was 12 nautical miles (NM) out from the main runway as it approached the radar cursor, "Twelve miles out, turn left, new heading 0-6-0. Report established 0-6-0. Maintain 1,800 feet."

AFR311: "Roger 0-6-0." A few seconds later, "Established 0-6-0 and 1,800 feet."

AFR932: "Drifting right, turn left heading 0-5-6. Report established 0-5-6. Maintain 1,800 feet."

AFR311: "New heading 0-5-6...Established heading 0-5-6. Maintaining 1,800 feet."

AFR932: "On course, heading 0-5-8. Report established 0-5-8."

AFR311: "Heading 0-5-8...established 0-5-8. Altitude 1,800 feet."

AFR932: "On course. True airspeed 120 knots, 10 NM out, maintain 1,800."

AFR311: "Roger 120 kt."

AFR932: Two minutes later, the chopper radar return is steady under the moveable cursor, "Seven NM out, start descent at 300 feet per minute...maintain heading 0-5-8."

AFR311: "Heading 0-5-8. Maintaining 120 kt. Descending 300 feet per minute."

AFR932: "On course, five NM out...say altitude."

AFR311: "1,650 feet"

AFR932: "50 feet high...increase descent rate to 350 feet per minute (FPM)."

AFR311: "Roger 350 FPM."

AFR932: "Slight drift left, turn right, new heading 0-6-1. Report established heading 0-6-1."

AFR311: "Heading established 0-6-1."

AFR932: "On course, four miles out, say altitude."

AFR311: "1,300 feet."

AFR932: "On course. Descent rate is now 300 FPM."

AFR311: "Roger 300 FPM."

AFR932: "On course. Three miles from touchdown...altitude should be 1,000 feet."

AFR311: "Roger. 1,000 feet."

AFR932: "New heading 0-6-0. Two miles out, altitude should be 700."

AFR311: "Roger. 0-6-0 and 700 feet."

AFR932: "New heading 0-5-9. Report established 0-5-9."

AFR311: "Established 0-5-9."

AFR932: "On course. One mile out. Altitude should be 400 feet."

AFR311: "400 feet. 0-5-9 heading."

AFR932: "1/2 mile out. On course. Altitude should be 250 feet...Any joy."

AFR311: "250 feet. No Joy."

AFR952: "Over landing lights. On course. 150 feet."

AFR311: "We see the lights and the runway...landing assured." Thirty seconds later, "Air Force Rescue 6-5-3-1-1 is safely on the ground. Thanks Nav. We will see you back at the O' club. Out."

AFR932: "Roger. See you there."

With that, I returned the VHF radio back to the pilot and gave him a heading to Clark AB. About 55 minutes after we arrived, the Jolly crew entered the O' Club and immediately joined the King crew. They informed us that RCC radioed to them that mother and son were doing well. We celebrated a great mission together. My money was "no good" as the chopper guys made sure I had any and all the drinks I wanted.

The copilot of the Jolly crew was the resource manager of the HH-53 pilots. We were always arguing during staff meetings about providing training time for my navigators. He wanted the available and severely limited training time and funds to be spent on the helicopter pilots and very little to be used for the Navs. After completing this mission where his very life depended upon the competence of an HC-130 navigator, I asked him if he still wanted to restrict Nav training. He sheepishly agreed that Navs needed their training time as did every other crew position on both aircraft.

The funniest part of the mission was described to the King crew by the Jolly FE. After describing the turmoil created by placing the reluctant patient and her husband aboard the chopper while on Bataan Island, he continued, "After we took off, the woman was moaning in pain and her husband, sitting on a folding chair in the center aisle, was holding her hand and kept his eyes tightly shut. Remember, they had never seen an aircraft before, let alone a Super Jolly (which grossed out at 44,500 pounds and whose rotary wing extended almost 67 feet in length). Finally, the husband decided to open his eyes right in the middle of in-flight refueling procedures! All this poor bastard saw in front of him, filling the windshield, was the ass end C-130 lit up like a fucking Christmas tree. That dude let out the loudest, most piercing scream I ever did hear. We all heard him . . . even over the roar of the engines! Well, after he stopped screaming, he closed his eyes again and did not open them until we were on the ground at the Manila airport!"

The best part of the mission was learning that the woman gave birth to a healthy boy that night. Both mother and son were doing well. For the next week, my feet never touched the ground. Two other side notes. First, my radar the next day returned to the washed-out state it was before we changed call signs, and I wrote it up as a "red X" item (a necessary maintenance item which needed to be repaired before we would be allowed to fly again). It was a miracle when we changed call signs from King to Air Force Rescue that the radar came to life and when we returned to our King call sign, the radar failed again! Secondly, six years later, when my father passed away, they found a copy of the newspaper clipping which chronicled this particular mission in his wallet. He was proud of the fact that my prowess as a navigator saved the lives of two people. Judaism teaches us that "to save one life is to save the world."

The second mission was a real rescue mission to Iwo Jima. My pilot this mission was again, Capt. Randy Dill. We were playing golf while on "alert" when notification over the UHF "brick" that we all carried was activated. We were told to report to operations immediately. About 15 minutes later, the crew was assembled in the alert aircraft. Over the radios we were informed that we were looking for two Coast Guard servicemen who took a small craft out of the bay located on the island of Iwo Jima. Both the tides and prevailing winds pushed the small craft westward away from the island. They were missing for about two hours when we took off. It took us about 3 1/2 hours to reach our search area.

During our transit time, local fishermen noticed some apparent activity on a very small island approximately 30 NM North of Iwo Jima. We made that sighting our starting point to initiate our search pattern. I directed the aircraft to overfly Iwo Jima and then proceed to the small unidentified island. We flew a sine curve pattern to that island in order to search all possible routes that the small craft might have taken. By the time we reached the target island, it was around four o'clock in the afternoon. This island was maybe a half mile in diameter with a 1,500-foot volcanic cone in the middle. There appeared to be some movement on the beaches surrounding the volcanic cone. Randy took the aircraft down to 1,700 feet and brought us to within 1/4 mile from the shoreline. We circled the island at this low altitude in order to see if any survivors were on the narrow beach. We saw some apparent movement. In response, Randy brought the aircraft closer to the shore at an altitude of five hundred feet. From the surface to about 3,000 feet MSL, we experienced a very strong easterly wind which was blowing about 90 knots in speed. We discovered that the movement we noticed from afar was the flapping of abandoned equipment which was left on the beach. There were no survivors.

Moreover, when we got in the lee of the volcanic cone, we experienced severe to extreme mechanical turbulence due to the strength of the wind blowing from east to west. We took three orbits in order to ensure that the island did not have any survivors located on it. At the end of the third orbit, number one engine started to overheat. Randy increased our altitude to above 7,500 feet in order to get out of that hellacious wind and the turbulence it was causing. The engine continued to overheat and Randy was afraid that if we did not shut it down, it could start an engine fire. Randy called for the shutdown checklist which he and our flight engineer, *MSgt. Ruben Alarcon* followed. However, after shutdown procedures were completed, the propeller would not feather. That meant we could not alter the angle of the prop in order to reduce the speed of rotation. An unfeathered propeller will spin faster than the mechanism holding it in place can tolerate. The faster the aircraft goes, the greater the speed of the unfeathered propeller around its shaft which creates the condition known as a "runaway prop." What makes the situation potentially fatal is this fact: If the propeller speed exceeds red line, the prop can come off its moorings and literally tear the airplane in half. In addition, the faster the prop goes, the more drag it creates for the aircraft making it difficult to stay airborne. If the speed is increased to create more lift, then the danger of the propeller coming off its moorings was also increased. If thrust is reduced then speed is also lessened. But slower speeds also reduce lift. If lift is lowered too much, the plane falls out of the sky! In summary, the "safe" window of speed was only a few knots . . . exceed this "window" and the prop comes off its moorings . . . go lower and the plane ceases to fly. The AC and the FE had to find that very narrow "window."

I knew at once that this was a very dangerous situation. I gave Randy a heading of 1-8-0, taking us to Iwo Jima and the airport located in the center of the island. Randy and Ruben were working furiously, attempting to feather the propeller, without success. They experimented with the airspeed we could fly without causing the prop to over speed and still stay airborne. We found that about 143 knots was optimal speed. Even then, we were not sure that we would reach the island, as we were having trouble maintaining altitude. On the back page of my navigator checklist folder was the form containing the standard ditching message. That consisted of the following: Our present position, altitude, ground speed or true airspeed and our magnetic heading for a specific time. Our radio operator was in contact with Rescue Coordination Center (RCC) via HF radio. I gave him the page I filled out and told him to inform RCC. While he was doing that, I gave Randy further headings to intercept the two-mile final for a straight-in approach to the Iwo Jima aerodrome. It was a race between how slowly we could lose altitude and still possess sufficient flying time in order to reach Iwo Jima. By the time we were on a two-mile final, our altitude was just under 500 feet. Just inside one-mile final, the prop finally feathered, and we landed without incident. Ruben made the comment that maintenance would have to clean up five "brown spots" on the five seats located in the cockpit. We all laughed nervously just happy to be alive and able to walk off the airplane. Unfortunately, the lost "Coastees" or Coast Guard personnel were never found.

We had to wait about a week for maintenance to fix our number one propeller. When they took it off, they measured it and the centrifugal force created by increased speed of rotation caused the propeller to increase its size by 1/16 of an inch! Meanwhile, the forced downtime gave the entire crew a chance to visit this World War II battlefield.

The island is approximately eight square miles in area and is shaped like a diamond with its highest point in the southern corner. That highpoint is Mount Suribachi which is the place where the Marines planted the flag on the third day of the battle to take this island. The photograph of that event became the most iconic picture of World War II. The statue commemorating that flag raising adorns the Tomb of the Unknown Soldier located in Arlington National Cemetery. The island reeks from the sulfur fumes emanating from the volcanic forces which created the island. During the battle, which occurred thirty-three years before I arrived, approximately 107,000 men met and fought on its eight square miles. The number killed and wounded exceeded 30,000 soldiers. The Japanese garrison was defended by approximately 22,000 men. Only two hundred sixteen soldiers of that defensive garrison survived the five-week battle. The men stationed there when I visited the island, both American and Japanese, were still finding bodies located in the deep crevices of the Suribachi volcano and the many caves found all over the island. Many of the gun placements were left to rust as they were buried by debris caused by the battle which was fought more than three decades before. My entire crew climbed Mount Suribachi and looked over the landing sites of the American Marines. There was no cover. Those men took that island which included the fortified Mount Suribachi. Our Marines accomplished this feat with unbridled courage. I do not have words to convey the overwhelming respect I have for the warriors who fought there. I now advocate a position that no one should be allowed to vote in our national election without first climbing Suribachi and seeing with their own eyes the cost of freedom.

On the top of Mount Suribachi, there are two monuments, one Japanese and one American. Both are dedicated to their respective forces who fought gallantly on that island. In 1968, our government turned over control of Iwo Jima to the Japanese government. The Japanese forces on the island maintained the aerodrome and the monuments located there. I saw with my own eyes, that the Japanese preserved both monuments meticulously. They respected the courage both sides displayed in that monumental battle. I am glad that today Japan is a functioning democracy and one of our stronger allies.

I was stationed at Kadina AB for eighteen months. Both Gary Blokland and I rotated back to the states in March of 1979. We were ordered to join the 55th ARRS at Eglin Air Force Base, Florida. We were leaving a great organization which was well led (the 33ARRS) and joining the exact opposite in Florida.

18

55TH ARRS

In March 1979, I departed Kadina AB. The Air Force granted me a month's leave which I used to go stateside and see my father and JG and his family. My father was much grayer than I remembered. He lived continuously in Florida, and so that was my first stop. He was enjoying playing golf and taking it easy. Unlike my experiences in Southeast Asia, I was able to tell him about flying rescue. I gave him a copy of the newspaper account of the Filipino rescue where we saved a mother and her unborn child. Remembering that Jewish tradition teaches us that to save one life is to save the world, and on that night, I helped save two lives, really touched my dad and was a source of pride for the old man. That meant the world to him and because I loved him so much, his reaction and pride in my accomplishment meant the world to me.

I spent a week with Dad talking about old times and some of the funny things that occurred while I was flying rescue. He missed having Mom around, and he knew that his time was short. The doctors told him that his heart was severely weakened by two previous heart attacks.

We got to play several rounds of golf together which we both really enjoyed.

The second week of leave I went north to visit JG and Hope. I arrived at LaGuardia Airport where Hope picked me up and took me back to their home in Suffolk County. I would spend the next ten days with them. It was about two o'clock in the afternoon when we arrived. Both children were attending the local elementary school and were due to be dropped off about an hour after we got there. We had some time to talk by ourselves. Hope had put on about 15 pounds, and her hair had a few gray streaks in it. Her eyes were as bright as ever and so was her mind. She had developed a thriving practice as a psychiatric social worker. She limited her outside work to about twenty hours a week in order to devote time to raising her two children.

She told me that JG was enjoying tremendous success. He was now a full partner in a rising law firm. He ran all operations on Long Island and on occasion, the firm needed his expertise in major cases that were heard in New York City. He was on a first name basis with the Democrat Party hierarchy on Long Island. He helped the party raise money and provided free legal advice. The problem for Hope was he was so busy that his time for his family was very limited.

Daniel, now ten years old, was an up and coming baseball player and spent a lot of time playing little league baseball. Elizabeth Mae was seven years old and her interests were playing soccer and dance lessons. She was quick and agile which served both interests well. The soccer coach of the girls under-ten years old travel team watched her play recreational soccer and was impressed. She wanted Elizabeth Mae to play on her squad. Moving up to travel soccer would require a great deal more practice and more time away from home. Hope adjusted her schedule in order to make this happen. Both children were doing very well in school. Given who their parents were, that fact did not surprise me.

A little after three o'clock that afternoon, Hope and I walked to the nearby bus stop where the children were dropped off. We didn't have to wait long when the yellow bus stopped and four children got off. Daniel and Elizabeth Mae saw me standing next to their mother. They ran yelling that "Uncle" Blake was here, which made me feel really good. After giving both of them an exuberant hug, we walked back to the house. Hope asked the children about their day, and they excitedly told us what they were learning and the various things that were occurring in the school. I also found out that Elizabeth Mae liked to be called just Mae and Daniel answered best to Danny. They made sure that Uncle Blake understood how they like to be addressed.

That afternoon, Mae was going to have a soccer practice and Danny was going to play a Little League baseball game. JG had an Austin Healey sports car that he liked to drive on the weekends. Hope gave me the keys and directions to Mae's practice field. She took Danny to his game and gave me driving instructions to meet her at the baseball field with Mae after the soccer practice was over. Usually his baseball games were scheduled for 6:30 in the evening, but today the game was scheduled for five, as Danny's coach had to leave early the next day on a business trip. Both he and the opposing coach agreed to the new start time. Hope was worried that she would have to choose between the two, but my being there made that choice unnecessary.

Elizabeth Mae got in the front seat with me, and we proceeded to her practice field which was only a couple miles away. She got excited when she saw her teammates. I pulled in and parked next to the other cars. There was a half-dozen moms located on the sidelines watching their girls and their friends gather for the practice. I was the only male there, as the coach was also a soccer mom. I introduced myself to the coach and the other moms, and they were curious as to my relationship with Elizabeth Mae, JG and Hope. After answering their questions, I concentrated on watching the practice. After twenty minutes or so, I noticed that the team needed work on proper spacing, quicker passing and shooting techniques. I waited until the first break and asked the coach if she would mind if I ran a few drills to help in this regard. I told her of my background as a player and as a coach. I think she was curious as to what I would do so she told me to run the next half of practice. I placed the girls into separate lines, and we did two quick passing drills. It took the girls a while, but they started absorbing the technique, and as a group, they were passing much better. I took them through two of my favorite shooting drills. Some of the players had problems keeping their shots low to the ground. I demonstrated a couple techniques which allowed the player to keep the shots under the cross bar. By the end of the drills, all of them were shooting better. Finally, the last fifteen minutes, we did a full-scale scrimmage, where I could emphasize proper spacing and decision-making. I went about twenty minutes longer than they normally go, but nobody minded. In fact, the coach asked me to assist her as long as I was going to be in New York. I agreed to her request, as I really enjoyed coaching again, and the parents I met seemed to be fine people.

After the practice was over, I took Elizabeth Mae to the baseball game where we watched Danny's team play. Hope saw me drive into the parking area and waved to me. Elizabeth Mae ran from the car and excitedly told her mother what happened at her practice. Hope asked me, "Are you sure you really want to do this? I mean, that's a lot of time from your vacation."

I answered, "Of course I do. I had a ball, and I really like and enjoy the kids on Mae's team." I looked over and saw that Danny's game was in progress, and I asked how the team, and Danny in particular, were doing. It was the bottom of the fifth inning, and Danny's team was coming up to bat with the score tied at two runs apiece. Danny was scheduled to bat fifth. He came up with runners on second and third and two out. He hit an outside pitch to the opposite field for a single which scored both runners. The team held on and won the game 4-3 in a very exciting game. We left the field about ten minutes before seven and I followed Hope back to their home.

As I pulled in the driveway, I saw JG, already changed out of his suit, coming out to meet us. Danny ran out from his mom's car, and Elizabeth Mae jumped out of the Austin Healey. Both ran to their dad excitedly telling him about their afternoon. He gave both of them a hug and laughingly said, "One at a time."

Hope told them, "Let's get inside and wash up. Supper will be served in ten minutes. You can tell your dad all about it after we are sitting at the table. Now move!" Both children ran into the house and did what their mother asked. Hope had prepared a wonderful beef stew in a slow cook pot. She had baked potatoes in the oven and a fresh salad in the fridge. Ten minutes after we got inside, she had the meal on the table. JG, with all of us seated, said, "Now, let's hear all about it!"

Danny, being the oldest, went first. He described the game in detail and in particular his game-winning hit. I added, when he was done, that it was a fine piece of hitting as he took a pitch over the outside corner and drove it to the opposite field. That really impressed me as a hitter, a baseball player and a fan of the game. Danny beamed with the praise. Elizabeth Mae then told her dad about the practice and the drills I was running. She was thrilled that I would assist the coach for the next five practices and for her first two games of the season. JG smiled. Because I flew For the Air Force and was away most of the time, I missed most of the normal milestones of a growing child. In the next ten days, I would see Danny play two more games and assist in coaching Elizabeth Mae's team. It really helped me bond with my godchildren.

I told the children that I had a surprise for them. During a two-week TDY mission on the Korean Peninsula, I purchased two flight jackets that were made for the children. I had the Korean tailor embroider the jackets with navigator wings, 33rd ARRS patch and their names. The children loved their gifts and couldn't wait to show them off to their schoolmates the next day.

Hope took charge of the children and supervised their homework duties and made sure they took a complete and thorough shower. While she took care of the children, JG showed me the addition that he had built onto the existing house. It was there that he had his personal office and Hope had her waiting room and a treatment room for her patients. The addition also had its own complete bathroom and a guestroom which became my room for the next ten days. JG also showed me his recently installed tennis court and in-ground pool which were completed about a month before I got there.

After the children were put to bed, the adults returned to the den where JG and I had a couple beers as Hope sipped a glass of wine. They asked about the missions I was doing while flying for the 33rd ARRS. They were really interested in the mission that I flew in the Philippines where we saved a mother and her unborn child. In turn, Hope told me that her practice was as full as she wanted and that she had patients on a waiting list. She could go full time to pursue her career, but motherhood trumped that aspiration.

I asked Hope how the Steins, her next-door neighbors, were coping with the loss of Lisa, their daughter and only child. Hope liked them both and was becoming very attached to them, particularly Mrs. Stein. Hope told me that both were making some progress accepting the death of their daughter. I asked, "Do you think it would help if I said something to Mrs. Stein? I really liked Lisa, and I truly wish that I'd had more time with her. I don't want to do harm, but I would like her to know how I felt about her daughter."

Hope answered, "I think Edna would appreciate your taking the time to see her. I'll call ahead and make sure it's okay. If it is, I will set up a time when you can go over there." That seemed acceptable to me, and that's what we did. Hope got up and went into her treatment room. JG and I filled the time talking about sports, baseball in particular, as he was an avid Dodger fan, and I was just as committed to the Giants. About fifteen minutes later, Hope came back into the den and told me that Edna Stein would like to talk to me after breakfast. I told her that was fine with me.

JG then told me that he was now a full partner in his law firm. He ran the family law operations which was centered in Mineola, Long Island. About once or twice a month he would be involved with the more extensive portion of the practice which dealt with major lawsuits in New York City venues. His expertise was both as a trial attorney and, more importantly for the big cases in the city, the firm's expert in picking jurors. His uncanny sense to "read" people gave his firm a huge edge in trying cases. He was almost always correct. Once his boss, now his partner, asked him how he did it. JG answered honestly that he didn't know. It was a gut reaction, but it was almost always the right decision. I truly understood how he felt, as my "gut" kept me alive in combat and also resulted in making the proper life-and-death decisions that a fire control officer in an AC-130 gunship must make.

About 9:30 that evening, JG and I decided to go for a walk while Hope stayed behind to take care of the dishes and the children. The outside was the only place that JG could smoke. Hope didn't smoke and did not tolerate it in the house. She thought rightly that seeing any adult smoke was not a good example for the children to emulate. I gave up cigarettes while I was still stationed back in Kadina AB on a dare issued by Col. Watkins. I stopped smoking by going "cold turkey." However, the urge to smoke was still very strong within me. It was a chilly evening and I put on my flight jacket while JG wore his Marietta sweater. We walked around his neighborhood. As soon as we were out of view from JG's home, he lit a cigarette and drew a deep inhalation. The street was wide and had almost no traffic which made for very good walking conditions.

JG told me that he spent one or two weekends in the city when they have very lucrative cases. He was now pulling down over $300,000 a year. His end-of-year bonus would more than double his salary. His partners wanted him to move to the city full time as the lead trial lawyer, but he resisted that suggestion because he wanted to be close to his children, and he did not want to move them. If he moved to New York, it would really hurt his family. The practice offered to literally double the salary, but JG held firm.

He then told me that he was carrying on an affair with two women. One was a young housewife who suffered from an abusive husband. JG was representing her in her divorce proceedings against her husband. I asked, "Isn't that dangerous?"

JG laughed and said, "I know my customer. She's not serious about me and besides, I am taking her case pro bono. She's very happy with my representation and the comfort I provide her. She is beautiful and totally sexy . . . a walking wet dream!"

"Who's the second one?" I asked.

"Another lawyer. Her name is Rachel. She works in the city for an opposing firm. We usually get together on those weekends that I have to spend in the city. Rachel likes my sense of humor and knows that I am married. In fact, that makes me very attractive to her because I will not make demands outside the bedroom. She likes her independence, and she likes to fuck. She was a gymnast in college. Rachel still works out and her body is incredible. One day when I knew she was coming to the firm's New York City apartment, I placed two placards under the bed before she got there. It was fairly late when she arrived, and so we went straight to the bedroom. The sex was truly incredible. Afterwards, Rachel asked me just how good it was. I reached under the bed and pulled out the two cards which I had placed there earlier. One card had a nine and the second card had an eight. I gave her a 9.8 just like they do in the Olympics when rating gymnastics. She howled with laughter. Then she hit me on the chest and said to me that we'd experienced a 10.0. I agreed and told her that I had anticipated a rating based on the last time we were together. We laughed again!"

"How do you keep all of this from Hope?"

"So far it hasn't been a problem. I work long hours, and I bring home an enormous amount of money. Besides, Hope is busy with her practice and our children."

"I think Hope is a wonderful woman and a great wife. If it were me, I would feel too guilty to do that."

"Blake, I feel sometimes that I married too young. Hope was the first woman that I have ever slept with. I still love her, and I would never want to get a divorce, but I feel that I missed out on having some kind of adventure in my life. When I was in high school, it was always the other guys who got the pretty girls—never me. Now I can have all the women I ever wanted."

I looked at my friend of almost twenty years. His light brown hair was thinning. His blue eyes were too close together to be considered handsome. He weighed probably thirty pounds more than he should.

Hope, after giving birth to two children, had a matronly body. She was no longer the lithesome girl I remembered in college. Yet, both were beautiful to me. Is it a quirk of mine that a person's personality and persona affect how they are perceived by me. If I like someone's personality, then they become physically attractive in my eyes. The reverse is also true. When I know someone well, I can no longer be objective regarding how he or she looks.

Hope, being the kind, gentle and intelligent person that she was and is always appealed to me. The longer I knew Hope, the prettier she got in my eyes. This was also true for JG's dad, who became more and more enthralled with Hope as he got to know her better. The beauty of her soul and her conversion to Judaism led to the old man's rapprochement with his son. Hope took to the religion because of its ethical basis and its emphasis on doing good works. All this passed through my mind before I answered JG.

"I think you're risking losing her. Frankly, it's a risk I would not take. Hope is the real deal. I hope someday you realize how lucky you are and that she will never find out about your cheating. I love both you guys. Your children are wonderful. You should appreciate them and not let lust destroy your family."

We walked about ten minutes in silence. JG decided to change the subject, and he asked me about coaching Elizabeth Mae's soccer team. I told him how much I enjoyed the experience and how it also gave me the opportunity to know her as a person. In the next twenty minutes, on the way home, I filled him in regarding the team and how Elizabeth Mae would make a fine striker. I told him what we were going to work on regarding the skills and decision-making abilities that each teammate must acquire. He listened intently to my uninterrupted layout of how I was going to make them a much better team. He told me that he would make it his business to attend the first two games as the team would be under my influence. He told me to use his Austin Healey as my own. Then JG informed me that he'd arranged a temporary membership in his racquet club which was about five miles from where he lived. The club was mainly for tennis but did have an active racquetball membership.

I played racquetball in the morning and coached in the afternoon. It didn't take me long to find able opponents in the racquetball court. I played at an advanced level, and the club manager arranged for players who could challenge me. I would generally play for two to three hours each day. The club had excellent facilities, and I would shower there and change into dry clothes. JG was an advanced tennis player. That game was too slow for me, and I couldn't get into playing it. I loved the speed, the power, the quick anticipation and especially the sound of a well struck 'kill shot' which echoed like a gunshot! Tennis was way too tame for me.

The second day I was there, I visited with Mrs. Stein. It was not easy because I really appreciated just how much she had lost. I wanted her to know that I really enjoyed Lisa's company. I told Mrs. Stein that I wanted to spend more time with her daughter. She responded, "I know. Lisa told me that you invited her to accompany you to an Air Force school somewhere in the south."

"That's true, ma'am. I hoped that spending time with me would help her get free of the drugs. In the time we spent together, Lisa was clean which gave me hope. I told Lisa at the time that she could not use if she was with me and that I would help her in any way I could to free her of that horrible addiction. I asked her to accompany me to Montgomery Air Force Base in Alabama for two months if she could remain drug-free. She chose to remain in San Francisco. I still regret her choice, but I could not change her mind. I wish I had that ability to do so."

"So do I. Oh God, so do I!" she sobbed. The tears were now flowing freely. Mrs. Stein struggled to regain control of herself and continued, "When my husband and I found out that Lisa was dating an Air Force officer, we were thrilled. We hoped against all hope that having a stable relationship with a truly decent and strong person would help her kick the habit. I want you to know how close you came. Lisa called me for the next to last time about two days before she died. She told me about your offer and how she really wanted to go, but she was scared that she could not remain clean for two months. Both her dad and I encouraged her to go with you. We wanted her out of the San Francisco environment. Lisa really enjoyed the time she spent with you. I heard it in her voice. We are grateful that she found some happiness in her short life before she was overcome by drugs."

I again passed on my condolences and told her that if she needed anything, Hope would know how to find me. She wished me well and thanked me for coming. I told her it was the least I could do. I would always remember Lisa fondly and that I still missed her. We hugged and I said my goodbyes. I walked back to JG's home.

Hope was waiting for me. She asked how it went. I told her, as accurately as I could, all that transpired. I also told her how sorry I was for Mrs. Stein. I think it helped her to hear something positive about her daughter. I told Hope that I felt I did some good. At least that is what I thought. Several days later, after meeting with Lisa's mother, Hope told me that my visit benefited Mrs. Stein who was grateful I took the time to tell her about her daughter. I told Hope that when I found out that Lisa died from a drug overdose, I felt both the emotions of loss and anger. A loss because I would never see Lisa again and anger that drugs killed a person for whom I cared deeply.

The days passed quickly. When Danny had his games, I would also be in attendance. It was fun spending time with JG's family and especially getting to know the children. They'd changed so much. The time we spent together also made me want to have a family of my own. I was approaching my 40th birthday within a couple years and felt that the time had come . . . if I met the right person.

JG was true to his word. He attended both games and saw his little girl score three goals. He was thrilled. I gave the coach some pointers on how to improve the team and the drills that she should use to accomplish this goal. Before I left, the girls on the team gave me a signed soccer ball with all their names on it and a picture of the team.

I departed New York in the last week of March, 1979. I arrived at a small airport near Eglin Air Force Base. I rented a car and drove onto the base. I signed into the VOQ (Visiting Officers' Quarters) and my squadron, the 55th ARRS, otherwise called the "double nickel." They gave me another week to find off-base housing and to buy a car. I bought a three-bedroom ranch at the urging of my real estate agent, who told me correctly," . . . to buy a house that would be easy to resell, it must have three bedrooms, a two-car garage and a fireplace." The ranch I purchased had all three. I purchased a brand-new Toyota because I had sold all my other vehicles before going overseas.

I reported for duty to my new squadron. Unfortunately, as well led as 33rd ARRS was, in contrast, the 55th was just the opposite. Both the commander and the operations officer were career staffers with no combat experience. In Jimmy Carter's military, staffers were promoted over warriors. The only saving grace about being in the squadron was the fact that Gary Blokland, my pilot in the 33rd, transferred to the 55th at the same time I did. I continued to fly with him for most of my missions in our new squadron. Our morale as a unit was further deteriorated by the fact that more than 90% of the pilots and navigators either had their dates of separation (DOS) established or were in the process of requesting separation from the service.

By the time I had spent a month in the 55th, I realized how poor the leadership was and how most of the crews were dangerously inexperienced. *Lt. Col. Jennings*, the operations officer was my reporting official. He was the polar opposite of Col. Frank Watkins who was my direct boss in the 33rd. Where Col. Watkins was a great pilot, a gifted officer, and the personification of leadership: Col. Jennings was an inept pilot with virtually no leadership capabilities whatsoever. It was difficult for me to serve under a man for whom I virtually had no respect. Col. Jennings made it abundantly clear that my lack of staff work would preclude me from being the navigator resource manager as I was in the 33rd. We constantly bumped heads as to how to complete various mission requirements. This undertow of a personality conflict, mixed with a totally different view on how to accomplish a mission, made my time serving under this man hard to endure.

Matters came to a head in July, 1979, approximately four months after I got there. At this time, the Nicaraguan Sandinistas were in conflict with the Contras. There was a risk that this war would spill over to the neighboring country of Panama. The president ordered the military to beef up the area around the Panama Canal. Our squadron was tasked to establish a forward operations area on Howard Air Force Base which was located near the Canal Zone. Two things occurred which cemented in my own mind that it was time to leave the United States Air Force.

The first was the fact that intelligence reports indicated that the Sandinistas had access to the handheld SA-7 SAM (surface to air missile). This was the very same weapon used to shoot down Spectre 11 which I experienced first-hand on June 18, 1972. After my return to Ubon, I helped develop the tactics which defeated this weapon system every time it was used against the AC-130 gunships. Part of these tactics was the deployment of a decoy flare which would cause the missile to track it, rather than the aircraft. In the rescue version of the C-130, the system used to deploy the decoy flare was the ALE-20 Flare Dispenser. The control mechanism of the ALE-20 was located on the navigator's desk. We went into a potential combat situation where none of the crews knew how to detect or defeat the SA-7 SAM, and none of the ALE-20 systems were ever checked to see if they worked under real flight conditions! In my whole squadron, there was only one other rated officer who had actual combat experience besides me. This lack of experience was hard to believe only six years after the Vietnam armistice was signed.

After being in Panama for a week, I developed a severe case of strep throat. My temperature rose to 104°, and I was medevac'd to Eglin Air Force Base. I was seriously ill and hospitalized for almost a week. Finally, the temperature broke, but it took another week to sufficiently regain my health in order for me to return to flying status. By the second week of August, I was placed on alert for possible redeployment back to Panama. My pilot was Capt. Ralph Zeller who was the only other combat experienced flight officer in my squadron. We arrived at squadron headquarters at 0715 for a 0730 brief which lasted approximately fifteen minutes. We were then bussed to the alert aircraft where we proceeded to preflight our equipment. When I turned on the radar, I noticed that it was not "painting" weather returns. In accordance with existing regulations, I "red Xed" that airplane which meant that it could not be used as an alert aircraft. Radar was considered a "no go" system. If it did not operate properly, the airplane was considered unflyable. This was especially true if the track would go across the Gulf of Mexico in August. The Gulf during this time of year was literally covered with severe and extreme thunderstorms. Aircrews depended upon radar to safely navigate around them. There is so much power in a well-developed thunderstorm that it can literally rip an aircraft to pieces due to the tremendous forces encountered when experiencing simultaneous and violent updrafts and downdrafts.

After I "red Xed" the airplane, we climbed back on the bus and returned to squadron headquarters. Before the bus was parked, Col. Jennings came out to meet us. He was fuming. He looked directly at me and shouted, "You obviously made a mistake in your preflight of the alert aircraft! Go back and do it correctly. You understand me, Capt. Blakeman!"

"Yes sir," I responded. The rest of the crew departed, and the bus driver then took me back to the airplane. The crew chief was waiting for me. He started the auxiliary power unit (APU). I turned on the radar and attempted to tune it so that it would "paint" the thunderstorms which already surrounded our base. The onboard radar was still not capable of painting a line of thunderstorms approximately ten miles from our position, so I "red Xed" the airplane again. The bus driver took me back and Col. Jennings was waiting for me again. "Capt. Blakeman," he yelled at me as he got on the bus, "you obviously need help in preflighting the radar system, so I am sending a radar technician to accompany you in preflighting the onboard radar. Now go back out there and do it right!"

"Yes sir!" I responded. The colonel left the bus and the radar technician came aboard. Back we went to the alert aircraft that I was assigned to fly. The crew chief turned on the aircraft's APU, and I proceeded to turn on the radar as the technician watched my every move. When the radar was on fully, I turned to the technician and said, "Look at the line of thunderstorms approaching from the west." I pointed toward the front of the airplane where the "boomers" were located. I then said to the technician, "Do you see that line approaching us on the radar?"

He responded, "No sir, I do not."

"Well, I need the radar to paint boomers at least forty miles out. If it can't do that, then the aircraft is unsafe."

"Yes sir."

"Let's go over to the other alert aircraft, and I'll bring up the radar and you'll see the returns, and you'll also see what I am looking for." We shut down the radar and the APU and walked over to the second alert aircraft. The crew chief attempted to bring up the second aircraft's APU and could not do so, so we "red Xed" the second aircraft. Then the technician and the alert crew chief brought over a mobile power cart to provide power to the second aircraft. Now that aircraft had power, I could (and did) bring up the onboard radar. The scope showed not only the first visible line of boomers, but two other lines directly behind it. The first line was the only one we could see from the ground. That is why radar is so important for weather avoidance . . . the crew needs to be able to see beyond the first line to remain reasonably safe in a thunderstorm-filled environment. The radar clearly showed not just a single line of thunderstorms, but three separate distinct lines of boomers headed our way. I turned to the technician and said, "When the first aircraft's radar looks like this, I will accept it and you can remove the red X." We powered down the aircraft and returned to the squadron.

Col. Jennings was there to meet us, and he was beyond furious. Now we had "red Xed" two alert aircraft. That meant we had no available aircraft to respond to an emergency or rescue situation. The technician, caught between two warring officers, was clearly uncomfortable. He confirmed that the radar was indeed not usable on the first aircraft and that the second aircraft needed an APU replacement. Both jobs would take at least several hours to complete. I told Col. Jennings that I was going to the officer's club to get some breakfast and that he should call me when the aircraft was ready to be preflighted again. He wasn't happy, but he had no choice.

I went to the club. There I joined Capt. Ralph Zeller (nicknamed Zelly) for breakfast. I told him what had occurred. We both had a good laugh thinking about Col. Jennings' reaction when he learned that he had two "red Xed" aircraft, not just one! Zelly told me that Col. Jennings tried to pressure him to overwrite my "red X." He would not do so. Zelly was the only other combat experienced flight officer in my squadron. Both of us would not put a crew in danger by accepting an aircraft to fly the Gulf without radar. I felt much better having my pilot's backing.

After a leisurely breakfast, I returned to the squadron to see how far they had come in repairing the radar system aboard my alert aircraft. A few moments after stepping out of my car, Col. Jennings, accompanied by eight maintenance officers and NCOs, literally dragged me into a dark room in the basement of the squadron headquarters. There Col. Jennings attempted to bully me into removing my "red X." He accused me of being incompetent.

Frankly, I was furious. This was the last straw. I pulled off my nameplate from my flight suit which contained my name and wings. It was attached just above my left pocket using Velcro tape. The nameplate came into my right hand, and I thrust it into the colonel's hand. He was stunned by my reaction, as I said to him, "If you think you can navigate this fucking aircraft better than I can, here are my wings. You fly the fucking airplane!" With that, I turned and left, leaving Col. Jennings with his mouth wide open holding my nameplate.

I returned home and awaited the phone call I knew was coming. About six hours later, an operations NCO notified me that the alert aircraft was ready for pre-flight and that I would be met by Capt.

Zeller. We would pre-flight the aircraft again. I told the NCO that I was on my way. It took me about 20 minutes to get back into my flying suit and return to squadron headquarters. There I met Zelly, and together we were bussed to the alert aircraft. This time the radar came up as it should, and I signed off that the aircraft was ready for flight. Zelly had put his signature over the "red X" and that made the aircraft legally fit to fly.

After they dropped us off at squadron headquarters, Zelly and I went to the officer's club for supper. I told him what had occurred with Col. Jennings. I found out from Zelly that the colonel tried to pressure him again. We were both furious that a senior officer would act in such an amoral way. The fact that he would risk an entire crew and wantonly abandon the written regulations regarding safety of flight was, in our opinion, absolutely unforgivable. We were the only two combat experienced officers in the entire squadron. For the next two hours Zelly and I discussed our options, and we decided that next morning that we would put in our requests for dates of separation (DOS). And that's what we did. The next morning, while still on alert, we went to the personnel office. There we filled out the forms needed to separate from the service. I was told that the earliest date I could get was June, 1980. Zelly's earliest DOS date was a month later.

For the next 14 months, I performed my duties as a squadron navigator and nothing more. When I was not taking required training, flying missions or sitting alert, I spent my time preparing to leave the service. I was either going to return to Sacramento or go back to my roots in New York. As it turned out, one of my father's contemporaries, Mr. Moshe Zester, found out that I was leaving the service. He needed somebody he could trust who knew the trucking business and who could manage men. Mr. Zester wrote to me in Florida and offered to pay my way to New York to be interviewed. I informed Mr.

Zester in my written response that I would be available for an interview the Friday following Thanksgiving if that was agreeable to him. He responded that it was indeed most satisfactory and that he was looking forward to meeting me. He enclosed his business address, phone number, driving directions to his office and a check which more than covered my expenses in traveling back and forth to New York.

By the time all this transpired it was already well into October, 1979. After I made my plane reservations to LaGuardia Airport, I called JG's home phone and Hope answered. I told her that I was returning to New York for Thanksgiving and I asked her, "Would you like some company?" Hope squealed with delight and asked if I needed a ride from the airport. I told her I did indeed.

On Tuesday, November 26, 1979, I arrived on time, and JG was there to meet me. A little after ten at night, we made our way to his home. JG was driving his Mercedes which was his regular automobile. He told me that, as before, I could use his Austin Healey for the week that I would be staying with the family. He was excited about my job interview because, if I landed the position, I would, once again, be near my best friend and his family.

Traffic was light that night which made conversation possible. I asked how he was doing. JG told me that he'd just finished spending the weekend in New York City because a huge class-action suit was being heard. He spent Friday, Saturday and all of Monday helping the senior partner select a jury. The case was on hold, as the trial judge had to make several rulings regarding objections by both sides. The case was going to be resumed the following Monday morning. JG was free until Friday morning when he had to go back to the city and sit second seat to the senior partner. If they won, JG's share of legal fees would exceed one million dollars. We could spend Wednesday and Thursday together, but by early Friday morning, JG would take the train into the city and not return until after I departed. I told him that I appreciated even the two days that we could share together.

I asked how things were going with Hope and the children. JG's immediate response of silence was ominous to me. I was worried that his philandering would destroy the relationship he had with his wife. After about half a minute, JG told me, "I haven't had intimate relations with Hope in over six weeks. We had an argument about some minor issue, and it got blown way out of context. At first, she withheld sex from me. About two weeks ago, she wanted to make up and I withheld sex from her. I will not tolerate the use of sex as a weapon. I saw the effects of that tactic on many of the divorce cases that I handled."

"How long are you going to keep this up?" I asked.

"Until she agrees that sex can no longer be used as a weapon in our relationship. Hope can be stubborn, as you know, but I think I am winning my argument."

"What about the other women you have been seeing?"

"I have been so busy with this case that I have not seen my Mineola office for over three weeks. On occasion, when I am in the city, I get a phone call from Rachel seeing if it is possible for us to get together. Over the past six weeks, I've seen her three times."

"Does Hope suspect anything?"

"No. She knows that I have been working as much as twenty hours a day on this case. She also knows that if I win it, it will make our family financially secure for a long time."

"Dammit, JG! Don't risk it. Put an end to it. You have a great family and you're acting in a reckless manner. Do you still love Hope?"

"Oh God, yes. More than ever. Sometimes I wonder why I do what I do."

"If there's anything I can do, don't hesitate to ask. I would do anything to help keep you guys together."

"Thanks Blake. That means the world to me."

"On a more pleasant note, tell me about my godchildren." JG then proceeded to tell me how well they were doing. He also told me that both Danny and Elizabeth Mae really enjoyed my last visit. They kept talking about it long after I left. And they both enjoyed having a unique flight jacket with their names embroidered on the front just like the flight jacket I wore.

It was just about eleven o'clock in the evening when we arrived, and Hope was there to welcome both of us. JG got a kiss on the lips, and I got a hug and a kiss on the cheek for my welcome. Hope was tired as she had to get up early the next morning and the children still had a half day of school on Wednesday. She told me to make myself at home and then excused herself so she could go to bed. I could see JG was also very tired and so was I as I flew a practice ride early that morning. We said our good nights to each other, and I took my suitcase to the guest room in the back. I took a shower and went right to bed.

The next morning I was awakened by the normal sounds made by children. I quickly got dressed and made my way into the kitchen where both Daniel and Elizabeth Mae were eating their breakfast. They both ran into my arms as I entered the kitchen. I gave them hugs and, at their mother's urging, they went back to their food. Hope told me that we would eat after the children got on the bus. They wanted me to take them to the bus stop wearing my flight jacket. Hope thought it was a good idea and urged me to do it. I agreed. After breakfast, they put on their flight jackets, and I put on my official Air Force flight jacket. They wanted their friends to see a real Air Force officer accompany them to the bus stop. Frankly, I got a kick out of doing what they requested.

After the kids were safely on their way, I returned to the kitchen where Hope was making breakfast for both of us. After the usual pleasantries, I asked Hope how Mrs. Stein was doing. Hope felt that she was turning the corner and finally able to accept the death of her daughter. Hope also sensed that my visit was beneficial to Lisa's mom. It was the least I could do.

I noticed that JG's Mercedes was not in the driveway. I asked Hope where he had gone. She told me that he got called to the office because there was a problem in the class-action suit that the law firm was pursuing. One of the jurors took ill and had to be replaced. JG went into the city to help the firm sit the final juror. When that was done, he would return to Long Island. As before, he left me the keys to his Austin Healey and a temporary membership in his tennis club. Hope told me to enjoy myself at the club and to be home by one o'clock in the afternoon because she planned to take the children to see the "Star Wars" movie. It had been out for more than a year, but now the children were old enough to see and appreciate this futuristic movie without being overly scared.

I went to the club and, as luck would have it, I found a very good racquetball player who was looking for a game. We played for several hours, splitting four games. We both got a really good workout, and I made an arrangement to play with him on Saturday morning. I showered at the club and changed into my Ohio State sweatshirt and blue jeans. I returned to JG and Hope's home by 12:45 that afternoon. We both waited at the bus stop for the children to arrive. About fifteen minutes later, the bus rolled up and four children got off. Danny and Elizabeth Mae ran to Hope and then to me in order to get a welcoming hug. We retired back to the kitchen where the four of us shared some tuna salad sandwiches and soft drinks.

After lunch, we went to the local theater and saw the first "*Star Wars*" movie. The kids loved it. When we got home, JG was waiting for us. The kids ran to their father and told him all about the movie. He smiled seeing how happy his children were, but I knew JG better than any person in the world. I saw a twinge of sadness in his face because he missed seeing his children so thoroughly enjoy an unusual experience. Watching them enjoy that movie really enhanced the whole experience for me. How much more meaningful and poignant would it have been for the person who was actually their father? I sensed his loss and sadness.

For the next two days, JG was totally devoted to spending time with me, Hope and his children. Thursday, the day of Thanksgiving, Hope was up early preparing a large turkey dinner. The house smelled delicious. As a result, I went around the house being in a perpetual state of hunger. Finally, about three o'clock in the afternoon, we sat down for a family Thanksgiving dinner. It was magnificent. Hope had become a great cook. She even baked an apple pie, knowing it was my favorite. When she brought out that magnificent pie and a large pot of coffee, it brought to mind something that occurred to JG and me when we were still students at Marietta College. I reminded JG of the incident and we both laughed. Hope and the children wanted to know what was so funny, so JG and I took turns telling this tale.

This occurred after the fall semester in our senior year. We would travel back to New York in my little Saab automobile. We left Marietta College about ten o'clock that evening. We took Route 22 through some of the Pennsylvania Dutch country. There was a truck stop there which was about halfway between Marietta College and Long Island. We both were hungry, and I needed coffee to stay awake as it was about three o'clock in the morning. JG and I went to the counter where there was one other truck driver. There were two waitresses who were serving food for the counter patrons. We five were the only people in the building. The waitresses were a young, very pretty girl, approximately twenty years old, and her mother, who was about fifty. JG started teasing the young girl and everyone joined in. It was great fun, as JG's humor was usually dished out without even a trace of malice. Even being the butt of one of his jokes, anyone could sense that he was laughing with you and not at you. We spent the next two hours laughing hilariously at some of the humorous remarks made at the young girl's expense. Even her mother joined in, telling us some of her daughter's peccadilloes. The young lady who was the subject of this "abuse" really enjoyed being the center of attention. We spent almost two hours there and had a great time. It made the rest the trip much more endurable as we laughed all the way home.

After JG and I finished our rendition of that chance meeting in the Pennsylvania Dutch country, I added this comment: "The strange part was when I related this experience to my father. He then asked me exactly where this truck stop was located. I gave him the approximate mile marker on Route 22 and he laughed. I asked him what was so funny. Dad told me that he ate at that same truck stop many times when he used to drive that route. Dad also told me what he remembered about the full-time waitress he encountered some twenty-five or thirty years ago. I do believe it was the young lady's mother whom Dad described!" I related that to JG and he smiled. He thoroughly enjoyed the coincidence.

After a remarkably good meal, JG and I retired to the den where we watched football. Thanksgiving without football is almost a cardinal sin! We talked sports for the rest of the evening.

The next morning, I had an early breakfast with JG and Hope. I went back to my room and changed into a suit and tie. I took my attaché case with me and drove the Austin Healey to my appointment with Mr. Moshe Zester. His trucking business was located in Franklin Square, Long Island. I arrived about fifteen minutes early, as I gave myself extra time to find his location. His building was a two-story warehouse with an extensive dock in the rear and offices located in the front of the building. I parked the Austin Healey and found my way into the main entrance. As I entered the building, I saw that the office door was on my immediate right. I entered and encountered a middle-aged woman behind the desk. She looked up and said, "Hello, are you Mr. Norris Blakeman?" I told her I was.

She then pushed the button and said into the interphone that I was in the office. A gruff voice said to her, "Bring him in." She opened the door to the inner office and indicated with her right hand that I was to enter which I did.

Mr. Zester was sitting behind his desk. As I entered, he rose and offered me a firm handshake and a genuine smile. He was about my height and weighed about 190 pounds. His thinning hair was brown with many gray highlights. He had warm brown eyes and a generous mouth. He offered me a seat facing his desk.

"I know your father, Norris. I know him well. He and I started our businesses about the same time. In fact, on some of the bigger contracts, we pooled our resources in order to bid them. Your dad is a man of his word. When he gave you a handshake on a deal, you could take it to the bank. I spoke with his foreman, Ike. I asked him about you and if you were like your father. Ike regarded you very highly as he did your dad. That meant a lot to me. The past several years, my business, ZM Distribution, has grown, and I need help in managing it. I understand you know the trucking business, and in particular, how a well-run dock should be operated. Is that true?"

"Yes sir. My father taught me well."

"Good. Besides competence, I need somebody with leadership abilities and above all other things, someone who is patently honest. Running a dock with all the various things that find their way onto it is a very tempting target for somebody with a less than stellar character. I need someone whom I can trust and who can manage a loading dock. Are you up to that job?"

"Yes sir. I live by the officer's code, and I can manage men."

"Good. Call me, Moshe. When you work for me, you will no longer be in the service. "

He then described what my job would be and what he expected. I told him that the earliest I could start would be June of next year. That was a time the Air Force indicated I would be allowed to separate. I also told him that I applied to the National Guard so that I could continue flying on a part-time basis. Moshe was a World War II veteran, and he appreciated that I wanted to continue, even in a limited way, my service to my country. I told him that was basically one weekend a month, and I would use my vacation time for my required annual, full-time, two-week stint. Moshe was agreeable. He offered me the same money I was making as a captain on flying status. He showed me around the operation and introduced me to several men that worked for him. When I got out of the military in June, I would supervise all operations on the loading dock.

Moshe asked about my service, and I told him some of the things I did in the past eight years. I talked about my gunship days, and I asked him not to mention this to my father as I never informed him about what service I rendered when I was in Southeast Asia. I did this because I did not want to worry him or my mother. Moshe understood my reasons and agreed.

Moshe drove us to a local Greek diner for lunch. He was greeted warmly as everybody who worked there knew him. He asked our server for a table in the back away from most of the other customers. She took us to a table that was in an enclave separated from the main dining room. We placed our orders and Moshe told me about his son, Michael Zester. Moshe had three daughters, all married, but Michael was his pride and joy. He hoped that someday Michael would have joined him in running the business. Michael was supposed to take Moshe's place after he completed his military service.

At least that was the plan. Michael joined the Marine Corps when he finished high school. Unlike many of his friends, he wanted to serve his country. Moshe, a combat infantryman with wide experience in World War II, was very proud of his son. In 1968, during the first Tet offensive, Michael was killed defending the city of Hue in Vietnam. That happened more than a decade earlier, and yet I could hear the palpable grief which resonated in his voice.

I gave him my heartfelt condolences. I then told him about the second Tet Offensive which occurred around the city of An Loc, Vietnam. I described to him how we defended the city and, in particular, during the last day of the siege, when two gunships laid waste to both enemy forces besieging that town. I went on to say, "That stopped the second Tet offensive dead in its tracks. It taught our enemy that he could no longer amass a large fighting force in South Viet Nam or the bordering countries without making these forces a target rather than a military capability. That battle gave the United States government the means and the path to ensure the safety of the South Vietnamese government and people. In addition, maintaining the presence of the gunships in Southeast Asia and the B-52s in Guam would make it impossible for the North Vietnamese and their communist allies to assemble in the numbers required for any future offensive thrust. That, in turn, also provided protection for all those forces in Southeast Asia which aligned their fate with our national interests, including the Cambodians that supported Prince Sihanouk, and the Hmong tribes who were the natural enemy of the Pathet Lao (Laotian Communists)."

"Then why did Saigon fall?" he asked.

"After President Nixon was impeached, the Democrat Congress defunded all monies going to the South Vietnamese government and also defunded the gunships' presence in Southeast Asia. The last gunship left Thailand on December 15, 1974. Saigon fell four months later, followed closely by the ascendancy of the communist forces in the neighboring states which resulted in at least three million civilians being slaughtered mercilessly by various communist regimes in Cambodia, Laos and Vietnam. We had the war won and the Democrats gave it away."

In my attaché case, I had retained a copy of the letter that Prince Matak, a cousin of Prince Sihanouk, wrote to his friend Ambassador Gunther just before he was killed by the Khmer Rouge. It was published in one of the local papers that I read. I kept a copy of it because I was so moved by what Matak wrote. I handed it to Moshe. This is what he read:

Dear Excellency and friend,

I thank you very sincerely for your letter and for your offer to transport me towards freedom. I cannot, alas, leave in such a cowardly fashion.

As for you and in particular for your great country, I never believed for a moment that you would have this sentiment of abandoning a people which have chosen liberty. You have refused us your protection, and we can do nothing about it. You leave us, and it is my wish that you and your country will find happiness under the sky.

But mark it well that, if I shall die here on the spot and in my country that I love, it is too bad, because we are all born and must die one day. I have only committed the mistake of believing in you, the Americans.

Please accept, Excellency, my dear friend, my faithful and friendly sentiments.

Sirik Matak

Moshe read and then reread this letter and with tears in his eyes, he vehemently said, "Those bastards. Their actions nullified the sacrifice that my Michael and all the others who fell in battle made in order to secure some form of reasonable government in that region. I hope they all rot in hell!"

"I know exactly how you feel. Seeing Saigon fall was like a dagger in my heart. I'm not sure that I will ever get over it completely. Not seeing the war to its full conclusion, in my opinion, was the cruelest blow of all. When I returned from Southeast Asia, I remember being spat upon by civilians at the airport. I remember one child asking me how many children I killed. But through all of it, seeing Saigon fall and the last chopper leaving was the hardest for me. And then seeing the slaughter of the very same allies whom I supported during my tour there just drove me to further and deeper depression." He reached across the table and placed his hand upon mine, telling me in effect that he understood how I felt.

He then said, "I want a copy of that letter. When we get back to the office, would you mind if I copied it when we return? There are some people I know who need to read it!" I immediately agreed to his request. Then Moshe raised his hand to signal the waitress. She came over to the table and gave the bill to Moshe. He gave her his American

Express card and told me that he had to get back to work. When we returned to his office, he had his secretary make a copy of the Matak letter. A few moments later, she returned, and she gave me back my copy. Then he said to me, "Norris, you got the job. It's yours as soon as you leave the service. Just let me know the earliest you can start." I told him that was more than agreeable to me. We shook hands as I was leaving to return to JG's home.

I stopped at a large mall located in Huntington, Long Island where I purchased Hanukkah gifts for JG, Hope and the children. I had the clerks in the stores wrapped the gifts for me. My leave extended to December 3, which was the first day of Hanukkah. I was scheduled to leave the next day on December 4. I found a stationery store where I purchased Hanukkah cards, and I filled them out in the store. I taped each card to the appropriate gift. One of the stores also gave me a large bag which I used to transport the gifts I'd bought.

When I pulled into the driveway, I noticed that Hope's minivan and JG's Mercedes were not there so I took my bag filled with gifts and went into the living room. Hope had all her gifts under a large coffee table located in the front of the sofa. I placed the gifts that I'd purchased under the same coffee table. I then went to my room and changed from my suit into dungarees and a sweatshirt. About twenty minutes later, I heard the children noisily enter the house. I left my room and was warmly greeted by Danny, Elizabeth Mae and Hope. They had returned from a shopping spree of their own and lunch in their favorite restaurant which was a locally owned pizzeria. Just after they told me about their day, JG returned from a tennis match at his club. After we all said hello to each other, we went into the spacious den.

It was there that I informed them of the latest news. I would leave the service in June. I would return to New York and work for Mr.

Moshe Zester. After a loud, spontaneous outburst, they all had many questions. I answered each one and they were all glad that I would be a greater part of their lives in little more than half a year. That night I took the entire family to one of the better restaurants located in the immediate area. It was my treat.

Saturday, JG and I went to his club and spent the day there. He played tennis and I played racquetball. We had lunch there and, in the afternoon, we entered a duplicate bridge tournament in the club's spacious card room. Both of us were very good bridge players, but neither of us, or anyone we played, could come close to my mother's ability to play the game. Most of the hands we had as East-West partners were defensive in nature, and both of us excelled in that aspect of the game. We came in first and won some tournament points.

On Sunday, JG and I watched NFL football. Both of us were Giants fans and, as usual, we were already disappointed with the season. It had been sixteen years since the last time the Giants made the playoffs. At least we got to see some really good games which were televised nationally. The Giants were so inept that the league forced their ownership to accept the leadership of George Young to manage all aspects of the team, particularly hiring the coaches and selecting the players in the draft. Mr. Young's first choice was Phil Simms who became our franchise quarterback. In 1981, Mr. Young selected the greatest football player ever to play the game, Lawrence Taylor, and the rest, as they say, is history!

On Sunday evening, we attended the local synagogue to celebrate the first night of Hanukkah. The congregation had a special service designed for the children. They enacted the story of Hanukkah and passed out noisemakers for the children to use. When the storyteller mentioned the Maccabees, the children cheered. Both Danny and Elizabeth Mae really got into it. As for me, I really enjoyed watching their reaction. The kids really enjoyed the songs which are associated with that holiday.

This was the first time I'd entered a synagogue since April, 1973. I had just returned from a combat tour in Southeast Asia when I went to pray in the local synagogue closest to Mather Air Force Base. I was still awaiting my whole bag shipment from overseas, so the only formal clothes I had to wear were my uniforms and in particular, my class A blues. That's what I wore when I went to pray. Not a single soul in that congregation would talk to me. I was shunned by my own people. I walked out, never to return. The only reason I entered this Long Island synagogue was to be with JG and his family.

I enjoyed watching the joyful exuberance of my godchildren. During the noise and laughter of the Hanukkah celebration, my thoughts went to my Spectre comrades, and in particular, those who did not return. In many ways, being in this house of worship, I felt like Robert Heinlein's *A Stranger in a Strange Place*. I looked around me, and in that whole congregation there probably was no one, besides myself, who really understood and knew the cost of war. To them, it was just words and nebulous actions… To me and my fellow combat veterans, it was a reality that existed under a small veneer of civilization. Always there and never far away. One can never completely go home. This is particularly true for a Vietnam combat veteran because the bonds which tie the soldier to country were broken by those he fought to defend. These thoughts darkened my mood. Only after we left the synagogue and returned home, did I feel a little better.

That night we opened our Hanukkah gifts. The children went first and they did very well. I bought Danny a first-rate, professional grade, baseball glove. I purchased a brand-new, lightweight, racquet-ball racquet for Elizabeth Mae with the added promise that when I returned to New York to live that I would teach her how to play the game. With her speed and quickness, she would become a very good player. She loved the racquet, but I think she liked spending time with me even more. I gave Hope a gold Jewish star so that she could put it on her charm bracelet. I gave JG a box of the best Dominican cigars that I could find. Hope, in return, gave me a beautiful attaché case, and JG gave me a $250 gift certificate to one of the best men's stores in the area. He told me, "Now that you are entering civilian life, you have to dress for success!"

The next morning, JG drove me to LaGuardia Airport so I could catch a return flight to the Florida Panhandle. He told me that he would keep his eyes open for houses close to my future place of employment. I told him that if he found one, to act on my behalf. If he made a deal for me, I would honor it. I hugged him goodbye and went toward my airplane. I had a little more than six months to go in the Air Force before I could resume civilian life. I figured that not too much can happen in my remaining six months in uniform. Events proved me wrong!

19

GETTING OUT

It was just after New Year's, 1980, when I attended my first stop smoking support group. The last cigarette I smoked was in September of 1978. I was smoke-free, but the desire to smoke was still in me, so I attended an off-base support group sponsored by a coalition of the local clergy in the Niceville, Florida area. The meeting was conducted by Dr. Schneider, a female psychologist who was about fifty-five years old. She was a matronly woman with a pleasant voice, a ready smile, kind eyes and a rapier-like wit. My group contained a woman about ten years my junior. She had fiery red hair, blue eyes, a pleasant face and a great smile. She appealed to me, and I made it my business to talk with her during the twenty-minute recess which divided the three-hour weekly session. In the first hour, Dr. Schneider had us introduce ourselves to the rest of the group. The woman I was interested in knowing was named Katie. She was a recently divorced mother of two children, a boy and a girl.

When it was her turn, she said that she was born and raised in the Florida Panhandle. Her slow speech and locally produced twang and accent fully proved that point. I liked the fact that she described her "ex" in humorous terms and without any perceived rancor. She stood about five foot, four inches and was a little on the plump side, but then birthing two children will do that to a woman. The more she talked, the more I liked her, and the prettier she became in my eyes. When it was my turn to speak, I could see that she was interested in what I had to say, particularly the fact that I was a single captain on flying status.

During the break, I started talking with her when we both were getting a cup of coffee and a couple of cookies from the display table in the rear of the room. The oatmeal cookies were delicious, and I commented to that effect. She smiled and said that she had baked them. She added, "Both of my children love these cookies. They always ask me to make a batch whenever I have the time."

"How old are your children?" I asked.

"Tiffany is ten years old, and Brian is seven years of age," she responded.

"That's the same age as my two godchildren. But in my case, Daniel is ten and Elizabeth Mae is seven."

That broke the ice, and we exchanged stories about the two sets of children. She then asked, "You like children, don't you?"

"I do. Someday, I would like to have some of my own."

"I'm surprised that you haven't married already," she responded and the tone of voice indicated that her statement was as much a question as it was declarative.

"That is a long story which I cannot go into now, but if you have dinner with me some night, I will go into it in a lot more detail. Hopefully, I can answer any and all questions you may have."

"Are you asking me for a date?" Katie asked with a smile on her face and a twinkle in her eye.

"In a word, yes. Absolutely."

"Good. Then I accept!"

This was Monday night, and I knew her children had to go to school. "How about Friday night?" I asked.

"That would be perfect." With that she gave me her address with driving instructions. We then returned to the group.

That Friday, I arrived at her house at the appointed time. We navigators are sticklers for maintaining accurate ETAs (estimated time of arrival)! I rang the doorbell, which was answered by a large, teenage girl. I looked up at a fit and very pretty girl who was every bit of 6'2" in her stocking feet and was very athletically built. "Good evening. I hope I am in the right place," I said.

The girl smiled and said, "You must be Blake." I confided that she was right. "My name is Esther, and I babysit for Aunt Katie when she needs me."

Two very lively children ran into the living room to meet the man who was taking their mom to dinner. Both children had light brown hair, blue eyes and slender builds. They were understandably curious about me. I told them that I was an Air Force officer, a navigator in particular, and that I flew rescue in the squadron located at Eglin Air Force Base. They asked what a navigator does. I told them that I tell the pilot where he is and how to go to where he wants to go. I direct search patterns in order to look for survivors who need rescuing. I also use airborne radar to direct in-flight refueling of some very large helicopters. They asked for some stories about my flying experiences. I told them that I would do so when I had more time. With that, Katie came into the room and told them to say good night as we were leaving for dinner. Katie gave Esther some final instructions and kissed and hugged both children and told them to mind Esther. Frankly, I didn't think Esther would have a problem dealing with these two delightful youngsters!

I took Katie to a local upscale restaurant. After some casual chit-chat, she asked me, "Why is a good-looking guy like you not married? What's wrong?" I laughed and told her that it was a matter of bad timing. She smiled and I could see by the expression on her face that she wanted more details. My personal inclination when I dealt with members of the fairer sex was staying silent regarding the tragic loss of my fiancée. But with Katie, there was something in her persona that overcame my reticence. I told her how Sandy and her family were wiped out by a drunk driver while I was attending survival training. I also related how many times I wished I had taken her with me to that school. After telling Katie, with a fair amount of detail, how my relationship with Sandy had developed and what she meant to me, I said to her, "I still miss her. Not a day goes by that I don't think about her."

Katie reached for my hand and squeezed it. She looked directly in my eyes, then said, "That was almost ten years ago. I'm sure there are others. You are too good looking not to attract female attention."

"Yes, they were others, but my timing was always off. When they were ready, I wasn't and vice versa. Besides, I'd like to know what happened with you, if I might ask."

"Turnabout is fair play," Katie continued. "I married my husband, Jamie Ray Hendricks whom everybody calls JR just after we graduated high school. I was already knocked up with Tiffany, and my family did not take kindly to men who walk away from children they fathered. You might say we had a typical Southern shotgun wedding. I loved the guy, so it was okay by me. I don't think JR minded too much either, at least for the first five years. JR got a job just after we were married in a local factory here making decking supplies. Our home, the one we're living in now, was given to me by my granddaddy as a wedding gift. Even though JR did not make much money, we got by because we did not have to pay rent. Well, about four years ago, the recession really hit our industry with a terrible blow. JR got himself laid off and started drinking. We started arguing more often. The final blow came when he hit me and knocked me unconscious. He did that in front of the children. Maybe I could forgive him for hitting me but not when he did it with the children watching. That was the last straw. I told him to leave."

"Did he leave?" I asked. "He sounds like he was a mean drunk. Why would he listen to you?"

Katie smiled and said, "My cousin Perry is the deputy sheriff here in Niceville. Esther, my baby sitter, is his daughter. Perry stands about 6'7" and weighs damn near 350 pounds. He played offensive tackle for the Gators. I called him when JR just laughed at me about leaving. Cousin Perry came over immediately and took one look at my face. I could see his eyes narrow with anger. He turned toward my husband and strode over to him. Perry picked JR up off the ground by his throat and told him that if he did not leave, he would throw JR in jail for battery. He also informed JR that if he ever laid a hand on me again, he would not only beat him to death, but hide his body in the Okeechobee swamp where nobody would find it. Well, JR considered his options and made the wise choice. He left the house, and I filed for divorce. Cousin Perry made sure that he did not contest it. The final decree was issued about a year ago."

"Does he pay you child support?"

"Yes, he does. The court told him to pay four hundred dollars a month. Cousin Perry makes sure that my money arrives on time. I could've asked for more, but I settled on a minimum if JR agreed to not see his children unless properly supervised. I can't have them driving with a drunk."

"Have you been able to make it financially?" I asked.

"Oh yes. I have a full-time job working in a local supermarket. I work there as a cashier and the company allows me to buy food at a pretty good discount. They also provide complete health coverage for the children and me. The house is paid for, and so we live fairly decently. I take the money that JR pays me and put most of it into a trust fund for each child. I want to use those monies to pay for their education if they want to go to college or to help start a business if that's their hankering. I kinda hope that they choose education, but that's the decision they will have to make for themselves."

After the dinner was over, I took Katie onto the base where we watched a movie being shown in the base cinema. After the movie, I asked if she wanted to go to the club for a drink. Katie said to me, "I'd rather see where you live, if you don't mind."

"Not at all." I responded.

I drove us to my ranch-styled home. I took her around the house and gave her the full "Cook's tour." She loved the house. We then went into my living room, and I asked if she would like some coffee or tea, or something else to drink. She thought a cup of tea would be perfect. I brought over two cups of tea so I could join her. I could see that she wanted to be kissed. I reached out for her, and she fell into my arms. We kissed slowly and then more passionately. Then she got up and held out her hand. I took hers in mine and let her lead me to my bedroom.

"It's been more than two years since I've been with a man. I almost don't remember how to do this!" Katie uttered.

"I do," I responded. Katie laughed and kissed me passionately again. I picked her up and placed her gently on my bed. I slowly undressed her and kissed the parts of her body as they became visible to me. In between, I undressed myself. Katie moaned loudly as the years of frustration were released. Her body shuddered as I entered her. Her nails dug deeply into my back. She came quickly. I stayed in her and continued to slowly penetrate her. Slowly, she was building for a second orgasm which occurred within seconds of my first. After I came, I kissed her gently on her mouth and rolled on my back. I picked her up and held her against my body. She rested her head on my chest. I ran my hand gently over her back while she regained her breath.

After about five minutes of silence, Katie picked up her head and looked at me directly. She said, "I don't know what you think of me. I have never done this before. In fact, JR is the only other man that I have been with."

I looked her in the eye and said, "I absolutely believe you."

Katie smiled. "Damnation! When the sex is this good, I really want to light up!"

"I hear you, girl. It's absolutely the same thing for me. I mean, the three times that I really want to smoke is after a really good meal, really good sex, and that first great cup of coffee in the morning. That's when quitting and staying smoke-free is the hardest."

"I guess we're in the same boat," she said as her head returned to my chest.

"What about birth control? I got caught up in wanting you, and I never asked."

"That is not a problem for me anymore. I had a really difficult delivery with Brian and the docs had to remove some female plumbing which left me sterile. I wanted to have more children, but God chose a different path for me. I just have to be thankful for the two I have." I heard the sadness in her voice and felt her loss. I continued to caress her back as I felt a tear fall onto my chest. I continued to hold her in silence because there are some hurts that are immune to being eased by words.

It was now almost one o'clock in the morning. Katie said to me, "I got to get going. My niece has to drive home, and I promised her mother that I would not stay out too late." We quickly got dressed, and I took her home. Esther met us at the door. She told Katie that the children were well behaved and that she had no problems complying with Katie's instructions. She took her money and wished both of us good night. I kissed Katie good night and left shortly after Esther.

From that time on, Katie and I became a regular item. Most of the time we would stay at Katie's place. The kids were comfortable there and in order to keep secret our liaison, I would never sleep over. For the next six weeks, I spent a lot of time with Katie and her two children. I helped them with their homework and when it was bedtime, they wanted both of us to kiss them good night. Sometimes they would come over to my place where I would prepare a meal for the four of us. Once a week, we would go on base for a meal at the O' Club, which the kids really enjoyed. I got permission from my commander to give Katie and the children a tour of the flight line and let them climb aboard an HC-130H aircraft. I became really attached to those children. Everything was going well until fate reared its ugly head.

On Saturday, February 23rd, I was on a date with Katie. We were having a meal at the O' Club. I was the alert navigator that weekend, so I carried a large portable UHF receiver which we called "the brick." That allowed base operations and/or the Rescue Coordination Center

(RCC) to communicate immediately with the alert rescue crew. It was about nine o'clock in the evening, and Katie and I were having a final cup of coffee. All of a sudden the brick came to life and a deep voice said, "Alert navigator, RCC. Over."

I punched the talk button and said, "This is the alert navigator. Over."

"Roger, Nav. Your crew is activated. Report to base ops in one hour, pack for at least thirty days and make sure you have all your cold-weather gear. Do you copy? Over."

"Roger. I'll be at base ops within the hour. I will bring all my cold-weather gear. Can you tell me where we're going? Over."

"Negative. Mission is classified. Over."

I signed off and quickly paid my bill. I drove Katie home and immediately proceeded directly to my house. I changed into a flight suit and packed up all my cold-weather gear. I drove to base ops and parked my car. I arrived two minutes ahead of my deadline. The alert pilot was Capt. Zeller. He was already in the planning room when I arrived. "Hey Zelly, where are we going?"

"Fucked if I know, Blake," Zelly responded.

"If I am going to flight plan this mission, I have to know our destination."

"Let's go to the operation board and see if someone will tell us what's happening." I followed Zelly to the scheduling board where the commander was standing. Zelly went up to him and asked what our destination was. The commander informed him that they were not sure at this time exactly where we were going and that we should hold tight for further information.

Finally, almost two hours later, we were informed that our destination was Keflavik, Iceland. Now, both Zelly and I came from the Pacific theatre. In that operational area, we used Pacific chart number one which contained all the exit points and entry points for North and South America, and literally all of Asia. Zelly and I spent the next forty minutes looking for Atlantic chart number one. Finally, a senior pilot popped his head into the planning room and said, "Why are you guys not flight planned yet?"

Zelly told the senior officer about our difficulty in finding Atlantic chart number one. The gentlemen laughed and said, "You need Low Canadian chart number 13."

"You're shitting me!" I uttered in amazement.

"Welcome to the Atlantic theater!" the senior officer said with a laugh as he departed.

I found Low Canadian chart number 13 and opened it up. Sure enough —it contained all the exit and entry points for the eastern portions of North and South America and the western portions of Europe down to Africa. Who knew? In thirty-five minutes, I completed a full ICAO flight plan, filled in the required entries on my navigational log and drew our course on the appropriate navigational charts. Our aircraft was loaded with 75,000 pounds of aviation fuel and could make the 14 ½ hour flight without stopping. We departed Eglin Air Force Base at 2:30 in the morning, local time.

It was evening by the time we reached Keflavik, Iceland. We landed at 2200 hrs. Zulu time. The sun had already set, and total darkness was almost upon us. I followed the aircraft's position to ensure that we were correctly following the published approach procedures listed in the manuals. That was part of my navigational duties. The flight itself was rather peaceful. I basically followed the coastline of the

United States and eastern Canada until Nova Scotia. At that point, we went over water passing just south of Greenland. The weather was clear, and it gave me a great opportunity to practice my celestial navigation which I did not let go to waste. I completed my quarterly quota and then some of the required celestial fixes. The landing was smooth and uneventful with some moderate turbulence that we experienced between 3,000 feet and 1,000 feet above the ground.

The runway itself was clear all the way down to the surface. However, the taxiways and ramp area all had eight inches of hard glare ice. When we deplaned, walking on that surface required extra concentration to keep upright. A bus took us to the housing set up for visiting crews. Basically, it was a bare-bones barrack. We got our assigned rooms, and the entire crew went directly to sleep. All of us were exhausted.

The crew assembled at 1000 local time. After eating, the crew underwent a training session detailing local procedures that we were to follow. The next day, we were placed on full alert for potential rescue situations in the North Atlantic region. Our PJ's had to have special diving suits that would insulate them from the freezing waters if the situation required dropping them into the ocean. For the next month, we sat alert with two days on and one day off. Even when we were not on active alert, we were on backup alert which meant that we were still restricted to base.

Keflavik AB and the surrounding area was totally covered by ice. The winds blew constantly between thirty and fifty knots, sometimes with gusts exceeding seventy-five knots. After a couple of days, I grew accustomed to the howling wind, and it became just background noise. It was so pervasive that the water in the bathroom toilet bowl developed a "wave" like action. Let me put it this way: When you took a dump, the released turd looked like it was "hanging 10!"

In the month I was there, we actually got alerted twice. Both times it was to locate and assist fishing boats in trouble in the North Atlantic seas. In one situation, we found our target. We experienced severe turbulence as we had to go down to seven hundred feet above the raging sea in order to find and assist the distressed craft. Flight visibility was barely a mile. It constrained the kind of search pattern I could employ. We were in touch with the Icelandic version of the Coast Guard which came to assist the men on that boat. They saw us circling the distressed craft. They took the crew aboard their ship.

The second mission was not successful as we could not locate another distressed fishing boat. We searched for three days without finding any trace of potential survivors. We were part of an armada of planes and boats searching for the lost fishermen. Unfortunately, none of us had luck in finding them.

After a month in Iceland, we were ordered to Midenhall RAF base located in eastern England. After landing and taking a day of rest, we received the required training in local procedures that applied to flying in England and, if necessary, the European continent. Again, we spent a month on alert with two days on and one day off. As before, we could not leave the base as we were again on secondary alert . . . even when we were off the schedule. The weather and the beautiful English countryside seemed almost balmy compared to what we'd just left in Iceland.

I must admit that this was the first and only time that I ever drank alcoholic beverages while on alert. I had a pint of "bitters" with one of the suppers that I enjoyed in the O' Club located on base. The RAF does not consider having a pint or two as drinking on duty. As the saying goes, "When in Rome..." That was a peaceful month of alert duty. We got alerted only three times for routine missions. After a month of not doing much, we received new orders sending us to a remote temporary air base located in eastern Turkey, very near the Iranian border. The flight planning to cross over Europe was extremely intensive as American military aircraft were restricted to very particular air routes and altitudes. The planning had to be meticulous. Any deviation would result in an international and diplomatic uproar. Zelly and I went over our route carefully to make sure that we were on the approved routings all the way to Turkey. That was the longest flight planning stint that I ever did for any mission. When we were done, both Zelly and I were confident that we had a good flight plan.

The next day after that marathon planning session, we flew to our destination which was a set of coordinates in the arid region of eastern Turkey. As we flew east of Istanbul, I was amazed how the color brown dominated the landscape below. We reached our destination and landed on a hastily constructed runway. Our quarters consisted of preassembled huts. The officers and enlisted men ate our meals together in a common mess hall. Again, we underwent local training procedures and were finally briefed on our real mission. Unlike the other deployments, we carried the armaments that would be placed on two HH-53C Super Jollys. This included four 50-caliber machine guns and two Gatling 7.62mm mini-guns. We also carried the hand-held weapons that the crews would be issued if deployed. The problem was that we were in violation of Turkish law. If one of their officers saw what we carried, we would all be imprisoned.

On the morning of April 24, we were given our final briefing. Our mission was providing rescue, if needed, to a commando raid to free the American hostages held in Teheran. During the night, maintenance personnel took the armaments we were carrying and placed them in the helicopters. Now both Super Jolly's were armed for a combat rescue mission.

I received, as the alert navigator, detailed charts of Iran. The hut we were staying in was only a couple hundred meters from our aircraft. On April 25, we were ordered to stay in our quarters until 0600 hours local time which was sunrise in eastern Turkey. After that point, we and the two Super Jolly crews were ordered to sit alert in our aircraft. About six hours later, we received the abort message. It was imperative to take back the "illegal" ordnance and to depart as soon as possible for Salerno, Italy. While the armaments were being reloaded back onto our aircraft, Zelly and I planned and filed an ICAO flight plan to leave Turkey within the hour. By the time we returned to the aircraft, the ordinance was loaded, and we departed immediately.

It took us almost 4 1/2 hours to reach Salerno. We stopped there as we were out of crew duty day as defined by Air Force Regulation 60-16. We spent the night in Salerno and departed the next morning for the Azores. The squadron let us stay in this resort area for the next two days as a reward for the months that we were away. The entire crew thoroughly enjoyed the off time. However, all of us were puzzled at the conflicting orders that we received. I just figured that I would never know the whole picture which is not unusual for a company grade officer. I was as wrong as I could be.

About five weeks after we returned, and about a week before I left active duty, our entire squadron was called into a large briefing hall. Every person's ID was meticulously inspected, and the room was guarded by two dozen security police (SPs) all armed with M-16 rifles and side arms. The windows were totally covered and taped down by some black material. After being granted admission, we were told to find a seat in this large auditorium. I sat next to Zelly who, like myself, was due to leave the service shortly. We were extremely curious as to the nature of this briefing. All we knew is that our presence was ordered, and we were now in compliance with that order. At precisely 0900 hours, the squadron commander entered the auditorium from the rear. He took two steps into the aisle and ordered the assembly to attention. Behind him strode a four-star general who made a beeline to the podium that had a microphone placed on top. He was alone on the stage.

General James A. Hill was a large man with an impeccably tailored uniform. I judged that he was in his late 50s or early 60's and physically fit. His dark hair had turned mostly gray, and his countenance was very serious. He looked around the room and seeing that all the security preparations were in place, said, "Seats!" All of us in the audience immediately sat down. We were extremely curious as to why a four-star general wanted to address our rescue squadron. We soon found out. The general took a few moments and looked around the room. He tried to make eye contact with every individual member of my squadron. The general then spoke:

"I am here to offer both an apology and an explanation. I know, based upon thirty-eight years of serving in uniform that sometimes you are ordered to do things that you do not understand. Most of the time, no one offers you an explanation of what might seem inexplicable orders. Normally, I would not take the time to do this, but I have personally witnessed incompetence on a scale which defies human imagination and borders on criminality. It cannot be ignored. It must be exposed for what it is.

"By this time, you all know about the colossal failure of our attempt to free the fifty-three hostages held by the Iranian government. Eight good men lost their lives needlessly. Your squadron was part of that mission, and you deserve to know why it failed and the mistakes that were made. You also deserve an apology for those of you who were put in harm's way and who had to endure three months of displacement.

"All the mistakes that were made and the colossal incompetence starts and ends with the President of the United States. I am going to explain to you why this is true. His first mistake occurred just after President Carter took office. One of his first acts as president was not replacing the H-53 helicopters. All the services have the Super Jollys in their inventory. Virtually every chief of their respective service implored the president to spend $4.5 billion to replace these Vietnam era helicopters. When we brought these helicopters into active service in the mid-60s, the Sikorsky Company, who manufactured the Super Jolly, told the Defense Department that the shelf life of such a large helicopter with so much power would only be ten to fifteen years at most. The stress of such a large rotary wing moving at speeds in excess of Mach 2 at the tips would cause vibrations that over time would weaken the structural integrity and would damage the instrumentation and transmission of these helicopters. The president ignored the advice of every chief of staff of their respective service and decided to spend $1.5 billion to refit all the Super Jollys. So, instead of replacing the H-53 with the new H-60 Sikorsky helicopter, he did save the taxpayers about $3 billion. When it came time to use them, the Super Jollys were not reliable enough to do the mission. Virtually every one of them, except Marine One, suffered battle damage in Vietnam. The normal reliability rate of the Super Jolly was less than 15% of all those that still remained in service. The mission called for six of the ten Super Jollys employed to be on station and operational over our embassy at the time of the raid. We actually had five able to go which was three times greater than the normal reliability rate for that particular weapon system.

The second reason why the mission failed goes back again to the President of the United States. His goal over what he hoped would be two terms in office was to unite all the services and combine them into one military. He wanted to eliminate service rivalries, so he insisted that helicopters be used from every service. Unfortunately, the only in-flight refueling capable H-53 helicopter was operated by the United States Air Force. All four chiefs told the president that only the Air Force HH-53 choppers should be used, as they could be refueled in the air. He personally denied this request, so we were forced to plan a land-based refueling event in the mission sequence. That one decision led to the death of eight good men. I'll talk more to that point later.

The third reason that the mission failed was when it was scheduled. Again, all the chiefs recommended a December timeframe. The perfect time was December 21, the winter solstice, which gave the raiders the maximum amount of night time and reduced the amount of daylight available to the defenders. During that time, the Iranian weather system is controlled by the Siberian high which would allow you to fly in cold stable air and would greatly reduce the potential wind and dust damage caused by greater surface winds. It took him months to make a decision. President Carter finally decided to go in April when the area is dominated by Coriolis storms. At this time of the year, the sun crosses the equator. That solar movement creates large atmospheric pressure changes which result in vast areas of excessive wind. That, in turn, causes both sand and dust storms in the very area that we had to fly. Three, possibly four, of the five helicopters unable to complete the mission were made inoperative by these excessive sand storms.

"The last reason was the most egregious of all. I am referring to command-and-control errors. The President of the United States insisted that he, and he alone, would control the mission from the White House. Special satellite and HF links were put in place to allow him to make changes in the plan in order to compensate for any unseen and unplanned problems. The events that occurred are the perfect example of Murphy's Law: If it can go wrong, it will! Virtually every military doctrine that I know dictates that operational and tactical decisions be made at the lowest possible level. The President of the United States, an academy graduate of Annapolis, who learned this doctrine as a midshipman, chose to ignore it. The same Coriolis storms which took down our helicopters also created gaps in his ability to communicate with the forces in theater. One helicopter pilot needed a special clearance to continue the mission, and since he was unable to reach command-and-control, he aborted his part of the mission. The only one authorized to grant him such a clearance was the President and at that point, he was unable to communicate with this vital portion of the mission.

"Compare our attempt at rescue to the Israeli raid to free the Entebbe hostages. The Israeli high command presented a plan to Prime Minister Golda Meir. She approved it at once and turned over all operational control to the on-scene commander, Lt. Col. Netanyahu. He practiced for two or three days and then executed the mission. The only casualty was Lt. Col. Netanyahu. All the hostages were returned safely. Mrs. Meir might not have graduated from the academy, but she's a much better military leader than our president. She found someone she could trust and turned over the mission to him. That's real leadership.

"Now, about the loss of life. What I am about to tell you is our best conjecture of what happened during the early morning hours of April 25 in the Iranian desert. As I told you before, we could not use the Air Force HH-53's because the president wanted helicopters from every service to be used to complete the mission. So, in order to refuel, each Super Jolly had to be directed to a position besides the C-130 which was the on-scene tanker. Each chopper took its turn to refuel while the others waited. It was pitch black out there. An airman was placed on the ground facing the choppers lined up to be refueled. Because we had to keep secret our presence in the Iranian desert, the use of any kind of illumination could not be allowed as it would be seen for many miles giving away our position. The only light used was done by a loadmaster facing the front of the Jollys. This airman used dimmed, red-tinted flashlights to direct the helicopters in order to enable each Jolly to get close enough to be refueled. We *think* that a sand insect bit this airman's neck. He went to flick the insect off his neck, forgetting for the moment that the signal light was in his hand. The helicopter pilot saw the light move to his right and followed it right into the Hercules. Because of radio silence procedures, the airman had to watch in horror, as there was no way to warn the helicopter pilot of the mistake that was made. Eight men died in the ensuing explosion. That airman, who was a loadmaster, was one of those casualties. If we had used the Air Force HH-53s, we would have refueled in the air, and those men would still be alive.

"Finally, I want all of you to know that I am resigning my commission and retiring after I finish going to every unit that was involved in this tragic mission and give them the same briefing you are hearing today. I will not serve under a President that I do not respect and personally loathe. Retirement is the only honorable path left to me. I want you all to know that having served with and commanded men such as yourselves for the past thirty-eight years has been the highlight of my life. I wish you all, Godspeed. That is all!"

As the general left the podium, my squadron commander called us to immediate attention. The entire audience complied. The general, head held high, marched out of the hall and departed using the rear entrance. When he left the briefing room, our squadron commander ordered, "Seats." We sat down again. The commander then told us, "The briefing you just received was top-secret and not to be discussed by anyone not in this room." He took several moments to look around the room to emphasize that point. He then continued, "The general informed me that you would be allowed to discuss this among yourselves, provided you are confident that no one is overhearing your conversation. Are there any questions?"

No one said a word and after approximately a minute of silence, the commander left the podium. The squadron's First Sergeant who reported directly to the commander, shouted, "Squadron, Ten Hut!" Everyone came to the position of attention. When the colonel cleared the back door, the Chief Master Sergeant yelled, "Dismissed!" The group slowly dissipated.

I looked at Zelly, and we nodded our heads at each other. He said to me, "Well Blake, at least now I understand what happened on that three-month deployment."

"I hear you, Zelly. I'm getting out next week on June 6. I'm taking terminal leave so I can start a new job on June 10. Are you still getting out also?"

"You bet, Blake. I'm leaving about a week after you. I got a job offer to fly for a small airline located in Alaska. The pay isn't great, but at least I won't have to put up with assholes like Colonel Jennings. Someone as incompetent as him would've been 'fragged' in country when I was flying in Vietnam. You know when you and I leave, they will not be one rated officer (pilot or navigator) with combat experience in this fucked-up squadron."

I nodded my agreement and then said, "Zelly, I really enjoyed flying with you. The company that picks you up will get a great pilot. I wish you nothing but the best."

"Blake, you are one hell of a navigator. I don't know if you know this or not, but every crewmember really respects your ability as a celestial navigator and the way you use radar to keep us out of weather. It was a pleasure serving with you." We shook hands. That was the last time I spoke with Zelly.

In the meantime, I had a wonderful reunion with Katie once I returned. We departed the Azores on May 2 which should have been a twelve-hour ride back to Eglin Air Force Base. But the winds were much stronger than forecasted. Fifteen hours after taking off, we made an emergency landing at Jacksonville Naval Air Station. We did not have enough fuel to make it safely back to Eglin Air Force Base. While maintenance loaded 10,000 pounds of aviation fuel into our aircraft, I called Katie, even though at this time it was just after ten o'clock in the evening. She squealed with joy when she heard my voice. I told her that I would be back on base in about an hour. She said she would wait up for me and that was fine with me. I told her I would be at her place sometime before midnight. She told me, "I'll keep the lights on for you!"

We landed at Eglin Air Force Base around 11:15 PM local time. Formal debrief was put off until the next Monday and so after putting my gear way, I went to my car and hoped that it would still start. It did. I immediately drove to Katie's home. When I knocked on her door, she flew into my arms. We kissed passionately and I told her, "I haven't showered in almost two days. Let me clean up first so I don't stink you out of house and home." I think getting close to me showed her the wisdom of my request.

I took my suitcase into the master bedroom and undressed in front of her. I asked how the kids were doing, and she said they were fine and sleeping in their bedrooms. Normally, I would never sleep over as Katie was concerned about how that might look to the children. Besides, she did not want to set a bad example. That night was the only exception. The next day was Saturday and the children would sleep late. We decided to set the alarm clock for seven o'clock in the morning which is well before the children would normally wake up. I would put on a fresh flying suit, and we would pretend that I just came in that morning. When that was decided, Katie joined me in the shower. I think we finally fell asleep somewhere between two and three o'clock in the morning. I was still tired after the alarm clock awakened me. I really wanted to sleep more, but I respected Katie's wishes and dressed quickly. Katie got up and started making breakfast. The smell of cooking bacon and eggs awakened the children. When they saw me, they ran into my arms.

They wanted to know all about my travels. So did their mom. That night Katie and I did very little talking. After three months of forced celibacy, I was not particularly concerned about talking or any other kind of verbal communication. After satisfying our physical needs, we fell asleep almost immediately. At that point, neither Katie nor her children knew much of what occurred when I was away. I told them as much as I could without compromising classified information. It took over two hours to finish eating and to satisfy their collective curiosity. I had packed my bags and loaded them into the car before the children awoke, so when breakfast was finished, I asked Katie if she would like to go out that night and she agreed. She would call Esther to babysit the children. I would return to her place about five o'clock that evening, and we would go out together.

I went home. I took another shower and fell asleep for an afternoon nap which lasted until almost 4:30 PM. I shaved and put on my civilian clothes. I proceeded over to Katie's. When I got there, Esther opened the door for me. The children gave me a warm welcome, and I said that I had a surprise. I had made reservations at the O' Club for five. I was going to take Katie, Esther and the children to the club for dinner. They all liked the idea very much. I told Esther that after dinner I would drop her and the children back home while I took their mom to the movies. That seemed acceptable to everybody and so we loaded everyone in my car and went to dinner on base.

By this time, I knew the children were very well behaved and so I was not nervous at all about bringing them to the club. They seated us at a roundtable with the children on my left, Katie on my right, and Esther seated across from me. After the server took our orders, I asked Esther why she called Katie her aunt. It seemed that Cousin Percy was her dad and even though they were related, Katie was not her blood aunt. She continued, "But I love her to pieces, and I do it because I respect her so much."

"Katie told me that you are a very accomplished athlete. What sport or sports do you play?" I asked.

"I play tennis in the fall, basketball in the winter and softball in the spring. But my main sport is tennis."

"Katie also told me that you may be a scholarship recipient because of your athletic ability. Is that true?"

"Oh yes! But I have a problem that I've been pondering."

"What is it?" I asked.

"Well, if I play on the girls' team, I will not get much competition. But if I play on the boys' team, I will play against competition equal or better than my own abilities. I know if I play on the girls' side, I could probably win a state championship. But playing with the boys would make me a much better player."

"My advice then is to challenge yourself. You may have a real future in tennis and playing against competition that doesn't challenge you will not let you advance your skill level. I suspect that you will learn more in one year playing with and against the boys than you would playing four years with the girls."

"That's just what my daddy says."

I chuckled as I responded, "Well, your daddy is right! Besides, I just read an article in today's paper about a female athlete at San Diego State University who is a gifted volleyball player. Both the men's and women's volleyball teams from that school are competing for a national championship. The young lady had her choice whether to play on the men's or women's team. She decided that she wanted to play on the men's team because it had a higher-level challenge. Do you know anything at all about this young lady?"

"No, I don't," she responded.

"We'll guess where the opposition for her doing this arose."

Esther thought silently for a moment and finally said, "If it's anything like my experience, then the women on campus would have more of a problem accepting this than the men did."

"And you would be right. That's exactly what happened. The men were very open to her playing on their team, as she's a great player. The women were upset because her absence from their team severely reduced their chances of winning a national championship. Even many of the other coeds who did not play sports resented her choice. Almost all the male students on campus celebrated her decision."

"I think I'll play with the boys' team!"

"Good for you," I answered. The server came with the main course. "This reminds me of something that happened to me when I was over in Japan flying rescue. Would you guys like to hear about it?"

They enthusiastically indicated their interest in hearing what I had to say. I went on, "This happened about two years ago. A wife who was married to one of my copilot's became interested in playing racquetball. Her name was Sharon, and she stood just under six-foot tall. She was taller than either the copilot or me. Sharon was also a very good athlete. Like you, Esther, she lettered in three sports over a four-year high school education. When we got on the court to play mixed doubles, Sharon would not, for whatever reason, follow the common courtesy of the sport. In particular, if you made a bad shot and put your opponent in position for a kill shot, etiquette calls for you to get out of the way and allow your opponent to make a shot unhindered by your presence. Every time Sharon would drive the ball to the left wall, she would drift front of me, preventing me from making my kill shot. This happened ten times in a row. Every time she did this, I would call a "hinder," and we would replay the point. Each time I would tell her that she was in violation of racquetball etiquette but to no avail. Finally, I'd had enough. On the eleventh time that she blocked my shot, I did not call a hinder. I just took my normal kill shot off the back wall. When I hit a racquetball correctly, it goes well over one hundred miles an hour. I hit the shot perfectly and less than a second after I swung my racquet, the ball hit Sharon squarely in her left tush. She must've jumped literally four feet in the air. There were tears in her eyes.

The next day, her husband told me that she had a well-developed bruise on the left buttocks. I told him what went on and that if she really wanted to learn the game, I would teach her. But she had to follow the rules, even the unwritten ones. He thought that was a great idea. For the next two weeks, I worked with Sharon to develop her game. Being the great athlete that she was, she learned quickly. At Kadina Air Base, we had open courts in the afternoon where everyone played doubles. As long as you won, you stayed on the court. Sharon became my regular partner and we very rarely lost. By the end of my tour there, we became very good friends. We played together every day that I was not flying or needed in the office. By the time I left, Sharon was easily the best female player on base. The moral of the story is if a woman plays with men and follows the rules and etiquette of the game then she will be treated as "one of the boys!"

I also found out, from our table conversation, that Katie was coming out of her self-imposed shell after being divorced. She was taking more of an active interest in what was occurring at the local Baptist church which she attended regularly. In addition, she became more involved with her extended family and what they were doing. Katie had quite a few aunts, uncles, cousins and close family friends all living in the Florida Panhandle. Since she met me, her whole countenance started to brighten, as she looked toward the future instead of ruminating upon the past. Katie was now enjoying life, and it couldn't happen to a nicer person.

After dinner, I dropped Esther and the children back at Katie's home. We never did make it to the movies. Katie wanted to go back to my place and have some alone time with me . . . most of it spent in bed. I finally returned her home before one o'clock in the morning. Katie paid Esther and she left. I kissed her good night and left. I went home and slept twelve hours. I was one tired puppy.

I put my house up for sale and sold it within a week. I heard from JG. He found a place for me to buy located in East Meadow, Long Island. I had given him my power of attorney before I left, so he closed the house for me, and I had a place to go when I went north. It was a small, three-bedroom ranch and the price was right. JG made sure that the house was structurally sound and there were no major problems. The money I made selling the house in Florida was more than enough to pay the closing costs and the down payment on the new house. JG laid out the money needed to close the New York house. I would repay him when I got up north.

For the next month, Katie and I spent as much time together as we could. The last time we were together was the evening of June 5th. I was on light duty as I was leaving the next day. I took care of those duties in the morning which left most of the day to spend with Katie and the children. There was a carnival in town, and I took them there. I received a lot of pleasure watching the children enjoying the rides. Later, I took the kids and Katie to the local Denny's. That was the children's favorite restaurant. For whatever reason, which I can't begin to comprehend, their favorite meal was the Denny's "big" breakfast. That's what they ordered, and that's what they had. Katie and I ate more moderately, but then we were no longer growing, except maybe sideways.

It was about 8:30 in the evening when we returned to Katie's home. She allowed them to stay up until 10 o'clock so they could talk with me some more. They did take baths at nine in the evening and when they were clean and, in their pajamas, we all got together in the living room so I could say goodbye to them. As hard as it was to leave Katie, it was even harder to leave Tiffany and Brian. They insisted that I tuck them into bed which I did. By 10:15 that evening, both were fast asleep.

Katie and I went back to her bedroom and made love for the last time. I cared deeply for her, but I wasn't in love enough to commit to marriage. I also knew that the fact that I was Jewish was hard for her family to accept. I was lying on my back with her head on my chest. Katie said, "Blake, I met a man during a church social. He asked me out, and I accepted. I've seen him off and on since you went away on that long trip. He is 45 years old, a successful businessman with two children of his own. The last time I saw him, he asked me to marry him."

"What did you answer?" I asked.

"I told him that I would give him his decision after this weekend. I wanted to spend one more day with you. I think I am in love with you. I am sure that I will learn to love Jim, but not the way I love you. You came into my life at exactly the right time. After the divorce and being left sterile, I didn't think I was much of a woman. You made me see that I still have much to give and much to live for. Whatever happens, I will always be grateful that I met and loved you."

"Tell me about Jim," I said.

"Well . . . he's about six foot with a bit of a pouch. He's probably the most successful builder in the Florida Panhandle. His children are in their first and second years of college. His wife died about five years ago from cancer. Jim is a very kind and generous man. He's a deacon in the church. He met Tiffany and Brian, and he is crazy about them. He told me that if we marry, he wants to formally adopt them. They seem to take to him as well. If I marry him, I will secure my children's future."

"Katie, I am almost forty years old and I'm going to change my profession. My life, right now, is totally unsettled. I have my feet firmly planted in the air! You need stability and right now, I cannot offer that. I care deeply for you and the children, and I'll respect whatever you decide."

"I will marry Jim. Part of me will always love you and wish you well, but I think you should go."

I got out of bed and quickly dressed. Katie threw on a housecoat and walked me to the door. I kissed her for the last time. She had tears in her eyes. "Vaya con Dios," I whispered in her ear as I turned toward my car. I got in and drove away. I did not look back. I was leaving the next day.

June 6th was a very busy day for me. I closed the Florida house. I called Moshe and told him that I would be starting my new job on

June 10th. He was more than happy with that. The movers put my household goods on the truck and told me they would meet me in the new house on June 9th. I had several hours of papers to sign in the personnel office on base. By one o'clock in the afternoon, I was on the road not only going back to New York but returning to civilian life.

20

CIVILIAN LIFE

I rolled into JG's home about four in the afternoon on Saturday, June 7th. I called him while I was on the road and told him the approximate time that I would arrive. I noticed both cars in the driveway, and I went up and rang the doorbell. JG, dressed in his Marietta sweatshirt and shorts, opened the door, gave me a big hug and said, "Come on in! All of us were expecting you."

I looked around and coming toward me at a rapid rate were my two godchildren. I gave each a hug and a kiss on the cheek. Hope, not quite as agile as her children, followed them to my side and I received a long hug and a quick peck on the mouth. She held me at arm's length and looked in my eyes, and said, "You're out! You are really out! A free man at last! Free to come and go. You'll never know how much and how often both JG and I worried about you."

I saw the tears of joy and relief in Hope's eyes. She held onto my arm and directed me toward the den. She said, "There are eight other people here that want to say hello." Much to my surprise, as we walked into the den, I saw Lou and Nancy Lee, their four children (all girls), and Mr. and Mrs. Stein, Lisa's parents. I personally greeted each surprise guest. This was the first time I'd had a chance to meet Lou and Nancy's four children. The girls' ages ranged from four to thirteen years old. They were very shy, as they had never met me, but by the end of the evening they had warmed to my presence. Lou's thick black hair had streaks of gray. Nancy Lee was probably ten or fifteen pounds heavier and her eyes, which still sparkled, seemed tired. Raising four girls in this modern age was not easy. It was apparent to me that they were still a very good couple. They would finish each other's sentences. Both were content with what life offered, both good and bad.

Mr. and Mrs. Stein stood back from this reuniting of the three college roommates. I went to them last. I shook Mr. Stein's hand and accepted a hug from his wife. It had been less than a year since I'd spoken with Mrs. Stein, and although she'd physically aged, I could sense that she was finally at peace with herself. I knew that when a couple loses a child, particularly an only child, it dramatically alters their relationship. Many marriages do not survive such a loss. In other cases, couples become even closer when enduring a devastating blow. With the Steins, it was the latter, not the former. Their friendship with Hope helped them work through their grief. They were attached to me as they regarded my relationship with their daughter, and the time I spent with her as something positive in an otherwise wasted life. They were also drawn to me because I shared their sense of loss.

JG asked me if I was hungry. He suggested that we retire to the dining room where the food would be served. He had the meal catered by one of the local restaurants because he wanted Hope to be able to participate without having to worry about preparing and serving a meal. His normally large dining room table was augmented by one provided by the caterers. All of us took our seats as the caterers served a mouth-watering meal. They also provided beer and wine during the meal and coffee afterwards. Since I was staying with JG, I went with Coors light beer, one of my favorites.

During the meal, we all had a chance to catch up with what we were doing and how life had treated us over the prior decades. Lou and Nancy Lee were doing quite well. During the last couple years, Lou was teaching history and economics in a fairly well-to-do neighborhood north of New Orleans. On the weekends, he would sit in on some of the better jazz bands in the area. He made more money doing two "gigs" per month than he did teaching. Since he loved doing both, the extra time that it took was not a chore for him. I did find out that Nancy Lee's mom had passed away due to breast cancer, so she was now undergoing an extensive exam to see if there were any early signs of the same disease. The tiredness I saw in her eyes really was due to a deep sadness from the loss of her mom. I could commiserate on a very deep level as my mom also passed away due to cancer only a couple years before. My words couldn't help her, but the sure knowledge that I knew the enormity of her loss seemed to help. I asked Nancy Lee how her daddy took the loss of his beloved wife. She told me that he believed he would see her again when "Jesus called the faithful to Him." She was also comforted because she shared her father's faith. Besides, the girls were doing well, and they became the focus of her life.

The Steins told the assembled group that in four years, by the end of 1984, Mr. Stein would fully retire, and both he and Mrs. Stein would immigrate to Israel. Both turned to Judaism, the faith of their fathers, which helped them deal with the loss of their daughter, Lisa. They left the reform temple and joined a modern orthodox synagogue. Mrs. Stein was in the process of renewing her nurse's license so that she could work in a refugee camp located just outside of Jerusalem. Mr. Stein was going to help teach English to some of the children in the camp. Because of his religious training, Mr. Stein was able to read Hebrew. Presently, he was taking courses in conversational Hebrew so that he would be totally fluent by the time they went over to Israel. They were going to work as unpaid volunteers. After he retired, Mr. Stein would have more than sufficient funds to allow them to live comfortably for the rest of their lives. Both wanted to make a contribution to society and to mankind as a way of making some sense of the loss of their only child. It was their way of coping and I suspected, though I did not know for sure, that Hope had something to do with that decision.

JG told us that he was now a senior partner in the law firm. He spent less than one day a week in the Long Island office because the firm had several major class-action suits in the works. The man who started the firm and brought JG into the fold needed JG's services in the courtroom more than he did supervising the Long Island office. A junior partner was being groomed to take JG's place by the end of the summer. Then JG would be working exclusively in the main office located in New York City. The firm would provide JG with a chauffeured limousine to take him back and forth to work. That limousine had a fairly complete office in the rear of the car, so JG would be "on the clock" from the time he left the house until the time he came home. The firm still wanted him to move to the city, but JG would not consider it until his children were both in college. Even then, he would not do it unless he had Hope's blessing. I was really happy with my best friend. He'd achieved the financial success that he always sought.

Hope was doing very well herself. Her practice was flourishing, and she had a long waiting list of people who wanted her services. With JG's success, money was never an issue, so she worked on those cases which she thought she could do the most good. Knowing how smart and how compassionate she was as a person, I thought she would help most if not all of her clients.

The attention turned to me. I told the group about my last year of service. I went into a lot of details regarding that first day of the three-month deployment when we departed Eglin Air Force Base to Keflavik, Iceland. They especially enjoyed the description of a turd "hanging ten" due to the persistent and strong surface winds that blow in that G-d-forsaken environment. JG then asked me how I felt about leaving the service. I took my time with that question. Finally, I responded, "It's very complicated. To say that I have mixed feelings is a massive understatement. Flying, crewing an aircraft, and doing a mission that may be very important and life sustaining was part of my life for the last decade. It is very difficult to leave. I am happy because I can now be with my second family and my friends. I can pursue a civilian career in a civilian life. I want to do these things. Someday, I might have a family of my own. I would like that. Now, since my time is my own, maybe that will happen. But if I see a C-130 above me, part of me will ache to be aboard. It's in my blood. In my last command, I served under inferior leadership. That was my personal breaking point." I then told them in detail what happened when Col. Jennings tried to force me to accept an unsafe aircraft and place it on alert. That was the straw that "broke the camel's back."

I also informed the group about my new job and the fact that I was excited about working for a friend of my father who was in the same business as my dad. My first day of work would be this coming Tuesday, June 10th. On Monday, I was moving into my new digs and that was okay with my boss, Mr. Moshe Zester. Besides, there was a rescue squadron that flew for the National Guard located at Suffolk County Airport on Long Island. I would try and join that unit after I was established in my new job, so at least I could scratch the inevitable "itch."

After dinner was over, the group broke up and there were separate conversations going on all over the house, the backyard and particularly in the patio. Finally, about ten, the party broke up and all the guests left. Since I was staying for the next couple of nights, I just moved my bags into JG's guestroom. It was about 10:30 at night when the caterers finally left, and Hope was satisfied that her home was clean and all the dishes put away. The children were asleep and the three of us went to the den. JG told me that he paid for my membership in the racquet club for the next year and that he supervised the rebuilding required of the house that he purchased for me. I asked him how much I owed him and he told me. It was well inside my budget. I wrote a check that night as promised. JG did not want to take the money, but I insisted. I told him I really appreciated what he had done for me, especially the membership in the racquet club which I planned to use on an almost daily basis. I would stay with JG and his family until my whole baggage was scheduled to arrive.

I asked Hope how Daniel and Elizabeth Mae were doing. Both were getting along splendidly, and Elizabeth Mae was especially looking forward to my coaching her team. She also wanted those racquetball lessons which I promised. I told Hope, in regard to those promised lessons, that it was a "done deal!"

The conversation went on to politics. JG was now one of the leading Democrats of Suffolk County. He made large contributions to the party, and his firm did some of their legal work. He virtually knew every politician in both Nassau and Suffolk Counties. The downturn in the country's economic situation really worried him because he felt the party was vulnerable to a Republican sweep in the upcoming elections.

"God, I hope so!" I responded.

"Why would you say that?" JG asked incredulously.

"Because of what I've witnessed in the last 3 1/2 years since Carter was inaugurated as our president."

"What do you mean?" he asked. I first made both JG and Hope promise not to say a word about what I was going to tell them. After they agreed to that stipulation, I related to them what I learned from General Hill's briefing. I emphasized the fact that the mission's disastrous ending was caused by the criminal ineptitude of the President of the United States. For once, JG was stunned into silence. Finally, he asked, "Aren't you concerned about Ronald Reagan? From what I read, he's a right-wing nut!"

"JG, I was in California when he was governor. Hands down, no lo contendere, the best governor that California ever had. I think he won re-election with somewhere around 60% of the vote. Besides, with what I witnessed in the service; he couldn't be worse than what we have now. In fact, you know I played racquetball in the base gym almost daily in the year before I left. I got to meet servicemen from all branches of the military and from every ethnic group while playing racquetball there. We all talked about the upcoming election as it was on all our minds. After all, whoever is elected president will have an enormous and direct affect upon those who serve in the military and their families. Not a single member of the military, and I mean not even one of all the other servicemen I encountered, was going to vote for that asshole. In the twelve years I served in the Air Force, I never saw such unanimity of opinion on any political issue or any politician. I honestly believe that he will not receive a single vote at Eglin Air Force Base in the upcoming election!"

"My God! I had no idea. Is it really that bad?" Hope exclaimed.

"Frankly, it's worse. There are so many instances that I could go into that it would take the whole night. Just one example: When the general stated that the reliability rate of the Super Jolly was 15%, he wasn't exaggerating in the least. I was the navigator resource manager in the 33rd ARRS. The reliability rate we reported was 18% and that also included numerous times when the helicopter just lifted off, hovered for a few seconds, and then landed back on the ramp. It couldn't fly the mission, but we got credit for an on-time takeoff. The actual reliability rate of the HH-53 helicopter, even with excellent maintenance, was less than 10%. When going to war or some kind of combat mission, declared or undeclared, it is necessary to go with what's in the inventory. At that point, there's no time to restock or retool. From what I heard in every command, our military will be woefully unprepared for a shooting war or some other kind of combat mission. All this decay in only seven years after the Vietnam War! I personally believe that if we are to recover our footing as a great nation, we need a new president. I like what I heard from Governor Reagan. If he keeps his word, he will be a very good or even great president."

After some stunned silence, JG said, "I guess we have to rethink how we vote this next election."

"JG, I don't know much about the local issues or local candidates, but I do know without question that this country desperately needs new leadership. If you know you're going down the wrong path, then you must change direction in order to get to where you want to go. I'm not guessing about this. If you spent one week in my shoes, you would come to the same conclusion."

It was getting late and I was tired because I left a South Carolina motel about four o'clock in the morning in order to get to JG's home around the time I told him to expect me. We said our good nights and all of us went to bed.

The next morning, I awoke to the sounds of excited children playing. It sounded good to me. I got up, put on shorts, a T-shirt and sneakers, and made my way to the kitchen. Hope was making a batch of scrambled eggs, turkey sausage, rye toast and best of all, really strong, black coffee. I joined the children as we ate our fill. On Sundays, the family let JG sleep until noon. It was only nine o'clock in the morning, so I figured it was a good time to start Elizabeth Mae's first racquetball lesson. Hope agreed, and after breakfast, I drove Elizabeth Mae to the racquet club. I called ahead and reserved a court. Mae had the racquet I gave her and was anxious to learn. I taught her some basic fundamentals in footwork and how to strike the ball. Little Mae took to the game like a duck to water. The girl was an absolute natural. She had speed and very quick response time. When she hit the ball well, she would let out a high-pitched screech that only a very young female member of the human race could accomplish. It was a joy for me to see her getting into the sport. Before we left, I stopped in the pro shop. There I bought Mae a racquet glove and eye protectors. I purchased the best ones they sold.

We returned home just before noon. Mae excitedly told her mother all about practice and proudly showed off her new equipment. I told Hope to take her to practice at least a couple times a week. Every Sunday, I would take her for a lesson. That started my Sunday morning tradition as a civilian. My job with Mr. Zester was a six-day-a-week job, especially while I was learning the ropes. I would not have the time to give Elizabeth Mae lessons during the week, but I did have the time on Sunday mornings. And that's what I did almost every Sunday for the next year.

About half past noon, JG, dressed in his typical Marietta sweater and denim shorts, entered the kitchen. While he had his breakfast, I had another cup of coffee and a bagel with a "schmear" (cream cheese).

Having a real New York bagel was a treat for me. We finished JG's breakfast and my snack, climbed into JG's Mercedes and drove to East Meadow so I could see my new digs.

We entered a development that was built probably in the mid-50s. The homes were small ranch houses that had quarter-acre lots. My "new" house was built twenty-five years ago. When JG saw the listing, he knew it was a major fixer-upper. He put in a very low bid which was accepted by the sellers, as they were in the process of going through a highly contested and messy divorce. Through his many contacts, JG acquired the services of a home contractor he'd earlier represented in his own messy divorce. JG did very well by the contractor and the grateful client provided me, through JG, a very good price to restore the house. The house had good "bones", as the foundation was poured concrete and the support joists far exceeded code. The exterior was all red brick. In addition, the contractor put on a brand-new roof and installed a brand-new heater/air conditioning unit and water heater. The drywall was all new and painted in a uniformly off-white color with beige carpets throughout. The kitchen had brand-new linoleum floor and new appliances. There was a small laundry room just past the kitchen which led to the side door. JG had a brand-new washer/dryer unit installed. The master bedroom was fairly large at 18 x 15, and the other two bedrooms were 12 x 13 feet. It had an unfinished full basement. There was no garage, but it did have a carport on the left side of the house which opened into the laundry room. All in all, I loved it.

JG and I went through the house carefully. We examined all the possibilities as to where to put my furniture. He'd already arranged for the phone company to come on Monday and provide my own phone line. He signed for all my utilities. He could do this in my name because he had my power of attorney. I was very grateful. We spent several hours in the new house. I was now looking forward to moving into my new home. As we were leaving, I thanked JG again. He really came through.

From there, JG and I went to his club so he could play tennis, and I could get a pick-up game of racquetball. We played several hours there, then showered and changed our clothes. We went to JG's home where we picked up Hope and the children. I treated the family to supper at a local Italian restaurant. The next morning, I packed my car and departed for my East Meadow home. It was less than a twenty-minute drive which made saying goodbye to JG and his family much less dramatic than it had been before.

At nine o'clock Monday morning, the movers came with my whole baggage and furniture. They were still there when the phone company technician came to hook up my phone line. By 1:30 in the afternoon, I had both my furniture placed and a working phone. I immediately called Hope and gave her my new number. I then called Mr. Zester and after giving him my new phone number, I informed him that I would be at work early the next day. He was looking forward to showing me around and informing me what my new duties would be. I took an hour break and found a local restaurant that appealed to me. There I had lunch and then returned to my new home to finish putting away all my belongings and to hang all my pictures and certificates that I wanted to display.

Later that afternoon, I found the nearby grocery store and stocked up on food I needed to keep in the house. I had supper at another restaurant. By the time I finished getting the house the way I wanted, it was well past nine o'clock that evening. I took a shower and read for several hours before going to sleep.

I awoke the next morning at five o'clock. I got dressed in my work clothes. I found a Greek diner on the way to my job. I stopped for breakfast and tried the food. It was excellent and the coffee was strong and tasty. This would become my daily routine as the food was great and the service was quick and reliable. As we say in the Air Force, "If it ain't broke, don't fix it!"

I arrived at ZM Trucking just before 6:00 AM. Two minutes later, Moshe Zester arrived. We shook hands and again, he insisted that I call him "Moshe." I agreed. He then showed me a small office which would become my own. It had a desk, a phone and a calculator. On the wall, just left of the desk, was a listing of useful phone numbers of vendors who sold our company most, if not all, of the supplies that we consumed in providing a service to our customers. On the desk I had a rolodex address book which contained customers in one section and employees in another. Moshe told me I could put whatever wall displays that I thought was appropriate in order to make that small office feel like my own.

Moshe took me around to the loading dock. I would follow him for the next week and see how his business operated. Moshe was about the same age as my father. He had three married daughters and to put it mildly, he did not trust any of his sons-in-law. He wanted to spend less time with the business in order to semi-retire, and he needed someone reliable and trustworthy to make that goal possible. For the next week, I shadowed Moshe and asked a lot of questions. I saw how he constructed the routes, assembled the various loads, and how the trucks were loaded. Moshe told me that the men who drove for him had fairly standard routes. He went over the criteria that he used to change and/or augment routes and drivers. He showed me where all the various supplies were located and which vendors he'd use to resupply when the inventory was low. By the end of the week, I was also doing forklift duties, and I helped some of the dockworkers build the loads carried by the truckers.

Moshe told me that I did not have to get my hands dirty. He wanted someone to direct the men and run the dock. I told him, "When I was a fire control officer on a gunship, I made sure that I did my part in helping my gunners clean up after each mission. I personally shoveled over 20,000 rounds of 20mm casings. My gunners followed my orders precisely, without question, because I shared not only the danger, but the backbreaking work of completing a mission. Moshe, I promise you this: No one on the dock is going to outwork me. Period. You can take that to the bank. And the men who work under me will see that. Where I come from, we lead by example." Moshe thought about it for a while and let me have my own way. For the next two weeks, I spent half my time loading and building loads. When the men went home, I stayed and did inventory. I completed ordering the necessary supplies for the next week. I also went over my suggestions with Moshe for the inevitable changes that occur when compiling the loads. We discussed these thoroughly. I was interested in getting his input on these suggestions so that I could follow his reasoning as to how and why he made decisions.

By the fourth week I had the routine down fairly well. I was running the dock while operating a forklift and even on occasion, manually assisting in building a special load with some of the other workers. I was averaging over twelve hours a day. After I completed my second month, Moshe was taking half days off and on occasion he extended his weekends by several days. He began to rely on me more and more, and I did not disappoint him. By November, I decorated my office with a large picture of an AC-130A gunship, and a brass plaque with the Spectre emblem and a listing of the members of crew number one . . . my crew. I felt sufficiently accepted there to personalize the office.

The slow season for the trucking industry occurred just after Christmas and before Easter. The heavy schedule and the amount that

I had to learn did not leave me a lot of spare time. To that point, I didn't mind, because I was so busy learning my new profession. But after six months I wanted to have something of a social life. I really enjoyed the Sundays that I spent with JG and his family. I dedicated the mornings to improving Elizabeth Mae's skills in playing racquetball. I would also play with some of the better competition in the club, and Elizabeth Mae liked watching me do so. We would discuss certain points on the way home and why I employed a strategy that I used. The girl had a quick mind and internalized my thought processes and strategies in order to make it part of her own game. I enjoyed my Sunday meals with JG and his family where we discussed what was happening to all of us. I also found a partner to play racquetball at my level on Tuesdays and Thursdays, generally from eight to nine in the evening. The racquetball and the work that I did on the dock really kept me in good shape.

Of course, I had my Thanksgiving meal with JG and his family. Once the meal was complete and JG and I retired to the den to watch football, he told me about his partner who started the law firm. His name was Joseph Isakson. He was a 'landsman' (fellow Jew) who was one of the most respected and feared litigators in the New York court system. He lived on a five-acre plot which included a large manor house located in Great Neck, New York. His daughter, Allison, was a student at American University in Washington. She was a fifth-year senior who had just broken up with her boyfriend. JG told me that she may be the most beautiful girl he had ever seen. He met her in her father's office. Allison came in while they were discussing a case. Joseph was scheduled to have lunch with her, but he couldn't get away, so he asked JG to fill in for him. JG readily agreed.

JG took Allison to one of the upscale restaurants on Fifth Avenue near where the partnership had its main offices. During lunch, he sensed that she was a very troubled and unhappy young lady. She was very quiet and very reserved. Little by little, he got her to be sufficiently comfortable so that she could tell him something about herself. JG concentrated on what was on her mind, not on her attractiveness. Allison was not used to a man being interested in what was between her ears, instead of what was between her legs! During that lunch, JG sensed that the more Allison related her opinions on different topics, the more she was attracted to him. That crazy gift he possessed of accurately reading people screamed at him that he could "get into her pants" if he so desired. It wasn't anything outwardly that she did; it's what he sensed. JG had become quite the ladies' man and normally might have accepted this unstated invitation from a magnificently beautiful woman. But this was too close to the most senior partner in the firm. As JG put it, "I don't want to shit where I eat." So, he asked me if I would try my hand at having a relationship with an absolutely beautiful Jewish girl. At this point, I hadn't dated anyone in almost five months as I was so busy learning my new job. Therefore, I immediately accepted.

The Saturday after Thanksgiving, I picked Allison up at her mansion in Great Neck, New York. The structure was so big that it contained at least twenty rooms. It was built on a five-acre lot in the most expensive real estate section on Long Island. I parked my car on the curved driveway adjacent to the front door. A butler let me in and had me wait in the study which had four chairs and wall-to-wall books. Each chair had a reading lamp next to it. I'd waited about ten minutes when Allison opened the door, entered the room and extended her right hand. I looked at one of the most beautiful women that I will ever see in this lifetime. A perfect oval face, light brown hair, eyes so blue that they were almost purple, and a slender athletic body. I shook her extended hand and she said to me, "You're JG's friend, Norris Blakeman, I presume."

I took her out first for dinner, and later a movie. Two things became apparent. First, by the questions she asked, I could tell that she was thoroughly and completely attracted to my best friend, JG. The second revelation I had after spending some time with her is something that I sensed, not deduced . . . a totally visceral reaction. There was within her an abiding sadness that lay way beyond my meager powers to reach or to alleviate. By the end of the evening, after we shook hands goodbye, I felt very sorry for this very beautiful and rich young lady. As pretty as she was, I felt no sexual attraction for her whatsoever. All I felt was pity. When I told JG what I had observed regarding Allison, he was not surprised. About six weeks later, when Allison was back in school and preparing to come home for the intercession holiday, she committed suicide. I knew the girl was in trouble; I just didn't know what to do about it. That was my only date in the first six months since I returned back to New York.

What I didn't have time to do was bar hopping in search of women to date. I read about a new service being offered in some of the upscale areas of Long Island. It was called video dating. Single men and women would make a video presentation of themselves answering some standard questions. The company would show the women members the video recordings of the men that they thought were appropriate for that individual member. Then the company would show you the tapes of women who indicated an interested in you. When both a male and female client agreed that they wanted to meet each other, the service would arrange a date. I liked it because it provided me a way of meeting eligible women who were interested in having a long-term relationship with a man and were interested in getting to know me better. It was both time and cost effective to do it this way rather than rely on random searches in bars and discos or some occasional or accidental encounters. Early in 1981, I enrolled in this video dating service.

The first three arranged dates I had led to some fun times and, generally after the third or fourth date, to some casual sex, but nothing that had long-term implications. That was okay with me. After all, I still had my Sundays with JG and his family. Besides, I was very busy then in my new job. Moshe gave me more and more responsibility.

By this time, I applied to fly in the New York National Guard as I told Moshe I would do when he gave me my initial interview. The unit I was interested in was the 106th ARRS located in Suffolk County Airport on Eastern Long Island. My application to be a navigator on the HC-130H aircraft was quickly accepted. I checked out operationally in only three missions. Between the job and flying for the Guard, I had very little time.

It was the fourth person who I met through the video dating service when I struck gold. Her name was Betsy, and she was three years younger than I with a daughter who was six years old. She lived in Oceanside which was not far from where I worked. The day after I received her phone number from the dating service, I called. She sounded very nice, and I arranged to take her out on Saturday night for dinner. This was the middle of May, and the weather was almost perfect. The temperature was quite mild, and the skies were absolutely clear. I arrived at her place at 6:30 in the evening wearing slacks and a decent dress shirt. I knocked on the door, and it was answered by a little girl who I guessed to be my date's daughter. This precocious girl with light brown hair, very large blue eyes and a bunch of freckles looked up at me and said very earnestly, "Are you here to marry my mother?"

I was taken aback for just a second and then answered, "I think I should take her to dinner first!"

I heard a pleasant-sounding laughter coming from the stairs behind the young girl. Betsy came downstairs and said, "Hello. Please don't mind my daughter. She has a habit of saying what is exactly on her mind. I hope you're not embarrassed. Why don't you come in?"

I said, after entering the house, "No way. I think she's cute."

Betsy hugged her daughter and told her to get Grandma. A few moments later, Betsy's mom came in from the kitchen, and Betsy introduced me to her. Her name was Hannah, and she was a small elderly woman with a very gentle manner. I told her mom where we were going and that I would have Betsy back around midnight. We chatted for about ten minutes while Betsy got her wrap. Her mother wanted to make sure that she would stay warm in case it got colder that night.

A little before seven we finally got to leave. Betsy was 5 '4" and weighed 124 pounds. She had a classic hourglass figure, dark curly hair, big brown eyes and a very nice smile. I took her to a well-known seaside place called the *Ship's Inn* located in Long Beach. The food was good, but the conversation was better. Betsy was your typical, old-fashioned, nice Jewish girl. Now that I was very close to forty years old, I think I was finally ready for such a woman. She was exactly what my mother would have ordered for me if she could.

We spent three hours eating and talking. I found out that she divorced her husband about three years earlier because he was emotionally abusive. Some women take that, but not Betsy. The girl had moxie, and I liked the fact that she would stand up for herself and her daughter. She asked why I wasn't married. I told her about Sandy and the fact that my timing was never very good. Also, the lifestyle that I had as a flying officer in the United States Air Force, moving from place to place, exacerbated my difficulty in finding a long-term relationship.

After the meal was over, I asked if she wanted to see a movie or go to the boardwalk and take a stroll under a lovely evening sky. She chose the stroll which was my choice too. We walked and talked for several more hours. Finally, just after midnight, I drove her home. I kissed her good night and told her that I would like to see her again. She felt the same way, so I told her that I would call her on Monday after I checked my schedule at work. I phoned her that Monday, and we went out again. That was the start of a courtship that would last twenty-five months and culminated in marriage in June, 1983. I had finally found my lifetime partner and mate.

After seeing Betsy for three or four months, my life got both complicated and simplified. It was complicated because now I had to find time between work and flying in order to see Betsy. I also had to adjust my time with JG and his family because Saturday night and Sundays were the only time that I could see Betsy and her family for any extended time. For me, the complication was making all these demands upon my time come together in some reasonable way. My life got simplified by the fact that I did not want to see other women.

The biggest problem was with JG. He got used to me being around on Sundays and so did Elizabeth Mae. That was hard. My biggest ally in smoothing things out with JG and his daughter was Hope. She made JG see that this was a good thing in my life. JG and I shared one peculiar trait. We do not like change. And this was one big change. Elizabeth Mae got used to our Sunday morning racquetball court time. However, she was now old enough to play travel soccer which was played on Sundays. I was still assisting her soccer coach several days a month. Also, I managed to attend about half of her games. That seemed to mollify Elizabeth Mae.

The next couple of months were hectic, but satisfying. Work was becoming much more routine. At this point, I was running the entire operation. Moshe was a happy man, as he was basically retired. He would stop in the office about eight to ten times a month in order to check the books and relieve me on Wednesdays so that I could fly for the Guard. Moshe was spending more time fishing which was his passion and what he could not do before I came along because he could not leave the business. In addition, I found different ways to increase the loaders' productivity by changing the way we put the route loads together. I was a hands-on manager who worked alongside his men. I was the first one on the dock and generally last to leave, except on Wednesdays when I would fly for the Guard.

If we had a really good month, I would buy lunch for all the loaders. Moshe had the same policy regarding the union as my father did. If the big trucking companies suffered a strike, our men would get paid retroactively the new rate starting the first day of the strike. Like my father, Moshe never had to suffer any kind of work stoppage. When I had discipline problems, I took them directly to the union to be resolved, and they always decided the issue in my favor. I had twenty-two men working for me, and they all made a good salary. Our company was a distribution hub for several dozen major producers. We were just more efficient than any of our competitors. The company was well into the black, and on my first anniversary working there, Moshe gave me a $10,000 a year raise. That was in addition to my first bonus which was $5,000 given to me at the beginning of the year.

The summer of 1981 was a good time for me. Besides doing well at work, I started flying for the 106th ARRS. They flew the same aircraft that I flew for the 33rd ARRS and the55th ARRS which of course was the HC-130H. The mission was the same that I flew the last four years and so, except for learning local procedures, I was right at home in that aircraft. The only problem I had was with the chief navigator, Lt. Col. Emory, and I wasn't sure why. I suspected that he probably talked with Lt. Col. Jennings and heard nothing encouraging regarding me. I stayed out of the man's way and just did my job. The pilots and crews that I flew with seemed very satisfied with my competence. That's what really mattered to me.

I was spending any spare time I had with Betsy and her family. She lived in a converted ranch that when originally built was one story. When she divorced her husband, her mom and dad let her build a second-floor apartment for her and her daughter, Molly. Betsy was an only child and her daughter was the only grandchild for her parents. Molly became the center of the lives of the three adults that also resided in the home. Betsy's dad, Harold, was an obese man who at sixty-five years of age was fully retired. He never made much money in his life, but he was as honest and forthright as any person I've ever met. Her mom needed to work because Harold, her husband, never made much of an income. She, like her husband, was a very honest and forthright person. And until Molly came along, Betsy was the absolute center of their lives. As I got closer to Betsy, I also got closer to her mother and father. By the summer, I was calling them "Mom" and "Dad."

At least twice a month, Betsy and I would go out with JG and Hope. When we did, the conversation was lively and provocative, especially for me, as I was the only conservative in the group. Many times, we would drive to JG's home as it was well set up for entertaining. Eventually the women would talk about child rearing and issues like that while JG and I would walk together so that he could smoke. During that summer, JG told me that the firm was taking on a major class-action suit against the airlines. His firm was representing the stewardesses who were forced to maintain strict weight limits and had to be more than presentable in the way they looked.

For the next six months to a year, JG was going to interview the stewardesses from virtually every major airline. He was looking for about a dozen of them to testify in court. The meetings were arranged so that potential witnesses could be interviewed in the home offices of the law firm in New York City. That made it convenient for the stewardesses, as many stayed in the city on the layover time between flights. These interviews were so intensive and numerous that JG was staying in the city generally around five days a week.

I asked, "How is Hope coping with this situation?"

"She does not like it. We fight all the time about the amount of time I spend away from home. Finally, I told her that I would take her and the children during the first summer after this case is resolved to whatever resort or vacation spot of her and their choice. The senior partner promised me a full month off once the case is completed. When I told Hope about the time off, she seemed mollified, at least for the moment."

I sensed JG was harboring a deeper problem. "There is something else going on. What is it?"

He laughed and said, "No one knows me better than you. You're right."

"Well, what is it?" I asked.

"It's like this. Some of the stewardesses have come on to me. I brush it off nicely because I don't need a conflict of interest. One of them, however, has really got me going. Her name is Sylvia, and she is not only beautiful, but she possesses a first-rate mind. I did the preliminary interview with Sylvia last week. Her situation, which I will not divulge, is possibly germane to the case. She is more than presentable, and my first inclination is that she will make a first-rate witness. At least I think she will."

"Did she come on to you?"

"Big time."

"What did you do about it?" I asked.

"Nothing yet. However, I think she knows I am interested in pursuing a relationship. I won't know until I give her the more in-depth interviews and see where that takes the case and my interest."

"When do you think that might be?"

"It'll take me another six months to go through all of the preliminary interviews. I'll get the second interviews which are much more detailed and in-depth, sometime around February or March. I want to be in court trying this case sometime around May or June of next year."

"JG, you know how I feel. I think what you're doing is wrong. So far, you've been lucky. Hope has not found out about the others. Just stop it while you can. If all of this came out, you would devastate your family. Damn it all . . . it's not worth the risk!"

"You're right. I know you're right, and yet something propels me to do it." JG puffed on his cigarette and continued, "It's like these fucking cancer sticks. I know that I should stop smoking, but here I am puffing away."

"Maybe you should talk to someone who could help you break both bad habits."

JG laughed. "Hell man, that's why I talk to you."

"Seriously JG. You have been talking to me about this for more than two years. I'm always there for you. Nothing will change that. But you got to talk to someone who knows how to deal with this kind of problem. Frankly, this is beyond me. At least think about it."

"Okay. I will give some thought to what you just said." JG put out his cigarette and said, "We better get back before our women send out a search party for us!" I laughed, and we walked back to his house.

By the end of the summer of 1981, I realized that JG and I were moving in opposite directions. I believe that I'd found my soul mate in Betsy. Our relationship was deepening as I learned to trust her implicitly. Sometimes we would fight, but it was always open and forthright arguments. No games. When we had disagreements, we would listen to each other's side and almost always find that middle ground acceptable to both. Moreover, whatever disagreements we had, they were never about the big things, the basic things...the core values. These we shared together. We also fit well together, as my weaknesses were her strengths and vice versa. For example, Betsy was very accomplished in the language arts and limited in mathematical reasoning. I, on the other hand, am very good in math and deductive reasoning, but my language skills left much to be desired.

Just when I thought my world was coming together, disaster struck. It was October 8, 1981. Moshe and I were meeting with his accountant to discuss last month's profit and the end of the third quarter financial results. The company had the best month and the best quarter in our history. During the meeting, Moshe complained that it was too warm in the office. He was sweating profusely even though the temperature was 70°. That morning, before the CPA arrived, Moshe complained that he was getting arthritic pains in his left shoulder. He laughed it off by saying, "Thank God, when I go fishing, I cast with my right arm!"

I was getting worried, so I said, "Moshe, let me take you to the hospital."

"Nah. I'll be all right!" We continued the meeting. I had his secretary drop the temperature to 65°, and yet Moshe continued to sweat profusely. His words started to slur.

I got up and said, "Moshe, I'm taking you to the hospital now. No argument. Now!"

He rose out of his seat, grasped his chest and fell over. I rushed to his side and yelled for his secretary, Mrs. Birnbaum. She heard the vehemence of my request and came running into the office. While I was tried to make Moshe comfortable, she saw the situation and put her hands over her mouth as she said, "Oh my God! Oh my God!"

"Call 9-1-1 now! Mrs. Birnbaum . . . CALL NOW!"

She nodded her head and ran to the phone to make the call. Meanwhile, I had Moshe on his back with his arms at his side. His open eyes were no longer seeing. I felt for a pulse and could not find one. I put my ear just outside his mouth and could not hear any breathing sounds. I moved his head to clear the breathing path. Still no breath sounds. I started CPR. I remembered the ABCs of CPR taught to me by the Air Force. Fifteen compressions for every two breaths. Ten minutes later, I heard the soulful wail of the siren announcing the arrival of the ambulance and its crew. Two EMT specialists dressed in their blue uniforms and pushing a collapsible stretcher came into the office. They shooed me away as they took over. I watched in horror as they tried to find a pulse. They could not. They tore off his shirt and tried to restart his heart with a defibrillator. They tried three times without success. My friend and mentor died that morning in the office of the business that he started over forty-five years before.

Moshe had three daughters ranging in age from twenty-eight to thirty-seven. All three were married, and Moshe did not trust any of his sons-in-law. His shining star was his lost son, Michael. His wife predeceased him by ten years, and so the three daughters stood to inherit the entire business. Two days after he died, I met his best friend and lawyer, Mr. Edward Zuckerman. I knew of him, but that was the first time I had a chance to actually meet him. He came into the office and introduced himself. He told me that Moshe and he grew up together. They became fast friends from the beginning, as they were always paired together since their last names began with a letter Z. In those days, teachers usually paired children together using some kind of alphabetic structure. Frankly, not unlike my own Air Force experience.

Mr. Zuckerman was a tall and distinguished man. His voice had a deep resonance to it. He had wavy gray hair, deep brown eyes and was dressed for success. After the usual introductions, he said that I should call him by his nickname, Mr. Z. That was fine with me.

Mr. Z did not waste time and got right down to business. He said, "Moshe held you in the very highest regard. In my opinion, having known him almost all my life, you were starting to take the place of Michael, the son he lost in Vietnam. He was getting ready to restructure his will so that you would continue to run the business and profits would go to his daughters. In fact, earlier this week we had a long talk at my office on just how to do this. I was preparing the necessary paperwork to make this happen when I learned that my best friend had just died. I'm sorry to tell you this, but I am forced to use his old will as a matter of law."

I responded, "I want you to know that I also liked and respected Moshe. The man was a mensch in every sense of the word. I knew you two were close because Moshe spoke of you often and with much affection. You have my sympathy, sir."

"Thank you. He was a good man, and I will miss him grievously. The business now passes to the three daughters. None of them, nor their husbands, want to get their hands dirty running it or taking charge of it. They have instructed me to sell the business. There is a serious offer already on the table. I think Moshe's daughters are going to accept it. The reason I am here is to tell you a circumstance that you need to know. I think that's what Moshe would want me to do. Before I go on, I must have your word that what I am about to tell you never leaves this office and that you will not tell anyone. Period!"

"You have my word, sir."

Mr. Z nodded and continued, "The people buying this business have ties to organized crime. They want this company because its function is distribution of products made by different sources. That could be legal as well as illegal contraband. Besides, it's a great way to launder ill-gotten profits and make money spendable. If you stay doing what you're doing, you run the risk of being tainted by being involved with what I think will be a criminal enterprise. I know this to be true because they have made significant offers to buy this company for the past several years. In fact, six months ago this conglomeration offered Moshe sixteen million to buy ZM Distribution. That was five million over the assessed value of the company. Moshe turned them down, but his spoiled children will accept."

"What do you recommend that I do?" I asked.

"That's up to you, Norris. I'm sure they will offer you significant money to stay. You have two options. You can stay and hope for the best and that somehow, if I am right, you will not be involved with underhanded and illegal dealings. Or you can opt to resign, in accordance with your contract, by giving them a minimum of two weeks' notice. Those are your choices."

I thanked him for the information and told him that: "If the business is sold to this group that you mentioned, I will resign. If the daughters keep the business or sell to a reputable company, I will stay." Before he left, I asked him to be able to talk over what he told me with a woman that I was dating. He asked, "Is the relationship a serious one?"

I answered, "Yes sir, it is."

"Then tell her, but no one else. If you two are going to make a life together, then you do not need to start by having secrets from each other. Neither Moshe nor I would want that!"

I thanked him. We shook hands as he said goodbye and left the office.

About a week later, on Friday, October 17, I was notified in writing that the company was being sold to the group mentioned by Mr. Z. That weekend, when Betsy and I got together, I swore her to secrecy, and then I shared with her the entire conversation that I had with Mister Z. I told her that I had to resign from the company because I did not want to work for the people who were purchasing it. I was going to look for employment elsewhere. I would give my two weeks' notice as soon as I had secured new employment. I remembered the old adage, "It's easier to find a job when you already have one!"

The following Saturday, I noticed an article published in *Newsday*, the paper of record for Long Island. In this article, the author stated that New York Center, part of the air traffic control system of the United States, was looking for people with aviation backgrounds to fill in for the fired controllers. During the summer of 1981, many air traffic controllers all across the country went on strike in violation of the oath they swore as a precondition of employment and against the expressed orders of the President of the United States. I called Mrs. Birnbaum and told her that I would be late to arrive on Monday morning. I asked her to tell the foreman to proceed normally and that I would be there by one o'clock in the afternoon. When she asked why I was taking this time, I told her it was a personal matter.

With copies of my DD form 214 in hand, I went to the air traffic control center in Ronkonkoma, Long Island. I met with the personnel people and filled out an application. Because of the strike and the resultant need for people with aviation backgrounds, the normal process for hiring was shortened from six months to two weeks. After completing the necessary paperwork and application forms, I was then interviewed for over an hour. The managers with whom I spoke were duly impressed with my background. If I passed the necessary security check, I would start in two weeks. That was fine with me because it gave me the time to fulfill my contractual obligations to ZM Distribution. My starting pay would be about a third of what I was receiving at my present job, but the location of the center was closer to Suffolk County Airport where I flew for the Guard. I could increase the amount of time I flew which would allow me to make my financial ends meet.

When I returned to work, I had Mrs. Birnbaum type my letter of resignation. I signed it and told her to send it to Mr. Z. She asked me why and I told her that I didn't want to work there without Moshe being my boss. That she understood. That night, I went over to Betsy's home and told her what I had done. At first, she was annoyed with me because I did not discuss this with her before submitting my letter. She was concerned that I would not make enough money to support a family. I told her that this was just the opening pay and that I intended to take the test for air traffic control in order to become a full-time controller. If that occurred, I would earn more than the minimum income needed to support a growing family. I also reminded her that I was warned to leave the company by Moshe's best friend and lawyer. I told her that I did not want to get involved with any company with ties to organized crime. That totally mollified her objections. We would face this situation together.

21

NEW YORK CENTER

Monday, November 2, 1981, I started my career with Air Traffic Control (ATC). I reported to New York Center at eight o'clock in the morning and received a week of instruction on air routes, ATC procedures, and a rudimentary knowledge of how to operate the main ATC computer which controlled all the individual positions and every radar scope in all sectors of the center. I was assigned to Area F, which covered the northern and western approaches to both LaGuardia and JFK Airports.

My boss and direct supervisor was *Joseph Maguille* who was called Joe by all who knew him on the floor of the center. Joe was about my height, proportionally built, with jet black hair, a black goatee, deep brown eyes, and a very winning personality. He was not only an excellent supervisor but also a first-rate controller. As soon as I hit the floor, I made it my business to help the controllers do whatever they wanted done without hesitation. I also made it my business to learn as much as I could about ATC procedures, controlling techniques and the main computer.

The controllers I worked with and for really appreciated my attitude and my aviation background. One of the first things I learned about functioning in a busy ATC center was that acceptance by co-workers was imperative in order to survive in this professional and pressure packed environment. Comparing it to a combat unit's type of camaraderie is not a far-fetched metaphor. The two things you needed to prosper in the ATC world (as well as in a combat unit) were doing your job well and being very honest. Mistakes were not well-tolerated in either world. When traffic was slow, I asked questions on why something was done the way it was done. By my second month there, the controllers trusted me enough to do procedures that were well beyond my grade level. I was like a sponge in that I absorbed as much information as I could. I was both very intelligent and well-motivated which resulted in my ability to absorb a great deal of information in a relatively short amount of time.

I also listened as the controllers discussed the strike which failed. I received an insider's view on what really occurred. The controllers' union was called PATCO (Professional Air Traffic Control Organization) which had its beginnings emanating from New York Center. In the late 1970s, the president of PATCO, *Mr. John F. Leyden*, cautioned the membership not to strike. He saw correctly the preparations that ATC management was undergoing in order to prepare for a strike, i.e., management increased the relative number of supervisors and trainers so that one out of every three controllers was either a supervisor, a trainer, or a member of the staff. Those positions were considered part of management and therefore these controllers could not be part of the union. Mr. Leyden saw this and advised that they could not succeed in striking the people and the government of the

United States. He also advised that a strike would be illegal, as every controller had sworn an oath to the government of the United States that he or she would not strike.

The fever for striking among many of the controllers got the best of them. A majority felt that they should earn at least as much as an overseas airline pilot. They thought they knew better than their union president and so a cabal of lower ranked union officers contrived a situation which forced all union leadership to resign their positions within PATCO. What Mr. Leyden did not know was that his resignation was the only one that the Union's ruling board accepted. He was replaced, using this underhanded method, by *Mr. Robert E. Poli*, the new president of PATCO.

Mr. Poli, also a controller from New York Center, took several months to coalesce his power by getting all his people in various offices within the union structure. By the spring of 1981, Mr. Poli had secured his total control of PATCO. He then led a nationwide controller strike in violation of the oath they all swore to the people and to the government of the United States. President Reagan, after advising the controllers that they were in violation of the law and the oath they swore, told them that if they did not report to work on a date certain, they would be fired. The controllers in my area told me that many of their fellow controllers, thinking that they were irreplaceable, just laughed at the president.

When the date certain passed, President Reagan kept his word and fired all the striking controllers. What Mr. Poli did not comprehend, and what Mr. Leyden fully understood, was that there was on hand a sufficient workforce available to handle the nation's air traffic. This workforce was comprised of the following: an overabundance of supervisors, staff members and trainers; the floor controllers with sufficient common sense who did not strike; and military controllers who were melded into the system to augment their civilian counterparts. In addition, when other unions offered to join the strike, Mr. Poli told them that it was not necessary and not wanted. He was under the impression that the controllers who worked the centers, the terminal approaches, and the towers were absolutely irreplaceable. He didn't need anybody else, and he didn't want any other organization to share his union's glory! The controllers with whom I worked told me that the strike was "hubris gone amok."

ATC management, responding to the reality of the strike, used flight station personnel to run smaller towers. That freed the smaller tower controllers, who remained true to the oath they took and did not strike, to be moved to larger towers and approach controls. The military controllers were placed in various centers and approach controls, and they performed brilliantly. The FAA management restricted the use of ATC services to general aviation which was comprised of the individual and corporate pilots. There was some inconvenience as the procedures for getting a clearance for an instrument flight was a little more rigorous than it was in the past but still very doable. The controllers worked ten-hour days, but still had one hour off for every hour on duty controlling traffic. As a result of all of this preplanning, air traffic moved fairly well for the next several years until a sufficient number of new air-traffic controllers were trained and put into the system. Within three years, all air traffic returned to prestrike capabilities, rules and procedures. As a side note, Mr. Poli lost his job. Mr. Leyden, who resigned from the union, retained his position, and he was placed in another center. He was fully retired a couple years later after the strike. Every once in a while, in life, justice is served!

I took the test for air traffic in December, 1981. I received the highest grades of any of the test takers in the eastern region. I knew that I was too old for consideration for tower, approach or center controller options, but I could qualify to serve as a controller in the fight service option. In addition, I also was supposed to go to the top of the hiring list because of the points I received from being a combat veteran. For the next three months, I heard nothing, so I kept working at my job, expecting to hear from the agency.

One of the most memorable characters that I met at New York Center was a controller named "*Fat Jack.*" This man, about forty-five or fifty years old, who was about 5'10" tall and weighed around 300 pounds (thus the name Fat Jack) was, by all accounts, the "best damned controller at New York Center." Fat Jack demanded perfection of himself as well as the other controllers and assistants who worked with him. He had absolutely no use for affirmative action. When working for him, he demanded the same level of performance, regardless of race or gender, which he expected of himself. He was easily the most difficult controller that I ever had to work for and with, but the man had no equal in doing his job.

One day, during a busy traffic period, the entire computer system which generated all radar images failed. Fat Jack didn't blink an eye. At this time, he was working twenty-five airplanes in his sector. He got out of his chair, pulled two maintenance pins on either side of the radar which allowed the radar scope to be moved away from the console and be rotated so that the radar screen was now horizontal and parallel to the floor. A center radar is about forty inches in diameter and when pulled out from its console, it is shaped like a large kettle with the flat top being the radar screen. Once the computer failed, the only thing remaining on the radar screen itself were lines which represented the published airways used by aircraft flying through this particular sector. Fat Jack had his assistants help him make twenty-five "shrimp boats" which are small plastic holders about one inch long which contained a piece of paper with the aircraft ID and altitude written onto it. Fat

Jack, while preparing his scope and the corresponding shrimp boats, never stopped talking to the pilots. Within minutes, he had a shrimp boat for each of the twenty-five aircraft he was controlling. As he talked to each aircraft, he moved the corresponding shrimp boat. He continued to take on traffic as well as passing on traffic which was exiting in his sector. This situation continued for a little more than thirty minutes when the computer was reset and restarted. When the computer was restored, every, and I mean every, aircraft that Jack was working was covered by its appropriate shrimp boat. It was a tour de force of air-traffic control. His belligerent attitude was tolerated because the man had no peer while safely and efficiently controlling traffic.

A second incident occurred on Sunday, March 14, 1982. Joe and I were working the Hancock sector which feeds traffic going and coming from LaGuardia and JFK Airports. It was just past eight o'clock in the evening, and we were a little more than halfway through our shift. We only had four airplanes in this sector so Joe and I were working it alone. By this time, I knew the computer as well as most controllers. Some of the controllers to whom I gave assistance also let me give directions over the radios to pilots to see how I would handle it. I also knew all the handoff procedures for most of the sectors and in particular, the sector that Joe and I were working. Ten minutes after we started, the printer went crazy. It started generating strip after strip. Each one represented an aircraft about to enter our sector. Joe looked around and did not see another journeyman controller. He called over another assistant, like myself, and told that assistant, "I want you to stuff for Blake." "Stuff" was the terminology used for placing the strips into plastic holders and then putting the plastic holders in the proper incoming bay. Joe turned to me and said, "Blake, you do the handoffs and strip marking. Are you up to it?"

"Yes sir! I know where all the traffic goes and who I have to call," I responded. The calls started coming in. The controller operating the sector who was passing us the traffic would call me on the interphone and ask if we had the aircraft in question on radar. Joe would hear the question, I would point to the aircraft on the radar, and Joe would nod. I would then tell the controller on the interphone, "Radar contact," meaning we had the particular aircraft in question on our radar and we would accept control. I made sure that Joe had his eyes on every aircraft I accepted. As Joe talked to these aircraft, I made every single entry on the strips. Again, each strip represented a particular aircraft. I knew all the accepted shorthand used for strip marking. When the aircraft was ready to leave our sector, Joe would give me a hand signal and point to the particular aircraft in question. I would nod my assent and then contact, through the interphone, the gaining sector's controller and get his final instructions needed for him or her to receive the oncoming traffic. I would put that information on the strip and point to it. Joe would see my visual signal and nod. As soon as he could, he notified the aircraft in question via VHF radios and passed on the final commands to the pilot of the departing aircraft. I would place a checkmark next to the information on this strip which indicated that the instructions were passed to the pilot and acknowledged. And then I would call the gaining controller. He would hear my voice and say the aircraft call sign followed by "radar contact." That meant he now controlled that aircraft, and I would take the strip out of the holder and place it in a bay designated for traffic that was handled and passed on.

For the next hour and a half, Joe and I worked this way. Joe never stopped talking during this time. He was issuing command after command after command. I wrote each one on the strips using the prescribed symbols and abbreviations. I was so into what we were doing that I was oblivious to anything else going on around me. The concentration required to do this type of job is not anything that I can relate in words to someone who has not done it. I honestly believe that if a bomb had gone off behind us, neither Joe nor I would have noticed. Any outside stimuli that did not pertain to handling this traffic was summarily ignored.

What I did not know until the next day was that about forty-five minutes into this never-ending stream of traffic, the Air Traffic Manager (ATM) of New York Center (and I mean the nine hundred-pound gorilla who ran the facility) was standing right behind Joe and me. In his company was another F area supervisor named *John Sullivan.* John told me the next day the entire story that occurred after the ATM and he watched Joe and I work together for more than 30 minutes. The ATM asked John, referring to me, "Who's the new controller doing handoff procedures for Joe?"

John answered, "That's Norris Blakeman, sir".

The ATM asked, "When did Blakeman graduate from the academy?"

John meekly, and with some trepidation, answered, "He's a stuffer stripper, sir." (A stuffer stripper was the colloquialism used to describe a GS-7 level assistant. Handoff duties, by rule, are supposed to be performed by a fully qualified controller which is a GS-14 level position.)

The ATM continued to watch me flawlessly perform handoff duties. He turned to John and said, "I want Blakeman to go to the academy as soon as possible. I mean, if there is an opening tomorrow, I want him there tomorrow!"

John said in response, "I'm sorry, sir. But Blakeman is almost forty years old, and the law would not allow him to attend that school."

The ATM then said to John, "You better find a replacement for him. I mean a GS-14 replacement, even if you have to go to the break room." After John agreed to do this, the ATM stormed off to his office. Center ATMs are **not** used to not getting their way. This is especially true for New York Center.

John, about ten minutes later, found a journeyman controller (GS-14 type) and told him to replace me and take over handoff duties. That controller came over and just stood behind me. He plugged in the instructor side to hear the conversations I was having with controllers from other sectors. He watched from more than ten minutes until he had a full picture in his mind of the traffic that we were working. When he could safely take over for me, he tapped my shoulder twice which was his signal that he now would assume the position. I gratefully got out of my seat and let him take over. Joe covered his microphone boon and said to me, "Good job, Blake. Take the rest of the night off!" I still had over two hours to go before my shift ended. Even though I was covered with sweat from head to toe, I felt great.

In the meantime, my personal life was quite hectic. Air-traffic control schedules are not just Monday through Friday, but must cover the entire work week for the entire year. That meant having days off which rotated through the days of the week. About every other month, I would have weekends off. My shifts were either 6:00 AM to 2:00 PM, 2:00 PM to 10:00 PM, or 4:00 PM to midnight. I also worked about ten hours of overtime per week. Because of my diminished pay, I needed all the work I could get. I augmented my income by flying for the guard two or three times a week. That left me little personal time. I would see Betsy several times a week, but my time to assist Elizabeth Mae's soccer team was reduced to two or three times a month.

About a month after Joe and I worked that memorable night handling the Hancock sector together, I was at work discussing with my two supervisors why I wasn't being picked up for work in an air-traffic station. I had passed the test with flying colors, and I was concerned when others were selected ahead of me. Joe told me to speak to a supervisor whom we all called, "*Fuzzy.*" (I do not know the genesis of that particular nickname.) I found Fuzzy working another sector, and I told him about my situation. Fuzzy was a huge African-American supervisor who stood well over six feet and was somewhat north of 250 pounds. As large as he was, he was still quite a gentle man. But the unique thing about Fuzzy was that no one on the floor or even in Eastern Region knew more about ATC personnel procedures than he did. He told me that the Vietnam veterans being hired were those who did not have a college degree with only two exceptions. I asked what those exceptions were. Fuzzy told me that those veterans who received the Purple Heart and/or were disabled enough to receive compensatory payment due to military service were the two exceptions. I told Fuzzy, "Then I'm doubly qualified!"

"What do you mean?" he asked.

"I have the Purple Heart and I receive a VA 20% disability check based on my prior active duty."

"You have the Purple Heart and you're compensatory!?"

"Yup!"

"Oh boy! I better call Eastern Region because somebody's in trouble."

Right in front of me, Fuzzy, using the speaker phone, dialed a number he already knew by heart. I overheard the conversation as he talked to somebody named *Dave*, an Eastern Region personnel special-ist. He cited the applicable regulation to Dave who responded that I was not eligible because I had a college degree. Fuzzy told Dave that there were two exceptions to that rule. Dave took his time and smugly told Fuzzy that the only exceptions were receipt of the Purple Heart and/or being a compensatory veteran.

That's when Fuzzy said, "Dave, he is both!" After a stunned silence, Dave asked again that his understanding was correct. Fuzzy answered again, "Yes Dave. He is doubly qualified, and he received the highest scores in eastern region. One word to the IG (Inspector General) and someone is in trouble. What can we do for this young man?" Dave told Fuzzy that he would look into the situation and get back to him or to me within the week. That was more than acceptable for me. I thanked Fuzzy profusely for helping me out.

That conversation occurred on Thursday, April 19. A week later, I had that Thursday off, and Betsy and I were doing chores together all over the Island. Molly was in school so it was just the two of us. It was just after one o'clock when we were passing close to my house, and I told Betsy that I wanted to stop by and see if I had any mail. Just as we walked in, the phone rang. I answered it and to my surprise, it was Dave, the personnel officer at Eastern Region.

DAVE: "Mr. Blakeman, we have an opening at Elmira Flight Service Station (ELM FSS). If you decide to accept this position, you must be at the academy located in Oklahoma City by Sunday, April 22. Classes begin promptly at 8:00 a.m. on Monday, April 23. Do you want that position? I need an answer right away. "

ME: "Can you give me an hour? This is so sudden."

DAVE: "I'll call you back at this number in one hour. Let me know either way."

Betsy and I talked it over. We thoroughly discussed the pros and cons. I told her if I successfully completed the school and attained journeyman status as a controller in a station, then my pay would be as a GS-10 which would be sufficient income to provide for a family. I would have only the one job and not be whipsawed between flying, working and trying to have a private life. Both Betsy and I were denizens of Long Island. This is where we wanted to be, but I needed a profession with a future. This position offered me stability and would let me retire after thirty years of federal service or twenty years of control time. I already had more than twelve years of federal service in the bank, and I only needed eighteen more years to secure a generous retirement. I told her that I would not accept the position unless she would move to Elmira with me. By this time, we were a solid couple, and I had every intention of marrying her as soon as it was financially possible. I told her my intentions, and my Betsy said that ". . . it was more important to be together than where we lived." That was the answer I sought.

Dave called precisely one hour after we hung up. I told him that I accepted the position. He told me that my orders and travel vouchers would be available the next day at New York Center's Human Resources office. That office would also arrange my flight to Oklahoma City and provide suitable housing near the academy. Friday was a work day for me, however I would not have to be on the floor because the FAA would give me paid time to get my affairs in order before going to the academy. I was glad that I was picking up my material I needed to travel at the center. It gave me a chance to say goodbye to the controllers and the supervisors in Area F who were so good to me.

Betsy and I returned to her place. I shared an early supper with Betsy, her parents and Molly. It was then that we told the family about the conversation I had with Dave and my decision to go to Oklahoma City.

Molly asked, "How long is the school?"

I answered, "Fifteen weeks. When I get back, I will have three weeks off before reporting to Elmira Flight Service Station (ELM FSS)."

I explained to the family that if I was successful in completing the school and obtaining my journeyman qualification, it would provide sufficient income to support a family. All of us discussed the pros and cons about this position, but they saw that Betsy and I were pretty well decided on a course of action. Her parents were concerned about us having to leave Long Island. I told them that Elmira was a level II facility and once I got checked out, I could bid Islip Flight Service which was a level III facility. In fact, the FAA encouraged relocation as part of a promotion. That seemed to placate them.

After dinner was over, I called JG and Hope. I told them the news. JG was devastated. He really liked having me around. We had been best friends for more than twenty years. Besides, he needed to have someone to whom he could confide without the slightest fear of betrayal. I told JG that I would bid Islip FSS as soon as I could in the hope of returning to the Island. I made plans for Betsy and me to go out to dinner with JG and Hope on Friday night. JG had some business in the city, but he told me that he would have his secretary rearrange his schedule in order to see me then. He did not do that lightly. I knew this was important to him. I certainly knew it was important to me.

While Betsy and her mom were cleaning up after dinner, I had a chance to talk to Betsy's dad. I told him that I loved his daughter, and I wanted his permission to ask her to marry me. He smiled, then laughed and said, "My Betsy doesn't really need my permission. My girl absolutely makes up her own mind. But I really appreciate the fact that you asked me for her hand." I promised him then, as I do now, that I would take care of Betsy to the best of my ability, now and forever. He was very satisfied with that answer. That night, after Molly went to bed and Betsy and I were alone, I asked her to marry me and she quickly agreed. We would marry as soon as I became a journeyman controller.

22

ELMIRA FLIGHT SERVICE

The Friday before I departed for Oklahoma City, Betsy and I went out with JG and Hope. We had a posh dinner at JG's tennis club and went back to JG's home after completing the meal. We arrived at the house a little after nine o'clock that evening. Mrs. Stein, Lisa's mom, was babysitting the children. She greeted us warmly and told Hope that the children refused to go to sleep until they said goodbye to me. I went with JG and Hope to their individual rooms and kissed them good night and told each that I would miss them and that I loved them. I would see them as soon as possible after I completed the air-traffic control program which was "only" four months in duration. Now, to an adult, that is a short time, but not to a thirteen-year old boy and a ten-year-old girl. Elizabeth Mae was particularly upset at my leaving as I did spend more time with her than I did with Daniel. Besides her interests, both in soccer and racquetball, coincided with my own. Also, I loved her ruthless attitude when it came to playing sports. The girl was totally into competition and did not like or appreciate coming in second. Literally, a girl and an athlete after my own heart! I promised her that I would attend as many summer soccer practices as I could and at least one racquetball competition sponsored by her dad's racquet club. Even at a tender age, Elizabeth Mae had enhanced capabilities which greatly outdistanced the girls her own age. She now competed with boys in her age group and older.

In fact, during supper, JG told Betsy and I about an incident which occurred about a week before. They were having their evening meal at home when Daniel and Elizabeth Mae got into an argument about which was a better sport. Daniel, like his dad, was very big into tennis. He was near the top of the competitive ladder for his age that they used in the racquet club in order to rate the abilities of all the various members. Elizabeth Mae was at the top of her ladder for racquetball as it related to girls and near the top in the boys' ladder. The argument became pretty heated as they both passionately loved their individual sports. On top of that, their sibling rivalry was intense as they were both very competitive. JG and Hope listened, with some amusement, as the kids went back and forth with each other. Both JG and Hope watched intently as the children worked out their own sibling relationship. Daniel, trying to get an edge with his sister, reverted to some personal "button" issues that he used to tease and torment Elizabeth Mae. That really angered the little girl. Elizabeth Mae stood up, hands on hips, stared at her brother and said angrily, "Well, tennis is a game for pussies!" Both JG and Hope told us that they were in the middle of chewing their food when their daughter made that statement. Both spit out the food and were doubled over with laughter hearing their daughter making such a declaration. JG told me that they were laughing so hard they both had tears in their eyes. After they regained control of themselves, they attempted to admonish their daughter, but not too effectively.

After relating the story, JG looked directly at me and said, "I wonder where Elizabeth Mae picked up that language?" I tried to look as innocent as possible. I was not too successful.

When the children were safely asleep, JG and I excused ourselves from the women and went into his home office. It was not only very large but also very well appointed. The room was completely sound-proofed to provide privacy for the occasional client who he would see there. We talked over what I wanted to do with my house. We went back and forth on whether to rent or sell. Renting had the bigger upside but was fraught with economic peril. A risk I could not take. I told JG to sell the house, and I also gave him complete power of attorney in dealing with any and all issues as it applied to me. I told him to put the house up in June. By that time, I would know if I was going to succeed at the academy.

I asked JG how his huge, class-action suit regarding the airline stewardesses was coming along. He told me that he expected to go to court sometime next summer and he expected to win. That was not unusual . . . he almost always won.

We were sitting on opposite ends of a large sofa placed in the back of his office. The room was not only soundproofed but also had its own air filtering system. He had it built this way in order to allow him to smoke in this room. JG lit up, inhaled deeply and took his time exhaling. He was enjoying that rush from the first cigarette consumed after eating. He carefully chose his words, sitting with his back to the armrest and facing me, "Do you remember my telling you about Sylvia?"

I answered, "I think I do. She was the really pretty one that you were thinking about using as a witness."

"That's the one." he responded and then continued, "She is a magnificently beautiful woman. Unfortunately, or fortunately, in regard to this case, Sylvia has no problem maintaining a weight standard. She is 5'6" tall and weighs 118 pounds, and that does not vary more than a pound, regardless of what she eats. That's the problem. The standards are easy for her to maintain, so she would not make a good witness to the case that we're trying to make. However, there is an upside."

"What is that?" I asked.

"She flies into New York about twice a month, and I see her when she stays over in the city. The sex between us is absolutely phenomenal, so much so that I have lost interest in any other woman. She's an absolutely free spirit and does not want to get bogged down with a permanent relationship. Sylvia told me in no uncertain terms that I was not the only one she would see. She lives life on her own terms. Sylvia really likes my sense of humor, and we share many of the same sensibilities particularly when it comes to music and art. She made it abundantly clear to me that she does not practice exclusivity as it relates to sexual activity. I either had to accept a limited claim on her time or none at all. I chose to accept those limitations rather than not see her. Besides, there are some built-in benefits for me."

"Like what?" I asked.

"Well, I am no longer seeing or having relations with any other women besides Sylvia and Hope. It makes my life a lot simpler, and that is the upside. As a result, I've been spending more time with the family in the past several months. Hell, I heard Elizabeth Mae calling tennis a 'pussy' sport because I made it a priority to be home as much as possible. Now that I am a full partner, I can make my hours conform to my family's needs. Sylvia is the last hangover to a lifestyle I no longer wish to pursue. I suspect that someday she will give me my walking papers, and that will be the end of that."

"JG, you have a great family. Don't put it at risk. But I have told you this many times before. I just hope someday you listen."

He laughed. "That day may be sooner than you think. We better join the ladies before they start looking for us." I agreed and we returned to the den. Betsy and I left JG and Hope about an hour later. Two days later, I arrived at the airport in Oklahoma City.

My time at the academy was spent going to class and studying about three hours every night. During the weekend, I studied six hours a day on Saturday and Sunday. A lot of my classmates spent their off time in bars and places of entertainment. I took the school seriously. I was happily engaged to be married, and I wanted to be able to provide for my new family. I found a study partner who shared my proclivity to hit the books and do as well as possible.

Her name was *Joan*. She was a single mom of three children, and graduating this school and obtaining her full performance level (FPL) rating was her only goal. I enjoyed studying with her, and as a result, we became good friends. Sometimes before it got dark, we would take out our study cards, and while walking, asked each other questions regarding routes, air traffic procedures and weather phenomena. Most of the other students had spent significant time in a flight service station before attending the school, so they were well ahead of both of us when it came to the basic procedures regarding the flight service option. By the end of the first month, both Joan and I had caught up to the rest of the group. After the second month was completed, both Joan and I were in the top 20% of the class.

In the third month, we studied in-flight procedures which was considered the most difficult phase of training. Both Joan and I aced the exam and the flight simulator check ride. There was only one major test regarding weather phenomena and the emergency procedures check ride left to finish the course. Joan and I went to a Chinese restaurant to celebrate acing the in-flight check ride which was considered the hardest and most difficult graded event in the entire program. Joan had an old beat-up Dodge sedan that may have been older than she was, but it still ran. At any rate, we went to a nearby Chinese restaurant and ordered our meal. Joan was very careful to tell the server that she was highly allergic to any kind of shellfish. The server, a Chinese national, nodded his head and indicated that he understood. After we ate the meal, we left for her place so that we could study together. As we went to her car, Joan told me to drive as she was not feeling well. We got to her place about five minutes later and went into the kitchen in order to study. Right after Joan sat down, she complained about being dizzy. I asked her if she wanted to go outside and get some fresh air. She agreed. We got maybe a few feet past her door, and she said to me, "I think I'm going to pass out!"

I looked over my right shoulder and saw her starting to fall. I caught her, picked her up and carried her in my arms toward her old Dodge sedan. I opened up the passenger door and, as gently as I could, placed her in the seat. I still had her keys. I got in the driver's seat and drove like a maniac to Baptist Hospital in downtown Oklahoma City. I had gone there about five days before because I had extensive numbness on my left side. The doctors told me that the damage I suffered when I was blown out of the airplane was causing the numbness and that I could no longer jog in order to stay in shape. I also had to take aspirin until the numbness went away. At least I knew where Baptist Hospital was located . . . Thank God!

I made it to the emergency entrance in less than ten minutes. I parked illegally in front of the large double doors used by ambulance personnel when bringing in severely injured or gravely ill patients. I carried Joan in my arms into the emergency room. She was completely unconscious. A nurse and a doctor came running toward me and said, "What is her problem?"

I explained, "I think she's having allergic reaction. We just finished eating at a Chinese restaurant, and she told the waiter that she was highly allergic to seafood. I don't know what was in her food, but I suspect that they had some shellfish in it."

An orderly brought a stretcher with wheels, and I placed Joan on it. The doctor placed his stethoscope on the unconscious woman and said, "I don't have a pulse!" He asked for a specific type of drug. A nurse handed him a syringe, and the doctor immediately ejected the medicine into Joan's arm. It was like magic. She immediately woke up. She was dazed and unaware of where she was. She recognized me, and I told her that she was in the emergency room at Baptist Hospital. I stayed with her for the next two hours as her mental acuity returned. About that time, Joan returned to full consciousness and was ready to leave the hospital. The doctor insisted that she stay the night and be closely observed for the next twenty-four hours. Joan was a very strong-willed woman, and it took some time to finally convince her that the doctor was right. She finally agreed but only if I would take very careful notes and go over everything that was discussed by our instructors the next day. I agreed and gave her my solemn oath that I would do my best so that she would not miss a single fact or concept emanating from the class. She was appeased enough so that she was able to go to sleep, get her rest, and recover from almost losing her life.

The next day, when class was completed, I drove back to Baptist Hospital and picked her up. We went back to her apartment where we studied together for the next four or five hours. The only break we had was eating, and we stayed as far away from seafood as possible! I could tell by the way she studied that Joan was fully recovered. By the end of July, both of us had finished in the top 10% of the class. Joan returned to West Virginia and her babies, and I returned to Long Island to spend time with Betsy, her parents and Molly before going on to Elmira, New York. Once again, I was in awe on how God (or fate) worked. If I did not have a problem with extensive numbness on my left side causing me to go to Baptist Hospital about a week before, I would not have known the way. The doctor told me that she was within one or two minutes of extensive brain damage or death, or both. If I had to stop and ask directions or even call for an ambulance, Joan would not have survived.

I returned to Long Island on Friday, August 6, 1982. Betsy picked me up at LaGuardia Airport and drove me back to my house. Once we were safely in my home, I told her about the training I had just completed. I told her what had occurred with my study partner, Joan. Betsy asked, "What kind of relationship did you have with Joan? I mean, you're such a good-looking guy that it is hard to believe that she didn't make moves toward you."

I laughed and said, "Believe me when I tell you, Joan was all about the work. It's one of the traits I most admired about her. That girl was mission oriented which suited my needs perfectly. The two of us were probably the most serious students in the class. Besides, she wasn't the one who made a pass at me."

"Oh really? Then who did?" Betsy asked with raised eyebrows.

"We had one young lady in our class who was an absolute knock-out. She was pretty and had a great figure, and she knew it. Well, every guy in both sections of our class made a pass at this young lady. That is, every guy except me. I made it clear that I was engaged and not available. So, I was the one that she chose to have a relationship with which was an offer I politely turned down. That seemed to make her try harder and harder. I never understood it. Every guy except me wanted to get into her pants and yet, I was the one that she pursued. Go figure."

Betsy laughed, and I knew at once that she believed me. Right from beginning of our relationship, Betsy and I were always honest with each other. That still continues to this day. She then said, "She wanted you because you are the one guy that she could not have! It's basic human nature to desire what you can't have, especially when you're used to getting what you want when you want it. If she was as attractive as you say, and I believe you that she was all that you stated, then she was probably used to getting her way by just using her looks. I've known women like that, and they panic when their sex appeal doesn't work for them."

The next day, Betsy threw a party for me at the house she shared with her parents celebrating my completion of the academy training and, coincidentally, my birthday. JG, Hope and the children attended the party. Also attending were many of Betsy's relatives and friends. It was there that we announced formally our engagement. I spent the better part of the afternoon getting to know Betsy's friends and relatives. They asked a slew of questions because they wanted to know as much as they could about the man who was going to marry Betsy. I answered all their questions as honestly as I could.

I had three weeks off before going up to Elmira. I made sure that I attended two of Danny's little league games and coached two soccer practices for Elizabeth Mae's team. JG arranged a buyer for my house, and we were due to close by the end of August. I put most of my personal belongings in storage and kept enough furniture to fill a small apartment. Betsy and I went up to Elmira together about a week before I had to formally report to my station in order to find a suitable apartment. That trip took about three days. While we were there, I signed a six-month lease for a nice apartment about a ten-minute drive to the Elmira Airport where I would work. After completing the task of finding suitable housing, Betsy and I returned to the Island. By the end of August, I moved all my personal belongings that were not in storage to my new apartment in Elmira, New York.

On Monday, August 30 1982, I reported to work. Elmira Flight Service Station (ELM FSS) was located in the tower at Elmira Airport. The flight service station occupied the second floor of the tower. The station at that time was manned by eleven controllers (including myself), one supervisor and one air-traffic manager (ATM). Dress code for this station was a white shirt and tie. This was true because many of the weather briefings we gave pilots were done over-the-counter, person-to-person. In the center, all communication was over the radios, not face to face. Consequently, management correctly insisted on having professional attire.

The ATM was *Jerry Racine*. When I knew him, he was a man in his 50s with dark hair, dark eyes and a goatee. The one supervisor was *John "Robbie" Robinson*. Robbie was a retired naval NCO. He was a few inches taller than me, heavyset with a kind face. Both of these men insisted on every controller doing excellent work on any task assigned. When traffic turned really heavy, both men would be on the floor helping the controllers on duty work the increased demand. They provided the best operational environment that I experienced in over twenty-five years working as an air-traffic controller.

I was friendly with all my coworkers. But in particular, the one I befriended most was *Frank Malinowski*. Frank was a retired Air Force NCO. He was considered too old to work in a tower, so like me, he went into the flight service option. He graduated the academy about a month before I did. As a result, we were very close in our stages of training. Frank was about 5'10", heavyset, with dark-haired tinged with gray. He possessed a booming voice mixed with an infectious laugh. Frank and I were the only Vietnam War combat veterans. Frank was the tower chief at Tan Son Nhut Airport which was located just outside downtown Saigon. He ran that tower for several years. That, at that time, was probably the most difficult tower in the world to operate due to both the amount of traffic and the huge performance differences in the aircraft that they controlled. For example, you may have, as a controller, to work a C-141 Starlifter, an F-4 Phantom, and an O-2 observation aircraft in the same pattern. A controller at LaGuardia Airport works lots of traffic, but they're all basically airliners. The Air Force controllers who Frank supervised in Tan Sun Nhut worked aircraft whose approach speeds varied from sixty knots to two hundred knots. He knew more about controlling aircraft than anyone who worked in the Elmira tower, bar none! But the FAA said he was too old. The tower's loss was flight service's gain. Frank was a great controller, and he was well-liked by his fellow workers and virtually every pilot who we dealt with at Elmira.

We both quickly checked out in the flight data, teletype and weather observer positions. By the end of the year, we had both checked out in pre-flight duties. Pre-flight is basically briefing the pilots on current and forecasted weather conditions along their proposed route of flight. The pilots called on the phone or came there in person to receive their briefings. Elmira FSS had three briefing positions. Two of these positions were located on a long table and each controller sat side-by-side, answering the phone. The third position was located on a counter where the pilot would enter to receive a live briefing. Frank and I really enjoyed working together and our training needs coincided, so Robbie usually scheduled us together, and we would partner up on the phone briefing table more than any other set of controllers.

The wonderful thing about working at Elmira FSS was the intimacy between the controllers and the pilots. We knew most, if not all, of the pilots who flew out of Chemung County Airport (AKA Elmira Airport). Many times, we would receive the pilots' "N" number (the ATC assigned number for a particular aircraft), and we would know what kind of airplane he or she was flying and its operating characteristics. After a while, we could tailor our briefings to the exact needs of our local pilots who received the information. It made us a very efficient organization. Those pilots who were unfamiliar to us or who were flying out of the area received an excellent standard weather briefing virtually from every controller working at Elmira FSS.

To monitor proficiency, the FAA and the National Weather Service (NWS) personnel would call all the different stations throughout the country. They pretended to be pilots and asked for a weather briefing. After the briefing was completed, they would ask for the supervisor and get the information regarding who briefed them. The graded briefing, accompanied by a recording of that briefing, was then sent to the supervisor, regardless of the grade. The passing grade was satisfactory in every facility except Elmira. At our facility, outstanding was the only truly acceptable grade. We were consistently rated the top briefing facility in the Eastern Region. That was true every year I worked there. The habit of excellence that I acquired at Elmira FSS served me well virtually in every facility in which I worked during my time with the FAA.

The importance of the weather briefing that a pilot receives before he or she flies cannot be overstated. In the 1950s, the FAA determined that more than 90% of the serious aircraft accidents were caused by weather phenomena. The National Weather Service (NWS) did not have the personnel to brief the rapidly growing number of private and corporate pilots. Instead, they trained flight service personnel to do these briefings. Upon successful completion of the training, the controller would give a graded briefing to an NWS weather person. If the

NWS evaluator thought that the briefing was acceptable, the controller received a briefing certificate issued by the NWS which allowed him or her to legally brief pilots. The briefing background that we received at the academy was equivalent to a major at any university in weather phenomena. That is why the academy's length of time to train a flight service specialist is literally 150% longer than either the tower or center option.

When a specialist briefs a pilot on the weather he or she will encounter, the emphasis must be upon safety of flight. One of the factors in how the specialist shapes the briefing is the experience level of the pilot receiving the briefing. Generally inexperienced, low-time pilots fly under visual flight rules (VFR). When a VFR pilot's route of flight takes him or her into unsafe weather conditions, we use the specific term "VFR flight is not recommended." We also put a "VNR" abbreviation adjacent to the aircraft N number on our briefing log. When the briefer does this, it denotes that the pilot was warned of imminent danger due to weather. If pilots who receive the VNR statement still fly, they do so at their own risk and without any flight insurance. Once that statement is made to the pilot, it alleviates any financial responsibility from almost all, if not all, insurance companies who provide aviation policies. It is a very strong inducement to keep the pilot on the ground rather than risk his or her life flying into unsafe weather conditions.

Sometimes a briefer has to use his or her imagination to make his or her point. An example will serve: I was briefing a VFR pilot who was departing Elmira on his way to Binghamton Airport. It was a trip of approximately twenty-five minutes in his Cessna 172. Between his departure and his destination was a line of level VI (the most severe) thunderstorms. I told the pilot several times that "VFR flight was not recommended," yet he continued to indicate that he still wished to fly the route. I told the pilot, "Please hold the line while I get the accident report."

The pilot responded, "What do you mean by the accident report?"

I answered in a matter-of-fact voice, "Well, when the plane crashes and burns, and the pilot is killed, we have to fill out this report. In this accident report there are a lot of questions that we cannot answer because the pilot is dead. So, what I'm proposing is that you and I fill out the accident report together while you're still alive, and I will be able to fill out all the answers. When my boss comes to work tomorrow, he will have a completed accident report on his desk. Now please hold on while I get the report. It will only take me about a minute."

"You are serious, aren't you?" he asked.

"Yes sir. I need to fill out this report before you fly. Now would you hold on while I get the proper form so we can fill it out together?"

"Well, maybe I shouldn't fly."

I thought to myself, "DUH!!!" But to the pilot I said, "Yes sir. You should NOT fly!"

"I think you're right. I'll keep it on the ground," he said and then hung up. I felt really good. If he had flown, he would almost surely have been killed by the enormous power contained within level VI thunderstorms. The good briefer keeps the pilot in a safe envelope of flight . . . in some cases that means NOT FLYING! The good briefer will find a way to convey the danger to the pilot. Good briefings break the chain of events required to have an aircraft accident.

Several other humorous incidents come to mind when I think back on my experience at Elmira FSS. The first occurred in the first few months of 1983. By this time, both Frank and I were now checked out in preflight and were allowed to brief pilots without supervision. On this one day, during the day shift, Frank and I were sitting side-by-side at the briefing table answering the phones and briefing pilots. I heard Frank answer his phone by saying, "Frank's friendly flight service. May I help you?" The alliteration appealed to me and so for the next month or so as we worked side-by-side, both Frank and I were answering the phone using that phrase. That is until Jerry Racine called the facility and I answered the phone using "Frank's friendly flight service. May I help you?" Well, Jerry was not too pleased. As a result, I received a chewing out over the phone.

But I knew that Jerry wasn't too upset when he stated just before hanging up, "If you want to use that phrase, at least make it Jerry's friendly flight service!" I promised him I would never use that expression again and that seemed to satisfy him. After all, he knew I was an excellent briefer.

The second incident occurred when Frank and I were receiving our first formal introduction regarding the in-flight position. Robbie was giving both of us the initial overview, emphasizing different equipment, radios and interphones that we would use in the performance of the tasks required of that position. Both Frank and I were standing right behind Robbie listening to him as he talked about the equipment. It was around three o'clock in the afternoon in the middle of March, 1983. There was a fast-moving cold front approaching from the northwest during this time. The cumulous cloud cover was so thick that it was literally as dark as night over the airport. A line of steady-state thunderstorms was over the facility at the time that Frank and I were receiving our introduction to the in-flight position. Robbie was in midsentence, explaining how to operate the radios, when the facility got struck by a massive bolt of lightning. There was a loud explosion immediately followed by all the lights in the station going out. About three seconds later, the emergency lights came on. Robbie looked around and saw everybody except Frank and me. The bewilderment plastered on Robbie's face was priceless as he wondered where his trainees went! Frank dove under one desk, and I dove under the other. We both thought that we'd received an 88mm rocket attack. Everyone else was standing and looking around. The standing joke at my facility was: "How do you identify the two Vietnam combat veterans who worked at this facility? The answer was that they were under the desk!"

By mid-spring of that year, I knew I was going to check out as a full performance (FPL) controller. I brought Betsy back with me to spend several days looking for a suitable house for the entire family which included her parents and her daughter. We found a home for sale just off Water Street and just north of the Chemung River. I put a bid on the house which was accepted, and we planned to close on June 28. We picked June 26 as the date we would marry so that we could take title as man and wife thereby owning our new home jointly. Jerry gave me the last week in June and the first week in July as leave time. Normally, due to my low seniority, I would never have been able to get that time off, but my fellow controllers, understanding of how important it was to me personally, allowed me to "jump" the seniority list and granted me that vacation time.

Elmira, in the spring of 1983, was a quaint "city" of perhaps 40,000 people. Several decades before, it was a thriving industrial center, but it had been more than twenty years since Elmira had any major industry besides farming. As a result, the air quality was excellent and the southern section of town, where we purchased the house, was quite beautiful. Elmira College was located in the center of the city and had quite a bit of Mark Twain memorabilia including the gazebo in which he did most of his writing. Automobile traffic was almost never a problem as the streets and highways were constructed for a much larger population. This small city had wonderful restaurants and theaters which were well out of proportion to the size of its population. In short, it was a very nice place to live.

On June 23, I worked the midnight shift and did not have to report back to work until Monday July 11 at four o'clock in the afternoon. Right after work, I drove to Betsy's house and stayed there until we would depart for Elmira. On June 26, with JG as my best man, I married my Betsy to whom I would stay faithful for the remainder of my life. About eighty or so people attended, including my father, Lou and Nancy Lee, and JG and Hope. It was a modest afternoon wedding followed by a wonderful luncheon. It was the most we could afford. After the wedding was over, Betsy and I allowed ourselves a one-day honeymoon. On June 28, Betsy and I closed the new house, and we returned to Long Island. By June 30, we were busy packing up her family's belongings so that all of it could be transported during the Fourth of July weekend. On July 5, 1983, my new family moved into our Elmira residence. It was the only day of the year that the temperature exceeded 100°.

I spent the next week hanging pictures and otherwise making the house as comfortable as possible for her parents and Molly as well as ourselves. Frankly, it was a pleasure to get back to work! Doing ATC tasks, at that point, seemed easier to me. By the second week in our new house, we had fully settled in, and everyone in the family really enjoyed the new residence.

Life took on an enjoyable rhythm. My Betsy, well before she met me, obtained a Masters' degree as a reading specialist from Hofstra University. She had a unique personal "radar" which allowed her to accurately diagnose an individual's reading problem or learning disabilities. On Long Island, she tutored so that she could be home for her daughter. In Elmira, she could be a full-time housewife and mother. That was more than desirable to her. This way Molly had a stay-at-home mom, and I had someone who would take care of my physical needs while loving me at the same time. The money was tight, because I would not receive FPL pay until I'd spent a year as a GS-9. But it was doable and looking back, it was a very nice lifestyle.

The biggest problem I had was learning to be a stepparent. That is the single most difficult task that anyone could face. I was forty years old when I married, and I did not have any real experience raising a child. But like most people who are childless, I thought I knew all the answers. To be brutally blunt, my ability to stepparent was abysmal. I was way too strict in a household where discipline was not a priority. It took me several years to learn that a step parent has to come behind the parent to help out and should never . . . and I mean never . . . apply discipline! That is the job for the natural parent.

What exacerbated my problem was my PTSD which resulted from my combat service. I wanted and needed a great deal of Betsy's attention and affection. But Betsy was a loving and dutiful daughter of two aged parents and a wonderful mother to her daughter. These roles took their toll in both time and attention. It was a very hard adjustment for me to accommodate her other needs. Through counseling provided by the Veterans Administration, spread over the years, I finally could make that adjustment. But it wasn't easy.

When I got angry, I would take long walks until the anger abated. I had my mother's temper and it was not easy to overcome. Betsy let me take the walks, even when she wanted to continue an argument or a conversation, because she knew it was my best coping mechanism. Once the anger left, I could consider what she said and accept it. My Betsy was not only intellectually smart, but she had more than her share of wisdom. In fact, my nickname for her was "Bets Bear" because she "was smarter than the average bear!" That would make sense to you if you've ever seen the Yogi Bear cartoons that were prevalent in the

1960s. It took me a couple years, but eventually I got comfortable in my role in the family.

In late August, my father came to visit us. I picked him up at the Binghamton Airport and drove the fifty-six miles to our house. He stayed a week. Dad was very happy to see me settled. Betsy's parents were of his age and experience, and they got along wonderfully. This was Betsy's and my home, and I proudly showed it to him. I loved spending time with him. He and Moshe, my old boss, went back a long time. Dad told me some of the old tales that he and Moshe experienced together. Dad was an excellent bridge player, and we played with Betsy's parents almost every night that he was there. However, I noticed how frail he was and that worried me. We played a round of golf at the local community course. He used to really enjoy walking a course, but now that was impossible. So, we took a gas cart and played. I really enjoyed being with him. After the week was over, I drove him back to Binghamton where he got a flight to West Palm Beach. Before he departed, I hugged him and told him how much I loved him. Dad looked at me and said, "Norris, I am proud of the man you have become. I will always love you. Now I'm happy with your new family and your new home. May God bless you all the days of your life!" With that he left to go to his airplane. It was the last time I would see him alive. Five months later, I received a call from my brother saying that our father was dead. May God rest his soul. It was a Wednesday, January 4, about seven o'clock in the evening when the phone call came. My brother called and told me that our father had quietly passed away of a heart attack. His body was being flown back to Long Island where he would be buried next to our mother. The funeral was scheduled for January 6 at 2:00 PM. in a funeral home in eastern Long Island. I told him that Betsy and I would be there. I then called the chief pilot of Corning Glass Corporation whose name was *Rocky* and told him that my father had died and that Betsy and I needed to be on Long Island the next day. Corning Glass Corporation ran a daily shuttle flight, sometimes two, between Newark Airport and Chemung County Airport. Rocky told me that we would have guaranteed seats on the shuttle.

The personnel of Elmira FSS had a close relationship with the aviation branch of Corning Glass Corporation. Rocky was their chief pilot. He was a man of my height, a little on the heavy side, with graying hair and a generous disposition. We facilitated their needs for IFR flight plans and clearances whenever we could. We briefed all their pilots and shared the running of the annual Christmas party for both organizations which was usually held in the Corning Corporation aviation hangar. Rocky would come in to the station when I was working the midnight shift. Betsy, being the great housewife that she was and is, would pack a meal for me to eat and always included a generous helping of zucchini bread filled with chocolate chips. It was more than I could eat, so when Rocky would come in at four o'clock in the morning because he couldn't sleep, I would offer to share my bounty with him. He always accepted. We spent many a night sharing food that Betsy prepared along with a large pot of freshly brewed coffee. He enjoyed both the food and my company.

On Thursday, January 5, 1984, Betsy and I climbed aboard a King Air 200 (BE20) piloted by Rocky and flew to Newark Airport. During the flight, Rocky told the copilot to sit in the rear and bring up Betsy. He did as he was ordered. Betsy was given the copilot seat and a full tour of the aircraft and the terrain extending from Chemung Airport to the approach at Newark. When we got handed off to New York approach, Betsy returned to her seat. She was flush with excitement as she had never been in an aircraft cockpit before.

Once we landed at Newark, we got on the Corning bus shuttle which dropped us off near Penn Station. JG knew I was coming in and he had his limo driver pick us up and take us to his building. JG's office was in mid-town Manhattan and we reached it in only about fifteen minutes. I looked at my watch and saw the time was 11:45 in the morning. We took the elevator to JG's office on the 23rd floor which was fully occupied by his law firm. A secretary told Betsy and me that Mr. Gladon was expecting us and that she would take us directly to his office. This was the first time I saw JG's workplace. His personal office was approximately three hundred square feet with one glass wall facing the street. JG's desk was by the glass wall. There was a large sofa and three oversize chairs opposite his desk. JG stood up, came toward us, and hugged both Betsy and me. I was concerned about JG's appearance. He was significantly grayer, and he looked as if he was very tired. "I'm so sorry to hear about your dad. In all the years that I knew him, he showed me nothing but kindness, good cheer and wisdom. You and Betsy will stay at my house and we will go to the funeral together. Right now, I have to do some work so I can leave the office early today. I have a bad cold and seeing to your needs is a perfect excuse for me to leave early. However, I made reservations for you in the restaurant located on the first floor of this building. The food is excellent and will be charged to my law firm, so don't worry about paying the bill. Take your time eating and come back here in about an hour and a half, and we will drive to the island together. Hope is expecting you and so are the children."

Betsy and I thanked him. We went down to the restaurant and had a wonderful meal. JG was correct in that the food and service was absolutely first rate. We rejoined him after eating and left shortly after that. We used the firm's limo, so JG, Betsy and I were sitting in the rear compartment. JG sat on one side and Betsy and I, with our backs to the driver, sat facing him. I was concerned for my friend. It was little less than half a year since last I saw him, yet the change was dramatic. But it did not affect his wonderful wit. He regaled Betsy with stories from our past and how my father helped him cope with his dad.

JG said, "Many a time I would drive to Blake's house when I had these horrible arguments with my father. Blake's dad and mom treated me like one of their own. One day in particular comes to mind. I was very angry and hurt after having a huge fight with my father. Frankly, it was so long ago that I don't remember the particulars, but I told the whole thing to Mr. Blakeman. He told me that my father loved me and had such high expectations for me that it colored everything else he did. He told me at that time I would be successful, and my father would come to appreciate me. He needed a little more time to accept the person who I was becoming. He assured me that would happen. Later, after he met Hope, Mr. Blakeman told me that she would pave the way to obtain my dad's acceptance. And he was right. Talking to him helped me be patient when dealing with my own father. I made my peace with my father before he died. I hope you did the same."

I told JG about my last meeting with my dad. Recalling that last talk at the Binghamton Airport, brought tears to my eyes. "I will miss him all the days that are left of my life."

It was a little after four o'clock in the afternoon when the limo dropped us off at JG's home. Hope and the children heard the car arriving and came out to meet us. Betsy and I received hugs from Hope and the children. Hope held me for a long time. She had tears in her eyes as she said, "Your father was a really good man. I enjoyed his wonderful sense of humor and his wisdom. I'm so sorry."

To change the mood, I asked about the children and how they were doing. They looked healthy and full of life, and I needed a dose of that at that moment. Both children were doing well in school and were excelling in their sporting activities. We walked into the house and Elizabeth Mae excitedly told me about how well their soccer club was doing. They won the last major tournament of the season and in that last game, Elizabeth Mae scored two goals. I told her I wished I could've seen it, but I was also very proud of her. JG chimed in and stated that his daughter not only scored the winning goals but knocked out two girls of the opposing teams. Not dirty play, but certainly hard-nosed, aggressive soccer. Yep, that little girl played the game the way I did.

On a cold and dreary Friday morning, January 6, we buried my father. It's kind of a weird feeling being the eldest generation of one's family. For my first 41+ years, there was always someone older than I. Now there was no one. I was next in line, age wise…a stark realization of one's own mortality. The next day, Betsy and I caught the Corning Glass Saturday shuttle which departed JFK airport, and we returned to Elmira.

23

THE LONG GOODBYE

About a week after we got home from burying my father, I called JG's office to see how he was doing. I was worried about him because of the nasty cold he endured while Betsy and I were visiting him and his family. His secretary got him on the phone. After the initial greeting, JG told me that the doctors gave him a strong dose of antibiotics and that he was now recovering. He was also excited about his major class-action suit. The verdict came in and his side won. His share of the financial reward would make him a wealthy man for the rest of his life. I congratulated him and said, "It could not have happened to a nicer person. I am absolutely thrilled that you won. Now I hope you take some time off so you can fully recover your health."

He answered, "I will. I promise. I have about two to three months' worth of negotiations to complete the case, and then I will take Hope and the children for a two-week vacation. I think I can coordinate my time off with their spring break."

"Good. I was really worried about you and not about your health alone. Let me put this directly to you. Are you still seeing Sylvia?"

JG laughed and said, "You're such an old fuddy-duddy. I have not seen her for at least two months now. The way our relationship worked was that she would call me when she was in New York. Frankly, I have never called her. Sylvia always initiated the contact between us. I won't lie to you. I miss her but I'm not devastated. Lately I've been spending more time with Hope and the children, and I'm finding that I'm enjoying them more and more. The kids are old enough now to have their own distinct personalities . . . such an amazing process . . . watching them grow from totally dependent babies into their own separate human beings."

"Good. Now you make me feel better. I can relax. I think you're over the hump!"

"There you go again, you old fuddy-duddy!" JG laughed and said that he had to go. We said goodbye as we hung up.

About two weeks later, JG called the flight service station and asked for me. I was working a day shift and in particular, the in-flight position at the time. Robbie heard the concern in my friend's voice and told him that I would be available in a few moments once he relieved me. Robbie told me who was on the phone and that it was important. He took over my position and with a great deal of trepidation, I went to the office phone to talk to my best friend. I closed the door so that my conversation could not be overheard. After the initial greetings, I could hear the concern in JG's voice. "I need to talk to you as soon as possible," he said.

"What's wrong?" I asked.

"I don't want to discuss it over the phone. How soon can you be here?"

"I am scheduled for a midnight shift tonight which will go from midnight to 8:00 AM. The second Corning shuttle takes off at 8:30 AM. If I get a ride on that aircraft, I could be in the Newark airport by 9:30 AM tomorrow. Let me put you on hold, and I'll call over to Corning to see if I can get a ride." JG agreed to be put on hold. I then called Rocky who was in his office and told him that my best friend needed me to be in New York the next day. I asked if it would be possible for me to catch a ride on the second shuttle which left at 8:30.

Rocky answered, "You're in luck. I'm scheduled to fly that King Air tomorrow morning. You will have a ride, even if you have to stay in the jump seat." I thanked Rocky and returned to JG's line. I told him that I would be at Newark Airport the next morning. He asked for the name of the fixed base operator who handled Corning Glass aviation flights. I gave him the information, and JG said that his limo would be waiting for me.

I called Betsy and told her what had transpired. We did have plans for the next several days, but she understood that I had to go to New York. Betsy told me that she would pack a bag as well as my lunch for my midnight shift. She wanted to know what was going on. I couldn't answer as I did not know myself. I just knew that it was important. She was not a happy camper because she hated giving up our time together, but my Betsy also knew that I could never say "no" to JG.

I returned to the floor and thanked Robbie for allowing me to take that phone call. Normal policy was not allowing personal calls on the floor while you were on shift. Robbie was the kind of supervisor who recognized that sometimes rules had to be bent in order to accommodate great personal needs. It was one of the reasons that I believe, even to this day, Elmira Flight Service was an extraordinarily well-run facility. I did tell him that it was indeed, a very important phone call. I told him I was taking the Corning shuttle to New York. I would leave tomorrow after my midnight shift was completed. I thought I would be back for my evening shift on Saturday, January 28. Robbie told me that if I needed leave, all I had to do was ask. He would accommodate any request, even if he had to work the shift himself.

The next morning, Robbie came in early and relieved me which gave me plenty of time to walk over to the Corning hanger. Rocky, true to his word, made sure I had a seat. We arrived at Newark Airport at 9:20 in the morning. The limo was waiting for me just outside the fixed base operator's building. The driver took me directly to JG's office building. I took the elevator to the 23rd floor and went directly to the receptionist. I told her who I was, and she said that I was expected and that Mr. Gladon's secretary would come and escort me to JG's office. About two minutes later, JG's secretary turned the corner and came into view. She greeted me and told me to follow her which I did. About forty seconds later, she knocked on JG's door and was told to enter. I followed behind her. JG was sitting behind his desk. He looked up and said, "Brenda, hold my calls. I don't want to be disturbed until I tell you unless it is literally a matter of life and death." He waved to me to come sit in a comfortable chair to the right of his desk. Brenda left the office and closed the door behind her. I took the seat that he offered, and he then sat in a similar chair facing me.

I had an opportunity to closely observe my friend. His skin was ashen, and he had lost a lot of hair. He looked really terrible. I was appalled and deeply concerned by his appearance. I noticed that he had lost at least ten pounds since the last time I saw him which was less than three weeks earlier. JG, in his usual manner, waited several moments before addressing me directly.

He sat quietly for almost a minute. I could see his mind working as he formulated his ideas and how he wanted to open this dialogue. That was JG's manner and, after more than twenty years of knowing him, I was used to it and waited for him to complete the process. I think one of the reasons we got along so well is that I always gave him time to gather his thoughts without asking any questions which would interfere with that process. Finally, he looked up and said, "What I am about to tell you must remain between you and me. No exceptions. Not even Betsy. Do I have you word?"

"Absolutely. Whatever you tell me will stay with me. Period!" I responded.

JG nodded his head in assent and said, "Four days after you left to return to Elmira, I received a call from a Dr. Nora Stanwicz, a physician who works for the CDC. She made it a point to call me at my office."

"What is the CDC?" I asked.

"It is the Center for Disease Control and Prevention. Its job is the prevention of an outbreak of any type of communicable disease any-where in the country. Dr. Stanwicz insisted upon seeing me either that day or the next. I was scheduled to come into the office at 9:00 AM. I told her to meet me in my office at eight the next morning. I arrived at my office at 7:55 AM and she was already waiting. I brought her into the office. She asked me if anyone could overhear us. I assured her that the room was properly sound-proofed. After we were seated, she asked me if I knew Sylvia Majors, the airlines stewardess with whom I had an affair. You remember me talking about her?"

"Of course, I do. I also remember telling you that I had a bad feeling about her, and that you should break it off. Yeah, I remember."

"Well, your intuition, as usual, was correct again." JG allowed himself a small smile before continuing, "My gift was reading people. Hell, I'm a walking talking 'lie detector' machine. I can really read people, and that's what made me a very successful trial lawyer. Your gift was being intuitive about situations. You were never a great reader of people, but you always did have an inexplicable feel for the unusual situation. I think we both made the best of our individual gifts."

"What about Sylvia?" I asked.

"It turns out that Sylvia died about two weeks ago from Acquired Immune Deficiency Syndrome otherwise known as AIDS. You know what that is, don't you?"

"I know that it is some kind of virus which attacks the immune system and is virtually a death sentence. I don't think there's any cure for it."

"You're right. It's a death sentence and a horrible way to die. The doctors are not even sure of how communicable this disease is. They're not sure if it is passed from one person to another by airborne exposure or intimate sexual contact, or both. Most American physicians were not even aware of this disease prior to two or three years ago. They are pretty sure that the fastest and most sure way of passing this disease from one individual to the next is a matter of sexual contact. At any rate, Dr. Stanwicz interviewed Sylvia before she died. Sylvia was forth-coming in naming all her sexual partners. It turned out that I am one of eight men whom she was sleeping with before she died. Dr. Stanwicz took a sample of my blood and warned me not to have sexual contact with anyone and to limit any personal contact with any other human being until they got the results. That's why when you came here today, I did not hug you or shake your hand."

"Did you get the results?" I asked with great trepidation.

"This past Tuesday, January 24, Dr. Stanwicz came to my office and told me that I was HIV-positive. The fact that I was getting over pneumonia was a strong indication that my HIV is turning into full-blown AIDS. I asked her how long I have to live. She told me to realistically expect maybe two or three good months followed by two to six months of constant deterioration. But that is all guessing. They are just starting to learn basic AIDS parameters. All they can do for me medically is make my passing as painless as possible."

I felt like someone had just kicked me in the gut. I wanted to scream . . . to rail against the fates. But that wouldn't help. All I could do was ask in a soft voice, "There's nothing they can do?"

"Nothing. Not a damned thing!" JG responded.

"What about Hope? Have you put her in danger?" I asked.

"I don't think so. Hope started to suspect my infidelities about eight or nine months ago, so she cut me off sexually. Thank God. We started to get close again when I got pneumonia and frankly, I wasn't up to having sexual relations with anyone. Dr. Stanwicz agreed to test Hope's blood under the pretense that the type of pneumonia I had was very communicable. She actually tested not only Hope, but also the children as well. When she called me with my results, Dr. Stanwicz also informed me that Hope and the children were free of the HIV virus."

"Thank God; at least they are safe for the time being. What do you intend to do?"

"This is all I've thought about since Dr. Stanwicz informed me of my HIV status. I had to put my priorities in the proper order. There wasn't any time for bullshit. I had to look inside myself and determine what was best for my family which was at the very top of my priority list. The most important thing is not exposing them to any danger or anybody else for that matter. It became imperative to limit my contact with others. Dr. Stanwicz told me that they were more than 90% sure that the virus was passed by the absorption of human secretions or bodily fluids. Of course, sexual contact is possibly the easiest way to accomplish the passing of the virus from one person to another. I told my law partners that I am extremely ill and needed several months to regain my health without telling them the particulars. I just won a jury award which will bring in the neighborhood of $50 million in fees and expenses to the firm. That buys a whole bunch of empathy."

"What are you going to tell Hope?" I asked.

"I am going to tell her the whole truth. No more lies. She deserves to know everything. Then I'm going to disappear. There is a very expensive medical resort in Mexico that treats only AIDS patients. The staff is well aware of the risks and how to prevent being infected. The care is quite good, and the facility also contains a hospice wing. You are the only person who'll know the name and location of this resort. Hope is going to meet me at my apartment in the city tonight. You remember the Steins who were supposed to go to Israel after burying their daughter Lisa?"

"I will never forget them and their grief."

"It turns out that Lisa's mom and Hope became really good friends as well as good neighbors. They needed a daughter and grandchildren to dote on. Hope, on other hand, as you know has absolutely no relationship with her parents because she married me and became Jewish. Hope was ostracized from her own family. She missed sharing her joy of parenthood with her natural mother and father. Over the past dozen years, Hope and the Steins have become very close. That relationship kept the Steins from immigrating to Israel. Hope is like their own daughter now, and they adore Daniel and Elizabeth Mae. Even the fact that you are my best friend helped cement that relationship. Hope loves you like a brother, and you were the best thing to happen to Lisa in her short adult life. Edna, Mrs. Stein to you, is going to babysit the children tonight so that I can talk unimpeded with Hope. In fact, the relationship is so strong that when I told Hope that we should buy a much larger house in Great Neck, which is considerably closer to the city, she said absolutely no. She loves her house, and she does not want to leave the Steins. She felt so strongly about it that I decided to just pay off the mortgage and be done with it. Besides, having a chauffeured limousine made available to me by the firm made commuting more palatable even over a larger distance."

"When are you leaving?" I asked.

"In three days, I will have completed everything that I can do. I scheduled a private jet to take me to the resort on January 30. I have to spend the next several days with my personal lawyer so that I can rewrite my will and prepare my estate to make it easier on Hope. I also must complete some of the preparatory work needed by my firm to negotiate the final payout with the airlines. Regardless, Hope will get half the estate and the children will share the other half. Since we own our home jointly, Hope will take sole possession without worrying about further inheritance taxes. She's going to want to talk to you at some length after she knows the full story. I know you'll make time for her and for the children. Just be fully honest with her. The time for deceit is over. The best you could do for me is to be the great friend to Hope that you were to me."

"You know I will."

JG nodded his head. He got up and walked to the window and just looked out. He would have this view for the next three days and then never again. I could sense his appreciation of the scene below and his love for the city. We were both native New Yorkers through and through. After a minute or two, he turned to me and said, "I have another confession I have to make to you. I have to get this off my chest before I meet my Maker."

"It can't be much worse than what you just told me."

"Remember all the arguments we had regarding the Dodgers and Giants?" he asked.

"Of course, I do."

"Well, it's time for me to confess." JG smiled as he looked at me and continued, "I have to admit it. I didn't want to, but Willie Mays is the best ballplayer that I have ever seen!" JG, always the Dodger fan, but for this day's disastrous foreboding would never, ever admit that a Giant, any Giant, could be the best in anything. We love talking sports, especially baseball, as we grew up in the New York environment of the 1950s . . . the absolute best baseball ever played anywhere at any time!

"I guess it's time for me to confess, too. Hands down, no lo contendere, Sandy Koufax is the best pitcher I ever saw play the game of baseball. I don't think he even has any competition!" We both started to laugh and then my laughter turned to tears. I was still in my seat with my hand over my eyes as the tears came. JG silently put his hand on my shoulder. I felt better.

"We will do lunch in my office, and then I will have my driver take you back to Newark Airport to catch the shuttle back to Elmira. I have some heavy-duty meetings to complete before I depart to Mexico." JG asked what I would like to eat. He reached for the interphone and passed the order to his secretary. She would bring up the food from the restaurant on the first floor of the building. We spent lunchtime eating and talking about the last soccer game I saw Elizabeth Mae play. JG was deeply involved with this class-action suit, and he missed that game. I gave him a running account. One of the things that I learned as a coach was recalling almost every play of a game that I either played in, coached, or had an abiding interest in the outcome. His little girl brought the same kind of intensity to her play as Lawrence Taylor did for the New York Giants. The girl took no prisoners. I think JG thoroughly enjoyed my replay of his daughter's game. After lunch, he walked me to the door. I hugged my friend goodbye, even against his protestations. "Vaya con Dios," I whispered in his ear as I left. It was the last time I saw the best friend I will ever have in this life.

The driver took me back to the fixed base operator's building. Rocky was there in the coffee shop. He told me that he would be happy to take me back to Elmira. I used the Corning phone and called Betsy. I told her that I would be home by 7:30 that evening. When I arrived at home, I was glad to hug my wife. Her embrace always lessened the tensions within me and allows me to find peace in her arms. I could not tell her what had transpired as I gave my word to JG, but Betsy knew that holding me helped me cope with whatever was troubling me. That's still true to this day.

Three months later, I received a large envelope which was postmarked from Mexico. The large envelope contained two smaller sealed envelopes. One envelope was addressed to Daniel and Elizabeth Mae. The second envelope was addressed to me. Both were made from superior materials. There was no return address. The letters were from JG. I open the one addressed to me:

My dearest friend,

The facility I am in provided me an English-speaking stenographer. I no longer have the strength to even hold a pen. I now have full-blown AIDS. I am past having any hope for a cure. For the last day or so, I have refused pain medication so that I could write these final letters with a clear mind. You can plainly see that I addressed one to my children and one to you.

I want you to hold the letter to my children in your possession until both of them are adults. When you think the time is right, get them in the same room and let them read the letter together. After they read the letter, I want you to answer all their questions as completely and honestly as possible. No more lies. Only the truth will serve.

Now I'm going to tell you something I had not previously related. About six months before I left for Mexico, I started seeing a shrink. I needed to know why I had this overwhelming urge to sleep with as many women as I could. Hope has always been, and always will be, the love of my life. Why then did I sleep around so much? What drove me? I needed to know. Then the receipt of this final diagnosis, this death penalty, really focused my mind. The shrink and I really got down to issues.

Part of my problem was that when I was in high school and first started dating, I was never the guy who got the pretty girl. That was my early background. Then after graduating college we had to deal with Viet Nam. Every young man had to face the fact that our country was at war, and each of us had to answer two questions: "Would I serve?" and "Can I do it?" Two very simple questions. You went and faced your fear and did your duty. You found out that you could operate bravely and effectively in a combat environment. You know that about yourself. While you answered those questions for yourself, I never did. For you it is the fact of your life. I am left with questions, not answers. That self-doubt exacerbated my need to boost my ego which led to the situation I am in presently.

Once I got my law degree and started practicing with a great deal of success, I found that attractive women wanted my attention. Frankly, I needed the ego boost. I used material success and sexual conquests to prove to myself that I was a man. I knew, as you told me many a time that such behavior might cost me the best woman ever to enter my life. Unfortunately, you were right.

Who knows? Maybe we'll meet in the next life. I wish you nothing but the best. You deserve a kind fate. Hope, the children and you were the best things in my life. Take care my friend.

JG

Two days later, on Tuesday, May 1, Hope called me at my home. When I got on the phone, she said between sobs, "JG died this morning."

I felt that horrid pit in my stomach after receiving her news. "I'm so sorry, Hope. Is there anything I can do?"

Hope composed herself and answered, "Not right now. It was only a half hour ago when I received the phone call from a Mexican facility where he was staying. They are shipping his body north today, and it should be here by the day after tomorrow. JG made his own funeral arrangements before he left to go to Mexico. The funeral home will hold a formal burial on Friday. I want a small service with only family and friends there. I don't think I could handle a large number of folks. When can you come down here?"

"I will be there by Thursday afternoon at the very latest. I will fly down if I can grab the Corning shuttle. If that's not doable, then I will drive. I have to call my supervisor to arrange my time off, but I will be there, come hell or high water. I loved him more than a brother. I will miss him every day of my life."

I heard Hope sobbing with my response. After several minutes, she said, "You two were always so close. I know no one will miss him as much as you do. Let me know when I can expect you. Will Betsy and Molly come with you?"

"She's in school now, and Betsy has to stay with her parents. They are getting on in age and need her assistance almost every day. I'll come down by myself, and I will let you know when to expect me as soon as I know." We said our goodbyes.

I immediately told Betsy as much of the conversation as I could remember. She wanted to come, but she agreed that she could not leave her daughter or her parents. All three needed her attention. I then called Rocky who told me that he would put me on Thursday's shuttle to Newark with a return on the Saturday flight from JFK. I thanked him profusely. I then called Robbie. He allowed me to use family leave as he knew how close JG and I were to each other. I called Hope and told her to pick me up at the nearby Long Island railroad station near her house sometime during the following day. I would call her as soon as I knew which train I would take.

On Thursday, I left Elmira at 7:30 in the morning on the Corning shuttle. I took the Corning bus to Penn Station where I grabbed the first available train to the Huntington Station. As soon as I got my ticket, I located the nearest phone booth and called Hope. I told her the scheduled ETA to the Huntington stop and asked if somebody could pick me up. She told me that either Edna Stein or she would be there to meet me.

It was a few minutes after noon when my train arrived. I saw Edna Stein on the elevated platform. I got off the train with my valise in hand and made my way directly to Mrs. Stein. She opened her arms and hugged me even before saying a word. "I'm so glad you're here. Hope really needs you and so do the children."

I could see she was teary. I picked up my valise and she held onto my left arm as we walked toward her car. I asked her, "How are they doing, Mrs. Stein?"

She answered, "Please call me Edna. They are doing as well as can be expected." Edna then turned and looked directly in my eyes as she said, "Hope told me everything. You know we have become very close. After I lost Lisa, Hope helped me cope with my grief. I love her both as a friend and as a daughter. She really helped both me and my husband accept our loss. Lisa was the only child that I was able to bear. That's why our grief was so completely devastating. Hope now fills the void created by Lisa's death for both Harry and myself. I love her now as much as if I bore her myself."

I responded, as we got into the car, "I'm glad that she has someone so close emotionally as well as geographically. I have loved her as a sister for more than twenty years. It is my wish that when all is said and done, Hope will find happiness. God only knows, she deserves it. Hope is one of the finest human beings I've met in this lifetime."

Edna nodded in agreement as she started the car. After we were safely on the road for the fifteen-minute ride back to where Hope lived, Edna said, "Before he left, JG told Hope about his infidelities. She was angry at you because you knew and didn't tell her."

I answered, "I couldn't betray JG's trust. I was caught between a rock and a hard place. If I told Hope, then JG would be angry with me. The reverse was also true. I was in an absolutely classic no-win situation. All I could do was tell JG to stop his hurtful behavior."

"JG, before he left, told Hope that you constantly advised him to stop doing what he was doing. I helped her see that it was JG's behavior that she should be angry with and not yours. She was completely devastated by the news of his screwing around. Then Hope had to deal with the news of JG contracting the AIDS virus on top of everything else! As a result, Hope was so angry with him that she would not even speak to him even as he left for the last time."

"Did she talk with JG at any time since he left?" I asked.

"No. And that adds to the hurt. Hope never had a chance to say a final goodbye. I know how that feels. My last conversation with Lisa was an angry one. I so wanted for her to leave the drugs and make a decent life. We argued and I hung up in disgust. It was the last time I spoke with my daughter. I will carry that guilt for the rest of my life. It may not be rational; it just is. Hope helped me work through the guilt and shame, and now I will help her in the same manner, as she must deal with basically the same problem."

"What goes around comes around . . . an old Air Force saying that I picked up in the military. How are the children doing?" I asked.

"They're too young to really understand what's happening. They know their father is dead and that he went away for a long vacation because he was ill. That's about as much as they can handle now. In fact, Hope sent Daniel and Elizabeth Mae to school today. She did this because she wants their lives to return to some kind of normalcy as soon as possible. Besides, I believe your presence will help that process along by providing the children with someone who loves them and who was a very big part of their father's life." I nodded as we drove the rest of the way in silence.

A little while later, we were at our destination. The main door was open and only covered by a screen door. I called out to Hope, and I heard her coming quickly to the front door. She was a mess. Her hair was up and covered by a kerchief. Her eyes, puffy from crying, were dull and almost lifeless. She told me to come in and I did. I dropped my valise, and Hope ran into my open arms. I held her tightly, and the tears came quickly. I continued to hold her. I was in no rush. I would let her regain her composure in her own time. After several minutes, she looked up at me and kissed me on the cheek.

Hope then held my left arm with both of hers as she led me to the sofa in the den. "Of course, you will stay with us in your old room. I will not have it any other way!"

"That's exactly where I was planning to stay anyhow, so we're both on the same page."

"Good. The rabbi is coming shortly so that we can discuss the final details of the burial ceremony. Also, Ben Rothstein, JG's classmate from Brooklyn Law and friend, is coming by this evening in order to discuss the will. You have to be here because you're in it."

"JG told me that he was leaving everything to you and the children. Why am I in it?"

"Ben will tell us this evening. All I know is that he asked if it was possible for you to be here."

"That's not a problem. I'm not going anywhere." I turned to look directly at her and said, "I don't have the words to express my sorrow and loss. I feel so damned helpless. I love you and the children, and there's not much if anything I can do to alleviate the pain all of you are going through. If there's anything you need, just ask."

"I will. Did JG tell you about the last time I spoke with him?"

"The only thing he related to me was the fact that you were very upset with him. He did tell me that he was going to be brutally honest in answering all your questions. He also told me that if you had questions for me that I should answer them as honestly and as fully as I could. I told him during the last conversation I had with him in this lifetime that I would do so."

"My last conversation with my husband occurred on Sunday night, January 29. I remember it like it happened yesterday. JG wanted me to come to the city three days earlier, but I had to cancel because Daniel was carrying a high fever, and I did not want to leave his side. JG said that he would come as soon as he could. The children were asleep, as it was past 10:00 PM and a night I'll never forget. JG arrived in the back of his limo. He told his driver to stay close by because he didn't know exactly when he was going to leave. We sat in the kitchen, and he told me that he was unfaithful and that as a result of his behavior, he contracted the HIV virus. He also told me that he had the doctor test me and the children, and that we were free of the virus. I was furious with him. I felt so betrayed. I really couldn't shout, although I wanted to, because I didn't want to wake the children. He told me that he was leaving for some unknown destination where he would be assured not to pass on this virus to anybody else. He told me that he loved me and that he would return only if he was cured or in a coffin." Hope paused for a few moments and continued, "Those were his exact words—cured or in a coffin. There was no in between. He told me that he could not risk contaminating either me or the children. He would suffer a lingering death alone. It was his way of at least partially atoning for his abhorrent behavior. He also told me that the children and I would be taken care of financially for the rest of our lives. He assured me that money would not be a concern for us. He hoped that someday I might find a way to forgive him. I asked him why he did what he did. JG said he didn't know at that time, but he was working through the problem with professional help. He got up to leave and I turned my back on him. He hesitated for a while and then left by the front door. A few moments later, I heard the limo pull away and that was the last I saw of my husband. Do you want to hear an absolutely unbelievable thing?"

"What's that?" I asked.

"I'm hurt. I'm still furious with him. But I still love him. I will always love him. I miss him terribly." Hope had trouble uttering the last sentences, as they came between convulsive sobs. I held her again as she cried herself out. Finally, again regaining composure, Hope asked me, "Why do you think he cheated on me?"

"I'll let JG answer for himself," I said as I got up and went to my valise. I opened it up and retrieved JG's last letter to me. I walked back to the sofa and handed Hope the letter. She quickly read it and then reread it.

She looked up at me and said, "Where is the letter addressed to the children?"

"In my bank vault in Elmira."

"Do you know what's in it?"

"I do not. I thought it inappropriate for me to open it. It belongs to them, and I will give it to them when I feel they are old enough to handle some very rough truths regarding their father. That was JG's last wish and I will honor it."

Hope smiled. It was a small smile, but a smile nevertheless. A small victory as she said, "You always do the honorable thing. It is one of your more endearing traits, even when it frustrates me." Hope handed the letter back to me and asked, "Can I make a copy?"

"Of course," I responded as I handed back the letter to her. Hope got up and went to her office. After several minutes went by, she returned with my letter and handed it back again.

Just then the doorbell rang. Edna Stein went to the door to welcome the rabbi. He was a portly man with thinning hair who was wearing a dark suit and a yarmulke. "Rabbi, this is Norris Blakeman, JG's best friend. Although everyone just calls him Blake. Blake, this is Rabbi Adelman." We shook hands. Edna went to the kitchen as the rabbi took the seat facing Hope and me.

The rabbi's penetrating brown eyes were focused upon Hope. He said to her, "I see that you are not going to sit shiva. Are you sure that is what you want?"

Hope responded, "Yes Rabbi. I'm sure. I'm still very angry with my husband, alive or dead. Maybe someday I will be able to forgive him. It's too soon."

The rabbi shook his head and said, "I understand why you're so angry. I believe that sitting shiva will allow you to find forgiveness sooner rather than later. But that is your decision, and I will help you in any way I can. If you decide to change your mind, I will tell you the traditions associated with sitting shiva."

"Thank you, Rabbi. If I change my mind, I will let you know."

"The funeral home director told me that all you want is a graveside ceremony. Is that correct?"

"Yes Rabbi. I just want the family and our very close friends. It should be no more than fifteen people. You can conduct the standard ceremony for a Jewish burial after all are present at the gravesite." I could hear the steel in her voice. I knew Hope almost as well as JG did as we all met at the same time. We had spent more than half our lives knowing each other. I knew at that instant that no amount of argument or reasoned approach would change her mind.

"I understand you wanted the ceremony to start on Friday morning at ten sharp. Is that right?"

"Yes Rabbi. The funeral director will have the body and the coffin ready for burial available at the gravesite by 9:30 in the morning. I want a very simple, dignified ceremony." After a pause Hope added, "And no eulogy!"

"If that's what you want, then that's what you'll get. I will see you Friday morning. I'll be at the gravesite at least fifteen minutes early. Please accept my condolences again. If there's anything you need further for me to do, you just need to ask." The rabbi got up. He bowed to Hope and said goodbye. I walked him to the door because I had a feeling that he wanted to say something to me. Perhaps it was the way he looked at me as he was leaving Hope's side. When we got to the door, the rabbi turned toward me and said, "Hope is carrying a great burden of bitterness. The sooner she forgives JG, the sooner she will heal. You may get through to her because she trusts you. She has a history with you. I hope you use it wisely. It was a pleasure meeting you, Blake, although I wish it was under more pleasant circumstances."

I shook the rabbi's hand and said, "I will follow your advice, but I know Hope. It won't be easy and it may take some time, but I will do my best."

"That's all any of us can do." With that the rabbi turned and left. I closed the door behind him.

About an hour later, the children returned from school. Hope and I waited outside. We saw them get off the buses. Daniel arrived first. He was a sophomore in high school, and now was taller than I. His light sandy hair darkened to a brownish color. His adolescent body was starting to fill out. He got off the bus and kissed his mom, then turned to me. We shook hands. His voice had deepened since the last time I spoke with him. He said, "Uncle Blake, it's so good to see you. I knew you'd be here."

I passed on my condolences to him. Hope quickly directed the conversation toward the normal occurrences of the day. She wanted her son thinking about the future and not the past. I followed her lead. I did not agree with it, but it was her call. Danny went inside because he stated that he had a lot of homework to complete before his baseball game. He seemed unusually quiet to me. At the time, I just passed that off as a form of grief.

About a half-hour later, Elizabeth Mae got off her bus. When she saw me standing next to her mother, she immediately ran into my arms. I gave her a big hug, and she kissed me on the cheek. Unlike her stoic brother, seeing me reminded her of her dad, as we were always together. She immediately burst into tears and said, "I miss my daddy."

I continued to hold her as she cried on my shoulder. I told my goddaughter, "I miss him too. I will miss him every day of my life for as long as God gives me breath to live." After a while, she turned to her mom, and they hugged each other. Seeing her daughter cry brought Hope to tears again. They walked arm in arm back into the house. Hope saw to it that her children carried on the day as normally as possible.

Daniel had a varsity baseball game scheduled for this day. He was the starting second baseman, and he had to be at the field no later than four o'clock in the afternoon. Hope asked me to drive using JG's Austin Healey. I gladly complied as I wanted to see him play. Danny, now dressed in his uniform, got in the car and was unusually quiet during the trip to the ballpark. I asked what the matter was. He responded, "I know what happened to my father. Mom doesn't know this. I remember the night dad came home just before he went away. Mom thought I was sleeping. I was just about to go to the kitchen for a glass of water when I heard the front door open, and I heard Dad's voice. I pulled back behind the kitchen door that leads to the bedrooms and listened to their entire conversation. They did not know that I was there, and I overheard my father telling my mother that he was unfaithful and suffering from AIDS. I knew why he went away and why he died."

The fact that Daniel knew the whole story surprised me. I pulled off the side of the road so I could face him directly as I responded. "Why did you keep it to yourself?" I asked.

"Mom has enough to deal with. I didn't want to add to her problems."

"It's my opinion that you should discuss this with your mother. The fact that you know and can deal with it will take some of the burden off of her. You're the man of the family now. Your mom needs to know that she can rely on you. Your mother is spending a great deal of her energy trying to protect both you and your sister. If she knows that you are aware of the situation, then all she must do is protect your sister until she's old enough to learn the truth. Besides, you'll be somebody who your mother will trust implicitly and that makes you very valuable as a confidante. You're going to have a great deal more responsibility than you should have at your age. If you handle it well, you will grow up faster and be a better man for doing so."

Daniel, like his father, thought about what I'd just said. Like his father, I quietly gave him the time to respond. After about a minute, Daniel said, "Thanks Uncle Blake. When I get home, I will tell mom about what I overheard."

"Are you still angry with your father?"

"Yes, Uncle Blake. If he were here right now, I'd spit in his face. I can't tell you the number of nights I heard my mother cry herself to sleep. Yes, I would say I am very angry."

"Let me tell you two things. First, bitterness and anger harm the soul. The sooner you put them in the past and remember the good things about your father, the sooner you will recover from his loss and your disappointment in his actions. The second thing is that it is not for the child to judge the father. That never works out. All of us are imperfect. I can tell you these things now and they're just words to you, but as you get older and hopefully wiser, you'll come to learn the truth of them."

Danny nodded his head in agreement. I then asked, "How about some baseball? I really want to see you play. You think we can do that?"

"Yes sir!"

"Good. Let's get going!" With that, I drove to the ballpark. Danny was about five minutes late. The team wasn't sure he was going to be there. When they saw us approach, they gathered around him and made it abundantly clear that they were happy knowing he was going to play ball. Danny introduced me to the coach and the players as his "Uncle Blake." The players ran back to the diamond to continue their warm-up, Danny included. The coach told me that Danny would play as much as he wanted. The team understood the situation. It was the coach's opinion that playing ball with a group of his contemporaries who totally accepted and liked him would be good for Daniel. I agreed.

I watched the game. Danny's team won 5-4. He had two hits in four at bats and made several good plays in the field. I really enjoyed watching him play, but what I really appreciated was how deeply he was into the game. I could see the pure joy on his face as he hit the ball well or made a good play in the field. For the 2 1/2 hours that he played, he was free from concerns of his personal life. JG would have loved to seen the game I just witnessed. He loved baseball as much as I did, and I know he loved his son.

I took Danny directly home after the game. He went to take a shower, and I told Hope what happened with the game. That brought the first true smile I saw on her face since I arrived. We had a quiet supper prepared by Edna Stein. Both she and Mr. Stein joined us at the table. After dinner, we retired to the den. There we watched TV to get our minds off the next day's events.

The doorbell rang at 8:00 PM. It was JG's friend and lawyer, Ben Rothstein. Hope let him in and made the introductions. He was about my height, with dark hair and dark sympathetic brown eyes. Ben had a local general practice. He also had a Masters' degree in finance. He was JG's lawyer, accountant and financial expert all rolled up in one. They'd attended Brooklyn Law together. JG trusted Ben completely. Hope took Ben and me into JG's private office. Ben asked her if it would be all right for him to use JG's desk. Hope told him that would be acceptable. He sat down in JG's chair. He placed some papers on the top of the desk and asked us to sit facing him. We moved two chairs to the other side of the desk and listened as he went over JG's last will and testament.

After we were comfortably seated facing Ben, he cleared his throat and began, "I want you both to know that I am aware of the enormity of your loss. JG and I were friends for almost two decades. I spent two long days doing nothing but setting up his estate in accordance with his wishes and his desire to maximize what he could do for his family. I met with him on January 28 and 29 of this year. His estate is estimated at around ten million dollars. Five million comes from a paid-up policy from his law firm. That policy was paid by JG in lieu of compensation and therefore, is not considered income. JG was wise enough to pay the taxes on his insurance payments. Three million dollars goes to Hope and a million to each child. JG and I set up trust accounts for these funds. After the funeral, I will go over with Hope, in great detail, all the ramifications, and why JG wanted to set it up the way he did. That will take about a day, so we will do that later. Is that okay with you, Hope?"

"Certainly. I probably won't change anything, because JG was very good at this stuff, but I do want to understand as much as I can."

"Good." Ben then continued, "JG had approximately 300,000 dollars in a joint checking account. You can use those funds, Hope, to run the household until the insurance money kicks in. There are no tax liabilities associated with those funds because you are the co-owner of that account. The other five million is basically liquid. That is to say stocks, bonds and mutual funds accounts. Before he died, JG paid off all his outstanding loans including the mortgage on this house. Since you (referring to Hope) and he owned the house jointly, there is no tax liability resulting from his passing regarding your home. This money will be put into a trust fund for charitable causes. The principal will generate income of approximately 300,000 to 400,000 dollars annually. That is a conservative estimate. Fifty percent of the net income is to be used to grow the principal, and 50% is to be dispersed by a committee of three. Each member of the committee will receive a stipend of $10,000 a year to pay for the time used in consideration of which charitable function would receive the largess. Hope, you, Mr. Blakeman and myself are the three that JG designated. Any decision must be unanimous in funding a particular cause. We are to meet twice a year. Hope will be the president of this Gladon Fund. I will be paid an additional $10,000 a year to manage the fund's assets. We can have our first meeting after the fund is totally established. Probably in about two months. Is that okay with both of you?"

Hope nodded her head in agreement and I said, "It is fine with me."

"Good. Now in regard to personal property such as jewelry, furniture and the like, Hope, you get all of it, except JG's Austin Healey. That car will become the property of Mr. Norris Blakeman as soon as the will is probated." Then looking directly at me, Ben said, "JG knew you really liked that car. I know he would want you to enjoy it."

"I will. Every time I get in it, I will always think of him."

"That basically is that. I know the funeral is tomorrow. The next time we meet, I will discuss everything in a lot more detail. I just wanted to cover the basic points of JG's will. This is not the time to go into a lot of detail, but I do have one request and that is I would like to attend JG's funeral if that's okay with you, Hope?"

"Absolutely. I know that you and JG were good friends." With that, we got up and returned to the den. Ben shook hands with both of us and departed.

At 9:30 PM it was time for Elizabeth Mae to go to bed. She asked if I would tuck her in. I told her I would. About twenty minutes later, Hope said that I could say good night to Elizabeth Mae. I went into her room. Elizabeth Mae was in her pajamas and covered by a blanket. I sat on the edge of her bed and looked directly into her light blue eyes. She was a pretty girl and someday would become a beautiful woman. I put my right hand on her cheek and she cupped my hand with both of hers. She asked if I would stay until she fell asleep. That's exactly what I did. It only took her a few minutes to fall into a deep slumber. I kissed her forehead and left the room closing the door behind me. When I returned to the kitchen and den area, I saw Hope in a deep conversation with her son. I decided to leave them alone and went into the den to watch TV.

I was watching the eleven o'clock news when Hope came into the den. I muted the sound as she entered the room. Hope sat down next to me. I then asked, "How is it going with Daniel?"

Hope replied, "I just spent an hour or so talking with him. He told me about the conversation he had with you on the way to the ballpark. I can't tell you how relieved I am. He was so sullen after JG departed for Mexico. His grades, as well as his behavior in general, deteriorated. I knew something was grievously wrong, but I did not know how to approach it. Because of your talk with him this afternoon, he has really opened up. Now I can help him. Hell, now we can help each other. For the first time, I treated my son like an adult. I think he really appreciated it."

"You remember Sandy, the girl I almost married and who died suddenly in a car accident?"

"Of course, I remember. Why?"

"She was only seventeen years old, but she was more of an adult than any woman I dated before her. The fact that her father deserted the family when she was eleven made her face a terrible situation as an adult rather than as a child. She grew up quickly, and she grew up well. The point I am trying to make is this: sometimes adversity will strengthen a girl into a fine woman or a boy into a strong man. I believe that Daniel, by helping you and by facing and dealing with his own problems, will become a man sooner and with greater resolve. I not only hope for that, but now I think it likely."

Hope yawned. "I think I can sleep now. You know your way around, so I'll see you tomorrow morning."

I got up and hugged her. She left for the master bedroom. I finished watching the news and went back to the guest room. I took a shower and went right to bed. I was tired, too.

The next morning, I was up at 7:30. I put on a pair of shorts and a sweatshirt and made my way to the kitchen. Hope was already up and making breakfast for the children. She asked if I wanted some eggs, toast and coffee. I told her that sounded wonderful to me, and I joined her and her children for breakfast. About eight o'clock in the morning as were just finishing up eating, the doorbell rang. It was Lou and Nancy Lee. They took the redeye flight from New Orleans to LaGuardia Airport. Lou rented a car and Nancy Lee drove both of them directly to Hope's home. Lou was now sporting more than some gray hair which looked good on him. His glasses were as thick as ever. Nancy Lee was probably ten or fifteen pounds heavier than I remembered her. Nancy Lee also cut her hair shorter as befitted her age, but she still had that elegant flair. After we greeted each other, both Lou and Nancy Lee passed their condolences to Hope and the children. Then they sat down at the breakfast table. Hope put on another pot of coffee as we spent the next half-hour catching up with each other. After about a half-hour, Lou and Nancy Lee waited in the den while Hope, the children and I changed into the appropriate formal clothes.

At 9:00 AM sharp, a huge black stretch limo, provided by the funeral director, was at the front of the house. Mr. and Mrs. Stein, Lou, Nancy Lee, Hope, Daniel, Elizabeth Mae and I all piled into this oversize limo. We arrived at the graveyard about a half-hour later. The driver took us directly to the gravesite. We had to walk about one hundred feet from where the limo was parked to where we would bury JG. We were joined at the site by JG's sister (his only living relative) and by Ben Rothstein and his wife. The casket was suspended over the freshly dug grave site by two thick straps which were connected to a pulley system that allowed the casket to be gently lowered into the hole. In accordance with Jewish tradition, the casket was made totally of wood. It had the Star of David carved into the middle of the top as its only decoration.

I looked up at the sky. After all, I was a celestial navigator. The winds were out of the northwest which indicated to me that a ridge of high pressure was building to the west of us. The sky was a magnificent opaque blue color with only a few puffy cumulus clouds sprinkled from horizon to horizon. At 9:45 the rabbi drove up and parked his car behind the limo and Ben's car. He was wearing a black rabbinical robe, a black formal yarmulke, a white prayer shawl, and he carried a small prayer book. He went directly to Hope who made the introductions.

The rabbi then gave each of us a black ribbon with a pin behind it. He told us that we were to pin the black ribbon which had a cut in the middle of it, upon the left lapel of what we were wearing. That was to symbolize the rending (tearing) of our clothes which was the traditional response of mourning for the loss of a loved one. He then led the group through about a half-dozen prayers which included the Sh'ma (Here O' Israel, the Lord is our God, the Lord is One) and the

23rd Psalm. Finally, the rabbi led all of us in the Kaddish which is the mournful and traditional prayer said for the deceased:

Yis'gadal v'yis'kadash sh'may ra'bbo, b'olmo dee'vro chir'usay v'yam-lich malchu'say, b'chayaychon uv'yomay'chon uv'chayay d'chol bais Yisroel, ba'agolo u'vizman koriv; v'imru Omein. Y'hay shmay rabbo m'vorach l'olam ul'olmay olmayo. Yisborach v'yishtabach v'yispoar v'yisromam v'yis-masay, v'yishador v'yis'aleh v'yisalal, shmay d'kudsho, brich hu, l'aylo min kl birchoso v'sheeroso, tush'bechoso v'nechemoso, da,ameeran b'olmo; vimru Omein. Y'hay shlomo rabbo min sh'mayo, v'chayim alaynu v'al kol Yisroel; v'imru Omein. Oseh sholom bimromov, hu ya'aseh sholom olaynu, v'al kol yisroel; vimru Omein.

The translation of that prayer goes as follows:

May the great Name of God be exalted and sanctified, throughout the world, which he has created according to his will. May his Kingship be established in your lifetime and in your days, and in the lifetime of the entire household of Israel, swiftly and in the near future; and say, Amen. May his great name be blessed, forever and ever. Blessed, praised, glorified, exalted, extolled, honored elevated and lauded be the name of the holy one, Blessed is he—above and beyond any blessings and hymns, praises and consolations, which are uttered in the world; and say Amen. May there be abundant peace from Heaven, and life, upon us and upon all Israel; and say, Amen.

He who makes peace in his high holy places, may he bring peace upon us, and upon all Israel; and say Amen.

Then the casket was lowered by several men using a pulley sys-tem to gently drop it into the grave. After the coffin was resting on the bottom of the grave, the rabbi got a shovel from one of the workmen and shoveled several shovel loads onto the top of the coffin. He handed the shovel to Hope, and she shoveled several loads. The shovel was passed to everyone there to mourn, and we took turns until the coffin was finally and totally covered. When it was my turn, I had to shovel with tears in my eyes. We kept shoveling until the wood that formed the coffin was no longer visible. At that point, the shovel was returned to the workmen who would finish the job. It was at that point when Hope totally broke down. She reached for me, and I held her tightly, and I let her cry on my shoulder until she was done. Between sobs, she said, "I thought we would spend our lives together. I miss him. God, I miss him." Sometimes there's nothing you can say. All I could do was be there and weep with my best friend's wife.

After a while, Hope regained her composure. I wiped the tears from my own eyes, and we departed the graveyard. We went back to the house where a catering company was already setting up food for the bereaved and the visitors who were yet to come. Hope, in the days just before the funeral, told all who wanted to make a condolence call to come to the house after one o'clock in the afternoon. All the food was laid out in buffet style. Lou, Nancy Lee and myself filled our plates and retreated to the kitchen. There we had a chance to catch up. Basically, they were doing really well. I was amused at how they both finished each other's sentences. But then again, they were a couple together for more than half of their lives.

About one o'clock in the afternoon, a parade of people made their way to Hope's home. JG was always my friend and that is the way I thought of him. I knew very little of his professional and political life. Most of the people who worked in his firm, including all the partners and the associates, paid their respects to Hope and the children. In addition, JG was an important man in the cogs of the Democratic machine that ruled Nassau and Suffolk Counties as well as the political action committee of the American Bar Association. JG also believed in doing pro bono work for those unfortunate people who really needed excellent legal representation, and who could not afford such services. All of these different aspects of JG's life were apparent and well represented by the numerous people who came to pay their respects.

There were so many people there that I felt uncomfortable. Ever since I returned from the war, I did not like being in crowded places. I am always aware of where the exits are every time I enter a building. I make it my business to know. I spent the first part of the afternoon with Lou and Nancy Lee, mostly reminiscing about our days at Marietta College, but they had to leave at 2:30 in the afternoon in order to catch a return flight back to New Orleans.

After they left, I first went to the guest bedroom and hung up my suit jacket. I then retreated to the patio. The temperature had climbed to the low 70s and the northwest breeze felt great. Here, at least, I found refuge from all the strangers I did not know. I was there for about a half-hour when Elizabeth Mae came up to me and asked if I would like to take a walk. All these people making their way through her home made her uncomfortable as well. I told her that I would love to do so if it was okay with her mother. Elizabeth Mae ran back into the house and about five minutes later, came back to the patio and said, "Mom thinks that a walk is a very good idea."

We exited through the rear gate onto a path which led to the street. There were cars parked on both sides of the road for more than a quarter-mile. We walked on the left side of the street, as there were no sidewalks in this housing development. I kept Elizabeth Mae on my left which insured that I would be closer to the oncoming traffic . . . not that there was very much traffic in that upscale development. We walked in silence for a while appreciating both the well-placed large trees which lined the streets and the beautiful sky above. I think we both felt some relief when we finally walked past the last of the visiting cars.

We continued to walk in silence for more than half an hour. Finally, Elizabeth Mae asked me, "Why did Daddy go away?"

"He was very sick and he didn't want you, your mother or your brother to catch what he had. So, he went to a place that could handle his sickness without getting others ill."

"What did he have? I mean what kind of sickness?"

"He had a very bad case of a viral infection."

"And there was nothing they could do for him?"

"Unfortunately, that is absolutely true."

"Do you think he missed us?"

"God yes! Let me tell you about the last conversation I had with your dad just before he left. I was in his office in New York City, and we were having lunch together. We had about an hour to spend before your dad had to attend several very important meetings. At any rate, we ate in his office. I had a pretty good idea that this was going to be the last time I would speak with your father who was also my best friend. Do you remember your last soccer game I attended . . . the one where you scored two goals and had a nice assist? You know the game that I'm talking about, right?"

"Of course, I do. I remember all my soccer games."

I smiled. Her ability to recall and replay a game in her own mind was one of the many things that I liked, admired, and loved about my goddaughter. "Let me tell you, Elizabeth Mae, that game was all your dad wanted to talk about. You know that I am also pretty good about recalling in my own mind the whole sequence of a game. It's a trait both you and I share. When I got to the part about you scoring a goal or having an assist due to a well-placed pass, your dad's eyes lit up. He had missed that game because of his business. When I finished, he had in his own mind a pretty good idea of what occurred. He was so proud of you."

"Let me get this straight. This was Dad's last conversation with you, and I was what you talked about?"

"It's true. You know that I would never lie to you. Your brother, your mother and you were the absolute center of his universe. The fact that he went away to die in loneliness in order protect you and the others says all that needs be said. Your father loved you as much as it is possible to love your own child. That you can take to the bank!"

We continued to walk in silence as Elizabeth Mae internalized and absorbed what I just told her. Her demeanor improved, and we started talking about her soccer travel team's prospects for the upcoming season. I knew most of the girls on the team, and so we discussed the best way to position individual players in order to maximize the team's ability to win.

We returned to the home around five o'clock that evening. Elizabeth Mae went to her room. I found Hope in the den. There were still about a dozen people wandering through the living room and the den. I caught Hope's eyes and signaled that I wanted to talk to her. She excused herself from a conversation she was having with two people and moved toward my direction. She asked how her daughter was doing, and I related the conversation I had with Elizabeth Mae. Hope asked, "What did you say to her regarding her father's illness?"

"I told her it was a viral infection. That's true as far as it goes," I responded. Hope nodded her assent as that answer was satisfactory to her. She then asked how Elizabeth Mae was coping. I told her that she seemed to be in a much better mood after I talked with her. Hope thanked me and then returned to her guests.

It was a little after nine o'clock that evening when all the visitors finally left. Hope allowed the children to stay up until midnight giving them time to unwind. We all went to bed shortly after that. The next morning, after breakfast, I said my goodbyes to Hope and the children. They were expecting a large number of people again to come on Saturday. I had to catch my flight with Corning Glass shuttle from JFK Airport. Edna Stein graciously volunteered to drive me. I hugged Hope and Elizabeth Mae. I shook Danny's hand. Hope thanked me for coming and asked me to give Betsy her best wishes. I told her I would do so, and then I left with Edna Stein.

I called Betsy just before I left, so she would know what time I would arrive. Betsy prepared a wonderful meal for the entire family. I told them all that had occurred and passed on Hope's best wishes to my wife. It was good to be home!

24

JOSHUA PAUL

One year and ten days after I returned from burying my best friend, I worked a midnight shift. It was Wednesday, May 15, 1985, and I returned home around 8:15 in the morning. Betsy had just gotten up as I entered our bedroom. She was still in her nightgown and just after I kissed her, she covered her mouth and ran to the bathroom. As soon as she got there, I heard her violently throw up. I followed her to the bathroom and saw my wife's head over the toilet bowl. I'd never vomited so vehemently even in my worst drinking days. I was extremely worried and thought she might have a particularly virulent stomach virus. Betsy looked ashen as she left the bathroom. I called our family doctor and made an appointment for that morning. I was exhausted from working all night, but I was more concerned about her health than I was tired. I helped Betsy get her daughter ready for school so that she could lie down for a while.

Once Molly was safely on the bus, I took Betsy to the family doctor. About an hour after Betsy entered the examination room, a nurse came into the waiting room to summon me. She led me to a private office where Betsy and the doctor were waiting for me. I sat down with some trepidation as I awaited what the doctor had to say. He looked at me and said, "Your wife is not sick, she's pregnant!"

I almost fell off my chair. I was told by my own doctors that the chances of me being able to father a child were fairly remote because of my exposure to Agent Orange in Vietnam as well as the radiation treatments I took to battle thyroid cancer. For a second time in my life, I was totally speechless. After the shock wore off, the doctor asked me how I felt about the situation. Finally, I said only one word: "WOW!"

Betsy chimed in, "Is that a good wow or a bad wow?"

I smiled and said, "It's a fantastic wow!"

The doctor wasn't sure how far along she was but, based on the fact that she had missed two periods, he felt that she was about 2 1/2 months pregnant. He told us to get ourselves a very good obstetrician because at Betsy's age (presently thirty-nine years and forty at the time of delivery) this would be, at a minimum, a fairly high-risk pregnancy.

As luck would have it, after I moved to Elmira, I joined the local racquetball club. My regular partner was an obstetrician, *Dr. Larry Dolkhart* whose specialty was high-risk pregnancies. Larry graduated from an Ivy League medical school. He and I were about the same height. He was about ten pounds lighter than I and had intense brown eyes and dark hair. He played a very tactical game of racquetball while I played a power game. It usually took over half an hour to complete each game that we played, as we were so closely aligned in our abilities to play the game. I called his office as soon as we got home and made an appointment to see him the next day.

Later that same afternoon, I received another surprise. A letter addressed to me from the nephew of *Paul Gilbert* arrived the same day that I found out my wife was pregnant with my child. Thirteen years earlier, I made a promise to myself, after being safely retrieved from the A Shau Valley, that if God gave me a child, I would name him or her after Paul. I had not heard from his family in more than a decade. The coincidence that this letter would arrive on the same day that I found out that my wife was pregnant astounded me. But that was only the first of several major surprises.

I was off the schedule for the next two days, so it was easy for me to accompany my wife for her first of many medical visits that her pregnancy would require. After Larry examined Betsy, I was called into his office. He told both of us together that this would be a high-risk pregnancy due to numerous factors: Betsy's age; the medical history of her family; the fact that she was RH negative, and I was RH positive; my medical history and exposure to Agent Orange. He told Betsy that he wanted to see her every two weeks before her seventh month and then weekly thereafter. Betsy and I agreed to comply with his request. He also told us that we would be having a December baby.

Betsy and I returned home and informed her parents that they were about to become grandparents again for the second time. Betsy's mother, Hannah, was more concerned about her daughter's health than her joy of having another grandchild. It would not be an easy pregnancy, but Betsy thought it was worth the risk. I totally agreed with her.

The next step was to inform Molly that she was going to have either a baby brother or a baby sister sometime before the end of the year. Now, that was not as easy as it sounds. Molly, being the only grandchild, was accustomed to being doted on by her loving grandparents. Molly is both extremely intelligent and perceptive. She would know instinctively and intellectually that her position of prominence within the family would be overtaken by the new arrival. New babies almost always dominate a family's attention, affection and interest.

Before we learned that Betsy was pregnant, Molly was campaigning for a puppy. I was the one that was not sure that I wanted to have a pet as I suspected that I would be the one charged with having to walk the dog on a daily basis. Now that Betsy was pregnant, I felt that if Molly was allowed to have a dog, it would be easier for her to accept the news that her mother was going to have another child Molly wanted a Cairn terrier (the same kind of dog that Dorothy had in the "Wizard of Oz" motion picture).

Mom, Dad, Betsy and I discussed this issue over the next several weeks. Together, we decided that it would be a good idea for Molly to get her dog. On the first week of June, we learned that there was a Cairn terrier breeder located in Binghamton, New York, approximately fifty-six miles east of where we lived. We called the breeder and found out that she still had several puppies available for sale. On Saturday, June 1, about 10 o'clock in the morning, Betsy, Mom, Molly and I traveled east to Binghamton. Mom sat in front with me and Betsy sat with her daughter in the back seat of the car. We were about five miles down the road when Betsy informed her daughter that she was with child. Molly broke out into unrelenting sobs. To put it mildly, she was not a happy camper!

That situation continued all the way to Binghamton. Molly was so angry that when we arrived at the breeder's house, she refused to get out of the car. Betsy made her do so as we made our way to the breeder's front door. We knocked and an attractive, middle-aged woman answered the door. Molly was hiding behind her mother. After some coaxing, Molly reluctantly entered the house. The breeder, Mrs. Smith, was a kind and gentle woman. She offered Molly her hand and said, "Follow me. There's someone who wants to meet you."

Molly, who was very curious, took her hand as Mrs. Smith led her to the rear of the house where her award-winning female Cairn terrier was playing with two of her puppies. Molly, with her eyes wide opened, saw the two puppies and forgot that she was unhappy. She immediately reached for the smaller of the puppies—a small female who easily fit in her hands. They took one look at each other, and it was love at first sight! I gratefully wrote Mrs. Smith a check for the full amount in order to pay for our new, small, reddish-brown, Cairn terrier puppy. Molly, on the way home, told us that she was going to name the puppy "Star."

It didn't take long, but after a few days Star became a complete member of the family. She was a very intelligent dog. So much so that I believed then, as I do today, that Star understood English. She was also adventuresome. To my dismay, I found out the hard way that Cairn terrier puppies, magically like the one in our family, had the ability to climb chain mail fences. However, the important and salient fact of Star's arrival was that it smoothed the way for my daughter to accept the new baby. Star also provided company for Betsy when Molly was in school and I was working. As she progressed in her pregnancy, Star became her constant companion.

In August of 1985, Larry wanted Betsy to have the amniocentesis test. This involved sticking a needle in Betsy's middle in order to extract the amniotic fluids needed to test the baby for any genetic diseases. One of the byproducts of this test is information regarding the sex of the baby. We had to travel up to a hospital in Rochester in order to safely perform this test. Now Betsy and I were discussing potential names for our child. Betsy came up with great names for a girl child, but her boy names were horrible. (Almost as bad as *Johnny Cash's, "A Boy Named Sue!"*) We made the following wager: If it was a girl baby, Betsy would name her and if it was a boy, I would have the pleasure of naming him. Betsy took the bet, because the children born in her extended family were almost always female.

I took the bet because of three reasons. First, when I was thirteen years old, I had a very strong premonition that someday I would have a son. It was inexplicable and yet it left an indelible impression upon me that it would happen. Before Betsy got pregnant, I occasionally thought of it and reluctantly dismissed it as something which would never come true. As soon as I knew that my "Bets Bear" was with child, that premonition returned in spades. The second reason I took the bet was that there was no downside. Betsy's names for a girl child were wonderful and I liked them all. The third and most important reason was that I wanted to keep the promise I made to myself when I was rescued from the A Shau Valley. I wanted to honor both my best friend and the pilot who saved my life. JG did not like his first name, so I used the first letter "J" and came up with Joshua, a great name from the Bible. The middle name, Paul, would be in honor of *Paul Gilbert*. Now Betsy wasn't thrilled with the name Paul because she thought it was "too Christian sounding," but Betsy made the bet anyway because she knew how important it was to me to keep my word and to honor the man that saved my life. Betsy and I were lying in bed one night discussing names. I put my hand on her belly and uttered for the first time the names in sequence, Joshua Paul. I knew instantly that it was a perfect fit. That would be my child's name if he was a boy.

About a week after the trip to the hospital in Rochester, Larry called us into his office in order to discuss the results. He was now relatively certain that we were going to have a healthy baby. He then asked us if we wanted to know the sex of the baby. We looked at each other. There was no dissent . . . we both wanted to know. Larry then told us, "There odds are greater than 95% that it is a boy." In that case, at that instant, I knew his name was to be Joshua Paul. As a side note, after

Josh was born, Betsy's favorite pet name for her son was "Paulie Cute Persons". So much for not liking the name Paul!

Just after we got home from seeing Larry, the second inexplicable coincidence occurred. I received a phone call from Paul's family. His nephew wanted to talk to me about his uncle. On the day that I found out my wife was pregnant; I received a letter from Paul's family. On the day that we found out that the child was going to be a boy and he would have Paul's name, I got a phone call from Paul's family. Those were the only contacts I'd had in the past thirteen years!

By September, Betsy was growing by leaps and bounds. I teased her that she was so big she could occupy two time zones simultaneously. I thought it was funny, but then again, I was not the one who was pregnant. Betsy also had another problem which occurred when she started laughing which caused her to lose bladder control. So of course, being the ultrasensitive guy that I am, my job was to make her laugh. I must admit, I had a lot of help from our new puppy. We all laughed at Star's antics. Betsy wore long, loose-fitting gowns without any underwear. That facilitated her ability to use the bathroom. Besides, it was getting difficult to find underwear that would fit!

Larry wanted Betsy to walk on a regular basis as her main source of exercise. I would take Betsy's arm, and we would walk to the dikes which guarded the Chemung River. These large earthen mounds were about four hundred yards south of our home and went on for miles. Betsy and I walked on the tops of them. Of course, we would take Star with us. Our puppy loved to run free over the dikes which were broad and high. It was always a contest to see who would water the top of the dikes first: Betsy or Star.

By the middle of October, as Betsy entered her eighth month of pregnancy, she developed toxemia. As a result, her blood pressure rose to dangerous levels. Larry told Betsy that she was to stay in bed as much as possible and that he would see her twice a week in order to monitor her blood pressure. It was touch and go for the last two months. The bed rest helped her keep her blood pressure down so that she could deliver a full-term baby.

By the middle of December, Larry told us that Betsy had to give birth within the next two weeks. Otherwise, her life and the health of our baby would be in jeopardy. If the baby came naturally before that time, then all would proceed normally. But if not, then Larry would induce labor.

On Thursday, December 26, 1985, I took Betsy to the Elmira hospital. The hospital staff put Betsy in the "birthing room" which was adjacent to a full-blown operating room in case an emergency cesarean delivery was necessary. The room was pleasantly decorated. That was where they induced labor by giving Betsy a shot of some kind of medicine. I was there for the entire procedure. Betsy and I practiced Lamaze techniques in classes offered by the hospital well before her due date. I was her birthing "coach," and I witnessed my son being born. Betsy grabbed my right arm and dug her fingernails into my flesh as Joshua passed through the birth canal. The marks she left on my wrist stayed there for three years after he was born.

The term labor is no misnomer. Giving birth is the single hardest "work" that any human being could ever do. It is the most amazing of processes, and I was glad that I witnessed it. When Joshua was delivered, the nurses cleaned him and wrapped him in a blanket. The head nurse offered Betsy a chance to hold her newborn son. My girl was so shaky that she could not lift her arms to embrace him, so the head nurse put my son in my arms. I looked at his amazing face, and I was quietly crying. My tears actually fell upon the blanket which wrapped my son. At that instant, I felt the most intense love of and for another human being that I had ever experienced in my life. There was nothing and no one that came ahead of that little boy that I held. It was true at 5:35 on the afternoon of December 26, 1985, the day of his birth, and it remains true to this day. His birth started me on a journey which will continue for the rest of my life. As I like to say, referring to myself, even to this day, half-jokingly half-seriously, "Joshua's birth was the end of a perfect thirty-year adolescence!"

Larry kept Betsy in the hospital for five days until her blood pressure returned to normal. Since Joshua was being breast-fed, he stayed with his mother in the hospital. On the first day of January, 1986, I took my son home. It was the first time that his maternal grandparents could hold their new grandson. Our dog, Star, went absolutely berserk running around the room until she could get close enough to obtain Joshua's scent. After she sniffed him, Star was quite content to leave him alone. Dad looked at his beautiful grandson, and I saw the tears well in his eyes as he was filled with absolute delight. Dad was in the sunset of his life. He suffered from obesity, diabetes and high blood pressure. Movement was difficult for him. Over the next four years, Dad watched as Josh turned from an infant to a child. That little boy became the absolute center of his life. Since we both felt the same way, it brought us closer together. After Joshua was about six months old, Dad, who'd wished for a girl baby when he found out that Betsy was pregnant, told me, "I never knew that little boys could be so cute!"

When Josh was two months old, I put him in a frontloading "papoose" cloth carrier which held him against my chest and allowed me to use my hands freely. Betsy would place a watch cap on Joshua which covered his head and his ears. Then Betsy dressed him in an insulated "onesie" before helping me place him in the frontloading papoose. I would then put on Dad's winter coat which was big enough to enclose both of us and zip it so that only a small portion of Josh's head would be above the end of the zipper. I felt his little hands around my chest and his feet around my side. I'd put Star on a leash and the three of us would go for a three-mile walk. It was winter in Elmira, New York. The temperature was usually between 5° and 20°F, yet my son stayed "toasty" under his grandfather's jacket.

We walked on Water Street, and our favorite destination was the Elmira Savings Bank. One of the tellers who worked in that particular bank was a girl named *Betsy* who shared the same first name as my wife which made it easy for me to remember. This Betsy was one of the three or four most beautiful women I have ever seen in my life—light brown hair, blue eyes, oval face and a perfectly apportioned body. Betsy was a very competent teller who loved babies and dogs. I had one each. Every time I came into the bank, she would come out from the teller's cage in order to play with my dog and my son. Betsy always had a treat for Star. I would spend about ten minutes in the bank and then walk back home.

When springtime came, my Betsy would take Josh onto our screened-in porch on the side of the house. This porch had small and thick covering comprised of smallish evergreen trees which encircled it. Those trees sheltered us from being seen by anyone outside the structure. When Josh was five months old, springtime had finally come to the Chemung Valley. A family of robins built their nest in one of the trees adjacent to our porch. Betsy would breast-feed our son on this porch and watch the adult robins feed their nestlings. I'd sit on the porch and watch both my son and the young birds being fed simultaneously. The family nickname for that porch was the "maternity room."

Betsy breast-fed our son until he was eight months old. By that time, he'd developed four front teeth which included two uppers and two lowers. While Joshua was sucking at his mother's breast, he would occasionally bite her nipple and smile devilishly when Betsy would jump. Betsy told me about what my son was doing. I laughed and said, "Well, now we know there can be no doubt . . . he is definitely my son!" Not that I had even the slightest doubt that it was absolutely true. Soon after, Betsy decided it was time to stop breast-feeding and time to use a bottle exclusively. That occurred in his ninth month of life.

By September of that year, we found out that the FAA was going to close Elmira Flight Service Station. We had the choice of either going to Buffalo, New York or Millville, New Jersey. The family decided that the Buffalo winters would be unendurable for my in-laws, so we decided to move to southern New Jersey where I would continue my career as an air-traffic control specialist at the Millville Automated Flight Service Station (MIV AFSS).

Betsy, Joshua and I drove to the Millville area in order to look for housing. We decided to build a house in East Vineland. When Josh was almost two years old, we moved into our new house and I worked traffic there for twenty years.

When Josh was three years old and living in his new home, two incidents come to mind. The first occurred when Betsy was putting our son to sleep. He looked at his mother and asked, "Mom, is life a dream?" Betsy knew the importance of that statement much more than I did. She came out of his bedroom somewhat shaken and said to me, "Blake, honey, you better start saving your shekels. Our son is going to need an exclusive school!" I just dismissed her comment as a mother's pride in her baby. Boy, was I wrong!

The second incident occurred three months before his fourth birthday. It was about 7:30 in the morning when Josh came down the stairs and asked if I would make him some breakfast. I asked if he would like some French toast. He thought that was a very good idea. I made up a batch of French toast slices and gave him three to eat. Just after he was done, Betsy came downstairs and asked if I would make another batch of French toast. I complied with her request. Joshua, still hungry, asked for two more slices which I gave him. Betsy, always the teacher, turned to her little blonde-haired, blue-eyed son and asked him, "Joshua, how many pieces did you have before?"

Joshua replied, "I had three slices, Mom."

Betsy then asked, "How many did you have just now?"

Joshua answered, "I had two."

Betsy, driving the point home, asked, "Then how many slices did you eat altogether?"

Joshua thought about the question, and then he answered his mom, "I had three slices just before you came down, and I had two more with you." The answer came to him as his blue eyes got as big as saucers, and with an astonished look on his face, he blurted out, "I had five slices of French toast!" Joshua hesitated for about two or three seconds and then said, with a perfect West Texas accent, "SUMMM BITCH!"

That took both Betsy and I by surprise. We were laughing so hard that we literally fell off our chairs. Then I stopped laughing. I looked up at my wife and said to her, "That's something Paul would have said. Where did our son come up with that?" Joshua had never used that term before and he never, to my knowledge, ever used it again.

When Joshua was three years old, we enrolled him in the Early Learning Center (ELC), a school for children ages three to six years old and a subsidiary of our local Jewish congregation. One of his fellow students was a little girl named *Erin*. She was the daughter of *Trudy*, a stay-at-home mom and a father who was a brain surgeon. They lived on our block about five houses from where we lived. They were not Jewish, but Erin's mom thought that the ELC School was the best in the area, so she sent her child there. Erin and Joshua became very good friends.

At the start of kindergarten, when they were five years old, Erin's father was diagnosed with end-stage brain cancer. As a result, Erin spent a great deal of time with my family allowing her mother time to deal with a dying husband and her two younger brothers. I would take Joshua and Erin to one of the local parks in Vineland where there was a small lake populated with numerous waterfowl birds including swans, ducks, and geese. The park also had a playground on the premises which they both enjoyed.

In early spring, 1991, Erin's father passed away. My daughter, Molly, helped Trudy by babysitting the children while she made arrangements to bury her husband. On this particular night, I got a call from Molly as she was babysitting in Trudy's home. Trudy was at the funeral parlor making final arrangements. Over the phone, Molly told me that Erin was asking for Joshua. She requested that I should bring my son over there so that they could be together. I told her that we would be there in the next five or ten minutes. I dressed my son warmly as it was both dark and cold outside. We walked diagonally across the street to Trudy's home. The main door was open and the space was covered by just a solid glass storm door. Molly, standing in the kitchen holding Erin's hand, waved for us to enter. I stood there a few feet into the hallway holding my son's hand when Erin noticed both of us. I must have reminded her of her dad as she burst out crying, "My daddy is dead! My daddy is dead!"

Joshua, without a moment's hesitation, ran to her side, and Erin threw her arms around my son. She was now sobbing on his shoulder as he held her. He comforted her by saying to her, "This will pass. Believe me, this will pass!" I was astonished that my five-year-old offered such adult advice. Erin, a very bright little girl in her own right, knew what she needed. At that moment, she needed my son, and he was there for her. That was my first indication of how good a person my young son was and the kind of man he would become. That incident was one of the most poignant moments of my life.

By June of that year, Trudy moved her family to Colorado, and I never saw any of them again. That summer, after Erin's family left New Jersey, Joshua enrolled in the local soccer club. I told Betsy that the kids were so young that I was not sure I could coach them. Betsy always urged me to be involved in everything that our son would try. She reasoned that childhood passed by so quickly that it was necessary to partake in all the various activities. You only get one shot at it. As usual, Betsy was right.

I suffered watching inept coaches for his first two years. In order for me to coach, I had to sign up for the day shifts at MIV AFSS. That meant less money and inferior supervision, but I only had the one son. I decided to coach and put up with the horrible supervisors on the day shift. That made my work life miserable, but in retrospect, a worthwhile sacrifice.

When Joshua was seven years old, he attended one of the local public elementary schools. One day he was talking to both Betsy and I about some controversy which occurred in his class. I asked my son how the blacks in the classroom responded to that particular set of events. Joshua looked up to me and said, "Dad, we have no black people in our class."

I knew that Vineland was thoroughly integrated throughout its educational system, so I asked my son, "What kind of people are in your class?"

"Well Dad, we have chocolate and coffee-colored people."

I asked, "What color are you?"

My son quickly answered, "That's easy, Dad. I'm peach!" My son did not see people as members of a race or an ethnic group. He saw them as individuals and as an artist would see someone to paint on a canvas. That was fine with both his mother and me.

In the fall before my son's eighth birthday, I became his soccer coach. For the next five years, I coached him and his teammates in the recreational leagues that the Vineland Soccer Association provided for children of his age. I had a core of six players, including my son, who wanted to transition to travel soccer, but would not do so until I was able to coach them at that level. The delay was due to my son's intensive Bar Mitzvah training. Travel soccer would have to wait.

When he was nine years old, Joshua's team was part of an under ten recreational soccer league. This particular group of young boys got along so well that they became one of my favorite teams over the years that I have coached. One of my players, *James,* was the son of one of my coworkers at MIV AFSS named *John.* Over the years, John and I not only worked together but became good friends. John was an ordained Baptist minister, a born-again Christian, who lived the life he preached. In order to get Sundays off, John had to work almost every Saturday. Unfortunately for John, Saturday was the day that we played our games, so James was almost always driven to the game by his mom, *Kathy.* John only got to see one game. That was the last regular-season game before the playoffs began. Kathy had to stay home and take care of their other son. John was at the game when James scored his first goal, a beautiful curving shot which enter the goalmouth just below the crossbar and to the left of the right upright. I really enjoyed seeing my friend's unabated joy as he witnessed his son's success. Seeing parents enjoy the exploits of their children was one of the great benefits of coaching.

That team went on to win the playoffs. The last game was a 2-1 thriller where we scored two goals in the last two minutes of the game to win the championship. After the game, the team went to the home of one of my players. These parents had a five-acre farmland in their backyard. It was the Memorial Day weekend. We purchased more than enough pizzas for everyone to eat. The temperature was in the low 70s, and there was a gentle northwesterly breeze. For the next three hours, we watched the eleven boys of this team play together in perfect harmony under a perfect spring sky. I had such a feeling of contentment watching my son play with his teammates. All the parents felt the same way as I did. I wish I could bottle that feeling that a parent gets when he or she sees their child having a spectacularly wonderful day playing.

As Joshua got older, particularly after entering puberty, his intellectual prowess, always at the top of his class, started to greatly expand. While others in the gifted program grew at a geometric rate, Joshua's intellectual growth was exponential. When he was eleven years old, we were at a Chinese restaurant awaiting delivery of our food. In the fifteen minutes that the restaurant required to prepare and serve the food, I taught my son how to compute the surface area and the volume of any solid. The only objects I used as teaching aids were a pen and a few paper napkins. Another customer, a middle-aged woman, sat in amazement as she watched my son absorb these concepts and quickly internalize them.

By the time Josh was thirteen years old, I realized that my son was a genius . . . a literal genius. My concern now was making sure that he understood the value of all people. I was alarmed when I realized just how far and by how much Joshua had eclipsed his gifted classmates. I reread Chiam Potok's masterpiece "*The Chosen*" which literally moved me to tears when I read, in the final chapter, the great Rebbe's explanation to his genius son as to why he raised him in silence. To which I quote in part:

"A man is born into this world with only a tiny spark of goodness in him. The spark is GOD, it is the soul; the rest is ugliness and evil, a shell. The spark must be guarded like a treasure; it must be nurtured; it must be fanned into flame. It must learn to seek other sparks; it must dominate the shell. Anything can be a shell. Anything. Indifference, laziness, brutality, and genius. Yes, even a great mind can be a shell and choke the spark."

Just after his thirteenth birthday, Joshua asked me to take his television out of his room. I asked him why. He responded that he "needed more room for his books." I never had to tell my son to do his homework. He would do quickly what the school required and then start reading and absorbing information at almost an alarming rate. Before his fifteenth birthday, Joshua was well into existential philosophy advocated by Nietzsche and Jung.

Six months after Joshua's thirteenth birthday, he completed his Bar Mitzvah--a highlight in our lives. We'd waited that long so the weather would be decent and all his relatives would be able to attend. Now Joshua and the other five teammates of my recreational league team would be able to play in the travel soccer league which required a much higher skill level. The age appropriate team sponsored by the Vineland Soccer Association was mired in last place in the lowest class of travel soccer. I challenged the head coach for his position.

The board members of the Vineland Soccer Association told me to attend the May meeting so I could be interviewed by them to see if they would change coaches. The meeting was held in a large trailer at the corner of the park where the games were played. There were about fifteen men in the trailer, and they all took their turns asking me questions. They wanted to know my qualifications and my philosophy in coaching soccer. One portly gentleman, whose nickname was "*Stubby*", asked me about the players that would accompany me to the travel team from my recreational squad. I told them, and Stubby in particular, that I was bringing six players who had the skills to play at the next level. Several thought that was not possible. Stubby told me if they had not played travel soccer before this, they would not possess the necessary skills to compete. I thoroughly disagreed and told all of them that the proof was in the pudding. Besides, the squad I would be taking over was a dismal failure. I could do no worse. Another board member asked me why I wouldn't wish to be the assistant to the present coach. My response to him was simply that as an air-traffic control specialist, I was used to doing things my own way. All successful air-traffic control specialists are, and were, classic type-A personalities. I ended my response by quoting Dante to the board: "*I would rather rule in hell than serve in heaven!*" For whatever reason, the board gave me the team. I was the new head coach for the Vineland Soccer Association under-14 Boys' Travel Team.

During this time, I also applied for the position of head varsity soccer coach at Sacred Heart High School which was located in downtown Vineland, New Jersey. I actually applied for the boys' team, but that position was already filled. The athletic director (AD) asked me if I would consider coaching the girls' team. I thought to myself that "soccer is soccer," and it did not matter what the gender of the team was. I accepted that job. By the rules governing high school soccer competition, I could not start coaching the girls' team until August 15, 1999. That meant, in my first year of coaching two teams simultaneously, I would concentrate my efforts with the boy's team during the months of May, June, July and the first half of August.

For the next three months, I held practice a minimum of three evenings each week and one long practice on Saturdays. I needed to get them to operate as one team. I changed the name of the team to "*Vineland Spectre.*" The six players I brought with me filled in nicely. They provided the strength the team needed to become a successful team. One of those players was my son who became the starting sweeper.

When August 15 rolled around, I started coaching the girls. Our first practice was a disaster. Of the twenty-two girls who signed up for soccer, I had two great players, about three or four decent players, and the rest look like the "Keystone Cops" trying to play soccer. It was apparent to me that my first job as coach was to improve the skill level of the players on the team. The school provided an assistant for me, but she was not available for the first two weeks of practice. I desperately needed an assistant to run simple drills with the bulk of the girls while I started teaching the game to groups of three and four. Luckily, the father of one of my great players, *Mr. Dave Tamanini*, offered to help me. His daughter, *Dana*, was one of the finest soccer players I have ever coached. For the first two weeks, all we did as a team was learn basic soccer skills. We didn't get into assigning positions until three days before our first scheduled scrimmage!

I remember after that first practice, one of my two great players, a freshman named *Carissa*, hesitantly told me that the stretching that I had my girls do was not sufficient. Remember, I was used to coaching boys, not girls. I told her to lead the team in stretching exercises for the next practice. Carissa, at five-foot three inches tall, was a thin, very pretty, blonde-haired, blue-eyed girl, and a tremendous athlete. She was easily the fastest girl on my team. Normally, I would never have a freshman lead a varsity team in any kind of exercise, but my instincts told me to trust this girl. As it turned out, Carissa was also an accomplished gymnast. She did stretching drills which put a human body in positions I did not think possible. From that time on until Carissa graduated, she led my team in stretching. That also included the summer practices where I could practice both teams simultaneously. There was not a player on either team who could stretch like Carissa!

In early September, my boys' team entered a huge soccer tournament as part of the Vineland Soccer Association's overall entry. This tournament attracted teams from all ages and both sexes, and from all over New Jersey and the neighboring states. Because of my team's poor past record, we were literally the last place seed in the tournament. These would be the first games that *Vineland Spectre* would play as a team. We won our first three games rather easily. The fourth game was the best game I ever saw my son play. Joshua was an absolute demon on defense. It was a scoreless contest until about a minute and a half left to play. The opposition got the ball inside our eighteen. Joshua tackled the ball, and while it bounced, he volleyed a perfect 60-yard pass to the right striker who beat the defender to the ball and took it directly toward the goal. The keeper came out to meet the challenge, and the right striker made a perfect centering pass to the trailing left striker who scored the only goal of the game. As a result of that victory, we were now in the championship game.

The team we would play for the championship was the top seeded team in the whole tournament. They averaged over five goals a game while not permitting a single goal to be scored against them. No one gave us a chance. As it turned out, we were the last remaining team from the Vineland Soccer Association and the only one that qualified for the championship round. Our game was attended not only by the parents of our players but by all the other teams and the board members of the Vineland Soccer Association, including Stubby.

That's when I made the greatest coaching move in my entire career. I knew Dana and Carissa, who played on the same travel team coached by Dave Tamanini, would be watching my boys' team play for the championship. Therefore, I introduced Carissa, my left striker on my girls' team, to *Derek,* my boys' team left striker. Both Derek and Carissa were 5'3"; both had blonde hair and blue eyes; both were the fastest players on their respective squads. As I said before, Carissa was a very pretty girl. All Derek could do, as shy as he was, was finally utter a muted "hello" while looking at the top of his shoes. But he knew that Carissa would be watching him play soccer, and he wanted to make an impression. Did he ever! He lit up that favored team for three goals and an assist. He played out of his mind, and we won the game 5 to 4. After the game, I found Stubby and I asked him again if he didn't think that these "rec" players could compete against experienced travel soccer players. Stubby, to his credit, told me that he was dead wrong. You see, Derek was one of those players who was on my rec squad and waited for me to be available before he moved to travel soccer.

My girls' team also did well. In New Jersey, a team must finish with a 500 record (win half their games) in order to be qualified for the state-wide tournament. Sacred Heart girls' soccer teams (*The Lady Lions*) had never, in the whole history of the school, ever qualified for that tournament. On Friday, October 22, 1999, we were going to play our last scheduled home game which, if we won, would qualify the girls' varsity team for entry into the state-wide tournament for the first time in the school's history. At the time, our record was eight wins, nine losses, and one tie. The team we were playing was a team that we had tied earlier.

It was a perfect fall day: cloudless sky' temperatures in the high 60s, a slight breeze coming from the northwest. Perfect soccer weather. Normal attendance at our home games was twenty or thirty folks who watched their daughters play soccer. Not today. There were well over five hundred people in attendance. All the major newspapers sent reporters to the game. Sacred Heart was a small school, but it had a major following throughout southern New Jersey, northern Delaware and the

Philadelphia areas. The school's reach and influence far exceeded its size. The possibility for this team to qualify for the state-wide tournament was a very big deal.

One of the girls who played for me was a senior named *Michelle*. This young lady was my starting right striker. She came from a thoroughly divided, ill-functioning home. Earlier in the year, she approached me and said that she had to leave the team because she would be spending a lot of time in family counseling. I told Michelle, "Do your schoolwork, your religious training, and family counseling. The team will take whatever time you have left over. You don't have to ask my permission to miss anything. Just let me know beforehand if possible. How does that sound to you?"

Michelle thought about it for twenty or thirty seconds, smiled and said, "I can do that!" I was glad that she decided to stay with the team because it was there that she found total acceptance and love from her teammates. Michelle really needed both, given the dismal state of her family situation. Michelle only missed two practices and one game in the course of the remaining schedule.

When I coached girls, I did not make physical contact with any of my players. When a girl did something really outstanding on the soccer field, I would tell her, "Consider yourself receiving a pat on the tush!" It's a verbal pat, not a physical one. My girls knew that's my way of saying, "Job well done."

The game started a little after 4 PM. My girls, the *Sacred Heart Lady Lions*, won the game four to one. Michelle played the best game of her career, scoring one goal and assisting on another. With about a minute to go in the game, I substituted for Michelle. Normally, when a girl left the game, she went and sat on the bench. When I pulled Michelle, she stood right behind me and stayed there. The crowd gave her a standing ovation in appreciation for the great game that she had just finished playing. About a minute later, the referee, who kept the time on the field, ran past Michelle and me. We both heard him as he counted down the final seconds of the game. At that point, Michelle knew that she and the other *Lady Lions* would be going to the state tournament for the first time in the school's history. She broke into convulsive sobs and in violation of my own rules and in front of more than five hundred people, including the school's principal and athletic director, I hugged one of my players tightly as she cried on my shoulder in pure joy. She stayed that way for several minutes. I let Michelle cry herself out and just before she left my embrace, quoting J.R.R. Tolkien, I said to her, "Not all tears are evil." It was then, and remains to this day, the absolute best moment I have ever had on the soccer field!

I coached both teams for the next seven years. Betsy complained that she became a "soccer widow." I suspected that she was probably right. Frankly, having to work day shifts at Millville was no picnic. The day supervisors were inept and made the job harder instead of easier. We did more traffic during the day shift, and received less money. But that's government work for you. Being my son's soccer coach and coaching the Lady Lions made it worthwhile.

When Josh was fourteen years old, he started getting massive migraines. I traveled all over South Jersey and Philadelphia seeking a medical cure for my son. The regular doctors were as useless as tits on a boar hog. Betsy and I, at the suggestion of my goalie's mom, turned toward holistic medicine. For the next two years, Betsy and I took Joshua up the holistic food chain. At the start of his sophomore year in high school, we found *Carl and Mae Jacobs*. Carl is in a class by himself as a holistic healer. Mae, his beautiful wife, was also his primary assistant. Over the next four years, Carl helped Joshua successfully overcome his migraines.

However, Joshua knew that he could not try out for the boys' varsity soccer team when he attended high school. It broke my heart to see him cry when he knew the headaches would prevent him from competing. He played on my team because I would adjust his practice and his playing time to accommodate dealing with those damned headaches. The upside of suffering migraines was that Joshua turned to poetry. He found, in Ezra Pound, a suffering and a poetic expression with which he could fully identify. Joshua self-taught himself how to structure various types of poetry. After a while, Joshua started writing his own poetry. This artistic endeavor helped him cope with his physical problems and emotional costs which emanated from his suffering.

In the spring of the year 2002, Betsy asked Joshua for his fifty best poems. She took those that he gave her and paid a printing company to make a hard-covered book of his poetry. She had six copies made, and they were printed on high-quality, glossy paper and bound with a high-quality leather binder. During that spring, Betsy and I decided to take Joshua on a tour lasting ten days where we would visit all of the colleges he might possibly wish to attend in the New England area. We had not been on a vacation for more than five years because of our financial situation. Somehow, we found the money, and we wanted to make this trip because we wanted Joshua to see what was in store for him when he graduated high school. We decided that all three of us needed to like a school in order for us to visit. For example, when I looked at the Yale University website, the opening paragraph of that site bragged about the number and percentage of those students they rejected for admission. Frankly, that made me sick to my stomach, and I exercised my veto as we did not visit Yale University even though it was directly on our route.

Over a three-year period, we visited schools that were apropos to my son's intellect such as the following: Brown University, Harvard

University, Dartmouth College, Middlebury College, Brandeis University, Amherst College, Cornell University, Oberlin College, Swarthmore College, College of William and Mary, Duke University, UNC, Vanderbilt University, Tufts University and Emory University.

All of these schools offered an introductory lecture which usually lasted about an hour followed by a guided tour of the campus which took another hour to complete. Joshua, at this stage of his life, was a skinny high school student who stood about 5'8", with brown hair and eyeglasses. He would not speak unless he had something meaningful to say. After the lecture was completed, Joshua waited to be the last person to talk with the individual who gave the introductory address. He would hand that person his book of poetry and see what his or her reaction was after reading one or more of his poems.

The school representative who showed the most interest in his book of poetry was the person from Brown University. She was a woman in her mid-50s who was very well attired and spoke without a trace of an accent. Her elegant diction was matched by her perfect use of grammar. I do not remember her name, but she was the assistant director of admissions at Brown University. I stood about five feet behind my son when he handed her his book of poetry. The woman read the first poem and asked, "How old were you when you wrote this?"

My son answered, "I was fifteen."

The woman read the next poem and asked the same question. She got the same answer. She read several more poems and asked the very same question again. And as before, she received the same answer. Then she and my son discussed the poetry department at Brown University. I think she was taken aback when she understood that Joshua knew who these professors were and read many of their writings. As we were leaving to attend the tour of the campus, I looked back and saw her writing furiously on the postcard-size document that each visiting high school student fills out before attending the introductory lecture. Of all the schools we visited over the next several years, it was Brown University that showed the most interest in this budding, brilliant young poet. When we took the walking tour there, my son stayed close to the tour guide. Betsy and I were a good fifteen to twenty feet behind him. Each guide led a group of about twenty people. Ten minutes into the tour, I saw the way my son was walking and looking at that campus. I swear to you that the joy he felt walking through that campus was palpable. At least it was to me! I turned to my wife and said, "Betsy, if the school accepts him, this is where he will go!"

My wife, who preferred that he stayed closer to home, immediately rapped my arm. She said angrily, "You can't know that. Do not say anything to Joshua. Let him make up his own mind!" Like any other husband, my response was a muted, "Yes dear." After eighteen years of marriage, I had learned that the title of "Dear" was the same as "Colonel" in the United States Air Force. After the tour was over, Betsy asked our son what he thought of Brown University. He answered, "I'm pretty sure that I want to attend this school. I'll look at the others, but I think this is the one!" I smiled at his answer. My wife is much better than I in quickly reading people, but Joshua is not just "people." He is my son. I sense what he's feeling. He is the one person in this world that I read and understand better than my wife.

After all the college visits, Brown University was the one that my son wanted to attend. However, Joshua's mother and sister kept harping that one visit was not enough to make such an important decision. Brown University had a program that allowed a potential student to spend the night in the freshman dorm and attend classes during the day. In order to quell the constant harping of our female folk, I called the admissions department at Brown University in order to arrange such a visit. This is the way the phone call went:

After several rings a woman answered, "Brown University admissions, may I help you?"

I answered, "Hi. My name is Norris Blakeman, and I want to arrange an overnight visit for my son."

With virtually no hesitation, the woman said, "When would you and Joshua like to visit our campus?"

I was taken aback because I had not mentioned my son's name, yet she knew who I was, and she was definitely interested in my son. I got over my shock and made the necessary arrangements for Joshua to visit during the first week of October just after the Jewish high holy days. Joshua visited the campus again and attended classes. There was no doubt now that Brown University was his first and only choice. He applied for early admission.

In late October, he filled out the extensive fourteen-page application which Brown required at that time. That was the most intrusive form that I have ever seen with the only exception being the one I had to fill out when I received my top-secret clearance. The last part of the application was an essay in which the school asked, "Tell us something about yourself that we would not otherwise know in less than 1,000 words." My son worked on this essay for several hours. He came into my home office and asked me to read it over. He handed me the page and left the room. This is what my son wrote as a seventeen-year-old high school student:

The Experience

I let out a groan. Something is clearly not right. Not unusual to me; I had a headache all day. Yet it had been tolerable, and I went to my soccer practice regardless. No longer tolerable. The pain in my head grew and craved my attention. I had to stop, as I could make it worse. A migraine cannot be ignored. It taunts you into forgetting that you're alive, that you can potentially have purpose. My body worn, I stagger to a car to sit down. I move slowly, each step as momentous as the next. The practice was scheduled late. Under artificial light, I feel blinded by my sensitivities. The grass appears eerily in my perception, leaving an unforgettable image. In the car, words come to me, as they often have since I began writing the previous year—the same time as the advent of my migraines. In isolation and relative silence, I anxiously want to leave, but know no place can possibly be comfortable. Anywhere, most stimuli are agonizing.

When I get home, I immediately wobble to my room, grabbing only a glass of water with me. There, as light is particularly bothersome, I turn on only the dimmest light I have, a small light on my desk. Sitting down on the chair at my desk, I grab a pile of blank, unadulterated papers and scribble the words that echo in my head. Finally, I can temporarily forget that I am capable of thought. No more words appear.

Having ensured preservation of my thoughts, I put Opeth's Morningrise in my stereo, and the music plays. I cannot relax. I take the most powerful drug for migraines available. It does nothing. Time passes without hurry, some seconds feeling almost completely still. I can only lay and listen, concentrating heavily on the music, my only comfort in the moment. I avoid thoughts of the pain in my head, which is noticeable whether I concentrate on it or not. Though I would look still to anyone else, the tension within me is enormous. Eventually, my body tires, I forgot all days, and I fall asleep.

The next day, I wake to a familiar pain, lessened by a night's rest. I stumble to my desk, only a few feet away. There, I see writing amassed on a sea of white, with pages no longer pure. I pick up the paper containing the poem I wrote; it's barely legible. I recall the only thought I was capable *of producing that night. Now coherent, I transcribe the words of the poet inspired by his inescapable pain and the unusual image he saw.*

Time would pass, and I would strengthen. Many nights I felt comparable pain, and I cannot forget these moments as long as the words still speak to me. With poetry, I will remember, and others, who may or may not have ever felt similarly, may understand this subjective experience as well.

I read his essay and then reread it. My eyes filled with tears. I gathered myself up and walked to my son's room. He was hunched over his books. I asked him to stand, and he did. I held out my arms and embraced my son and told him, "If they do not accept you after reading this, then Brown is not much of a school!" Joshua thanked me and returned to his books. As I left his room I said, "I am so proud of you, son." He nodded, and I quietly closed the door behind myself as I left. We mailed the application in the last week of October. Joshua had applied for early admission at Brown University. The school informed us that decision regarding early admission would be mailed and received to all students who applied on December 15, 2003.

I was a nervous wreck for the next two months. I wanted my son to get the education that he desired and deserved. I wished for this more than anything else in this world. December 15, 2003, was a Monday and as usual, I was working the day shift. The mail normally was delivered between one and two in the afternoon where I lived. Betsy and I were nervously awaiting Brown's decision. At 1:25 in the afternoon on that day, my Betsy called me at work and asked if I could come to the phone. The supervisor wasn't happy, as usual, but allowed me to receive this personal phone call.

I heard my wife's voice when she said, "Let me quote this exactly to you: Dear Joshua: I hope you are as pleased to get this letter as I am to send it to you. You have been admitted to the 241st class to enter the College of Brown University. I congratulate you on your record of academic and personal accomplishments, to which can now be added the honor of being accepted as an Early Decision applicant to Brown." Betsy then added, "There is more, but you can read it for yourself when you get home."

My reaction was simple. I let out the most unbelievable and loudest war whoop heard since Pickett's charge at the Battle of Gettysburg. All my fellow controllers looked at me on the phone waving my arms and screaming my head off. Two things happened at that moment. My fellow controllers all congratulated me on my son's achievement. The second thing that happened was the most amazing personal transition that I have ever experienced. All the animosities and hatreds and dark thoughts were vaporized into nothingness at the exact moment I knew that my son would be able to go to the school of his choice. From that moment to this day, I stopped living in the past and became fully engaged within the present tense. I have found myself at peace with the world, no matter what went before and what was to come. That was the exact moment that this war-torn and battered combat veteran finally came home.

EPILOGUE

Early in May, 1999, Anna gave birth to her second child. It was May 10th of that year when Alisa Joan Shellhorn was born. Alisa came into this world weighing six pounds and seven ounces and was a perfectly healthy child. Anna breast-fed her daughter as she had done before with her son.

Two weeks after the child was born, Liam's detectives came up with the probable name of her biological father. His name was Norris Blakeman. He was an air-traffic control specialist who worked in a station located in southern New Jersey. The detective agency put together a complete biography assembled from public documents without the subject being aware that he was at the center of an investigation. Liam asked the agency for a name using the parameters of his attendance at Sorbonne and as an Air Force officer. Liam made sure that he was the client and made no reference to Anna's family.

Once he had a name, he hired another agency to trail Mr. Norris Blakeman. Its job was to find out what kind of man he was and how he spent his time. The agency was also tasked to acquire some kind of residual DNA from Mr. Blakeman. All this had to be done without the subject's knowledge. Again, Liam was the client and as before, no reference was made regarding Anna or her family.

This second agency followed Norris into his racquetball club. While playing, Norris had a cut over his right eye when he was accidently struck by his opponent's racquet. The detective secured the bloody bandage which was placed over the wound and later discarded. Liam took the bloodied bandage and a sample of Anna's blood and brought it to a well-respected laboratory. He asked that the DNA be compared to determine if there was a familial match. No names were referenced in this request. All Liam wanted to know was whether or not there was a biological link. The lab results came back that there was a 99.7% chance that they were directly linked biologically. Frankly, with the evidence that he accumulated, Liam had no doubts. When he presented the same evidence to Anna and Mark, they both came to the same conclusion. Norris "Blake" Blakeman was Anna's biological father.

They read the complete dossier compiled regarding the life of this man. After they both read the report, Liam said to Anna, "I told you earlier that your mother would not pick a man who did not have high character. By what I have read, he seems to be a very decent man, living a fairly ordinary life. There is not even a hint of any criminal or immoral activity. He doesn't drink, smoke or run around on his wife. His life is completely and totally wrapped around his family and the soccer teams that he coaches. What do you want to do regarding this information?"

Anna pondered the question. "I really don't know what to do. If I announce my presence to him, I could disrupt his entire life. I would like to know him and see what Mom saw in him. What do you both think?" she asked of Liam and her husband.

Mark said, "I'll back you, whatever you decide. I do know after reading his dossier that this gentleman went through hell in Vietnam. He seems to be on a fairly even keel now. Knowing that you exist may have some disastrous and unintended consequences. I don't know. But whatever you decide is what we will do. Honey, it is all your decision."

They both looked questioningly at Liam who like Blakeman was a combat veteran of the Vietnam War. Liam responded by saying, "I agree with Mark. Many of the men I served with had a great deal of trouble reintegrating back into civilian life after fighting that war. Many of our own countrymen blamed the guys who fought there instead of the politicians who sent them. I couldn't guess the effect upon this gentleman knowing that he'd fathered a child that he never knew existed. What would that do to his family and his psyche? I just don't know the answers to those questions."

Mark added, "Anna, honey, take your time and think about it. There's no rush. You just gave birth to our beautiful daughter, and she needs you now. We can do something later, if that's your decision."

Anna responded, "You are right. I will think about this." Just then, as if on cue, Anna heard Alisa crying. The baby was hungry, and Anna looked forward to feeding her. Anna walked to the crib and retrieved her baby. She carried Alisa to the rocking chair where she exposed her right breast and allowed her daughter to drink her fill. She was not shy in Liam's presence because he was family. Both men appreciated watching this life-affirming process.

During the next several weeks, Anna gave the matter a great deal of thought. One of her considerations was the fact that her biological father was a Jew. Personally, that did not bother her. But for others in her social strata who comprised her life outside her family circle that would be a stigma, especially for her children. Too many times throughout history, people of Jewish descent were singled out and made a scapegoat for every social ill that beset mankind. If she announced her presence to her biological father, then her children's Jewish blood would become common knowledge. She desperately wanted to know the man that sired her, but she wanted to keep that lineage secret even more. She kept these thoughts to herself. She did not even speak of them to her husband or to Liam because she was ashamed of having them.

Anna did not speak of this with anyone for the next five months. She concentrated on giving her daughter a healthy head start in life. In the middle of October, 1999, when Alisa, now in her sixth month of life, was able to have foods besides breast milk, Anna decided that she would like to at least see her biological father. She talked this over with Liam and Mark.

Liam continued to monitor the life of Mr. Norris Blakeman through a local South Jersey detective agency. There were stories in all the local and major papers about the upcoming contest between the *Sacred Heart Lady Lions*, coached by Norris Blakeman, and another high school varsity team. Because of the widespread coverage, Liam felt that he could take Anna to this game, and she could see her biological father without standing out as somebody who did not belong in that environment.

The idea appealed to Anna. She talked it over with Mark. They decided that Anna and Liam would fly down to Philadelphia on Friday morning, October 22. They would rent a car and proceed to Vineland, New Jersey. They would watch the game, and then they would return that night back to the Boston area. Trudy, the nursemaid, would take care of the children, and Mark would stay home to help her out. It was a perfect excuse for Mark to spend quality time with both his children.

The plane landed at the Philadelphia International Airport at 11:35 in the morning. Liam and Anna quickly deplaned and went to the car rental agency located in the airport. Liam rented an SUV, and they drove straight to the Vineland area. The agency that was monitoring the movements of Mr. Blakeman recommended the *Olympia Restaurant* as an excellent place to eat. Liam got the location of that restaurant from the agency and took Anna there to eat lunch. The food was excellent. They left the restaurant by two that afternoon. Anna had Liam drive around the area to see what it was like. He drove to the eastern part of the city where the Blakeman family lived.

They parked across the street in order to watch the house. It was now about 3:15 in the afternoon. Liam and Anna were watching when the front door opened and for the first time, Anna saw her biological father. He was about five-foot seven, and he weighed about one hundred and eighty-five pounds. He wore blue jeans and a blue Sacred Heart sweatshirt. He was accompanied by a woman that Anna knew from the reports was his wife and by a thin teenage boy about one or two inches taller than his father who was her half-brother. They got into the family car, a Chrysler minivan, and departed for the soccer field. Liam made a quick U-turn and followed the minivan. In about five minutes, they arrived at the soccer field.

Anna watched as Mrs. Blakeman took two folding chairs to the spectator side of the field. Her husband and her son worked together to unload equipment from the back of the van. She watched as Norris Blakeman and his son, Joshua, her half-brother, carried several large bags of soccer balls, a small bag of soccer game balls, four flags, and a canvas duffel bag filled with assorted other equipment. The balls and the duffel bag were deposited on the home team side opposite where the fans were sitting. She saw Mr. Blakeman put the flags in the four corners of the pitch. At 3:30 a bus containing the *Sacred Heart Lady*

Lions entered the parking lot adjacent to the pitch. The girls emptied out and ran to the home-field bench where they placed their equipment. It amused Anna that every girl had painted her face blue-and-white to match their uniforms. The captain of the team, a girl wearing number ten, led the players in running two laps around the field. They did this without being told to do it.

The girls then circled a pretty blonde-haired girl wearing number two. She led them in their stretching exercises. Meanwhile, Mr. Blakeman was inspecting the field, the goal nets, and opening up the public bathrooms that were built adjacent to the field. Liam and Anna walked over to the spectator side of the field and sat down on portable stands that were erected for this contest. Many people were now streaming onto the field. Liam gave Anna some of the papers that he'd picked up in a newsstand adjacent to the Olympia restaurant. These papers had numerous stories regarding the importance of this game.

About 3:45 in the afternoon, another bus entered the park. That bus unloaded the high school team that the Lady Lions were about to face. Earlier in the year, according to the stories that Anna had just read, these teams tied. Today, only victory would serve the Lady Lions in their quest to qualify for the state championship tournament. These girls started with their warm-up exercises as Mr. Blakeman went over and introduced himself to the opposing coach. They talked for about two or three minutes after shaking hands. Mr. Blakeman then returned to his side of the pitch. By four o'clock in the afternoon, there were at least five hundred people, if not more, on the spectator side of the pitch. The Lady Lions had their blue uniforms on which matched the paint on their faces. The opposition was dressed in white with green trim. They were taunting the Lady Lions telling them that they were not going to win.

The game started at 4:10 PM. A blonde Lady Lion, wearing number nine, scored the first goal. The Lady Lions had a two-nil lead at the end of the half. The visiting team in white scored the next goal, making the score two to one. The Lady Lions roared back with two unanswered goals. The third goal was scored on a perfect assist by the same player who scored the first goal of the game. The score now was 4-1, with the Lady Lions comfortably in the lead.

Anna looked at her watch and knew that there were less than two minutes to play in the game. All this time she was watching her biological father. He seemed to have a very good rapport with the players on his team. Throughout the game, he would stand on his side of the midfield and yell encouragement to his players. When he substituted, the girl going in would stand in front of the scorer's desk at midfield. The girl coming out would go to the bench and sit. She watched her father make his last substitution for the player who wore the number nine. As a soccer player herself, Anna knew that the girl coming out of the game played superbly. Anna found herself clapping and cheering for this young lady who received a standing ovation from the fans, as they also greatly appreciated the quality of the girl's play. Even Liam was cheering for this young lady whom neither of them knew. She watched in fascination as the girl did not go to the bench. Instead, she stood right behind her coach who was Anna's biological father.

Anna did not watch the game at this point. The match was already decided, as there was less than a minute to play. She watched intently as the far-side referee, looking at his watch, passed by midfield on the players' side of the pitch. A few seconds later, that same referee blew his whistle and raised and crossed his hands, indicating the end of the game. The blonde player wearing number nine started sobbing. She watched as her biological father gathered the girl in his arms and let her cry herself out. The rest of the team and the spectators who watched the game were all yelling and screaming, jumping up and down, celebrating this crucial victory. While all this commotion was going on all over the field, her father just held the young lady as she continued to cry on his shoulder. Finally, the rest of the team, seeing the emotional impact the game had on the player wearing number nine, came over to where the coach was holding her. He finally let her go and the rest of the team embraced her. It was a beautiful moment, and Anna knew that it would stay with her for the rest of her life. Seeing this man have such a special moment touched her. She knew, without question, that the man that sired her had a good heart. Mom had chosen well. It was not Anna's place to barge into the man's life. She could live with that decision now. She turned to her lifelong protector and said, "Liam, take me home."